MISTER
NICK

For Alex with love Nick Axx

27. 9. 2015

MISTER NICK

Playing the field – Sailing the seas – Cooking up storms

NICK HUDSON

Bene Factum Publishing

Mister Nick

First published in 2015 by
Bene Factum Publishing Ltd
PO Box 58122
London
SW8 5WZ
Email: inquiries@bene-factum.co.uk
www.bene-factum.co.uk

ISBN: 978-1-909657-32-8

Cover and book design by Bene Factum Publishing.
Photos courtesy of the author.

Set in Borgia Pro.
Printed and bound in the UK.

Contents

Foreword

Nick Hudson has made more use of his life on earth than anyone else I ever met. His story is almost unbelievable – but it really happened in the amusing way Nick tells us in his book.

It will be the best adventure story of the year. You will enjoy it – I certainly did.

Michael Deeley
Oscar-winning producer of *The Deer Hunter*

Acknowledgements

Never was this traditional section of a book more appropriate than now.

At a dinner party I had been reminiscing with a fellow guest, Derek 'Puz' Russell-Stoneham. Towards the end of the meal he told me that I had a story to tell and that he would undertake to see that it was told; he would be in touch with me in the near future.

He was as good as his word, soon asking for the first few chapters of my memoirs. I sent them to him. These he passed on to Anthony Weldon, head of Bene Factum Publishing, who assessed them as being commercially worthwhile and offered to publish my book. A contract was drawn up and duly signed. Then the work really started.

I set to. I had determined from the outset that these memoirs would be honest and frank, but I had no inkling of the sometimes cathartic nature of matters with which I would be confronted. For example, the arbitrary termination of my career at sea in the Merchant Navy, the only career to which I ever aspired, affected me far more deeply that I had realised at the time. The disappointment had been pushed out of sight and mind into a recess of my subconscious, seemingly forgotten. When, in the process of writing these memoirs, I revisited that period of my life, there was that traumatic episode, as vivid and real – and as painful – as when it had occurred so many years ago. I was stopped in my tracks. Only when I truly accepted that this had been my fate, was I able to move on and continue writing.

In the course of my writing I have found myself forced to accept responsibility for selfish, even disloyal acts when, say, I have let down friends and business partners. I have had to lay those ghosts to rest, for they simply would not go away, returning – usually at four in the morning – to haunt me. I hope that if Leslie Williams, Paul Harman, Charles Longman or Robin Knox-Johnston read this book, they will find themselves able to forgive my transgressions. Heidi, my beloved Afghan hound, I am so sorry to have abandoned you.

These parts of my journey – the bumpy bits – I could never ever have managed to negotiate without the unstinting support of a group of literary friends who have gathered protectively around me, most of whom are themselves published writers. From the outset Patricia Atkinson convinced me that I could write and has urged me along. Michael and Ruth Deeley have never wavered in their conviction that my story was worth writing and have been a continuous source of inspiration and encouragement. Julia Watson and Martin Walker have offered valuable advice and sustained me with their love and warmth. Ingrid and Tom Beazley made their peaceful London flat available to me, which has been a marvellous place in which to work and to chill out. Philip Sturrock has made valuable suggestions to modernise my prose and make it more readable. Eddie and Janet Nimmo-Smith have never been far away, should my self-confidence waver. I thank you all fervently.

As the book has entered its final phase, Anthony Weldon, in a masterstroke, gave me Mary Sandys as my editor; she and I have enjoyed a most rewarding relationship, even as she littered the cutting room floor with tens of thousands of words of my prose. Dominic Horsfall of Bene Factum entered the picture. Although our ages are two generations apart, he grasped intuitively what I am all about and refined and polished my work with the greatest sensitivity. And always there is Puz, who started the ball rolling, giving it occasional enabling taps, usually in the confines of that musty time-warp which is the Chelsea Arts Club.

Finally and indispensably, there is that remarkable person who has been there from the beginning, who has endured all the ups and downs and uncertainties, and comforted me in moments of self-doubt and even self-dislike. She has never complained about my unsociable working hours. She has proof-read every word of the manuscript – offering comments and suggestions along the way. She has run our home in such a way as to allow me to devote myself to writing, and sustained me with scrumptious meals and timely snacks. She has borne far more than her share of the burden. I could not have completed this book without her loving presence.

She is my beautiful wife Veronica, to whom I dedicate this book.

Nick Hudson
Journiac, France
May 2015

To Veronica,
a sail not an anchor.

Prologue

It is 12th January 1971.

I am standing – barefooted, long-haired and be-kaftaned – high up in the hills of Barbados in front of my Jacobean mansion, in the middle of a country the size of the Isle of Wight.

It was never supposed to be like this. I was supposed to be answering the call of the Sirens, standing on the deck of a sailing ship, at one with the restless ocean. Instead I found myself surfing on the slope of a powerful breaking wave – the newly independent Barbados, relishing her freedom. Here I was to enjoy success and find adventure, flying and sailing myself around the Caribbean. I would meet people who strode the world stage – prime ministers, actors, rock musicians, artists, outrageous queens, and even the odd princess. *Tatler* magazine would dub me the social nexus of Barbados. And there were to be women – many beautiful women – with whom to make love.

I had arrived on the Island in March 1970, bringing with me a backgammon board, a Herbert Johnson hat with a snakeskin band, and second-degree burns. Now, on a balmy tropical evening less than a year later, I am awaiting the arrival of the first guests to my restaurant in the mansion behind me, Bagatelle Great House.

And I reflect again that it was never supposed to be like this…

I Was Really Meant To Go To Sea

E ver since I could remember, I was one of those fortunate people who know exactly what they want to do with their life. So I was going to follow in the four-generation family tradition and go to sea.

My great-great-grandfather had been a pilot with Trinity House at Greenwich. My great-grandfather, master of an Ellerman Line ship, died in his bed at a ripe old age, unlike four of his five sons. The first of these four to slip his cable was Frederick, known as 'Jinks'. In 1914 his ship was torpedoed by the Germans, and he survived several days in an open lifeboat in the inhospitable North Atlantic, nearly dying of exposure. He was torpedoed again in August 1918, just three months before the Armistice. Remembering his previous experience, he dashed below for some warm clothing. Whilst he was down there the ship sank, taking Jinks with her. In 1925 his brother Ernest met the most horrific death imaginable; as chief engineer aboard a Canadian Pacific merchantman, he was inspecting the interior of the ship's recently overhauled boilers when someone closed the furnace doors and fired up the burners. The next to perish was my grandfather, a colonel in the Royal Engineers, a big game hunter, extra master mariner in square rig, trawler owner, ocean yachtsman and father of four children. In 1931, with his partner Colonel Luard, he entered his yacht *Maintenees II* in the recently instigated Fastnet race. My grandmother set off from Yorkshire with her daughter Dot to meet her husband in Falmouth where the race finished, staying en route at the Lygon Arms in Broadway. Over breakfast she read in her *Daily Mirror* that her husband had been lost overboard near the Fastnet

Rock the previous day, and that she was now a widow. 'She simply fainted away,' I remember Dot telling me. Granny never recovered, and grieved in black widow's weeds to her dying day.

Then in 1945 Tom, aged fifty-nine, enlivened the proceedings of the Barnsley Conservative Association by dropping dead in the middle of a meeting.

The only surviving son was Archie, the youngest, who sailed before the mast as an ordinary seaman aboard clippers around the notorious Cape Horn. For these square riggers, going the 'wrong' way from east to west against the prevailing wind, and in Antarctic conditions, was truly hazardous. Uncle Archie was an unlikely Cape Horner, a little chap who looked just like the comedian Ronnie Corbett. Nevertheless, he survived the wave-swept decks and ice-covered rigging and the Spartan life in the forecastle below. Unlike his brothers, he intended to see in his sixtieth year. But he was not going to push his luck. So for a whole year he refused to leave his house until the fateful birthday was safely behind him, and lived for another twenty years, during which he enraptured me with his salty yarns.

In spite of this dismal family record, nothing but the sea would do for me. My father, too, was a seadog. He served in the Merchant Navy, then became a trawler owner in Hull. During World War II he served in the Royal Navy in mine-sweepers. In Liverpool, he told me, the biggest problem was not the Germans but the priests. When his crewmen returned home after a patrol, if they found a black umbrella hanging over the front doorknob, it meant that the priest was otherwise occupied within, and they had to come back later. This did not endear the Church of Rome to my father, and he never forgave it. Later he was reposted to Grimsby, where his intimate knowledge of the North Sea was invaluable in mine-sweeping operations.

When peace returned in 1945, he went back to his beloved trawlers. These deep-water vessels operated in the richly stocked fishing grounds around Iceland, the White Sea and Bear Island. The post-war years, before the invasion of mostly irresponsible fishing fleets from the European Union, saw the heyday of the British fishing industry. Fortunes were made and my father took his share.

Everything at home echoed life afloat. Silence was maintained during the BBC shipping forecast. Encoded messages from my father's skippers set our Teletext terminal in the hall chattering. All trawler owners had their own secret code – you didn't want rival skippers being told where your chaps had found fish – and the code book was kept under lock and key. My father's speech had a nautical flavour; if he wanted your attention he would call, 'Ahoy there!' When we left in the car, we 'set sail'; if we stopped on the way, we 'hove to'; and when we arrived at our destination, we 'came alongside'. Our holidays were spent afloat on the Norfolk Broads. Even our house was called The Moorings. So it's hardly surprising that the Sirens' voices cooed seductively in my ears. Strangely, my three brothers remained deaf to their song. I suspect that the wax of conformity, and the desire for a steady job, early marriage to a good Yorkshire wife, children, school fees and family holidays, had stopped their ears. I wanted none of that; I intended to spend my days on the ocean waves and make love to beautiful women. Nothing else, I thought, really mattered.

My dream was to live aboard a wooden sailing vessel. Not for me the charmless modern yacht, with its computer-generated angular lines, constructed from artificial materials. Wooden vessels are things of soft unforced curves, yielding beauty and organic grace, yet with enormous inherent strength. They flex and vibrate in harmony with the waves and the winds. They have a soul. To this day, at a yacht marina, I look out for a wooden mast in the forest of metal poles. When I see one, I hurry to find and admire the hull in which it is stepped. Wooden craft, safely away from land and lurking reefs, and with a little help from the Almighty, will ride out the worst storms. Lying a'hull or running before mountainous seas, they will yield obediently to the mighty forces of nature. One day I would have my own wooden boat.

Something my father drummed into us was that, whatever profession we chose to follow, we had to know it from the bottom upwards, to be able to do the job of anyone in our employ. So it was essential that I obtained professional qualifications to enable me to make a living on the sea. This meant joining an officer cadet training ship. The chosen establishment was

HMS *Worcester*, my father's old ship. This purpose-built school vessel was moored two hundred yards off shore at Greenhithe on the south bank of the Thames, upriver from the great docks at Tilbury. My father repeatedly asked if I was sure I wanted to join the *Worcester* – did I really want to go to sea? I was later to discover why he was so persistent, when it turned out that the *Worcester* was unusually tough. Just before my father joined her in 1922, the cadets overpowered the unpopular Chief Officer, bundled him into a laundry basket and chucked it into the Thames on the rushing ebb tide. Fortunately some alert bargees downriver intercepted it and hauled it out. King George V was greatly displeased when he heard of this and ordained that the naval crown be struck off the *Worcester*'s blue ensign. It was to be restored some years later. Even when I was there, a dispute in the tuck shop queue was settled with a knife in the back. It was a far cry from the leafy parish of Hessle, East Yorkshire.

The discipline of the ship's company had always been left in the hands of the cadets themselves. The ship had had a reputation for bullying since the mid-nineteenth century, when an old wooden-walled prison hulk was converted into the first of three *Worcesters*. The second-year cadets bullied those in their first year, who, in their turn, bullied the new arrivals. It was self-perpetuating.

I knew nothing of this lurid history when I joined the ship two months after my fourteenth birthday, wearing my smart officer cadet's uniform, perfectly tailored and fitted by Messrs. Gieves and Hawkes of Savile Row. I was the youngest cadet on board. Discipline was strict. It did not take much to incur the sadistic wrath of the junior and senior cadet captains. If, for example, after your first term, your front collar stud – we wore stiff collars, which were surprisingly comfortable – was visible above your tie, that heinous crime called for ritual punishment. Every evening we would have hot cocoa in the mess room, before slinging our hammocks and turning in. A junior cadet captain would tap his mug for silence and bellow, 'The following cadets fall in outside the senior cadet captains' cabin!' Those called would assemble as directed, be cross-examined, and inevitably found guilty as charged. They would then be ordered to bend over the end of a sofa, jackets raised, and receive six strokes of the cane. *Next!* I was terrified every evening. The thought of being beaten horrified me.

In the event, my name was never called, probably because the chief cadet captain – whose name somehow escapes me – rather fancied me. Well, what do you expect when two hundred virile young males are completely deprived of female company for twelve weeks at a stretch? Every night the metal bars from which our two hundred hammocks were slung vibrated like giant tuning forks.

The most sought-after berth was crewman in the Captain's gig, an immaculate six-oared craft, all gleaming white and gold. The Captain's cox'n stood proudly in the stern sheets, his hand on the gilded ram's head, the helm decorated with fancy rope work. When we heard the special piped tune, followed by the call ''Way Captain's gig!', there was always a buzz; it meant that our Captain Superintendent was either leaving or joining the ship. Captain Gordon Steele was a god-like figure who had won the Victoria Cross in 1919. He was in a Coastal Motor Boat that came under heavy fire off Kronstadt during the Allied intervention after the Russian Revolution; when the captain was killed, he took over the boat, managing to torpedo two Russian battleships before heading for safety. He now devoted himself to imparting to cadets the unfathomable mathematics and functions of the gyro compass.

We were taught how to calculate the mechanical advantage of combinations of blocks and tackles, how to estimate breaking strains of ropes, or which sorts of ropes to choose for different tasks. We learned navigation and became versed in spherical trigonometry, which was quite difficult for a fourteen-year-old – we had no calculators then. We learned to use the sextant, essential for celestial navigation. We had to be able to recite the Articles of the Sea off by heart. Outside the classroom we learned about anchoring, mooring, rigging and rope work, making complicated but beautiful knots such as a double diamond or monkey's paw. We were taught to row cutters with massive oars and how to handle sailing boats. We learned the layout of all the major docks in and around London – the East India Docks, Tilbury and so on.

We were encouraged to swarm up the rigging onto the main top platform. The safe way was to wriggle through the mockingly named lubber's hole, close to the mast. The other was to climb around the outside, hanging on to the futtock shrouds, feet searching for slender ratlines and your back towards the main deck sixty feet below. You then clambered round the bend onto the shrouds which supported the main topmast. It was easy – after the first time. And, anyway, there really was no choice. The lubber's hole? Never!

And, my word, did we dust off well when the situation called for it! At Divine Service on the main deck on Sunday morning, when Captain Steele actually descended amongst us mortals, we were immaculate in our No. 1 uniforms with the white flash on our lapels signifying the rank of officer cadet.

We enjoyed the opportunity ceremonial occasions gave us to show off our skills at drill. In 1973 President Tito of Yugoslavia visited London. He was not universally popular amongst the Yugoslav diaspora, and the safest way of getting him there was up the Thames on the presidential yacht *Galeb*. When *Galeb* came abeam the *Worcester*, we exchanged the dipping of ensigns, a courtesy recognised by maritime nations around the world. Since he was a visiting head of state, we dressed the *Worcester* overall, flying all the flags we could muster and manning the yards in the President's honour, balancing on the yard-arms, holding on to a wire behind our backs. The impressive effect was enhanced when we gave him three cheers, waving our caps so that with each 'Hurray!' our white tops flashed towards the quickly vanishing dignitary. We were just congratulating ourselves on how well it had all gone when we heard the cry, ''Ware wash!'

There is on the Thames, from the estuary up to the Pool of London, a speed limit of seven knots – eight miles an hour – which reduces the wash generated by passing vessels. Aware that he had many enemies in the United Kingdom, the President flouted the rules and had his ship go at full speed. We had rehearsed on calm water and were unprepared for the *Galeb*'s wash marching towards us in serried ranks of waves with breaking crests. The wash reached the clipper *Cutty Sark*, anchored abreast of us, and slipped silently under the perfect lines of her hull; stabilised by a deep heavy keel which gave her a low centre of gravity, she barely acknowledged the passing disturbance. The *Worcester*, on the other hand, in naval terms was a floating block of flats, and about as seaworthy, with a dangerously high centre of gravity. So when the wash hit her broadside, she rolled like a fat sow to port, then to starboard. Then back to port. And so on. I was on the main yard, a mere sixty feet above the deck, hanging on grimly. You may imagine the arc described by the higher yards and the cadets hanging on to them. No-one fell off, although much of the crockery in the ship's galley was shattered.

I was in my element. I had finished my first year and was about to enjoy the hard-earned privileges and ease of the second-year cadet, but without resorting to bullying, a long-practised tradition I despised. A life on the ocean waves was within touching distance. The *Worcester* had a reputation for turning out the best officer cadets in the country. Accordingly, we were offered officer cadetships with the most prestigious shipping lines – Cunard, P&O, Shaw Savill and others – whose fabulous liners we all dreamed of commanding.

My eyes had been tested as a matter of course before I joined the *Worcester* by a Board of Trade examiner. Now they had to be re-tested to make sure my eyesight still met the high standards demanded of a Merchant Navy deck officer. As I had just scraped through, I was taken to a consultant. He was of the opinion that my eyesight would deteriorate and that I should abandon any hopes of serving as a deck officer. My parents accepted his prognosis; he was a Harley Street specialist, after all. Perhaps, it was suggested, I might consider becoming a purser. Me – a seaborne waiter or hotel manager? Never!

So I was arbitrarily removed from the *Worcester*. As far as a career was concerned, I had no other ambitions. I had lost my lode star. I was adrift.

I do not exaggerate. I only discovered just how deep this cut had gone when I started to write this part of my story. I had to stop for two or three weeks until I came to terms with what had been taken away from me. No matter what successes I have enjoyed since, no other career could come close to replacing a life at sea.

Throughout my life, no class of person has caused me so much trouble as so-called 'experts'! Well into my sixties, I was passing Civil Aviation eye examinations for my private pilot's licence without difficulty. So much for Harley Street consultants!

Here I must add a postscript to this account of my early life. I often went riding with a girl called Veronica Nicholson. Then aged about ten or eleven, she was already exotically beautiful – her family came from somewhere around the Adriatic – and I was smitten. I sent her a Valentine card and a letter with S.W.A.L.K. – Sealed With A Loving Kiss – on the envelope. Only later did I learn that she never even opened them. She had noticed my preference for blondes in the form of her classmates Annabelle and Cynthia, and kept well away. However, I did get on well with her friend Jill Chatterton, who had long thick jet-black plaits tied with red ribbons. Remember these two; you will meet them again.

CHAPTER TWO

A Change Of Course

After leaving the *Worcester* I joined my two elder brothers, Peter and Tony, at a public school called Sedbergh, exchanging my fine officer cadet's uniform, which I really felt I had earned, for a shirt and shorts, since I was going to be climbing fells rather than rigging.

Sedbergh was a fine school, which in the seventeen years under the head-mastership of John Harold Bruce-Lockhart had undergone a radical trans-formation. It had been well known for its formidable rugger team, but by the time I was admitted in 1953 it was just as possible for a pupil to be awarded his school colours for playing the violin. I became a house prefect, played for the 1st XV and was the reluctant heavyweight boxing champion, a sport I loathed. My French improved enormously, the headmaster having been awarded the *Légion d'honneur* for his contribution to teaching that language. I was introduced to the Russian language by a remarkable teacher called Jack Hammer, igniting a flame which has burned brightly ever since.

I had quite a good treble voice, but just after arriving at Sedbergh I noticed that my top note was coming down semi-tone by semi-tone. At the late age of nearly sixteen my voice finally broke. I was devastated and I cried, for I really loved singing sacred music. I had to start shaving as well, surely the most tedious activity man has to endure.

I wish I could tell you that the subsequent loss of my virginity was con-summated in a flower-filled bower with frolicking cupids and beauteous maidens. The reality was less romantic. I was in the fish and chip shop queue – I absolutely loved the crispy scraps from the bottom of the fryer liberally sprinkled with vinegar and eaten off a piece of newspaper, prefer-ably the *Daily Mirror* – and standing next to me was a large girl a bit older than me. She asked if I would like to 'take a walk'. I eyed her promisingly taut blouse, and off we went to the woods on the outskirts of the village. In no time at all she had me out of my trousers and underpants and flat on my back. She hitched up her skirts, sat on me, took – stole – what she wanted, got to her feet and left through a gap in a hedge. I wish I could tell you more. I lay there, confused. I supposed I had been violated, robbed of I knew not what.

In fact, I had rather enjoyed the experience. The flame had been lit and demanded fuel. I heard that a girl called Anne was a sure bet, nearly unheard of then in East Yorkshire. I obtained her telephone number and we made a date. I picked her up in my mother's car and off we went to Jenny Brough Lane, a well-known trysting spot. As I switched off the engine, I had some concerns; I did not want a night of pleasure to turn into a lifetime of regret. But Anne had it all worked out. With swift fingers she cleared away all inconvenient cloth-ing, lowered her head and her halo of soft hair covered my loins. Lightning flashed. Thunder rolled. The earth moved. My word, I mused, sliced bread has a lot of ground to make up. I was beginning to think that becoming a tenor, albeit a disappointingly indifferent one, was not all bad.

When the time came to leave Sedbergh, my hopes of a life at sea having been dashed on the rocks of professional incompetence, my first thought was to take up farming. We owned a small farm in East Yorkshire on which, my devious little mind had calculated, I should be able to keep polo ponies. I was offered a place at Royal Cirencester Agricultural College and did sev-eral months' practical work on an estate in Norfolk. Then my call-up papers arrived, and any plans for the next two years were put on hold. In our family there was never any question of avoiding National Service by pleading flat feet or voicing conscientious objections. It was a duty and that was that. I elected to join the Royal Navy as a Russian interpreter. I would leave at the end of my time with a valuable university degree in my favourite foreign language paid for by the tax payer. Accordingly I went to the Admiralty building in Hull to offer my services.

As I walked down the corridor towards a door signed *Royal Navy*, I was confronted by an enormous poster depicting a man of blood-curdling mien wearing a green beret, his face blackened. Brandishing an ugly, stubby sub-machine gun, he was leaping fearlessly from an inflatable craft onto a rocky shore. That could be me. Without breaking step I turned right, and knocked on a door which bore the legend *Royal Marines*. Sitting at a desk was a colour sergeant with no neck. 'Yes?' he growled

'I want to be a Commando,' I announced. And so it came to pass. My service began as a recruit at the basic training camp at Lympstone in Devon. This was not meant to be easy, but, after my experiences on the *Worcester*, and meeting such fellow recruits as Dickie Beacham (brother of actress Stephanie Beacham) and the mercurial rugby international Richard Sharp, I thoroughly enjoyed myself. From there I went before the War Office Selection Board (WOSB) and was duly selected. Thence to the Duke of Westminster's Eaton Hall in Cheshire, an officer cadet training school where, in the last group to enjoy that magnificent pile, I was made into an officer. Whilst I was there I actually managed to get the splendid organ in the main hall working. It had a *campanella* – a peal of bells – a rarity indeed.

I was commissioned at Aldershot, and posted to Commando School at Bickleigh in Devon, where I gained the coveted Green Beret, just like the man leaping out of the inflatable craft at the recruiting centre! Finally I was sent to the Joint Services Amphibious Warfare School, where I was privileged to serve alongside such Royal Marine legends as Pat Gardiner, Mike Wilkins and Stuart Syrad. I would have liked to continue for a few years in the Corps with a short service commission, but that was not an option. With the Royal Marines it was all or nothing, unless you were dead or invalided out.

So I took the opportunity to reconsider my future career, and the medical profession was the lucky winner. I was going to be Dr Hudson. The first requirement on the seven-year trek to qualification was to obtain my first MB, which required 'A' levels in physics, chemistry and zoology. To achieve this I attended the Hull Polytechnic College.

At this time, just after my twenty-first birthday, I received some news of which I had no inkling whatsoever. I was to inherit, my parents told me, some money. It wasn't millions but I could have become a Name at Lloyds, an invitation I declined. I had absolutely no idea of the value of money and it would take years and many painful lessons before I did. Had I had a wife who required a dress allowance, children and their school fees and all the rest to pay for, it might have been different. For now my wealth allowed me to do as I pleased, buy what I wanted, and share it with my girlfriends.

The first thing I did was to buy myself a modest car, a Sprite, which I had supercharged. Within the year I had replaced it with a splendid Jaguar XK 150S. I exchanged the Jaguar for a Mercedes 300SL Gullwing which I saw in a saleroom after a good lunch at the Brompton Grill in Knightsbridge. This was to be the first of three such models that I owned over the next ten years. There was never a motorcar like it. It certainly raised the tone of the Hull Tech. car park.

I passed my first MB exams in spite of a near miss with the zoology practical, which required dissection of the seventh cranial nerve of a dog-fish reeking of formaldehyde. I dissected the *sixth* nerve. But I had to pass that section before moving on to the second MB at the London Hospital Medical School. Then inspiration struck. My teacher, Professor Wells, knew the examiner was something of a car buff and mentioned that the suppos-edly anonymous examinee who had dissected the wrong cranial nerve had a Gullwing, and implied that he could arrange for the examiner to take it for a spin. He did. I passed.

I went straight from Hull Tech. to continue my studies at the London Hospital Medical School, an idea doomed to failure from the beginning. In the early Sixties the City was taking off; businesses were flourishing; money was cheap; the Beatles had appeared on the scene. The miniskirt was in fash-ion, the Pill – thank heavens – was available, and the beautiful leggy English girls went wild. I was a well-off bachelor living in a lovely flat in Earls Court. And I was supposed to study?

It had been my intention to imitate Grimsdyke, a character from *Doctor in the House*, a loveable bounder whose aunt, as long as he was a student, sent him a generous allowance. So he was in no hurry to pass his second MB; he failed the first time and the second and the third, and was still in the school. I failed once but, unlike Grimsdyke, was summarily kicked out.

However, I had already invested three years of study in medicine. I found a private tutor, retook the second MB exam – and failed. I was surprised, because on this occasion I had given it my best shot and I am not an idiot. I heard later from a medical friend that I had never stood a chance of being readmitted. The Professor of Physiology, with whom I shared a mutual loathing, had it in for me. Apparently it all began when, late for a lecture, I roared into the school car park in my red Ferrari 250 Mille Miglia – I was between Gullwings at the time – and skidded to a spectacular halt in a cloud of dust. The dust settled to reveal the good professor, lightly dusted, standing by his bicycle. I suppose I must have appeared pretty repulsive to him, with a cavalier attitude towards my studies. He had a point. It looked as if the medical profession was going to have to scrape along without me.

I presented myself for interview at UNICEF, offering to work anywhere in the world for nothing, including my travel expenses. A horrid sniffy female turned me down flat. So, licking my wounds, for I really would have liked to work with children, I spoke to some friends in the wine business. They arranged for me to work in Burgundy, in Beaune at the Station Œnologique, a government-funded wine research institute, where I enjoyed a few months learning about the chemistry of wines and their making. I also discovered that I had a very good palate.

I returned to London and worked in some wine cellars at Tower Hill owned by the very knowledgeable Gerald Asher, who specialised in lesser-known wines, the only time I was to work for anybody but myself. It was time well spent and I learned a great deal. Then one evening I decided to eat at fashionable Nick's Diner, just down the road from my flat.

CHAPTER THREE

A Change Of Tack

I was comfortably installed with a book propped up against the ice bucket, a goblet of Côte de Brouilly to hand, enjoying the house dish, *filet de bœuf en croûte*. Suddenly there was a total eclipse and darkness fell, which was surprising in SW10. Nick Clarke, the owner – all seventy-seven inches and twenty-two stones of him – was looming over my table with a bottle of the very same wine. 'Mind if I join you?' he asked, sitting down. Politely I dog-eared the page and closed my book.

Nick was a self-taught restaurateur, whose only experience of matters foodie was as the catering officer in a Guards officers' mess during his national service. His fellow officers encouraged him to take his talent on to Civvy Street. With help from his mother, the actress Alison Leggatt, and from his godfather Richard Goolden, who for years played Mole in *Wind in the Willows*, he bought Annie's Café in Ifield Road, SW10, for £5,000, and re-named it Nick's Diner. It consisted of a three-storey building, a basement and under-pavement coal-holes that became cosy vaulted private dining rooms, and a good-sized garden at the back.

What Nick could never be bothered to learn was the boring but indispensable side of managing a restaurant – stock checks, controls and costing – but such was the Diner's success that there was always sufficient money to meet the bills – for the time being. Even before I arrived, it was supporting Nick, his wife Serafina and their daughter Susie, who was at a good public school.

Eventually Nick got around to what was really on his mind. He was having problems with his partner, one Peter Evans of Evans Eating House fame, who wanted to start a chain of Diners. Nick was against the idea. The partnership was therefore under strain and he was looking for a replacement. He must have talked persuasively because, by the time I came to pay my bill, I had agreed, due diligence notwithstanding, to buy out Mr Evans.

The next day I spoke to my father, who had his hands on my purse-strings, and later took him to see the Diner. With chairs on the tables, a smell of stale cigarette smoke, overflowing dustbins awaiting collection, all its shortcomings revealed in the hard light of day, the place was not exactly looking its best – no night operation does the morning after. Nevertheless this dear man gave his consent, subject to the approval of a professional accountant whom he sent in to examine the books. The bean counter agreed to the valuation that Nick and Serafina had put on the partnership. Money changed hands and there I was, a partner in Nick's Diner. I had a new career.

As Annie's Café, the Diner had been frequented mostly by lorry drivers – a transport café, in other words. The transition was neither smooth nor peaceful; when some of Annie's rougher latter-day clientele clashed with Nick's Old Etonian chums, nasty scenes ensued. It didn't help that across the street was the Ifield pub, where many of the lower orders quenched their thirst and willingly supplied reinforcements when a class war broke out. It was a good thing that Nick was as huge as he was. Eventually the Establishment won the battle, the increased prices and the lack of chips and HP sauce driving out the last of Annie's customers.

Shortly after the Diner opened something happened – quite unplanned – that added enormously to its 'you'll-never-guess-where-we're-taking-you' charm. Ifield Road was just in Fulham, and in those days Fulham was pretty seedy. Some slumming in Kings Road side streets was permissible, but Fulham was considered a borough too far. The first winter of business was very cold, so the street door, which opened directly into the dining area, had to be kept closed. To gain entry you rang the doorbell, a wooden peephole was opened and you were observed. If you had a reservation, or your social desirability or beauty were approved, you were admitted, as though to a speakeasy. Come the spring, the door was again left open, provoking well-bred squawks of disappointment. 'One absolutely *loved* ringing the bell of an anonymous house with dustbins outside in a seedy street in foul Fulham. It was half the fun. 'Lock the door again!' Nick was told, and locked it was, forever after, winter and summer.

Apart from slumming it and surprising one's friends, there were other good reasons for going to the Diner, even if the dim atmosphere of the ground floor dining room – a foggy admixture of cigarette smoke, candle fumes, Old Spice and garlic – was not to everyone's taste. Part of the attraction was that anyone from the royal family down to a local mobster might be hidden in the gloom.

The eclectic menu was unlike anything else available in London, and the cooking, although extremely basic, was adventurous. The wine list was well thought out, the degree of comfort adequate and the candlelight kind. And in the basement were Snitch and Snatch, the vaulted coalholes, conveniently curtained. The private dining room, hidden away in the nether regions beyond the tiny kitchen, was discreet, lockable from within and much used. On the first floor was Nick's bathroom, which doubled as the restaurant loo. On occasion we held board meetings in there, with Nick reclining massively in the bath covered with blessedly abundant soap suds.

A problem which was never solved was the lack of air extraction in the kitchen. Cooking fumes rose to the ground floor dining room and up to the higher floors. The staircase became effectively a chimney, and the customers' coats, hung alongside the staircase, became heavily impregnated with cigarette smoke, garlic and oil. The waiters – not by chance but by design – were cheeky, efficient and always slender and beautiful. They were one of the chief reasons for the Diner being the choice of many a female. We used paper tablecloths, so debs could write their telephone numbers and hide them under, say, a saucer for the waiter to retrieve when the birds had departed with their chinless wonders. Often the waiters were socially superior to the customers, perfectly at ease with anyone, from plumber to princess.

The head waiter was Nigel Douglas, who was particularly beautiful and whose wife Hilly wore the first miniskirt I ever saw. I nearly died of pleasure – she had endless legs. Their effect on me is exactly the same four decades later. One customer, wanting to attract Nigel's attention, clapped and shouted, 'Waiter!' Nigel strode across and stood tall, arching his lithe body like a matador, stamped his heels in a clattering *zapateado*, clapped his hands staccato over his head, and cried, 'Olé!' Laughter all round, except from the affronted party.

The legendary guitarist Davey Graham was partly the reason I was there on that fateful evening when Nick joined me. He played a few times a week, singing mostly blues and ballads, one of which was my favourite 'Baby Please Don't Go.' On your bill you would find *Music by Davey Graham, 1s 6d. If you don't like it, don't pay.*

An early manager was Charles Campbell, who left the Diner to open Oats restaurant in Hollywood Road, and later the Neale Street Restaurant. He gave the Diner a starter called Egg and Bacon Croquettes, a sort of superior Scotch egg with a tomato *concassé*, for which I would give my grandmother, if I still had one, to obtain the recipe. He died young. Moderation was not common in the Sixties.

Following my father's dictum, that to run a successful business you had to know it from the bottom up, I was soon working in the Diner's kitchen under the beady eye of Giuseppe 'Joe' d'Imperio, the head chef of a staff of three. Also in the kitchen was an awful slattern who did the washing up. Joe used to chase her around the tiny space brandishing a looped tenderloin into which he would stab a courgette and shouting, 'I agoin' to facka yow.' But in spite of the floor show we still managed to bang out more than a hundred covers a night of *à la carte* orders to an acceptable standard. To every bill was added a cover charge of two shillings, one of which went to Joe in cash, the other to the house. In a six-day week, averaging easily eighty covers a night, that added up for Joe. For additional income he worked in the Evans Eating House commissary in the daytime, where his sole job was to clean beef tenderloins on a piece-work basis. After a day of this, he came directly to the Diner to start the *mise en place* at three in the afternoon, working there until close to midnight. Joe was a tireless worker and he earned his large house in Shepherd's Bush.

Nick's menu writing was unique, descriptive and witty. It had to be, because many of the dishes were only to be found at the Diner and the waiters got bored describing every dish to every customer. One dish, not well known in Fulham – or anywhere else north of the Channel – at the time, was Steak Tartare. Often, when the dish was produced, the customer would say, 'Oh, I didn't want it *quite* so rare,' which was embarrassing for all concerned. So it was described on the menu as 'the best raw steak outside London Zoo', which saved many a blush.

Nick was self-taught, unshaped by any formal training. He did a great deal of research, and if he liked a dish he put it on the menu. One of his favourite discoveries was a starter from New Orleans called *la Médiatrice* – The Mediator – so called because, the story goes, if a man in that city had misbehaved, he would bring this home to his wife, who would eat it, then all was forgiven. If ever you need to seek such forgiveness, all you have to do is scoop out half a baguette, baste the inside copiously with garlic butter, then bake it in a hot oven until the crust is crispy and oozing. Shuck some oysters (mussels work well too), deep-fry them briefly, drain and stuff them in the baguette. Consume with copious quantities of guacamole. *Et voilà* – all is *couleur de rose* – divorce lawyers and alimony avoided.

Whatever else was on offer, the Diner's gastronomic popularity was built around the ever-present *filet de bœuf en croûte*, a dish of surpassing Sixties clumsiness. But with its crust of golden pastry in a pool of mud-coloured sauce, it looked good, it tasted good – and by golly, it did you good! With Nick's recipes, no complicated techniques were involved and no hard-to-obtain ingredients required. This meant that every dish could be repeated accurately and quickly, which was pleasing to the customers. This simplistic culinary philosophy I carried with me for the rest of my life as a restaurateur, and it has never failed me.

Everyone adored our side dish Garlic Spuds. Parboil potatoes, cut them into smallish cubes, dry them on kitchen paper, deep fry until brown and crispy, place in a bowl, season with salt and pepper, cover with plenty of crushed garlic and add an indecent amount of butter. Finally mix the whole shebang with a potato masher, sprinkle on some chopped parsley and serve. Satisfaction guaranteed.

When it came to puds, Caramelised Oranges Grand Marnier and Chocolate Mousse were popular, but the real champion was *crème brulée*. Many a customer would on arrival instruct the waiter to put aside sufficient *crèmes brulées* for the party, and only then consult the rest of the menu.

Nick's knowledge of wine was, unlike his consumption of it, relatively limited. He sensibly enlisted the help of well-informed friends, who brought imagination and innovation to the list that I inherited. Nigel Grant and the late Kit Bland of G.F. Grant & Co. advised him, especially on the wines of the Loire, which until then were mistakenly thought not to be able to travel. They added such rarities as Saché from La Sablonnière at Azay-le-Rideau, and a red Saumur-Champigny. Morley Richards, a lawyer and expert on German wines, introduced such treasures as St. Nicholas *Eiswein*. For Burgundy Nick turned to connoisseur Michel Couvreur, whose cellars were situated in the aptly-named Bouze-lès-Beaune. He was a purist, and his Burgundies were always fine examples of what was written on the label, as difficult to find then as now.

Finally there was the inimitable Ahmed Pochee, late of Baghdad, whose method of buying was to go around the big wine houses – Morgan Furze was a favourite – buying up wines of which they had too few bottles to list. He delivered his customers' wine in his Lagonda. His business was called Oddbins and it became bigger and bigger. Eventually it outgrew itself, and Ahmed found he was undercapitalised and forced to sell out to Augustus Barnett. Now it is no more.

As well as working in the kitchen, I took over the wine section of the business. One of the first things I did was to increase greatly the half-bottle section of the list, reckoning that for two people two bottles was a bit too much but a bottle and a half was just about right. One of my best acquisitions – from Ahmed, of course – was several half-bottles of Pontet-Canet 1926. One evening Tommy Docherty, the manager of nearby Chelsea Football Club, came to the Diner to celebrate an important victory. He selected and tasted this fifth growth wine and was thrilled. 'Get a whiff of this, Nick,' he said. I swirled the wine in the goblet with impressive skill and held it to my discerning nose, which is not small. Somehow my proboscis touched the wine and a ruby drop hung thereon. Tommy saw what had happened, shook his head and smiled ruefully, but he *did* drink that nectar.

The restaurant critic for *Queen* was the formidable Quentin Crewe, a man of immense influence who was a great supporter of the Diner in his column and a regular customer. Although wheelchair-bound – he suffered from progressive muscular dystrophy – Quentin had crossed the unfriendly Empty Quarter in Saudi Arabia. Unlike any other food critic I can think of, he had the courage to open his own restaurant, the Brasserie St. Quentin, thus exposing himself to other critics.

Nigel Dempster of the William Hickey column, promising anonymity, was always grateful for tasty scandalous snippets, for which the *Daily Express* paid five guineas. But this could backfire. Nick had rented the gatehouse to a property belonging to Pamela and David Hicks. He was invited to a party at the big house, and reported to Hickey something he had heard there. This was spotted by the Hicks. There was only one possible source; Nick had to leave the gatehouse.

In 1963 Joseph Losey filmed a sequence of *The Servant* at the Diner. This masterpiece starred a brilliant Dirk Bogarde with Sarah Miles, Wendy Craig and James Fox. The rather seedy image of the Diner which he portrayed is the one that many carry in their minds, but it did us no harm. On the contrary.

In those heady days anyone of consequence or fame ate at the Diner. Apart from a nod, their presence was never acknowledged, a lesson I took with me into future restaurant adventures. One evening a woman entered, mostly hidden in luxurious furs. The Russian hat was removed, and blond hair cascaded down, revealing the ravishing Julie Christie, direct from filming *Dr Zhivago* in Spain. The restaurant caught its breath. She was, in fact, godmother to the child of our manager, Peter Cramp.

Once in a while culinary heavyweights came amongst us. Elizabeth David and Margaret Costa were sometimes joined by Pamela Vandyke Price, she invariably wearing a pretty hat and gloves in case the well-known wine merchant André Simon, with whom she was head over heels in love, should drop by.

Or you might spy, hunched in a corner, Oliver Reed, fresh from his triumph in *Women in Love*. His face was scarred, as he had been the victim of mistaken identity by a pair of knife-wielding thugs in the Kings Road.

One evening Lindy Dufferin – Marchioness of Dufferin and Ava – asked a waiter to put a brown paper bag in a safe place. He hid it behind the bar. Later in the evening we took a peep. It was a glittering tiara. She had, we learned, come straight from a reception at Clarence House.

Clement Freud, an odd one who hid his insecurity behind a gruff aggressive façade, sniffed the air of the Diner one evening, detected aftershave, frowned and left.

Discretion was our watchword – well, almost always. One evening I saw a familiar figure ascending from the basement, and told my partner that the famous cricketer Ted Dexter was leaving. 'Good night, Ted!' bellowed Nick. Eyes turned towards the unfortunate willow-wielder. The lady with him was not Mrs Dexter. Probably his niece, we agreed.

I remember Mick Jagger and Rudolf Nureyev dining together. Both wore black leather, and ate voraciously and not very elegantly – my nanny would have had them over her knee. They did not exchange one word, yet somehow they created an invisible barrier, excluding everyone else. Years later I was to witness Ingrid Bergman and her children create exactly the same effect.

One day I arrived to find a fire engine outside the restaurant and hoses snaking through the front door and into the basement. The Beatles had been dining in one of the coal holes, and one of them – unidentified – had been meditatively sawing with his steak knife on a pipe in the ceiling which happened to be the water main.

I once received a surprising offer; Otto Preminger, the film producer, called me to his table and studied my face for a moment and said. 'Ven you vant to play ze part of a Roman centurion, you vill let me know.' So close to fame!

I read in one of Joanna Lumley's autobiographies that she used to enjoy the odd free dinner from Nick. Joanna was very slender, her face pretty and freckled. One evening her complexion was suddenly clear. 'Where have your gorgeous freckles gone?' I couldn't help asking. 'Oh, I just paint them on,' she said airily. She was one of many beautiful girls who enjoyed Nick's generosity. I never had an inkling of the extent of Nick's largesse but it was considerable.

Every Saturday a man came in with three friends. They always sat at the same table and had four *crèmes brulées* put aside before looking at the menu. They invariably ordered plain steak and Mateus rosé. One day I enquired, 'Nick, that man who comes every Saturday with three friends and has plain steak and Mateus – who is he?'

Nick clapped his hand to his forehead. 'He's called Jack,' he said, looking very cross with himself. 'I meant to tell you. Damn! Damn! I'm soooooo sorry – I forgot.'

'Forgot?' I asked, somewhat crisply.

'You know my Bentley?' Nick had recently acquired a rather nice R-type Bentley saloon, which, uniquely I think, had the gear lever low down between the driver's seat and the door. 'Well, the thing is, actually, what I meant to tell you is – er – well, I bought it from Jack on – er – nosh-credit…'

Nosh credit???

'It means Jack has to run up £900 worth of bills at the Diner in two years.' More clapping of hand to forehead and expressions of agony and remorse. 'Damn! Damn! How could I forget?' 'Jack' was none other than Jack Cohen of Tesco supermarkets. Heaven knows how many other nosh credit deals Nick had done.

Serafina and I had what might be described as a vexed relationship. I felt she and Nick rather rode roughshod over me, having always run the restaurant for themselves. Even after I put a great deal of money into the venture, nothing changed. One Bank Holiday weekend, she and her boyfriend Anthony Lindsay-Hogg dropped by to help themselves – as all we directors did – to whatever they wanted from the restaurant stores. But no-one had told Serafina that Little Joe, our helpful maintenance man, had removed the staircase. Serafina entered the restaurant, turned sharp left and descended to the basement rather more quickly than she intended. She suffered no serious bodily harm, though her pride may have got off less lightly. But I have met her since – she went on to great success as a literary agent – and found her, and she me, I believe, much more likeable.

I was told little about Nick's deals with criminal elements in south-west London. I knew that he had to pay so much a week in protection money, as it was euphemistically called, to ensure that the dustbins were emptied. But I have no idea how much was involved. I regret not being present when two Neanderthal thugs came in one evening demanding to speak to 'the gaffer'. Nick sussed out the situation immediately. 'Gentlemen,' he said, generously if inaccurately, 'do sit down. What would you like to drink?' Baffled – Nick was supposed to be terrified by these menacing halfwits – they sat and were given drinks.

'Pity about that brick you had through your window a few days back,' one of them remarked. 'Not good for business, is it, guv? Tends to upset people, know what I mean. But, tell you what, guv, if you was to hand over a pony (twenty-five pounds) each and e'vry week, we could make sure it don't happen again – see?'

Nick just smiled sweetly. 'There must be some mistake,' he told them. 'We haven't had a brick through our restaurant windows in living memory.'

The thug was taken aback. 'Bloody 'ell,' he moaned. 'They've done the wrong bleedin' place again!'

At that moment a powerful Irish voice boomed out, 'Hello dere, Nick. How're t'ings?' The source of the enquiry was a big man well over six feet tall. 'Christ,' said one of the thugs. 'You know Pete Scott?' They got to their feet and fled. Their manor was Battersea. Fulham and possibly Chelsea belonged to the Irishman. In the underworld you did not trespass.

Peter Scott was London's very own Raffles, an avowedly non-violent cat burglar of great fame, who wrote an autobiography, *Gentleman Thief: Recollections of a Cat Burglar*. He was also known as the human fly. Lance Callingham, a friend, fellow competitive water-skier, and son of the colourful Lady Docker of gold-plated Rolls-Royce fame, told me how, for a bet and still in evening dress, Peter climbed up the Park Lane façade of the Dorchester Hotel from pavement to roof. One of the most famous exploits of this charming middle-class criminal was nicking Sophia Loren's jewels in 1965, whilst she was working on the film *The Millionairess*. She was particularly upset by the loss of an uninsured £200,000 necklace. On the way home Peter stopped for a nap in a lay-by. A passing police patrol car spotted the car, recognised him, and found the Loren sparklers in the boot. Down the river he went – again. His marks were an illustrious lot, numbering amongst others Shirley MacLaine, the Shah of Iran, Judy Garland, and even Queen Elizabeth the Queen Mother. His last attempted heist was of a Picasso in 1998, which cost him three and a half years of freedom.

Once Nick told Peter that Serafina had been burgled, her jewellery stolen. Peter was terribly embarrassed. Fulham was his manor, and a friend of his being robbed on his turf was not on. Serafina got all her baubles back. When Peter died in March 2013, the *Daily Telegraph* gave him a full half-page obituary.

In the Sixties credit cards had not yet made an appearance, so bills were settled in cash or by cheque, or charged to one's account. Sometimes cheques bounced. To cover ourselves against this contingency we insured all cheques issued to us, for £65 a year. Our only requirement was to have the name and address of the issuer written on the reverse. Two instances rather dampened the waiters' willingness to ask customers to oblige. In one case the mother of Lady Elizabeth Anson (she had a terrific business called Party Planners) had taken the private dining room. When the waiter delivered the bill she wrote out a cheque. He asked if she would kindly write her name and address on the back. With a withering look she scrawled 'Anne of Denmark' which, by virtue of her second marriage, she was. Another customer, when asked by the waiter to comply, said rather tersely, 'See front!' The cheque had been drawn on Coutts Bank and he was John Coutts.

Those who signed bills but failed to pay within thirty days, or who told us once too often that the cheque was 'in the post', we passed to the tender mercies of the brothers Quatermain. These debt collectors had a most successful system. A well-spoken man would visit the reluctant payer, chat about the weather and politely request settlement. If the amount was paid as arranged, that was that. If, however, no subsequent payment was made, the next collector would be rather less refined. And the bloke after him would be heavier still, and nastier. We were always paid and asked no questions.

Nick's health was always a concern. His lifestyle consisted mostly of eating and drinking. As far as exercise went, except when he got lucky, he did little enough. I tried to get him a bit fitter. My first attempt took the form of karate, in which discipline, esoteric in those days, I was quite advanced. I built a small school in the garden. One of the exercises we practised was the reverse punch, which is a powerful technique. One day at a board meeting – not in the bathroom on this occasion – Nick stood up and said, 'I feel slightly tense' and, with a perfect reverse punch, slammed his fist through a nearby door. That ended the karate.

Next I took him to Ruislip marina, where David Nations, founding father of competitive British water-skiing, was coaching me in jumping. I thought that Nick might enjoy skiing. Made even vaster by his life jacket, he floated Leviathan-like close to the jetty. David came past in his mighty Bosch speedboat, its powerful engine rumbling menacingly. His look-out threw the towing handle to Nick. The tow rope tightened as the boat moved away. 'Ready?' enquired David through his electric loud-hailer.

Nick nodded to me, his hands gripping the handle.

'Hit it!' I yelled, and David unleashed a few hundred horsepower.

Somehow the towing line handle found its way between Nick's tree-like legs and, as the irresistible pull came, he began to yell and curse. His vocabulary was extensive and inventive, and I actually saw a woman clamp her hands over the ears of her innocent child. So that was the end of water-skiing, and of my attempts to improve his fitness. Nick's weight was to remain forever at twenty-two stones.

Running a restaurant day after day, being nice to people whatever your mood, is hard work. Added to this in Nick's case, none of the enormous amounts of cash generated over ten years had stuck to him. We were joined by Kem – more accurately Kemys-Tite Bennett, late of The Hole in the Wall in Bath, whose wife had recently been stolen by a Wimbledon sculptor called David Wynne. With Kem's considerable gastronomic know-how, we opened an outside catering business called Moveable Feasts, the commissary for which was housed in a former ladder factory in the Fulham Road. This venture, although successful, took too much time, and we eventually sold the name to Nick Huntingdon. The premises were taken over by Walter Baxter of Baxter's Pork Pie fame, who gave the building to his friend Fergus Provan, who in turn converted it into a restaurant called Provans.

One day a house across the road came up for sale. With financial assistance from Nick's mother we bought it and installed a restaurant, The Place Opposite. This never really took off, as people thought they were being put in the Diner annex. Later, in partnership with proven restaurateur Shura Shivarg, it became Nikita's, a Russian restaurant. But by that time, although still a shareholder, I had left London.

Nick died in a chiropodist's chair aged only forty-six. But he left his stamp on what, for one generation at least, were London's finest years – the Swinging Sixties.

I learned some valuable lessons at the Diner which were to stand me in good stead. I learned to devise simple yet satisfying dishes which only required accurate and speedy copying. I learned how to write an amusing and informative menu and wine list. I also gained the ability to work in the kitchen, which meant that professional chefs would never have me over a barrel, always a threat to non-cooking restaurateurs. I learned about financial controls and how, if they were not strenuously enforced, it was possible to run a busy restaurant and not make money. Finally I had found a profession which I could pursue anywhere in the world.

All in all, my investment in the Diner was to pay off handsomely.

CHAPTER FOUR

A Change In The Breeze

I began to consider the idea of supplying customers with wines they had enjoyed at the restaurant at home, but at wholesale prices. So I began Nicks' Diner Wines, which was soon renamed Savile Hudson Wines (the Savile was supposed to add a touch of class). The company was based in my flat, a lovely Victorian place in a block that stretched from Old Brompton Road to Egerton Gardens, where I lived with Heidi, an Afghan hound given me by Eve Britton, wife of the actor Tony Britton. Eve's bitch had produced an enormous litter of sixteen, which, Tony told me, left little room in the bed for them. Heidi was destructive, a thief, vindictive, fast as the wind, but beautiful, irresistible, and an occasional earner when she modelled for Woolmark. Although I lived in the middle of London, exercising her was no problem, since girlfriends literally queued up to take her walkies. I discovered why. As certain ladies in Paris knew full well, passing gentlemen used pooches as an excuse to introduce themselves. These encounters, carefully handled, might lead to an invitation to dinner, or better.

I found myself a secretary, Caroline Lloyd, all long legs, long hair and minimal mini – and a joy to work with. It was so refreshing each morning to go into the office – in fact my dining room – to be greeted by this smiling vision. She was very efficient, and she tolerated me. And – since you might want to ask – no, we didn't. And I had two cleaners, James Osborne, half-brother of James Aspinall, and a charming reprobate known as Mike 'Lunchtime' O'Sullivan, both of whom I was to meet again on the other side of the Big Pond.

The location of my flat was perfect, just ten minutes' drive from the Diner. Hyde Park was within walking distance, Knightsbridge tube station was minutes away, and there were numerous good restaurants close by – Au Fin Bec, Le Français, Parke's (later Mr Benson's Bar), and Patrick Lichfield's Tai Pan next door in Egerton Garden Mews. The most civilised hairdressing salon in the world, Gary Craze's Sweeney's, was in Beauchamp Place, sometimes known as Bankrupt Row, such were the exorbitant rates. There I would eat a toasted sandwich and drink coffee whilst having my hair looked after by Doug. One went there as much for the beautiful people – it was an early example of a unisex salon – as for any other reason.

But, most importantly, just down the road was Harrods, in those days the finest shop in the world. What a paradise it used to be before the phoney Pharaoh ruined it! Whenever we made a bigger-than-usual wine sale, I would dash off to that exemplary emporium to spend much more than the profit on the wine. First stop – by way of the ornate bronze lifts, their attendants singing out in a strange tuneless monotone, 'Lydees' 'aberdashery, 'andbags and haccesserories, mind the doors, per-lease' – was the book department, hoping for a newly discovered P.G. Wodehouse or C.S. Forrester. Next the second-hand furniture department, where they sold items not quite a hundred years old, which, not yet being 'antiques', were well priced. Thereafter to the piano department, where I would play some Chopin or Beethoven, which always went down well with the sales people and customers. I continued to the pet department, where I would have a love-in with an African Grey parrot who would coo sweetly while I scratched his head. I adore parrots.

Then down to the basement, The Green Man pub, and the gentlemen's loo, a pristine porcelain paradise maintained to polished perfection by a fellow in black trousers and crisp white tailored jacket with immaculate Brylcreemed hair. He doubled as a shiner of shoes, something he did extremely well; certainly the glacial perfection of his own defied description. As he worked his magic with brush and cloth, we would chat, but not about politics as with a taxi driver; water polo was his game. I became quite an expert after several years. The only other subject admitted to these Mensa-level discussions was his arthritis, so I waxed lyrical on the remarkable curative qualities of cod liver oil. I knew whereof I spoke, since my Dad was chairman of Seven Seas Cod Liver Oil Limited, and I had been brainwashed since childhood.

I would resurface like a mole into the Gentlemen's Outfitting, and set course for the Food Halls. In quick succession I gathered up brown bread, lemons, Normandy butter and Belgian chocolates, and hove to at the Scotch smoked salmon counter. Pale, smoky, almost transparent, with a melt-in-the-mouth quality – there was none better. It cost £10 per pound. Occasionally, if our wine sales had been particularly large, I might exit via the wine department and snare a bottle of Corton Charlemagne. Finally back to Egerton Gardens where I would lunch luxuriously, slipping Heidi a morsel or two.

I criss-crossed the country giving wine-tastings in offices and the homes of friends, who would invite their cronies and make an evening of it. I even flew to the Channel Islands and gave tastings there. From Ahmed Pochee I bought seven cases of Richebourg 1934 at a guinea – 21 shillings – a bottle, which Patrick Sergeant, then city editor of the *Daily Mail*, snapped up for a slightly increased price.

After a while, with increasing sales, I needed to carry more stock, so I rented the cellars beneath my block of flats. These belonged to my landlord, who had a carpet shop on the ground floor with windows on the Old Brompton Road. I was joined by Charles Longman, an Anglo-Frenchman of immense Gallic charm with a wide knowledge of wines, who had been working at Justerini & Brookes. Paul Harman, my accountant, completed the team. One of our selling techniques was to host lunches featuring our wines, in the hope that our guests might order a case or two before groping their way up the cellar steps. The combination of the Diner clientele and Charles Longman's customers meant that these events were never dull. I remember Sir John Ardizzone, President of the Royal Academy of Arts, his waistcoat covered in snuff and his great leonine head resting on his chest, sleeping quietly, a glass of port clutched in his hand. After one lunch we thought we had lost Paul Harman, only to find that he had, unnoticed, rippled off his chair and slipped under the table, where he too slept, smiling blissfully.

★

One day I saw in a showroom a rather splendid motorcar, sedate and upright. It was a Rolls-Royce 1936 Sedanca de Ville. I reflected that my days of hurtling around Europe in my Gullwing were likely to end in tears, for the roads were becoming increasingly crowded. In no time at all I had exchanged my Mercedes for the Rolls. I did a good deal, too, for I had bought my third and last Gullwing for £1,200 and was now getting £2,400 for it. What a clever fellow I was, I thought, doubling its value. The fact that Gullwings nowadays change hands for half a million pounds and more has not been lost on me.

A favourite Mayfair haunt was the Curzon Club, where the gambling subsidised the restaurant so you could dine well there for 25 shillings (£1.25). Next door was Cedar Travel, run by one Charles Riachi, who was also a member of the Club. Charles was the Mr Lebanon of London, and he ensured that his elite Lebanese clientele got whatever they wanted when they visited. In those days Lebanon was a stable, wealthy country, Beirut was 'the Paris of the Mediterranean', and its St. Georges Hotel was held in high esteem. We fell into conversation one summer evening over our pints of Pimm's, and within a few weeks I had purchased for £3,500 the remaining years of the lease on his mews house in Belgravia. This was not any old mews house. It was one of four in Chester Square Mews, a cul-de-sac with an arched entrance that I shared with Queen Juliana of the Netherlands and a concert pianist. I never met the fourth person. It was pure joy to arrive at the mews in the Rolls in pouring rain, pass under the arch, push the remote button which opened the garage door, and drive into the garage under the house. Somehow, after I left London a few months later, the lease, which I had been hoping to extend, slipped through my fingers thanks to some questionable professional advice – again.

It was terrific being part of the phoenix-like rebirth of a country. Britain had been bankrupted by war for the second time in thirty years, but had risen from the ashes of the *Blitzkrieg,* blockade**,** and rationing, to become again a leading nation with a thriving economy. Also we had the incomparable Beatles, we were world soccer champions and our beautiful mini-skirted girls were the envy of the world. What a time it was to be alive.

Thanks to naughty Lucilla 'Lil' Borthwick, whom I met through her brother Malcolm, I entered the world of debutantes and country house parties. As guests of Lil's parents, Algy and Bunty, we were left largely to our own devices. The range of activities was broad, what with backgammon, bridge, riding, hunter trials, tennis, croquet and piano-playing – and flirting. Lil always had pretty girlfriends, and, after we had retired, bedroom doors were opening and closing all night. I was asked to share a room with an Indian gentleman, a Parsee, who had once brought the Calcutta Symphony Orchestra to his mansion and spent the entire afternoon conducting them from the staircase. He took a fancy to me, and I found myself running around the bedroom trying to escape. I succeeded.

One weekend, between sets of tennis, one of the girls, with malice aforethought, asked if it was true that I did judo. I admitted I did. 'Go on,' she said giggling, 'do a throw on Hector.' Hector Kerr-Smiley, a 'debs' delight' unkindly known as Harpic (as in Clean Round the Bend), was extremely slight and fragile-looking. I executed a simple throw and laid him gently on the grass, whereupon he burst into tears. I felt absolutely awful.

Another setting for house parties was Dynes Hall, the home of my friend David Hart. His parents, Boy and Terry, had some amusing friends, but none more so than Ralph Richardson, the great actor, and Mo, his wife. Ralph loved motorbikes and used to ride around the grounds at huge speed on David's machine. Sometimes I would accompany him around the gardens with my camera at the ready. My Leica IIIc had a reflex housing which enabled me to take extreme close-up photos. I once took a photo of a bumble bee sitting on the hand of marble statue, its vibrant colours in marvellous contrast to the stone. Ralph loved the idea and thereafter called me 'The Poet'.

Of course, the reason parents sanctioned these house parties, and turned a blind eye to the shenanigans, was the hope that their daughters might land a suitable husband. Their good intentions were somewhat undermined by the arrival of the Pill. Girls could now assess the suitability of would-be husbands without the risks once associated with 'shooting before the Twelfth'. We all cashed in, girls and boys alike.

One of the great pleasures in the Sixties was travel. Car ownership was limited to the better off, so the roads were uncrowded, and there were no speed limits. Driving the Gullwing down to Lydd airport, flying it across to Le Touquet and roaring southwards to La Pyramide restaurant and Fernand Point was one of my great pleasures. The *Guide Michelin* was a quarter of the thickness of the modern version and infallible. You could be certain that the chef who had earned his rating was always there, not in his London or New York outlet. *Le Guide des Routiers*, a lorry drivers' guide to good cheap food, was likewise an essential travelling companion.

A favourite destination in France was the villa Boy and Terry Hart took for a month every year. It was situated on the Garoupe at Juan-les-Pins and belonged to Mr Heinz, the baked bean king. It literally had *ses pieds dans la mer*. The main salon looked out over the bay, and its huge window would, at the touch of a button, disappear into the ground. A casual breakfast was followed by a leisurely swim in the Garoupe bay. Blanche Kerman, wife of noted lawyer Isidor, would float around in an inflatable ring, holding a parasol to protect a complexion that had been the toast of inter-war Britain. She had memorably long slender legs, and was a fearsome bridge player. As noon approached, a butler would wade out to her with a tray bearing a gin and tonic embellished with plastic palm trees in a tall frosted glass. Lunch was the finest shellfish, lobster, crab or oysters, washed down with Chablis. Thereafter everyone retired for a short siesta. Bridge came next, until it was time for tennis at the Hôtel du Cap. Fast serves were frowned on, being not quite the thing. Sometimes, in the calm of the evening, a speed boat was hired, and I would show off my water-skiing skills. We frequently dined out, the then three-starred La Bonne Auberge being a favourite choice. Their *millefeuille au fromage* was my unchanging starter. The evening usually ended at the Juan-les-Pins casino, and eventually – richer or poorer – to bed. A couple of weeks of such hedonism were about all I could take.

Travelling by rail was enjoyable. There were first-class restaurant cars with wine lists to match, and porters to help with one's luggage. Taking the Red Arrow to Paris for a weekend fling was delightful. There was nothing quite like flashing through sleeping French towns at night, the window fully open, making love. Once I must have been with the gods, for my companion and I fell asleep entwined. We awoke to find the train had stopped at a station, and people were peering in at my lover and me with considerable interest!

Flying was effortless and BOAC was as good an airline as any, with young attractive cabin crew. The airports were never crowded, the VIP lounges were comfortable and their bars well stocked – and there were no tedious security checks. Blissfully, you could check in at the central London terminal on Cromwell Road, arriving at Heathrow unencumbered and at your destination refreshed.

One of the many bolts I thought desirable to have in my bachelor's quiver was the ability to fly an aeroplane. I enrolled at the Ken Gregory Flying School at Denham in Buckinghamshire, and obtained my private pilot's licence. I flew quite a bit around the United Kingdom, but it was in the next phase of my life that it really came into its own.

I did quite a lot of yachting out of the Royal Southern Yacht Club and sailed in the One Ton Cup. The high cost of that sport was something of an eye-opener. As if the boat itself were not expense enough, the owner was expected to pay for everything, including giving the entire crew dinner ashore. I could not help but notice that on many yachts the owner was scarcely welcome aboard his own vessel. He or she rather got in the way. Some patrons in polo suffer the same fate.

I would not have been in a position to so enjoy those heady days were it not for my inheritance. As mentioned, I had no idea whatsoever of the value of money, but I did have a very acute nose for a good thing, even if I sometimes failed to recognise its potential value at the time.

No matter on what unpredictable tangents my life took off, girls were the background against which all events were set. They influenced all my important decisions, and their intimate company was my principal pleasure. Indeed, I existed for them.

I had always hoped to become a more satisfying lover as I got older. I did have the advantage of learning at a comparatively young age the most important love lesson of my life. I had a girlfriend in Bournemouth called Maria, a ballet dancer, and older than me. You may imagine the positions the supple body of a dancer made possible. Once I lapsed smiling against the pillows in post-coital languor, thinking what a lucky woman she was to have been so pleasured, when a voice asked plaintively, 'What about me?'

I was staggered. What more could she want? 'I think,' said my lover, 'we'd better have a little chat.' Having gently soothed my battered ego, she proceeded to explain the differences between men and women. Essentially, she said, women took longer to – as it were – warm up, but if the man waited he would be well rewarded. It is so obvious with hindsight, but not then to a rampant young goat. I was never to forget what she told me. Thank you, sweet Maria. You changed my life.

I had masses of terrific – some truly outrageous – girlfriends. Sid James had introduced the moniker 'birds' to Britain. And it stuck, for it was the perfect description of those gorgeous, colourful creatures. Now they were finally flying free, liberated by the arrival of the Pill. They were not left – literally – carrying the baby. At last they had a choice. Some remained conventional and married. Some went wild. And some managed both.

There was none wilder than Sheila Oldham (sadly no longer with us), a red-headed flower child who wore fabulous floaty clothes, usually green or purple, and exotic bangles from Tibet. Her husband was involved in rock music. It didn't matter where we were, her devious mind was forever looking for ways to get a bit, anywhere, anytime, anyhow. Once I was driving her in her Lotus to Beauchamp Place, where we intended to lunch at Mr Benson's Bar. Suddenly she could wait no longer and dived down and attacked my defenceless person. Her aim was sure, and I was so distracted that I drove into the car in front. Never has clothing been adjusted so quickly, as pedestrians dashed up to offer assistance to a maiden seemingly in distress. It was a far from cheap thrill for me, since claiming insurance would have given the game away.

One day Sheila came up with an idea which thrilled her. Let's cause a stir at the French Horn in Sonning, a gastronomically terrific restaurant, if somewhat staid. Sheila loved to realise fantasies, and I was going to have to dress up for this one. I received precise instructions, and made a reservation for dinner.

That evening I strode into the dining room dressed in breeches and spurs, slapping my tall polished boots loudly with my whip. Sheila walked meekly behind, head bowed, wearing a flimsy shift and obviously nothing else. The restaurant went silent. I slapped her chair and pointed. She sat down. We somehow managed to keep straight faces for the whole delicious dinner; we always had the same things – a cornucopia of smoked salmon stuffed with thick yellow Jersey cream and lobster pieces flamed in cognac, followed by wild duck roasted on the spit over a fire in the entrance hall. Back in the car park we were convulsed with laughter. Then we were ready for bed again.

Another lover with whom life was never dull was the lively beautiful daughter-in-law of a baronet. She liked to make love on her fur coat and so did I. She also took a pragmatic view of her insufficient personal finances. In the hallway of her Belgravia house a bronze Buddha stood on a small console table. She would put her household bills between the wall and the Buddha which was gradually pushed towards the edge of the table. When eventually it fell off she would ring a Hungarian friend of a certain age. He would pay the bills and then enjoy the 'usufructs of gallantry', as Rex Stout, a favourite author of mine, put it. Buddha would be restored to his position against the wall and off they would go again.

Oh, how good it was to be a bachelor in the right place at the right time. When I thought of being married with a wife, children, school fees, family holidays, dress allowances – the fallout of the inevitable divorce – I shuddered.

Chapter Five

Off To The Sunny Caribbees!

One of our luncheon guests at the wine cellars was Robin Knox-Johnston, who had recently completed the first non-stop circumnavigation of the world aboard his yacht *Suhaili*. In conversation we discovered that we had both ordered a yacht hull from the same man, to whom we had paid our deposit as per a standard Lloyds contract. He had gone bust, or so he said, and we lost our deposits.

A friend of Robin's, a fellow single-hander of great renown, had also lost *his* deposit. He was Leslie 'Les' Williams, a lieutenant in the Royal Navy, who had been sponsored by Rudd Brothers to race a Gallant 53 yacht, *Spirit of Cutty Sark*, in the 1968 Blondie Hasler Single-Handed Trans-Atlantic race. Several days out from New York, he had been badly injured. He had also lost his self-steering gear, so was barely able to sleep, hardly daring to leave the helm. Courageously he carried on to the finish, gaining a commendable fourth place. The resulting publicity was so good for Cutty Sark Whisky and Les' fortitude so deserving, that Rudd Brothers had given him the boat.

Les, Robin and I decided to pool our resources and build a yacht to race in the inaugural 1971 Cape Town to Rio de Janeiro race, a monohull event. Having completed the race we would sail north, around the bump of north-eastern Brazil, and into the Caribbean. There we would charter the vessel with the accent on wine and food under my auspices.

In the short term Robin and Les would put into motion the design, finances, building, rigging, crewing, and sponsorship. They would take part in the two-handed Round Britain race, continuing to Malta for the Middle Sea race, finally sailing down to Cape Town, where I would join them and help with the refit before racing to Rio. My main input was to be financial. In the meantime I would go out to the Caribbean to look into the problems of licensing, water, work permits, local legislation, tourist agencies and so on. There I was to meet Ron Williams, the skipper of Les' *Spirit of Cutty Sark*, at the Friendship Bay Hotel on the tiny Caribbean island of Bequia in the Grenadines, and pick his brains.

Getting there meant flying to Barbados, changing aeroplanes and going on to the island of St. Vincent. There I would board an island schooner which would take me the twelve miles across the channel to Bequia, all seven square miles of it. I was not the best-prepared traveller, but then I never was. In this case I didn't even know where Barbados was, never mind the tiny island of Bequia, apart from its being in the Caribbean. I certainly didn't realise that it was only 200 miles from South America. Blithely I booked my flight and went on a shopping expedition for two items which I thought I would need.

The first was a backgammon board which I found at Messrs Abercrombie and Fitch. In Jamaica two years previously I had learned the game from Johnny (Earl of) Kimberley; I doubt if there was ever a better teacher. I took to the game and made money playing it. I sometimes played for quite high stakes. Backgammon is a widely played game, and I thought I might manage a rewarding rattle or two on my travels.

The other item I wanted was a broad-brimmed hat, so off I went to Herbert Johnson in Bond Street, in whose window I had spotted a rather dishy number with a snakeskin band.

There was a special person whom I was leaving behind – Carolyn Shaffer, the wife of Anthony Shaffer. He and his twin brother Peter were both playwrights of considerable repute. Our affair was gathering momentum, even though she had two enchanting young daughters, Claudia and Cressida, not my scene usually. Her marriage, she convinced me, was over (Anthony was later to marry Diane Cilento). Sometimes in the mornings we would drive her elder daughter Claudia to the French Lycée in South Kensington, where we would see many famous mothers in dressing-gowns, hidden – they hoped – behind dark glasses and headscarves, depositing their children.

She and I would dine together in our favourite restaurant, *Le Français* in the Fulham Road. Here the menu – and the wines – changed weekly from French region to region.

Anthony was frequently abroad, so Carolyn and I spent many happy nights together in their lovely house on the Wandsworth Bridge Road. The last time I was with Carolyn she woke me, whispering frantically, 'He's back!' I could hear a man paying off a taxi in the street below. He was supposed to be in New York for the opening of his play *Equus*! I grabbed my clothes and scuttled down the stairs as a key was being inserted into the front door lock. I dashed into the kitchen, opened the window and jumped out. I got a shock. Beneath the window was not the garden but a stairwell giving access to the basement. I fell into it, ending up in a heap, clutching my clothes but somehow uninjured. Eventually, I know not how, I dressed, found my way round the side of the house to the road, and retrieved my car.

Before I left for the West Indies, we discussed the possibility of Carolyn and her daughters joining me in the Caribbean after the transatlantic yacht race with Robin and Les. Obviously the whole concept was absolutely unworkable for any number of reasons. In any case, the torrent of events that was to sweep me off my feet in the next few months, and my own unforgivably selfish behaviour, put the three delightful females out of my mind. They were better off without me.

Another female whom I was to treat abominably was my Afghan hound Heidi. I left her with a kennel owner in Yorkshire and have never seen her again. Caroline, my loyal secretary, has never forgiven me.

Just as the Sixties were coming to a close, the day dawned on which I was to depart from my house in Chester Square Mews to do my fact-finding in the Caribbean. I kissed my girlfriend as she lay in our bed. She was gorgeous, with the longest legs I have ever seen; she worked as the Autocue girl at the BBC. I was leaving her as pure as when I had met her, which had been not my intention at all, so I was looking forward to our being re-united in a week or so. I never saw or heard from her again, though I was told she married an Oxford don. Anyway, I gathered up my meagre luggage, sufficient for a week or so – suitcase, backgammon board and the Herbert Johnson hat with its snakeskin band – and left for Heathrow.

Next stop: the sunny Caribbees!

CHAPTER SIX

The Hand Of Fate Takes The Helm

L ater that day I arrived in Barbados, where I had arranged to stop over at the Paradise Beach Hotel. I found the island surprisingly untropical – there was no sign of jungle, just acre upon acre of sugar cane. The road from the airport was narrow and bumpy, and the ancient taxi's suspension unable to cope. We passed small clusters of wooden houses with men slamming down dominoes on stout wooden tables in the shade of mango trees; no-one moved with any haste, for the air was humid and stifling.

The hotel was something of an oasis, its gardens bursting with luxuriant plants, with a driveway ending under a monumental *porte cochère*. As I checked in I was offered a welcoming rum punch. That evening there was a barbecue of roast suckling pig followed by a floor show, at which tourists were invited to make fools of themselves attempting to squeeze under the limbo bar. They obliged. I turned in early as I had to leave at dawn to catch a local flight to St. Vincent, a hundred miles to the west. From there I would take an island schooner to the island of Bequia – pronounced 'Beckwee' – to meet skipper Ron Williams.

The aeroplane approached St. Vincent from the west. Beyond the runway a mountain rose steeply – no taking off in *that* direction, I noted with a pilot's eye. I took an immediate dislike to the airfield because it had to involve a nasty downwind take-off, and to the island because it was looming – even claustrophobic – dominated at its northern end by the active volcano La Soufrière, which was to erupt eight years later.

In the capital, Kingstown, the air was still and stifling, the place crowded and bustling. I looked around and spotted Hazell's Bar – 'air-conditioned', it boasted! I went in and sat down. I had just ordered a *Cuba libre* – rum and Coke with lime – and opened my book, when a slender vision came weaving sinuously between the tables. From north to south there was a Panama hat, a striped suit in a pyjama-like material, and a pair of rather smart two-toned shoes. In its right hand was a silver-handled Malacca cane, held sword-like as if cleaving a path – as though anyone would dare impede the Progress. The face was patrician, the features refined, the nose slightly raised, the better to look down. This was my first sighting of the Honourable Colin Tennant, owner of Mustique Island, which he had purchased from the Hazels, a Vincentian family.

Before taking the island schooner *Friendship Rose* to Bequia, we were held back briefly as a cow was winched aboard, in a sling, lowered to the deck, and tied to the mast. This was Bequia's next week's meat supply, I was told. Most passengers were weighed down with 'Caribbean suitcases' – cardboard boxes – and caged chickens. Their island did not offer much food except fish, goat meat and sometimes, if the hunters had made a kill, whale meat. Bequia had once been a major whaling centre.

We motored out into the Caribbean Sea, the sails were hoisted and the engine cut. Peace! We breathed the trade winds, incomparably fresh after traversing 4,000 miles of the Atlantic. The channel was quite choppy and the movements of the *Friendship Rose* lively, too lively for some. A black priest on board went a most peculiar colour, and the cow mooed and bellowed. Under the lee of Bequia we found calmer waters, and were soon alongside and disembarking.

The jetty was stacked with hands of bananas, cartons of washing powder, bales of Pampers, tins of condensed milk, and mangos. A space had to be cleared to deposit the bellowing cow. I picked my way through to the harbour road, went onto the beach and took off my shoes to experience the sensual feeling of fine-grained hot tropical sand running between my toes. It felt so good that, for the next thirty years, except for regular visits to the bank to seek an increase in my overdraft limit, I rarely wore shoes. Bequia, with its colourful, easy-going capital Port Elizabeth, is one of the islands that make up the Grenadine archipelago. Together with St. Vincent – always referred to as the Mainland – they constitute the now independent nation of St. Vincent and the Grenadines. When I stepped ashore that day in 1970 it was still a colony.

The name Bequia comes from the Carib word *Becouya* – 'Island of the Cloud'. The Caribs were the fierce inhabitants of South American extraction who displaced, and in many cases ate, the creative peace-loving Amerindians, the first inhabitants in the Caribbean. The Caribs were in turn booted out by the Portuguese, the Spanish and the British, between the fifteenth and seventeenth centuries. Since 1903 they have continued their modern existence on the 3,700-acre Kalinago reservation – the Carib Territory – on the Atlantic coast of the nearby island of Dominica. It is self-administering and has its own Chief. The traditional Carib way of life is maintained to this day, although there has been some modernisation. There is now a model Carib village which tourists may visit, witness stage performances and buy local handicrafts, thereby helping the economy.

Bequia, with a land mass of only seven square miles, and a population of fewer than five thousand, was a peculiarly seductive island, especially to the international artistic community who had formed a colony there. Tourism, a notoriously fragile business, had only recently replaced whaling as the most important industry. The sea and her resources will forever remain the very lifeblood of Bequia and Bequians, traditionally splendid seamen and boat-builders.

Admiralty Bay, where the *Friendship Rose* was moored, was crammed with boats of every description swinging restlessly on their moorings. Modern vessels with soulless hulls of steel or fibreglass struck a jarring note amongst the timelessly elegant wooden skiffs and workboats. Local boys sculled dinghies with insolent skill, hoping to sell their wares to anyone who looked even vaguely foreign. Hung from lines slung between trees were fishing nets under which men sat in groups, repairing them and gossiping. Occasionally a bottle of Jack Iron rum, the local firewater which smelled like petrol, would be passed around. A sip sufficed. It was reckoned that one bottle would satisfy a team of carpenters for a day. Most Bequians made their livings supplying the needs of seafarers and now, increasingly, tourists. Several of the shops along the waterfront were chandleries. Others sold exquisite hand-made models of fully-rigged whalers and racing boats, famous for the meticulous attention paid to details – miniature oars, rowlocks, anchors, rudders, coiled ropes, harpoons – even down to the rounded stones on the bottom boards which, on racing days, were rolled up to windward after each tack as moveable ballast. There were examples of scrimshaw, delicate images of whaling activities carved into whalebone. Lean-to sheds under galvanised roofs were hung with garish pareos, sun hats, hideous Bermuda shorts and other tourist tat. There was no shortage of rum shops. Once in a while the crack of dominoes on wood would be heard, followed by a cry of triumph, and when darkness fell the players would move their game under a street light, the only source of illumination. But Port Elizabeth was far from bustling, apart from the brief upheaval caused by the arrival and departure of the *Friendship Rose*; sleepy is the word that comes to mind. The native Bequians moved steadily but with a strong intimation that there was always tomorrow – or the day after. People of the sea only bestir themselves when it is absolutely necessary.

My rendezvous was at the Friendship Bay Hotel, on the other side of the island. I found the island's only taxi driver asleep under a mango tree, a ragged straw hat tipped over his eyes. His taxi, a very old Studebaker, was suffering badly, as did all island vehicles – indeed anything not made of wood or glass – from the corrosive effects of the salt-laden air. We set off in the baking afternoon heat. The road, two strips of cracked and buckled concrete, wound up the western slopes and onto the central saddleback of the island, at which point I had to ask the driver to stop.

I knew exactly how stout Cortez felt when he fell silent on that peak in Darien. I, too, was rendered speechless. Away to the east a white line of Atlantic rollers was breaking on the outer reef. Scattered like jewels, on a sea of every hue from apple-green over the reefs to the deep blue of the channels, were the tiny islands of the Grenadines. These the driver proudly named for me. Closest, to the south-east, was Mustique, where Colin Tennant was king. Just north of it lay the uninhabited Baliceaux group. Further south were the islands of Canouan, the sublime Tobago Cays crowded with yachts, Mayreau, and, barely visible in the haze, Union, Palm, and Petit St. Vincent.

As I gazed over this idyllic scene, reality slowly penetrated my brain. *This* was my future life spread before me, not a pipe dream. With the help of my famously competent partners, Les Williams and Robin Knox-Johnston, I

St. Vincent and the Grenadines

would realise my life-long ambition, my only true vocation – a life at sea. My short-lived training as a Merchant Navy cadet would not be wasted after all. My vision was as clear as the sparkling waters before me. I saw myself cruising the Caribbean on our fine yacht, cooled by the trade winds, escorted by leaping, smiling dolphins. At noon we would anchor in some lonely bay and lunch under the shady awning. After a leisurely siesta, we would weigh anchor and sail for a while, trolling a fishing line astern, eventually finding a snug anchorage at sunset where we would stow the sails and break out the rum. Later we would barbecue freshly caught barracuda, the flavour of the tasty dark flesh and crispy skin enhanced with hot pepper sauce. This would be washed down with some wine purchased on nearby Martinique, a *département* of France. I would lie under the stars in my hammock, slung between forestay and mainmast, listening to the song of the wind in the rigging, conscious of the yacht tugging gently against her anchor, instinctively aware of the slightest change in the weather or sea conditions.

Enraptured, I climbed back into the taxi, now a veritable oven, and we rattled off across arid scrubland, inhabited only by goats and black-bellied sheep, from where we plunged down towards the south-east coast and Friendship Bay, my destination. The hotel was not in the least romantic, being constructed of concrete blocks, air bricks, ugly aluminium-framed windows with louvres, and a roof made from nasty corrugated asbestos, but it was mercifully camouflaged by rampant, many-coloured bougainvillea. The rooms were large, the terraces vast, the pillars massive, and the bar like a WWII Normandy beach bunker. Everything was oversized, as if designed by an amateur architect who wanted to make sure it could never fall down. Originally the hotel was built by a Bequian in the early Sixties. Later it was purchased by a colourful cigar-smoking American hotelier in Antigua, who had flown bombers in the Pacific during the war. He had dispatched the brothers Ron and Stan Young to Bequia to run it.

Ron, the elder brother, a big burly genial fellow in shorts and flip-flops, greeted me at Reception. I explained why I was there. 'I run the hotel side of the business,' he said. 'Boats? They're my brother Stan's department.'

Stan, it appeared, was out on a day charter in the hotel yacht but would be back before sundown. As I was to discover, wise sailors avoided navigating in the Grenadines after dark. Unmarked razor-sharp reefs, rearing vertically from the seabed, struck without warning. Of course, if you were engaged in the business of contraband, a popular pastime in those parts, which necessarily demanded an intimate knowledge of local navigation, that was a different matter. The central Customs and Excise authorities on St. Vincent did not have the resources to police the extensive national waters, so much profitable business was done between dusk and dawn. Brandy, Scotch whisky, cutprice cigarettes and even more exotic smoking material – Acapulco Gold was my favourite – were readily available at cut-throat prices.

Ron and Stan were yet another example of those who have found themselves in the Caribbean and wondered why on earth they would want to go back to the cold, rain, traffic jams, pollution, and pubs selling laughably small measures. Instead they could have sun, sand, the sea, beautiful people in very small bathing costumes, and rum at fifteen pounds a gallon. It was, if you were free to choose, a no-brainer.

The main problem was that the hotel had been built too soon. Its owner had been banking, not without reason, on an airport being constructed nearby in the early seventies. The parliamentary member for Bequia was the charismatic James Mitchell, known as Son, who owned the Frangipani Hotel and Bar in Port Elizabeth. He was elected Prime Minister in 1972, and I have no doubt that the construction of an airport would have been high on his list of priorities. The bumpy sick-making crossing from St. Vincent on the *Friendship Rose* was a strong deterrent for would-be tourists.

But by time the runway was eventually completed in 1992, both Ron and Stan were dead. Even as they lived in this paradise, both knew the sword of Damocles hung over them. There was a congenital weakness in the males of their family, aortic aneurism, a condition which medicine was unable to treat in those days. An aneurism occurs when the aorta, which carries oxygenated blood from the heart to the rest of the body, balloons under arterial pressure, eventually bursting without any warning. Death is instantaneous. Like their father before them, they were both to die from this inherited condition in the next ten years. In the meantime *carpe diem* was their philosophy. Nothing, they told me, was worth worrying about, least of all dying. I learned a valuable lesson from them.

As dusk approached I decided to wait on the beach for Stan's return. It was deserted except for three or four Sunfish craft pulled onto the sand, close by the stacked plastic beach furniture and folded parasols. I chucked off my bathing trunks and tee-shirt, and waded into the sea. There is no feeling like one's naked body floating weightlessly, caressed by the warm limpid waters of the Caribbean. It is, for me, a profoundly primitive experience in which you are freed of the cumbersome trappings of so-called civilised life. It is just the mood in which to watch the sun, its day's work done, sinking into the sea. On the fringes of the beach the fireflies were starting to show off amongst the sea-grape bushes, and the tree frogs and crickets were tuning up for their nocturnal symphony. As darkness came, the heavens revealed their crystalline splendour. Shooting stars streaked brightly and disappeared. The Milky Way and the constellations seemed so close. I was jolted out of this blissful reverie by the sound of slatting sails and creaking wooden blocks close at hand, as of a yacht coming into the wind. Above me a mast towered into the darkening sky. The sleek hull ghosted silently past under her genoa alone, barely disturbing the water, close enough to touch. I watched as Stan, in his element, walking the tack of the headsail out to windward to take off the weigh, unhurriedly laid her gently alongside the jetty. Such skill quickened the heart of a fellow sailor and I applauded silently. Stan made fast the moorings fore and aft and gracefully handed his charterers ashore. Some of them, thanks to Stan's powerful rum punches, needed to be set gently on course towards the hotel.

I pulled on my shorts, walked along the jetty and introduced myself. Stan was leaner than his brother, his body sinewy and taut. He had longish, receding blond hair, and a face the colour of mahogany. Frolicking around his feet was Nelson, his Jack Russell. As I helped Stan with the sunset ritual of erecting awnings, putting the yacht to bed and striking the ensign, I explained the purpose of my visit to Bequia. Of course he knew Ron Williams well – the yachting community in the Grenadines is tight-knit and supportive. 'I'll radio him in the morning,' he promised.

In those days radio was the sole means of voice communication among the boating fraternity. The cost of a new-fangled satellite telephone call was prohibitive – in the order of £7 a minute – and required a huge un-seaman-like antenna dish on board. Such things were generally confined to gin palaces chartered by tycoons and film stars. For sailors, the stand-by – default – radio channel was No. 16. Most sailors kept this tuned in all day, maintaining a casual listening watch. Eight in the morning and six in the evening were the best times when everyone was tuned in and listening. You made contact on channel 16, and then switched to another agreed channel where you would chat privately. At least that was the theory – sometimes the temptation to listen in was just too great.

By the next morning, Stan had spoken to Roy, who was sailing up from the island of Grenada; he would be at anchor in Friendship Bay the day after next and be at the hotel bar at noon. Would I meet him there? All meetings in the Caribbean seem to take place at bars. As I pondered a list of questions about chartering – fresh water availability, licences, work permits, travel agencies and the like – I looked at the bay below. A mile or so offshore was Whale Island, where, once a year and only once, a whale and her calf were hauled out up a ramp. They were taken at great risk, using a hand-held harpoon as tradition demanded, hurled from an oar-propelled boat. No rocket-propelled devices with exploding heads were employed here. The Leviathans, dwarfing the men who worked on them, were butchered for their meat, and the blubber rendered for oil. The sea near the ramp would be stained red for days. The enormous vertebrae made ideal bar stools, and a whale's jaw bones formed an impressive entrance to many a property. At lunchtime I sat down in the dining room – my book propped, as ever, against the ice bucket – to a delectable dish of cold red snapper with fresh mayonnaise followed by fruit. Ron and Stan took their food seriously. Afterwards I was tempted to take a siesta but decided instead to go for a sail. On the beach were several Sunfish, small sailing craft with a single lanteen sail. I stirred the somnolent water sports man into reluctant action and he dragged one of them into the sea for me. I clambered aboard, dropped the centre-board, locked the rudder into position, sheeted in the sail and away I went, downwind across the bay, the clear blue water slapping merrily against the flat fibreglass hull. The sun was warm on my shoulders, cooled by the flying spray. This was the life!

After a while I looked back, and was surprised to see the low-lying Bequia beginning to disappear below the horizon; it was time to head back. I hauled in the sail, went about and began tacking towards the distant shore. Immediately I was hard on the wind, the rudder popped up. This was not supposed to happen unless it struck an obstacle under water. I pushed it back down, locked it in position, and hauled in the sail again. The moment the craft gathered speed the rudder popped up again. This was not so good. Sunfish are not known for their ability to sail close to the wind; they tend to have much leeway – sideways motion. The rudder, fully down, helps the centreboard to counter this. The only way of getting back to shore was to make many shallow zigzags, each time gaining a little ground upwind. This would take the strain off the rudder and allow it to remain down. In theory, I should get back to the beach – eventually. I was hoping, sooner rather than later, to attract the attention of someone who could send out the ski boat to tow me in, but there was no-one in sight. The water sports man was probably back under his coconut palm with a bottle of rum or a female tourist, or both.

Two hours or more later, aided by a helpful shift in the wind direction – I don't think I would have made it back otherwise – I regained the beach and told the water sports bloke, now vertical again, what had happened. He explained that, because the rudders of the beached craft were left flopping up and down in the surf, the bronze locking portion – the very hinge of my fate – had become worn and ineffective. He would look into it tomorrow – or maybe the day after. In my room I took a shower and thought my skin felt rather sensitive; I saw in the mirror that it had a distinctly rosy glow.

I dried myself somewhat gingerly, put on shirt and shorts, and went down for an early supper of grilled local lobster – the spiny, clawless variety – with buckets of melted garlic butter, followed by a slice of key lime pie. Afterwards I took another long cold shower as my skin felt hotter. What could I expect, idiot that I was, not having used any sun protection whatsoever?

I fell into a fitful sleep under an idling fan, only to wake up not much later in great discomfort. I looked in the bathroom mirror and reeled in shock – who was that monster? What with the dreaded ultraviolet rays coming from all directions – the sky, the white sails, the white deck of the Sunfish and the highly reflective surface of the sea – I might as well have sat in a microwave for three hours. I was not a pretty sight. My chest, arms, shoulders, back and the tops of my thighs and feet were covered in huge semi-transparent, liquid-filled blisters. The skin that had been covered by my bathing costume was, by contrast, a ghostly pallid white, rather like the underside of a Dover sole. My weather-beaten face seemed to have got off lightly. But the worst part was the unbelievable sensitivity of my tense transparent skin. To touch it was agony. I needed expert medical help, which, possibly unfairly, I thought it unlikely Bequia would offer. What to do?

Then I remembered that the father of a girlfriend – not the one I had left in bed in London – was an eminent surgeon called Jack Leacock who lived on nearby Barbados. To get there I needed to go back to St. Vincent, either by taking the morning schooner or hitching a lift aboard any vessel thither bound. There I would hope to catch a LIAT flight to Barbados, not always the easiest thing to do. The wives of Caribbean ministers – because their governments held a few shares in the Company – had awarded themselves the right to use the aeroplanes like taxis. If they wanted to go shopping on another island, the ground staff, if they wanted to keep their jobs, gave them a seat, anyone's seat, and some unfortunate fare-paying passenger with a genuine booking was bumped.

In the event, the next afternoon found me back at Seawell airport on Barbados. My skin was still hyper-sensitive, but at least my bottom was unscathed, so I could sit down but only bolt upright. I telephoned the Leacocks and was told to get myself smartly to a private clinic in Bridgetown, the island capital, where Jack worked.

When I arrived on Barbados for the first time two days earlier I had been disappointed by the untropical landscape. Now, as I waited for a taxi, I had a good look around. The enlightened aviation policies of Prime Minister Errol Barrow were yet to be realised, and the airport was a minimal affair, a cheap building with a galvanised roof. You rather expected to see leaning against a wall one of Graham Greene's sleazier characters in a dirty white suit and battered Panama hat, picking his teeth and looking furtive.

Barbados' lush tropical forests were long gone. The first European settlers of the seventeenth century had chopped down most of the trees to make room for sugar plantations and for wood for building and furniture-making, something Barbadians became very good at. They were skilled copiers and, given the pattern books of such eighteenth-century English furniture makers as Chippendale and Hepplewhite, they produced excellent versions in Barbadian mahogany. Usually they added a little twist of their own which made them instantly recognisable and desirable to the connoisseur. It was a tragedy when antique dealers from Paris, who discovered this saleable resource in the 1970s and '80s, came to auction sales via Martinique, and plundered the Island's heritage, unhindered by any export control mechanism.

And so, from my taxi – a vast improvement on its Bequian counterpart – instead of noble mahoganies, towering royal palms, giant ferns and verdant bearded fig trees, I beheld only acres and acres of sugar cane. This commodity had been the source, thanks to slave labour, of the great wealth, influence and political clout enjoyed by the West Indian plantocracy, until a certain Mr Wilberforce made his voice heard in the 1830s. Disgracefully only one small parcel of the original Barbadian rain forest remains, at Turner Hall in the parish of St. Thomas.

★

For a newcomer to Barbados, one of the more striking features are the brightly painted wooden houses in which a large percentage of the population lives. In 1834, before the Emancipation of the West Indies (the abolition of slavery), most inhabitants – which is to say the blacks, who hugely outnumbered the whites – lived on plantations in 'tenantries'. This deliberately repressive system was characterised by insecurity of tenure, as the last thing the planters wanted was for slaves to put down roots. Their wooden homes were called chattel houses, because they could be dismantled when a slave was sold to another plantation and moved with him. By law this removal could only take place on a Sunday and is, to this day, something of an excuse for a celebration. Like a giant flat-pack, the house is dismantled and laid on a flatbed truck with the piano on top, so that a pianist can bash out hymns which are sung lustily by joyous movers and passers-by. At the new tenantry, the house is put together again. The law has since been amended, in 1956 and 1980, and now those living on tenantries have the right to purchase, at a controlled price, the freehold of the land on which they have erected their homes. One hundred and fifty years after emancipation they at last have security of tenure – and, critically, have been able to put down roots.

Chattel houses present problems. In days not so long gone, piles of stones at each corner had to suffice as foundations. Sometimes, when a house was moved, the owner would omit to tie down the ring beam which holds it all together, something which can be achieved simply with steel loops at the corners. So, when a strong storm comes, the roof flies off to land who knows where. The interior does not allow for any privacy, which leads to predictable familial problems. Also, being made entirely of wood, they are vulnerable to overturned kerosene stoves and offer a tempting target for arsonists seeking revenge. Increasingly Bajans are moving into stone-built houses, but by no means everyone.

In some cases, ownership of freehold – usually indicated by more permanent foundations – results in one finding on the famed Platinum West Coast, in the midst of the mansions of the rich and famous where the land is extraordinarily valuable, a chattel house. The occupier has refused monstrous amounts of money, being perfectly content to live close to the blue Caribbean, maybe fishing, maybe sitting under a coconut palm with rum to hand, or watching cricket on television; every chattel house has a television.

The thought of the Windies going in to bat on a Sunday morning at two hundred for two against England – their ex-colonial masters, please note! – is the West Indian idea of heaven. Even when a chattel house owner agrees to sell, it frequently proves impossible to find all the persons named on the title deed – Uncle Fred is in Toronto, Auntie Mame in Ulan Bator, Great-Aunt Eurene is God knows where – so title cannot be cleared and the sale cannot go through, a situation that tends to get lawyers, their clients, and realtors quite excited, and keeps the locals vastly amused.

Jack Leacock was a man I came to love and admire. Physically he was the complete ectomorph with a flat, slightly sunken chest, small shoulders, and a lean, wiry muscle mass. He was tall, inclined to stoop, and looked like the intellectual he was. He was down-to-earth, as doctors tend to be, sometimes shocking friends with his directness. He had no time for lay sensibilities. Once, during a cocktail party at his home, he took a syringe-full of blood from the arm of a departing guest, also a doctor, which he happened to require for analysis. There were bloodless faces all around. He was not given to histrionics and mercifully spared me a lecture on my stupidity. To his logical mind it was self-evident and I was paying the price for not having used some sun protection. He merely said, 'Second-degree burns', and went to work. I don't know what he did because I kept my eyes closed, grappling with the pain as best I could. Eventually he said, 'Your convalescence will take some time. You must come and stay with Margaret and me in our guest cottage for as long as it takes. I'll ask her to come and get you.'

Margaret duly arrived in her attention-grabbing beach buggy with huge chrome wheels and a VW engine. It had enormous, totally ineffective chrome silencers pointing heavenwards, stuck on the back. I had met her previously in England. She was stepmother to a girlfriend, Liz. She too was down-to-earth, a Geordie from a mining village in north-eastern England. She trained as a hospital theatre nurse, came to Barbados to work and, after a marriage or two, snared the Island's most eminent surgeon. Never were two people better matched.

We roared off through the shabby airless suburbs of Bridgetown into the breezy countryside, along endless tunnels of tall ripe sugar cane. Margaret drove at a fine clip, chattering away, and every bump was agony. Eventually, at the end of a cart track made up entirely of potholes, we arrived at their perfectly positioned home. When Jack, ever the pragmatist, decided to build a house for his family, he concluded that the optimum commuting distance between hospital and home, balancing being available for emergencies against getting away from it all, was seven miles. So he laid out an ordnance survey map on the kitchen table, stuck the compass point in the hospital, and described a circle with a radius of seven miles. From the locations over which the arc passed he chose Sharon Hill, an elevated piece of land, and therefore cooler, on a west-facing promontory that offered an uninterrupted view over the entire west and south coasts.

I found the first week or so painful, since there was no comfortable position for me to lie in bed except on my side. If I rolled onto my back or front, I woke up yelping. But Jack's healing balms did their work, new skin grew, and I began to feel myself once again. To this day only one doctor, a dermatologist in France, has spotted traces of the original ravages of that fateful afternoon.

Professionally Jack Leacock was as highly qualified as a surgeon could be, a fellow of the Royal College of Surgeons and a Master of Surgery. His family was amongst the founding fathers of Barbados. He was a Barbadian who, in spite of offers of university chairs around the world, devoted his life to his country. His daily routine, unchanged for more than forty years, invariably saw him ready for the first patient, in the consulting room behind the house, by seven o'clock. The queue actually began to form outside the gates at around five, but no-one was admitted until the Leacocks' fearsome Rottweiler, Hannibal, was locked up. Anyone could attend his surgery but they only paid if Jack thought they could afford it. He was a legend on the Island until the day he died. He should have been made Governor General, the Queen's representative, but his skin, unfortunately if understandably, was the wrong colour.

My convalescence in their guest cottage was the first of many valuable contributions that Jack and Margaret were to make to my new life. My admiration for them is boundless, and I shall be forever in their debt. Jack lived and died an atheist, which surprised me. As a Christian I believed that, about to meet his Maker, he would see the error of his ways and repent, but he did not. Heaven is lucky to have him.

It was Margaret's habit to chat on the telephone for the first part of the morning. She functioned as a sort of island switchboard for receiving, embellishing and distributing gossip. I happened to overhear a conversation in which a property was mentioned. She and her friend Billy Montagu had formed a real estate company, for which, with their social connections, there was every chance of success. I enquired about this property. Apparently it was just down the road, beneath Sharon Hill. Built in the seventeenth century, it had been the residence of several powerful noblemen. The first was the Lord Proprietor, the Earl of Carlisle. Later the Governor of Barbados and All the Caribbees, Lord Willoughby, owned it. It sounded about the right sort of place for the son of a Hull fisherman with modest aspirations.

I asked Margaret if I might view the house. We were there in five minutes. We drove between rusting gates up a fairly short drive overarched with wild bougainvillea. There, as the drive widened, I saw a magnificent if jaded house with a Palladian façade, and twin staircases going up to a long louvred gallery. Under the staircases was the dark cool entrance to the ground floor. In front stood two enormous evergreen trees, which in the past would have offered shade to carriages and horses. The jungle came up to the very walls and bougainvillea entered the house through the windows. I took one look and was in love. 'How much is it?' I asked.

The answer was 96,000 Barbados dollars – 20,000 pounds – plus a five percent transfer tax; five acres of land came with the house. There was no going back. I was going to become the owner of a decrepit Jacobean mansion in the middle of Barbados, a country the geographical whereabouts of which I scarcely knew a month ago.

At this point I heard from somewhere deep inside me a deferential 'Ahem'. It was my Head. 'Might I be permitted to say something?' it went on.

'If you must,' said my Heart abruptly, sensing something inconvenient coming on.

'Aren't you overlooking certain considerations?' enquired Head meekly.

'Considerations?' bellowed Heart. 'What considerations?' Heart had always overruled Head ever since they could both remember.

Head went on remorselessly, 'Perhaps you should consider what you would be leaving behind in England – your business interests, the wine company, not to mention your partners Charles Longman and Paul Har-

man. What's going to happen to them? And your 25,000-pound investment in Nick's Diner – what about that? Admittedly it's given you no
return whatsoever, but the company does own two houses in Fulham and
at least you now have culinary skills and a blueprint for a money-making
restaurant.'

Head had yet more to say. 'I suppose you expect Paul Harman to sort
out your messy affairs and unpaid bills, settle your debts, dispose of your
1936 Rolls-Royce and your personal possessions, and deal with your furniture. You also have a lease on a house in Chester Square Mews in Belgravia,
which ought to be very valuable.'

Head still wasn't finished. 'And maybe you should give some consideration to the girlfriend you left in bed, not to mention numerous others scattered around England. More poignantly, what is going to happen to Heidi,
your trusting, loving Afghan hound, whom you abandoned in kennels in
Yorkshire? And lastly, and of supreme importance, ought you not to think of
your parents, who have been so loving, generous, understanding and forgiving, no matter what you have thrown at them? You will have vanished from
their lives without a word. Your mother will be bereft,' concluded Head
reproachfully.

Heart could think of no satisfactory answers and sulked.

'If you buy this house,' Head persisted, 'how can you keep your commitment to Robin Knox-Johnston and Les Williams? They're depending
on you to help with the financing of the new yacht and to work on board
her later in the Caribbean as captain when she is chartered. And what about
that glorious vision you had on Bequia, when you saw the Grenadines, your
very future, stretched out before you? What about the life you dreamed of
at sea, of leaping smiling dolphins, of anchoring at sunset, of barbecuing a
barracuda? Was that so much hot air?'

Apparently it was. I have never met Robin since – thank heavens, for
I dreaded a chance encounter. Les was to drop by some years later, full of
forgiveness.

I should like to be able to tell you that I was filled with regret and
remorse by such disloyalty and unreliability. To my lasting shame, I
did not feel a twinge of either. The uncomfortable truth was that, the
moment I committed myself to buying Bagatelle and moving to Bar-

bados, these considerations were relegated to a mental oubliette. One minute they formed the whole structure of my existence; the next they counted for nothing.

There has to be a medical explanation for this behaviour which went completely against my nature, especially putting aside any consideration for my parents' feelings, for I truly loved them passionately. It was as if my subconscious, spotting a promising future, had ignored all such scruples. And it was right, although it did not tell me that at the time.

Here I need to digress slightly. I may have got away with my selfish behaviour forty years ago. However, when I came to write this book, all those matters which had conveniently been consigned to my oubliette were at a stroke restored to their original importance. They confronted me as if it had all occurred yesterday. I was stopped in my tracks, traumatised and quite unable to proceed. I tried sitting at the keyboard, hoping to find answers, somehow to expiate myself, and failed. Once, at lunch with my astrologer girlfriend Gloria Treloar, I met the successful feminist author Fay Weldon, who told me she was unable to write creatively on a word processor and always used longhand. So I had a go using pencil and paper. But manuscript didn't work either. Another, deeper, solution was required.

In the end I found the answer by chance. Waking early one morning, at the witching hour of four o'clock, with this section of my book tormenting my thoughts, I gave my subconscious free rein. The result was startling. That deeper level of my mind became clearly observable, a seething mass of guilt, selfishness, and self-dislike. I let it seethe. From time to time a concept would be singled out that I was able to observe, reflect on and, finally, write about. I may have given the wrong impression; this was not a passive process to be observed in a detached, curious manner. It was painful, and revealed aspects of my personality which I would rather have left unrecognised. It took several weeks, but I knew it was something I had to go through. In fact, once the process had begun, I don't think I could have stopped it even if I had wanted to. It was a difficult time. But it worked. I feel lighter now in spirit, relieved of a burden which I did not know I was carrying. I hope that, should they ever read this, Paul Harman, Robin Knox-Johnston, Les Williams, Charles Longman, Caroline Lloyd, the Autocue girl and any other being I hurt – and Heidi the Afghan too – will forgive me.

But forty years ago, I entertained no such reservations. All I could do was to ask myself: what was I to do with this broken-down mansion? Devious Heart knew full well but said nothing. I decided to go to Jamaica to think about it.

So I went to Bridgetown, to Billy Montagu's ABC Travel Agency, where that queen of travel agents, Graïnne Kearns, presided. A little while later, clutching my 40-day excursion ticket, I boarded a BOAC flight at Seawell airport, and was whisked off to Jamaica.

CHAPTER SEVEN

Interlude In Jamaica

T he flight to Jamaica was 1,100 miles. The Island is very different from Barbados, with a land mass of over 4,000 square miles, compared to Barbados' modest 168. Its highest point, Blue Mountain Peak, at 7,402 feet, dwarfs Barbados' pride and joy, Mount Hillaby, at a lowly 1,115 feet.

I was arriving in March to stay with my friends Peter and Janet Kerr-Jarrett on their estate, Tamarind. As in Barbados, I landed four-square on my social feet, for in many ways the Kerr-Jarretts were the Leacocks of Jamaica, a patriarchal family whose Island heritage went back eleven generations to the mid-seventeenth century. Both Jack and Peter had been educated in England and had returned to devote their lives to their native country and its people. Both had married 'Créole' women (in the Caribbean that means someone who lives in the region but was not born there). Margaret Leacock was industrious and organised, whilst Janet Kerr-Jarrett, who hailed from the United States, was exactly the opposite. She would emerge from her suite at noon, dressed in a floor-length housecoat, wave a languid hand at anyone she recognised, and then arrange herself gracefully on her chaise longue with a telephone close by. On Jamaica, telephone lines were scarce; the Tamarind area was served by a single line, and you might spend a quarter of an hour getting a dialling tone, if you were lucky. Not so Janet. The switchboard operator in Montego Bay had once worked at Tamarind, and at the appropriate moment she would open the line exclusively for Janet, blocking access to everyone else. Janet would then chat for the next hour or two, accumulating, amending, shading and distributing news and scandal, just like Margaret Leacock on Barbados.

I was looking forward to seeing someone I had met on my previous visit, a remarkable girl called Stuart (her parents, who lived on the nearby Tryall estate, had wanted a son). She had driven all the way to Tibet, which was accessible to foreigners then, in a Land Rover with her white cat, Moumas. She stopped at a monastery and was greeted with unexpected reverence by the monks. Pure white animals, she learned, were sacred to them, and the arrival of a stranger with such a creature was a good omen. She accepted their invitation to stay as long as she wished, and they taught her meditation. She also studied tai chi, Tantric art, and Buddhism. The monks named her Tara Devi – goddess of peace – which was apt, for Tara was possessed of great calm and spiritual insight. She could look at a person and see their future in their aura. On occasion she had to avert her gaze, not liking what she perceived. I have never met a mind like hers. A few years later I asked a Ouija board, 'Where is Tara?' and it spelled out unambiguously that she was in Calcutta, and coming to see me. A few weeks later, unannounced and unexpected – what idiot would believe a Ouija board? – Tara arrived.

The Kerr-Jarrett family home residence was set in the wooded hills above Montego Bay. It had a long cool veranda hung with brightly coloured Amerindian hammocks, and spacious rattan chairs and sofas scattered around. Fans idled under lofty ceilings, and the monumental mahogany furniture gleamed with a patina imparted by three centuries of loving care. The immensely long dining table was laden with silver candlesticks and massive epergnes, the polished purple-heart wood floor glowed warmly, and long snow-white curtains fluttered in the breeze. The house was surrounded by towering trees, giant ferns, bougainvillea, hibiscus and bird-of-paradise plants.

In the swimming pool one could float around on an inflatable plastic armchair, reading or snoozing, disturbed only by a discreet cough from the white-jacketed butler offering iced lemonade or rum punch. On the teak decking surrounding the pool peacocks strutted outrageously - this was the breeding season. They were less enchanting by night; the peacock's mating call is harsh and very loud. One night three cocks were competing cacophonously for the hens, each from their own tree close to the house, and sleep was hard to come by.

In the Kerr-Jarrett household the days were punctuated by excursions, picnics, lunch parties and, later, cocktails and elegant formal dinners. All one was expected to do was to arrive on time – Janet excepted, she was always embarrassingly late – appropriately dressed; elegantly casual as the expression was. It was the land of milk and honey, and I completely forgot why I had come to Jamaica in the first place.

Peter Kerr-Jarrett was passionately Jamaican. Like his forefathers he actively supported nation-building and local community development across the Island. His family had donated the land on which the Deep Water Harbour was constructed. He was a staunch Christian, who read his Bible each morning before going to work as a solicitor. He loved to end the day riding around the Tamarind estate on his favourite mule, which was not, by the way, one of your cow-hocked, sway-backed beasts as found in a cheap western, but had the conformation of a good horse with a lovely shiny coat. Peter maintained that muleback was the best way to oversee the estate; with the advantage of height, you missed nothing. I was sometimes invited on these rides, and he took the opportunity to pass on a little Jamaican history.

One of the north coast traditions was to take picnics on Sundays to the Martha Brae River, which emerges from the jungle as a glorious reach of crystal-clear water with waterfalls and pools. We would leave the picnic paraphernalia at the bottom, then drive or walk up to the topmost pool. Here we would dive in, swim to the head of the first waterfall, dive into the pool below, swim to the next waterfall and dive into the next pool. Several dives later one arrived at the lowest pool, where the picnic would have been set up by the non-swimmers. On one occasion I drove up to the top and pool-hopped down deliciously, arriving all bronzed and seal-sleek – rather God-like, I suppose – to find my fellow revellers well into the rum punch. Where was the corkscrew for the wine, they demanded? It was, of course, in my car. So I climbed back up to the top pool where I beheld a large jean-clad backside sticking out of my car. I peered in. A dreadlocked Rastafarian was absorbed in unscrewing the car radio. I tapped his muscular shoulder. 'Ahem!' said I. The mass of thick black dreadlocks revolved and there appeared a gleaming smile.

'A man has to live,' he told me with irrefutable logic. Having replaced the screws, he backed out, gave me resounding high fives, and loped off into the jungle. I drove the car plus corkscrew down to join the picnic. Two years later such a peaceful encounter would be highly unlikely.

The expatriates I met were a colourful happy-go-lucky lot, whose sole daily task was to amuse themselves. One was Juan Bacardi, son of the Cuban rum-making family, who, we were reliably informed, was paid a million dollars a year on the understanding that he kept away from the business. There was a gay ex-Merchant Navy steward who had made good in real estate. Ralph Chapman, who had sold his substantial holding in Britvic, was likewise of their number. He had married a very naughty Jamaican girl, Janet. However, the leader of the set, and my next host after I left the Kerr-Jarretts, was Johnny Kimberley. 'Colourful' is barely adequate to describe this man, and life in his house was always enjoyable. Our routine was simple. When we were not otherwise engaged, and Johnny wasn't selling real estate to wealthy Americans – how they loved to deal with 'a real English lord' – we played backgammon, drank bullshots or toppled into the pool to cool off. In addition, Johnny had an extremely beautiful Anglo-Indian companion. She was Janet Chapman's bosom pal and was known as Tiger, or, more formally, the Countess Cowley. Born Janet Elizabeth Mary Aiyar, she had married Denis Cowley in 1961. She tended to be careless with money, buying the odd Aston Martin and so on, and her husband had to put notices in the British national press disclaiming responsibility for her debts. Denis had died on the job, it is said, *à la* Rockefeller, whilst frolicking with a lady of the night in downmarket Bayswater in 1968. He was only forty-six years old. A little later Tiger somehow managed to grab Johnny just after the fifth of his six wives – a close call; the bed may still have been warm and fragrant. Not that Johnny ever allowed such trivialities as marital fidelity to get in the way. By his own admission he just couldn't get enough sex. Nor could Tiger.

Once, she and I were messing around in the secluded swimming pool at the Montego Bay Country and Racquet Club, when she indicated that I should come closer. 'Pussycat,' she breathed, 'I've got the water jet in exactly the right place – know what I mean? Talk to me.' Leaning against the rim of the pool, I put an arm across her shoulders and, as I whispered delicious depravities in her ear, noticed a woman of stern aspect and a certain age on a wooden reclining chair, glancing at us over her Herald Tribune. Soon Tiger began to get very agitated, her eyes became wild, she threw back her head, moaning, her back arched, she cried out and then, with a satisfied sigh, she slumped against my shoulder purring, 'Thank you, Pussycat, thank you.' To my astonishment, the lady of a certain age lowered her newspaper briefly, her stern face dissolving into a conspiratorial smile.

This den of vice *chez* Kimberley was something of a change from Tamarind and Bible-reading. Johnny was a great talker, and I listened because he had much to tell. His life got off to a flying start when P.G. Wodehouse stood as his godfather; he was a kinsman, Wodehouse being Johnny's family name. It is believed that Johnny's father, the third Earl, was the model for Bertie Wooster. In 1941, having inherited a fortune derived from, amongst other sources, the Kimberley diamond mines, Johnny set about squandering it. The money went towards paying his gambling debts and supporting ex-wives. His first marriage took place at St. George's Chapel at Windsor Castle in 1949. He knew it was going to be a disaster but dared not call it off because the King and Queen were amongst the guests; indeed the King proposed the toast. None of his wives remarried, preferring to keep the title Countess of Kimberley. His sixth wife, the delightful Janey, remained married to him until his death in 2002.

Johnny had a shocking reputation among his fellow peers as a glorious failure – he was the most-divorced peer in the four-century-long history of the House of Lords – but he did not lack physical courage. He served in tanks in the war, and was captain of the British four-man bobsleigh team, not a sport for the faint-hearted. He told me that, when negotiating the notorious Shuttlecock bend on the Cresta Run in Saint Moritz, the sledge left the track, and, having seen half a ton of metal fly over his head, he decided it was time to retire from the sport. He was an amusing and generous host, and I liked him enormously.

Tiger and I kept in touch after I left Jamaica. A few months later, in London, the telephone rang. 'Pussycat,' the voice purred, 'it's Tiger.' My heart rate went up a gear. 'I have to see you,' the husky and inviting voice went on. 'I've missed you so much and I need you. I'm in Johnny's house in Market Mews, next to the Hilton. Come as soon as possible.'

I'd always fancied her something rotten, so I hurried round to the mews house as fast as my legs could carry me, rang the doorbell and was invited upstairs. I galloped up the narrow staircase three at a time and headed for the bedroom door, guided by what sounded like a cocktail party from within. With some difficulty I forced open the door.

The room was full of handsome young men holding champagne glasses, standing around or sitting on the huge bed, laughing and talking. Bottles of Champagne, boxes of chocolates, and flowers were on every horizontal surface. Lying in the bed, her gorgeous Indian skin shown off to perfection by her white *décolleté* nightie, lustrous black hair spread magnificently *à la* Jane Russell on the snow-white pillow, was a beaming Tiger. If ever a cat had all the cream it wanted, she was it. 'Join the party, Pussycat,' she purred, tapping the ivory silk bedspread. I *think* I managed a smile.

And no, should you ask, I didn't get to lick up any of the cream. If only I'd been an earl! I did call Tiger later in the hope that the fan club had departed, but the party was still in full noisy swing. That was my last sighting of the rare and exotic Tiger. I hope the species never becomes extinct.

Following Ian Fleming's death, some mutual Jamaican friends, the Lindos, bought his house Goldeneye. Their son David, whom I had met in London, invited me there for lunch. Oracabessa was about 70 miles from Mo Bay, along the atrocious pot-holed tracks that the Jamaicans called roads. Three hours after leaving Mo Bay I found Goldeneye, hidden away on its private peninsula. I could hardly believe my eyes. A more perfect spot cannot be imagined, but the house was ugly, its walls constructed out of the cheapest possible materials. It sported, as its front door, a cheap wooden DIY job, on each side of which were frosted glass louvres in cheap aluminium frames. Hideous. Yet in it had lived a man, born in Mayfair of a banking family, whose creation James Bond was of famously expensive good taste. The door opened and there stood a smiling David Lindo. On the right side of the entrance the louvres opened, and two female heads, one above the other, peered out. One was David's mother; the lower one, a wizened crone, croaked, 'Who's that?'

'It's Nick Hudson, Granny; he's come all the way from Mo Bay for lunch,' replied David.

'Tell him to go away!' spat the crone.

So I did, in spite of having driven for nearly three hours over those awful roads. What else could I do? Neither a stunned David nor his mother said a word as I climbed back into the car and drove off. But once I was over the shock and disappointment I found I was hungry, so my thoughts turned to lunch.

Friends in Jamaica often pointed out that there was no Jamaican restaurant guide for tourists. Might I consider creating one? Passing the Jamaica Hilton on my way back to Mo Bay, it occurred to me that I might kill two birds with one stone and combine lunch with some research for the putative guide. I was soon installed in the poolside restaurant, with an enormous cheeseburger, a mountain of French fries, tomato ketchup, a copious salad and a bucket of Thousand Island dressing – not exactly a gastronomic test but I quickly disposed of it. I kept a critical eye on the nearby springboard, something I knew a little about, having received some instruction in the arctic Southside outdoor pool in Scarborough from a slightly plump boy called Christopher Wray – he reminded me of a seal – who was later to open a fabulous lighting emporium at Stamford Bridge in London. Here at the Jamaica Hilton there were two springboards, one a metre above the water, the other three metres. I noticed that everyone who dived off the three-metre board made an awful mess of it, generating an enormous splash which incurred my disdain. It was time, I decided, to show them how it should be done. I would demonstrate a vertical arrow-like entry that barely disturbed the water, then swim to the side with a powerful crawl, Johnny Weissmuller-style. I would flow in one continuous flowing motion up over the side and onto my feet, returning to my chaise longue, modestly unaware – like hell! – of the admiring glances of the onlookers.

Once on the three-metre platform I paused briefly, ensuring that all eyes were on me, inflated the manly chest, took the required three-and-a-half precisely measured paces – think Nureyev, strutting – hit the very end of the board, then launched myself into space, legs dead straight, pressed tightly together, toes pointed, arms high over my head, thumbs interlocked, fingers steepled heavenwards. Perfection! Then alarm bells started to ring. Something was seriously wrong. Instead of achieving an impossibly high zenith, way above the board, and rotating into the classic swallow-dive position, arms outstretched, back arched, my legs were overtaking me. Some halfwit had rolled back the adjustable fulcrum under the board so that it was not so much a springboard as a catapult. By the time I arrived at the surface I was horizontal, my back parallel to the water; indeed my feet all but got there first. I heard the crack as, from a height of maybe 20 feet, I hit the water and the air was knocked from my body. I surfaced and, with some difficulty, swam to the side. I hauled myself laboriously from the pool, tottered to my chaise longue and lay down gingerly, my back burning, my ego shattered.

For such a wealthy resort area, the north coast near Mo Bay boasted few restaurants, due largely to an iniquitous conspiracy between greedy hoteliers and travel agents. Tourists were offered the Modified American Plan (MAP), which entitled them to two meals a day in their hotel. This meant they had no desire to pay to dine out in a restaurant, and had to take or leave whatever was on offer at the hotel. Thus restaurateurs were denied many potential customers, to the extent that the viability of their operations was in doubt. Even worse, MAP was purchased abroad, so the Jamaican exchequer was deprived of the very lifeblood of the developing world – hard currency.

Nevertheless it was thought that a restaurant close to Mo Bay could be profitable, if it remained open only during the winter but closed in the summer. Janet Kerr-Jarrett put forward the idea of a restaurant partnership; she would put up the funds and I would run it. She knew, she said, just the place and would take me to see it, something best done in the evening for reasons which would become apparent. She drove me 20 miles eastwards along the coast to a village called Falmouth, and took me to a small warehouse, right at the edge of the lapping Caribbean. As a site for a restaurant, it could hardly be bettered. Janet led me out onto the wooden jetty which formed part of the property. 'Look!' she said. The water was alive, luminous with phosphorescence; fish left glowing tracks in their wake. As we stood admiring this phenomenon, a man rowed up to the jetty with the keys to the building. The spray from his oars generated a riot of coruscating colours, so strong was the phosphorescence in the water. The restaurant was a tempting proposition.

But in the course of the next day or two I recalled my main reason for visiting Jamaica, which was to decide what I was going to do with my newly acquired mansion on Barbados? The answer was suddenly obvious – convert it into a restaurant, of course! I have no doubt that perfidious Heart knew that from the start. The West Coast of Barbados, like its Jamaican counterpart, was devoid of first-class restaurants, and for the same reason as in Jamaica – the wretched MAP. I was going to try to rectify that. I had to decline Janet's kind offer. My future lay in Barbados.

As it turned out, I had, albeit fortuitously, made the right decision on two counts. First, not long afterwards, the aluminium giant Alcan built a plant on the Falmouth Bay. The resulting pollution killed off all the magical phosphorescence. Second, Jamaica fell into a terrible political decline, bringing violence, instability and poverty to the country. I had been lucky.

Meanwhile, at the far-distant south-eastern end of the Caribbean, two gentlemen were making their mark. On Barbados, in 1961, Ronnie Tree established the Sandy Lane Hotel, Estate and Golf Course, whilst on the minuscule island of Mustique Colin Tennant was creating an exclusive resort, eventually opening the Cotton House Hotel there in 1969. Both entrepreneurs sought the skills of the most talented bowerbird of the twentieth century, Oliver Messel. He did not disappoint them. The allure of his creations – a hotel and villas alike – proved irresistible to the well-heeled snowbirds that flocked there. For them, Jamaica, as the destination of choice, was about to be knocked off its perch. Nonetheless, although the Island's days may have been numbered, some remained. I was still enjoying blissful times, especially in the company of Johnny, Tiger and Tara. I eyed the expiration of my excursion ticket with dismay. There were endless parties lined up, and my appetite for backgammon and bullshots had not been sated. Also I had made my decision about Bagatelle, and a final fling was in order before turning my attention to its conversion. I told Johnny of my feelings as we hunched over the backgammon board. 'My word!' he said. 'Your ear looks sore.'

'My ear? It feels fine,' I said.

'Oh no, I can see from here that you have a middle ear infection. Dangerous to fly with that condition. It could be painful, even dangerous, at 30,000 feet. You might even lose your hearing.'

The penny dropped. 'Oh, absolutely!' I concurred. 'It could do permanent damage. But my ticket runs out in two days' time so I *have* to fly.'

'We can't risk it. You need to see Doctor Delisser right away.' Soon I found myself in the good doctor's surgery, where, after a cursory examination, he scribbled a note.

'Take this to the airport,' he said. 'The BOAC manager will authorise the extension of your excursion ticket until you are better.' What could be simpler? I made haste to the airport, note in hand.

'How may I help you?' the manager enquired solicitously.

'Doctor Delisser asked me to give you this,' I replied, passed him the note, and waited for one of those sympathetic smiles reserved for those suffering from the distressing symptoms of middle ear infection. Instead, his face darkened. He snatched up his telephone and dialled. He didn't even have to look up the number.

'Lord Kimberley,' he hissed furiously, 'good morning. This is the BOAC airport manager speaking. I have here,' he glanced at the ticket and glowered, 'a Mr Hudson. He has a note from Doctor Delisser. This, Lord Kimberley, is your third house guest this season who has contracted a middle ear infection just days before their excursion was due to expire. I suggest you ask Doctor Delisser to come up with rather more imaginative diagnoses in future.' With that he banged down the telephone. But I did get my extension.

Two weeks later, it really was time to drag myself away. I had achieved my aim, deciding to convert Bagatelle into a restaurant. It had to be ready in time to catch the season, which began at Christmas. At least 80% of the year's income was generated in the following months up to Easter. Starting from scratch, converting my ruin in barely nine months would be pushing it.

I went to Mo Bay's only florist to order some flowers for Peter and Janet and Johnny and Tiger. 'I would like to buy some roses,' I told the man. He made a sweeping gesture, embracing the whole shop. 'Alllll is roses,' he trilled.

'Actually I want those red roses over there,' I said, pointing at some beautiful long-stemmed blooms.

'Oh, man!' he exclaimed, 'you mean roses *roses*!'

I was sad to leave Jamaica but Tara had agreed to join me in Barbados later in the year. The day of departure dawned and I was driven to the airport by Johnny and Tiger, who were received with great deference – there were not a lot of earls and countesses in Mo Bay, after all. Johnny had arranged for us to be served farewell bullshots in the VIP lounge. Outside we could see the Barbados aeroplane being loaded with passengers. Eventually they were all gobbled up, and just the forward door left open. A man walked across to the lounge and announced, 'Lord Kimberley, the flight is ready for departure'. We hugged and kissed and thanked and promised and cried. Then I was escorted to the waiting aeroplane. Like royalty, I paused at the top of the steps to turn and wave goodbye to my kind friends, and entered. The door closed behind me. Once inside I turned left. I had been upgraded to first class. One could quickly become used to that sort of send-off.

Next stop: beautiful, beautiful Barbados – where a new life beckoned.

Chapter Eight

Starting From Scratch

My return to Barbados was a great improvement on my previous visit. Then I had been burned, blistered and wretched; now I was full of plans for Bagatelle. What, precisely, had my £21,000 bought me, apart from an old mansion in a deplorable state of repair that had survived more than three centuries of hurricanes? The house came with five acres of land, as was usual when plantations were sold off as sugar became less and less financially viable. The Tryhane family, planters who had owned Bagatelle, finding themselves in reduced circumstances, sold the plantation and the house separately and removed to the manager's residence close by. The land surrounding the house had reverted to jungle, in which could still be seen the remains of several terraces that, Mrs Sheila Parravicino *née* Tryhane told me, were the scenes of picnics and children's parties as late as the 1950s. Research revealed that my house had been built soon after 1629 by James Hay, first Earl of Carlisle, who received Barbados and all the Caribbean islands as a grant from King Charles I of England. Hay died in 1637 and the property was liquidated to help pay off his huge debts of £80,000. In about 1639, the year Barbados was awarded its own parliament, the house came into the possession of the fifth Lord Willoughby of Parham, who named it Parham Park after his baronial seat in Suffolk. Its name is *said* to have changed to Bagatelle when, in payment of a gambling debt, it was dismissed by the debtor as 'a mere bagatelle'. Lord Willoughby became Governor of Barbados and All the Caribbees in 1650, and was drowned in a hurricane off Antigua in 1666, after which, in the best traditions of Britannic democracy, his son the sixth Lord Willoughby succeeded him as Governor.

Bagatelle was so massively constructed as to be virtually indestructible, with walls several feet thick. There were no windows on the ground floor, just apertures high up close to the ceiling, and barred gates. The threat of flood damage, caused by the downpours that usually accompany tropical storms, had been averted by digging deep culverts in the hillside to divert the torrents around each end of the mansion. This floor was also ideally suited for a hurricane shelter, and almost certainly offered shelter to inhabitants of the nearby Redman's village in times of danger.

The house was one of the few on the Island with an upper storey pre-dating the great hurricanes of 1780 and 1832, which had all but blown Barbados off the map. It had been preserved by incorporating into its architecture some basic laws of physics. The success of these – it would have been irresponsible of me to meddle with them – merits explanation. The core of this floor consisted of six rooms, with sash windows protected by outside and inside shutters secured by bars. Unimpeded airflow was critical, because the high winds of a hurricane can generate a differential in air pressure between indoors and outdoors that can actually cause a house to collapse. So at Bagatelle no room or corridor, even with all doors closed, was isolated from its neighbour; each room was connected to the next by an aperture high up in the wall. Running along the north, south and east sides was a continuous gallery, probably added in the eighteenth or nineteenth century, enclosed by alternating sash windows and adjustable wooden louvres. These admitted the cooling winds from the east, so effectively that I never needed to install air-conditioning. Access from the rooms to the galleries was gained via double doors which could also be secured with stout wooden bars slotted into the walls.

Another air pressure-related danger threatened the integrity of the roof. The speed of air passing over its generally convex shape can give rise to a lifting force – the aerofoil effect – sufficiently strong to lift it off the house. So two additional features had been incorporated into the exterior architecture. First, the roof was divided into halves, making it a double-hipped structure; this reduced the surface of each roof and hence the lifting force. Second, a low parapet was built around the top of the outside wall to break up the flow of air as it approached the roof, causing turbulence, which greatly reduced the chances of the aerofoil effect developing. Although this is a modern concept, it is remarkable that the architects of the seventeenth century knew instinctively how to deal with the problem.

Bagatelle Great House remains to this day a monument to the ingenious solutions the early settlers found to problems that they had not encountered in temperate climes. My new home was indeed a rare and remarkable survivor, and I had thrown it a lifeline.

With the restaurant on the ground floor, I would live upstairs. The Leacocks would be neighbours. Margaret was thrilled. A new restaurant and a straight bachelor over thirty years old (an almost non-existent phenomenon on the Island) – what a juicy item for her morning's telephone bulletin! I told them that I had gratuitously renamed my property Bagatelle *Great* House, a nomenclature I had come across in Jamaica. 'The Bagatelle Great House Restaurant' had a sweet ring to it, and I felt it would be good for publicity purposes. After a very short time my international postal address became simply: Nicholas Hudson, Bagatelle Great House, Barbados. I rather liked that.

When I set out for the West Indies a couple of months earlier, I had, as I have said, little idea where I was going. All I knew was that the area known as the Caribbean was somewhere between North and South America, that Jamaica, Bermuda, and Barbados were islands where the rich spent the winter months, and that the natives were famously good at cricket. There was lots of rum, and handsome Harry Belafonte sang calypsos about his Island. Of the distances involved I had not the least idea; my impression was that the islands were all grouped together and not, as I was to discover, spread over a thousand miles. If someone had asked me to point out Barbados on a globe, I would have been unable to do so. As for St. Vincent and the Grenadines, I had only seen the names on those large triangular stamps in Stanley Gibbon's catalogue. 'Fools rush in,' my mother once said, 'but you at least do so with your eyes open.'

Everyone nowadays knows where Barbados is, but in 1970 it was something of a hideaway with a smallish airfield, and as often visited by liners,

Barbados. Her closest neighbour is St. Vincent, 100 miles away.
South America just 200 miles.

or Elders & Fyffe banana boats, as by aeroplanes. When I arrived the only airport was called Seawell, but in 1976 was to be renamed Grantley Adams Airport in honour of an eminent Barbadian of that name by his son Tom Adams, the then prime minister.

The part of Barbados which would involve me for the next twenty-eight years was a small part of a tiny island, containing three of its eleven parishes – St. Thomas, in which Bagatelle was situated, St. Peter and St. James.

St. Thomas was a wild part of the Island, unvisited even by many Barbadians, yet only 2 miles from Holetown and Sandy Lane. St. Peter played a role in my life because it contained several important houses – including that of Claudette Colbert, Verna Hull, and Eric and Sal Estorick's Nelson

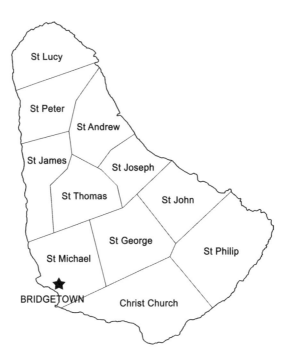

Barbados. 13°10' north – 59°32' west; 22 x 12 miles;
capital Bridgetown; London 4,200 miles.

Gay. The delightful Greensleeves restaurant and the commendable Cobblers Cove Hotel were also there. The beaches, though, were very narrow and often difficult to access.

St. James was *the* place. It is astonishing to consider the wealth and influence that were concentrated in this tiny area. Until recently the beach lands had been mosquito-infested swamp, plagued with outbreaks of dengue fever, and seemingly valueless, until a visionary called Ronnie Tree arrived in 1946 and changed everything.

It had been my intention not to bother doing any building work upstairs at Bagatelle for the time being. Meeting a Christmas 1970 deadline was my priority but I did want to make one slight structural alteration before moving in. To maximise the 'air-conditioning' effect I decided to remove the false ceilings in the galleries and open the space right up to the galvanised iron roof. I began by prising loose a panel from the hardboard ceiling, only to be deluged by foul-smelling bat droppings. Barbados is home to a huge number of bats, which are a protected species, and a great many had colonised the space above the false ceiling. Donning my Herbert Johnson hat with the snakeskin band, I dismantled the whole ceiling, and shovelled tons of malodorous filth down the steps to the parking area. Blessedly, that night there was a heavy rainstorm and it was all washed away down the drive, out of my life but possibly into my neighbours'.

With that nasty job out of the way it was time for me to leave the generous comfort *chez* Leacock and move into my new home. No pantechnicon would be required; furniture requirements were minimal. The last occupants of Bagatelle, a pair of wild bachelors, Reds Mackie and friend, had left a bed and a cooker. I purchased a fridge, a pair of sheets, a couple of saucepans, a gallon of rum, and some Coca-Cola. Limes – an essential ingredient for my favourite poison in those days, rum and Coke – grew on a tree in the jungle which passed as my garden. What else could a single man need in the tropics?

Overwhelmed by all this luxury, you may not have remarked the absence of a bathroom. There was a loo in a nook next to the cooker, which I always felt was rather spooky; I was later told by my housekeeper Mrs Nichols that a man had committed suicide in it. Bathing needs were met by a shower on the back balcony, where the monkeys took great interest in my ablutions. Hot water was provided by an unexpectedly functioning stone-age Ascot gas heater, which always announced it was working by letting off a series of small explosions.

One of the great blessings of West Indian life is that clothing requirements are minimal. In the daytime I wore shorts and maybe a top. In the evening I just dropped a kaftan over my head and was immediately ready for anything. Shoes were slightly more complicated. I used to walk to the bank barefooted, and put on my shoes to meet the manager – blessed Tony Thomas, who saved my bacon more than once. I would take my leave, remove my shoes on the bank steps, and head for home. My feet became incredibly thick-skinned – in time I could stand on a drawing-pin without discomfort – and wide. I developed what the Bajans – the local word for Barbadians – refer to as 'de yam feet'. This made buying shoes a real problem, as any that were wide enough were far too long.

Once, my hand was forced. Walking down South Audley Street in London, I stepped into a puddle, which resulted in a soaking sock; I discovered that the sole of my shoe was completely worn through. So I went into a nearby shop to buy another pair and could hardly believe the price – around £75, three times the amount I had paid sometime in the Sixties. I made sure they lasted. On another occasion I arrived early to join my friend Christopher Robinson for lunch at the smart Churchill's restaurant in Toronto, and asked the *maître d'hôtel* if I might sit at the table to await my host. 'But of course, sir,' he said. Cough! Cough! 'Forgive me, but would you mind keeping your feet well under the table?' I looked down and saw that I had forgotten to put on my shoes. That fellow had style.

Wheels are essential when living in the sticks, but the Island's public transport vehicles were driven exclusively by speed-crazed madmen. Margaret Leacock offered to sell me the magnificent chrome-embellished beach buggy in which she had first met me at the airport. It drew attention wherever I went. This was good, because I wanted to draw attention both to myself and hence to the about-to-be opened Bagatelle Great House Restaurant –entities as yet unknown on the Island.

My household inventory still lacked a cat, a dog, a piano and a guitar. But these shortcomings would soon be rectified.

I loaded my few possessions into the beach buggy, offered heartfelt thanks to Jack and Margaret, and drove the five minutes down to Bagatelle, ready to experience my first evening alone in my new home, listening to the tropical orchestra of chattering crickets and honking tree frogs. It was the hour of the sundowner. The air was full of the seductive scent of the ylang-ylang trees, and monkeys ran clattering over the roof, shouting noisily. I retired to my Berbice chair with a generous rum and Coke, put my feet up, and took stock of my new situation.

I was in a foreign country, with no knowledge of its history, its people, or how it worked – liquor licensing, work permits, planning permission, suppliers and the like. I knew no local restaurateurs from whom to seek guidance. I had no credit rating history to oil the wheels of commerce. All I had was a dilapidated mansion, high hopes, and a deadline to meet.

Yes! 'Starting from scratch' is a fair description.

Chapter Nine

The Hon. Janet & Other Kidds

A s a newcomer in Barbados, many people were extremely kind to me. Chief among them were the Kidds; there was always a warm welcome at their home, Holders House.

Strictly speaking Janet Kidd was a snowbird, only spending winters on-Island, but her presence on Barbados was such that she seemed to be permanently in residence. Her father Lord Beaverbrook had served in Churchill's War Cabinet with Ronnie Tree. In 1958 she was shown a plot of land on the newly opened Sandy Lane estate, bought it, and built a house there. Then in 1962 the adjoining plantation, Holders, comprising some 300 acres, came on the market, and she purchased it for BDS$200,000 – £42,000 in those days. The main house, a potentially elegant seventeenth-century residence, was in a poor state, but its west-facing location, half a mile from the sea, was perfect.

A memorable feature was a spacious veranda on the west and south sides of the house. Immediately below the terrace Janet added a swimming pool and a gazebo, under which was a round table that could seat twelve. The house was surrounded by a lush garden graced with tall royal palms where, in later years, Johnny and Wendy Kidd were to put on the now-famous Holders Festival.

Janet installed herself every morning on the veranda on a chaise longue, telephone to hand, and issued decrees. She was very much the *grande dame*. She had first married Ian Campbell, 11ᵗʰ Duke of Argyll, by whom she had a daughter, the Hon. Jeanne Campbell. Next she married the Hon. William Montagu by whom she had 'Billy' Montagu. In the grounds she built for him a wooden house universally known as 'the knock shop.' Billy, a kind man, was to die tragically young.

Janet was now married to Major Thomas Kidd, known as 'Cappy'. A formidable woman, she was nicknamed Bodie (as in Boadicea) by her friends. Cappy was subdued in her presence but quite different when you got him on his own. From time to time he would 'borrow' my exotic girlfriend Tara to accompany him to dinner parties. Janet preferred to stay at home where she was sure of having her own way. I attended many dinner parties at Holders. At one of these, at around nine o'clock, there was a sudden flick of her eyes and we saw a different Janet; she turned on my then girlfriend Chérie, who was very beautiful, and bullied her. I learned that this was not the first time she had done this. The victim was always pretty. Nora Docker used to do exactly the same thing.

Janet and Prince Philip were leaders in the hotly competitive sport of driving horse-drawn carriages. She drove a team of matched Icelanders with distinctive two-tone manes. On one occasion she arrived at the finish but was disqualified for not having on board the team with which she started – she had cut a corner rather too finely and left Rachel, her time-keeper, abigail and family treasure, hanging on a gate post, stopwatch in hand. Frankly, in a chariot race, I would have backed Janet to beat the Queen of the Iceni any day.

Rachel was precious to the Kidd family. She was Janet's intimate companion, helped to bring up her children and grandchildren, and remained after they had grown up. They adored and admired her, as did we all. When I last heard, quite a long time ago it has to be said, she was driving horse boxes full of Jack's polo ponies across Europe.

Janet had a useful mouthpiece for broadcasting her wishes, since her brother Max controlled the *Daily Express* and the *Sunday Express*. She would issue edicts, as when Oliver Reed was having a fling with her niece, the actress Laura Aitken. In those days the William Hickey column in the *Express* was the leader in the gossip business. Max was told to instruct Nigel Dempster – muckraker-in-chief – that the Laura/Oliver item was not to appear. It didn't.

I am not sure whether Janet or her son Johnny caught the helicopter bug first. At sixty-two she was the oldest person in the United Kingdom to qualify as a helicopter pilot. She was not, however, the best navigator. She once decided to drop in – literally – on a friend in Surrey for tea. Unfortunately she mistook the house and landed close to a herd of prize ponies which stampeded over much of Surrey. The results were predictably expensive.

Cappy and Janet had two children, Jane in 1943 and Johnny in 1944. Jane was like her father, a kind sympathetic girl, who married a young army officer with a hyphen who gave her a rotten time; none of us liked him, and the marriage did not last. Once, in the car park at Mr Nick's (a night spot I later added to Bagatelle), he tried to settle a dispute with Oliver Reed by kicking him in the balls – that was the sort of man he was. The actor parried the blow, and fortunately for his attacker made no more of it; Ollie was as strong as an ox and often drunk by that time of night.

Jane put this unhappy episode behind her and has since devoted her life to dressage, in which she is now a world authority. Her brother Johnny became a member of the British Olympic equestrian team. At polo he achieved a handicap of four, enough for him to turn professional. Very much the businessman, he involved himself in everything from telephones in Romania to flavoured vaginal douches. And whatever you were doing – building a space shuttle or seeking a career as a concert pianist – he would be happy to tell you how to do it.

In 1973 he married Wendy, who is a rock, albeit a very pretty one, and who bore Johnny three children: in 1973 Jack, in 1974 Jemma, and in 1978 Jodie. Jack, with enough charm for several Irishmen, has succeeded in the world of polo both as manager and player. Like his sisters he is very tall, and I think I know why. Once, Wendy and Johnny and I were chatting in their kitchen when Wendy demanded of the Filipino nanny, 'What are you putting on Jack's cornflakes?'

'Soy. We always put soy on our children's cornflakes at home.'

'*That*,' said Wendy tersely, 'is not soy. It's Baby Bio.'

The beautiful Jemma has created a successful cosmetics business and is now married to the Duke of Wellington's heir. She has already made her courageous contribution to that dynasty, bearing her husband Arthur twins. I believe it was a difficult confinement. As for Jodie, she has reached the very pinnacle of the modelling world and is good at anything she puts her hand to, from polo to driving Jeremy Clarkson's cars faster than most men.

Wendy had a sister, Vicky. Never were two sisters more different. Opinions tended to vary on Vicky, although everyone was agreed that she was a wild one. She eventually married a likeable Barbadian man called Shirley, a fruit machine tycoon, who was later to introduce me, albeit unintentionally, to the lovely Chérie, who was to play a critical role in my life.

Janet allowed the Barbados Polo Club to convert some of her cane fields into a polo field. Until then games were played on the Savannah in Bridgetown, where the military garrison had been based. She was later to make a gift of the field, under covenant, to the Club, an act of astonishing generosity. Fifteen acres of prime St. James land overlooking the west coast of Barbados, if it is to be had at all, does not come cheap.

Some fine houses were built along the western side of the field. In the early '70s two of the owners were especially colourful. One was Geoffrey Edwards, the noted arms dealer with strong connections to Saudi Arabia, whom I have to thank for introducing me to his house guests, three of my childhood heroes, Johnnie Johnson, Bolshie Bartley and Douglas Bader – all Battle of Britain legends. That *was* special.

The other was Colonel Harry Llewellyn, Dai and Roddy's dad. I was once walking along the beach at the Sandy Lane Hotel when someone said, 'Oh, here comes Harry Llewellyn.' Remembering the slender handsome colonel who, riding the nation's darling, Foxhunter, won Britain's only gold medal at the Helsinki Olympics in 1948, I turned to behold my idol. Oh dear! I saw a floppy denim hat, a somewhat florid face, a sagging torso, shapeless bathing shorts and Hush Puppies at the southern extremity.

But these disappointments counted for nothing. Harry was terrific fun. One did not see too much of Lady Llewellyn but Harry had a German lady friend, a vastly entertaining opera singer who sang arias at dinner. This was interrupted once when, at Holders, a man with a pistol dashed into the dining room and hissed, 'Stick dey up.'

'Good grief, man,' spluttered Harry, 'can't you see we're having dinner?' Shamefaced, the fellow slunk away, went upstairs, stole poor Rachel's money, and departed.

Janet died in 1988 at the age of eighty in the happy knowledge that, despite the odd bump, the tradition of her ever-achieving family was in good hands. Never was a life so devoid of wasted moments.

CHAPTER TEN

Setting Up Shop On Barbados

Bagatelle *had* to be open by Christmas, so there was no time to waste. Most of a restaurant's annual revenue on Barbados was generated between then and Easter; for the rest of the year you would be lucky to break even. Driven unthinkingly by the same force which had led me to abandon so callously my yachting partners and buy Bagatelle in the first place, I had not given much thought to finances. I had sent for the £21,000 to buy the property but somehow assumed that additional funds for the refurbishment would be found, heaven knows where. I bashed on regardless.

The most pressing job was the structural alterations. I needed an architect to draw up plans with a view to applying for planning permission, and it was suggested that I should approach the legendary Oliver Messel. He lived on-Island and was already familiar with the property, since his nephew, Anthony Armstrong-Jones, had considered buying the house and had asked him to cast his experienced eye over it. Fortunately for me the deal had not gone through. After meeting with Oliver I decided that he would be far above my financial touch – an expensive error, I fear, in that I only later became aware of the costly premium his name deservedly carried.

So I looked elsewhere. Ian Morrison was a young architect whose designs were taking Barbados by storm. While this talented young Geordie had been articled to the leading West Coast architectural practice, Robertson Ward, he did a spot of moonlighting and designed the world's most grown-up treehouse, Poachers, for some friends, the Vincents. This was such a success that he received further commissions and was soon able to open his own practice without even qualifying as an architect, something he has never needed to do. Ian has gone from success to success, being awarded several honorary degrees by his professional colleagues over the years.

He visited Bagatelle and immediately proposed that the massive walls be stripped of plaster to expose the beautiful coral stone beneath. This would be pointed with mortar made from the dust produced when coral stone is cut, which would dry to exactly the same colour. It was a laborious and noisy process, for coral stone dust is very fine and gets everywhere. The job took a long time, so it was expensive – but worth every cent. Atmospherically it was the making of the restaurant, creating an almost medieval ambiance.

In fact, stripping off the plaster solved a pressing problem. I did not want ugly surface electrical wiring but nor did I welcome the expense of channelling out stone walls. Instead we ran the wires in the spaces between the stones, concealing them with coral-dust mortar. The renovations revealed a secret of eighteenth-century wall construction, a method known as stone and rubble, consisting of two stone walls with a space of about twelve inches between them, which was filled with rubble and earth. The stone had been quarried close by in the garden, then sculpted into blocks and dressed – limestone can be cut like cheese with surprising ease using a special widetoothed two-man saw. The rubble and earth provided insulation against the heat but also a superhighway for the wood-eating termites that lived in the topsoil. Controlling these pests and other nasties was achieved by drilling holes through the walls into the cavity, into which an insecticide was injected under pressure by Mr Rentokil.

Ian solved another problem – who would do the work – by introducing me to Mr Prescott, an elderly Barbadian who led an equally elderly team of four men, whose combined ages fell just short of three hundred years. At first I thought they were working rather slowly, until, by way of making a subtle point, I tried sawing a piece of wood myself in the tropical heat and humidity. I began vigorously, a veritable blur of action, but was soon dripping with perspiration and quite worn out. The old timers simply worked steadily all day, stopping only for a tin of sardines at noon; Barbadian building sites were invariably littered with empty sardine tins. On the bigger sites, replacing the folding umbrella as the accessory of choice, construction helmets had come into fashion. It was customary to go to work wearing one, then carefully put it aside out of harm's way, only to put in on again when going home. The wearer thus avoided the stigma of being mistaken for a cane cutter, a despised job well beneath the dignity of the Barbadian male. It was left to workers brought in from the smaller, poorer islands to do this very hard work. The Barbadian women were also allowed to do it.

One of the Prescott team, Mr Worrell, was a stonemason on weekdays and a pastor at weekends. On Barbados, in addition to the Anglican parish churches, there were numberless non-conformist versions, for there was money to be made in that line of business; one church was honest enough to put a sign over the entrance – 'The Church of God Inc.' Pastor Worrell decided to open a second church, but soon discovered that even he could not be in two places at once, so on Sunday he had to delegate taking the collection in one or other of his churches. The result was that the money collected was rather less than projected. Being a pragmatist, the pastor changed his new church's Sabbath from Sunday to Saturday, thereby enabling him to preside at both Sabbaths, and the projected cash flow was realised. And flow it did – I found it prudent to avoid banking weekend restaurant takings on Monday mornings. If a couple of sack-carrying men of God were ahead of me in the queue and tipped out the contents onto the counter, it took ages to count. After lunch was a better bet.

Ian quickly drew up a basic plan, allowing Mr Prescott and his team to begin their work. In the meantime I roared all over the Island in my beach buggy, introducing myself to various suppliers of building materials. Fortunately, since my money had not yet arrived from England, on Barbados in those days a white person was automatically offered credit. Be it for building supplies or dinners in restaurants, you were simply handed a bill to sign and off you went. Barbados being the size of the Isle of Wight, there were few secrets. If you were a credit risk, it would soon be widely known.

From eight in the morning to four in the afternoon, Bagatelle's ground floor was all dust and noise. Upstairs I had much paperwork to occupy me. One requirement for a foreigner seeking to work in Barbados was obtaining a work permit. There were rumours amongst the ex-pat population of the necessity of bribing officials, something to which I never resorted. The authorities were interested, justifiably, in three factors: whether there was a Barbadian capable of doing the work for which the permit was being sought;

whether Barbados would benefit in terms of job creation, tax revenue, or enhanced tourism; and whether the investor would train locals, leading to Barbados being less dependent on imported know-how. Until very recently Barbados had been sugar, sugar and more sugar, which meant too many eggs in an increasingly unreliable basket. Now the Island needed to develop a working population with new and diverse skills. The Ministry of Home Affairs required me to produce proof of academic and professional qualifications, my police records if any, details of my investment, and my history as a restaurateur. How many people would I employ, and in what capacity? It was all perfectly logical, but time-consuming.

Obtaining a licence to sell alcohol was a nightmare in London. In Barbados you applied once a year to the licensing court in the parish where the enterprise was to operate. The police would come to assess your suitability and that of the premises, and then you attended a court hearing, hopefully getting the nod from the Beak. You paid very little, and thereafter were permitted to sell alcohol all day and all night throughout the year. The St. Thomas parish licensing court was to sit just before Christmas.

I designed the restaurant furniture to be basic, strong and lasting. The tables, made to fit the various nooks and crannies, were simple and painted black, and would be covered by cloths. The chairs for the bar were little tub-like things with low backs. The ones for the main restaurant were built from solid pitch pine, exceptionally unpretty, and weighed a ton. The Great Table chairs were even heavier and of generous size, though not generous enough for poor Harry Secombe who became wedged in one – we had difficulty prising him loose! Around the walls were stone banquettes, a typical Ian Morrison Costa Smeralda innovation. All the seats had black leatherette cushions, which were just as ugly and butch as they sound, but comfortable. On reflection, this 'interior design' was horribly masculine, the result of a man temporarily without a woman in his life. But thanks to kindly candle-light it worked, cost little and lasted for years.

Bagatelle, up in the hills of St. Thomas, was cooled by the blessed trade winds. However, during the hurricane season from late June to early October the winds die down and the air becomes humid and heavy. So I decided to install numerous ceiling fans, and purchased Japanese jobs for £20 each. They were turned on in January 1971 at idling speed and never turned off. When, several years later, I tried to do so in a rare fit of economy, the switches had seized solid, since the island air is full of salt. On my last visit to Barbados in 2007 those very fans – never oiled, never serviced – were still turning silently after thirty-six years of service.

As for selecting staff, I had no restaurant background or contacts on Barbados, so I was obliged to pursue a shamelessly selfish strategy. When I came across someone whose work in a restaurant impressed me I would invite them to join me at Bagatelle, and by the time Bagatelle opened I had put together a first-class team, which remained largely unchanged for the next twenty years. I had already spotted a barman, Randolph Blackman, the best there ever was, working in a dark windowless bar in Bridgetown, which had that nauseating smell well known to island travellers – stale conditioned air and rancid coconut oil. The bar was frequented by the staffs of embassies, consulates, high commissions and senior government offices. Consequently, when Their Excellencies came to the Bagatelle restaurant, Mr Blackman already knew their preferred drinks without needing to ask. He was author of the infamous Black Power cocktail. I had spotted my *maître d'hôtel*-to-be, Fitzgerald Smith, working in a hotel restaurant. He was exactly the sort of man I was looking for, so I invited him to join me and to bring with him four experienced waiters of his choosing. John Payne left his book-keeping job and took over the financial controls.

For the day staff – cleaners, gardener and so forth – I turned to Mrs Nichols, my fiercely possessive housekeeper, who lived in the next village, Redmans. She found me my chief washer-up, Eurene (sic) Drakes. Eurene managed to astonish me once; I dashed in from the bar with the blender in which we made banana daiquiris. I wanted it clean and ready to use – pronto! I thought she would take the bowl off the electric motor part, and wash it. Not a bit of it – bowl, lid, motor, electric plug and all disappeared into the soapy depths. And bang went that night's profits!

One day a human stick insect emerged out of the jungle, a skinny thirteen-year-old with blue-black West African skin and a smile to light up the universe. I could say that I adopted him, because he was still working for me nearly thirty years later, but in truth he adopted me. His name was Basil Bryan. At first he hung around, lurking and offering to help, a usual way of getting a job in Barbados. Eventually I started him as gardener, then made him a waiter, finally promoting him to wine waiter. He can do anything he puts his hand to. He went on to become a part-time magician, bar owner, restaurateur, preacher and driver of two-in-hand Haflinger horses. When last we met, he was teaching golf (I'm not at all sure he has ever played the game, but if he suddenly appeared at Augusta I would not be surprised). Basil is my unofficially adopted son, of whom I am immensely proud. When I go back to the Island, he and Margaret Leacock are the first people I look for.

Turning Bagatelle from a domestic residence into a restaurant meant increasing the capacity of the cesspit – 'the well', in local parlance. This was achieved by digging and blasting a hole until you found a fissure in the limestone bedrock. With more blasting this was enlarged to act as a drain into, I suppose, the bowels of the earth, although I have never felt inclined to enquire. The local well-digger arrived with pickaxe, shovel, rope, several sticks of dynamite and a box of matches. I showed him the existing soak-away. He heaved off the two sheets of galvanised iron and we peered into the niffy abyss. It was dry, thank heavens, not having been in serious action for some time. He tied one end of the rope to a convenient coconut palm, dropped the other end into the hole followed by the pickaxe and shovel, stuffed a stick of dynamite in his pocket and swarmed down. At the bottom he began hacking away with his pickaxe, looking for a suitable fissure – or suck, as it is onomatopoeically known. Eventually he made his choice and wedged in it the stick of dynamite.

There was none of that namby-pamby Hollywood nonsense, when John Wayne plunges the T-shaped handle of the detonator and the earth erupts miles away, endangering nobody but passing coyotes and rattlesnakes. The intrepid digger of wells looked at the dynamite stick, scratched his head thoughtfully, and snipped the fuse – a bit short, in my opinion. He then gave the rope a good testing tug. Satisfied, he struck a match, lit the fuse, seized the rope, and hauled himself up hand over hand. He clambered out, dragged the sheets of galvanised iron over the hole and chucked a couple of largish rocks on top. 'Run, man!' he shouted. I needed no urging. Not many seconds later, there was an enormous explosion, and the rocks were hurled into the air. For a brief moment I tried to imagine what would have happened if he had slipped or the rope had broken, but that did not bear thinking about.

As the dust settled the birds began to sing again. The well-digger emerged from behind his tree, cast aside the galvanised iron sheets and again swarmed down the rope into the smoking hole to examine the results. I peered down into the dusty dynamite-reeking chasm. 'We blast one mo' time,' came a voice from the depths. I decided I couldn't face another explosion – or, rather, its potential consequences – and left him to it. He did a good job – in all the following years I never had to call him back – but I still have disturbing visions of him being blown out of the hole like a human cannonball.

I had opened accounts with suppliers of building materials and Ian Morrison was finalising the drawings to be submitted to the town and country planning authorities. I was well advanced with the requirements for my work permit; tracking down evidence of 'O' and 'A' level passes was the hardest part, and I never did obtain a police report. Other considerations, such as sourcing food and liquor, designing menus and drawing up the wine list, would be spread out over the coming months. I was also going to have to find a chef who could supervise the execution, consistently and quickly, of my dishes, which were unlike anything a Barbadian chef had ever come across. I was even considering bringing in a chef from overseas, but that could be expensive and risky; besides obtaining a work permit for him, I would have to pay for his travel and provide accommodation. And who knew how he would work out? I had to find someone already living on-Island to fill this critical role. I began asking around.

Despite all this activity, life was not all work. I had established a cosy second base at the Sandy Lane Hotel, two miles from Bagatelle down on the coast. And at this point, dear reader, I propose to leave the building work at Bagatelle to proceed apace, and to introduce you to an extraordinary gentleman.

CHAPTER ELEVEN

The Genius Of Ronnie Tree

Ronnie Tree was born to an American mother and a British father in the United States and educated in England. He treasured his Anglo-American status. He was Member of Parliament for Harborough, and served in Winston Churchill's cabinet as a junior Minister of Information. He met Marietta Fitzgerald towards the end of the war. They had an affair, dumping their respective spouses in the process, and subsequently married in 1947. After the war a disbelieving world witnessed the colossus Churchill, and Ronnie with him, being discarded by an apparently ungrateful electorate. The nation believed Clement Attlee's Labour government's promise to create a fairer society and a welfare state. And the promise was kept, beginning with the creation of the National Health Service. But the new Leftist policies included increased taxes on the rich, so Ronnie decamped with Marietta to the United States. A city girl who liked to be close to the levers of power and to pull them from time to time, Marietta was bored by English country life and glad to leave. She was also a fervent Democrat, whilst Ronnie and his English circle were true-blue Tories. But Ronnie was restless in America. He toured the Caribbean where he considered living in Trinidad. Before making a final decision he stayed on Barbados with his friend Sir Edward Cunard at his West Coast mansion, Glitter Bay. Cunard persuaded him to buy 40 acres of land a short distance south of his own estate that enjoyed a similarly long sea frontage.

Ronnie put aside some 22 acres on which he was to build his home, Heron Bay, where he lived until he died in 1976 – there is still a pond where herons fish. Based on Palladio's Villa Maser, it was designed by Sir Jeffrey Jellicoe. Ronnie and Marietta moved there in 1947. Blessedly, they found time to produce a daughter, Penelope, born in 1949. I shall love her until the day I die. Not long afterwards Marietta returned to the United States to pursue both her high-flying career in Democratic Party circles and Adlai Stevenson, in whose two unsuccessful presidential campaigns she was closely involved. She had already stolen the heart of the film director John Huston and had not given it back.

The Tree pulling power proved irresistible to socialites on both sides of the Atlantic, and Barbados quickly became the place where society's *crème de la crème* wintered. Sir Anthony Eden, one of Ronnie's colleagues from Churchill's war cabinet, came with his wife Clarissa to stay at Heron Bay; they were likewise seduced by the Island's tropical charms and purchased the Villa Nova, some miles inland from the West Coast. There followed something of a stately stampede of British and American society to find land as close to Heron Bay as possible – ideally on the coast – on which to build a winter home. The Platinum Coast was born.

By the end of the Fifties the winter migration of snowbirds was such that Ronnie decided to build a hotel. It would provide, as the wags had it, a place for his friends to stay and pay. Ronnie chose, as the site for his hotel and an exclusive estate and golf course, the 400-acre Sandy Lane sugar plantation, which he purchased in 1958. The property had been declared bankrupt, for the heyday of the sugar barons was long past. The potential for development for purposes other than sugar production had gone unrecognised – hardly surprising, unless you were blessed with Ronnie's fertile imagination. The plantation included beach land – a whole bay, in fact – which, as I have already noted, was swampy; dengue fever and malaria posing an ever-present threat. The main West Coast road ran through the property next to the sea, which made development for tourism questionable. Indeed, so unappealing did the property appear that the beach land was thrown in for nothing by Colonel Jack Thorne, acting on behalf of his – the owning – family. Years later, seeing what Ronnie made of it, they never quite forgave him. This was the first of two own goals scored by the good Colonel. Other persons of substance, Barbadians and non-Barbadians alike, had an equal opportunity to invest at rock-bottom prices in the new Barbados no longer reliant on sugar, but few did. Among those who did catch the boat were Nick Parravicino and Bernie Weatherhead, who courageously took the plunge and have since reaped the rewards.

One who missed the boat was Atlantic Records supremo, the late Ahmed Ertigan. At a drunken party which he threw at the Bagatelle restaurant some years later, he told me that in the Fifties he had had the chance to buy a whole stretch of the West Coast from Sandy Lane to Coral Reef. At the time the land was measured in acres. The asking price was US$90,000 and he regretted having turned it down, thinking it unrealistically expensive. By the time of his party that land was selling not by the acre but by the square foot.

Ronnie had already thought out solutions to the two main problems – the swamp and the awkward position of the road. He took care of the former by draining, grading and landscaping the land in such a way that it would remain permanently dry. As for the coast road, he contrived a brilliant coup in a *quid pro quo*. He covenanted to the people of Barbados some land left over from his original 40 acres for a cricket ground; a more popular gift in the West Indies cannot be imagined. It is there today, called Trents, where cricket is played regularly. In return, Ronnie was permitted to move the road back about two hundred yards from the coast, so that the hotel, gardens, car park, pool and ancillary services were between it and the sea. Across the newly built road he created his Sandy Lane estate and golf course on land that hitherto had produced valuable sugar, but was now lying fallow – 'rab land', as Barbadians say.

Meeting Ronnie, you would never have suspected the exceptionally brilliant brain at work, certainly not in something as vulgar as commerce. At least, I didn't. He was a country gentleman, an affectionate and considerate friend, and had the air more of a bishop than a property developer. He loved nothing better than, as dusk approached, to sit in his high-backed cane chair close to the beach, sipping a rum punch and watching the sun sinking below the western horizon. A tinkle of his silver hand bell would summon a butler, Brown or Tull, in a moment with a top-up. Ronnie once told me, as we sat there, that he had chosen to locate Heron Bay close to the sea so that it was impossible for people to stand back and be awed by its grandeur. He was to ensure that the Sandy Lane Hotel was similarly positioned. He did not seek admiration, and created places not for their visual impact but because they were gracious and worked comfortably.

To design the hotel and golf course he turned to the local architectural practice, Robertson Ward. Jimmy Walker and Happy Ward produced a design embodying everything Ronnie stood for – understated elegance, luxurious comfort and perfect harmony with the landscape. The hotel was comparatively small, with only fifty-two rooms and, like Heron Bay, strangely unassuming as you approached it. But once in the foyer, you were overwhelmed by the beauty of the faintly-pink native coral stone of which the hotel was constructed. Out to sea the vivid blue Caribbean provided the most heavenly backdrop, lapping on the powder-fine white sand of the Sandy Lane beach, so recently a malodorous swamp overgrown with sea grape. From seaward it was quite difficult to spot the hotel, for the local building code stated that the height of a building on the West Coast must not exceed that of the coconut palms. Sadly, and to the detriment of the Island, this desirable stricture has been ignored in modern times and the West Coast is looking more and more like Miami Beach.

For Ronnie only the best would do. Accordingly he brought in an eminent horticulturalist from Kew Gardens, Richard Coghlan, to landscape the property. To ensure the smooth running of the hotel, he lured Helmut Kiertini from Claridges in London as manager. When it opened in 1961 it was without equal on Barbados. There were others, of course, but what none of them had, except possibly the Coral Reef Club, was the acreage. What they assuredly did not have was the jewel in the crown, the thousand-feet-long Sandy Lane beachfront land, which was owned by the hotel and its associates. All buildings on it were subject to a strict covenant, so there were no shacks or eyesores to be seen. The already narrow beaches to the north – including that at Heron Bay – tended to be eroded by winter storms, sometimes being washed away completely. To the south were less expensive hotels, villas and rum shops, cheek by jowl with each other. The Sandy Lane Hotel and its satellites reposed in lofty regal splendour.

Every day, as the sun rose, the Sandy Lane beach was raked, chaises longues and tables laid out, and parasols put up. Usually the bathing was safe. Only once in a while, as a result of winter storms in the North Atlantic, a huge swell was generated; then, unless you knew how to handle the steepling waves and powerful north-running currents, it was wiser to stay on the beach. From promontories at each end of the beach reefs extend out to sea, providing – when the sea was calm – marvellous snorkelling opportunities.

Very importantly, not least for public relations, the beach was not private. No beach on Barbados is. The Queen's Chain, a statute unchanged in the post-colonial era, stipulates that one chain – 22 yards – above the mean high water mark is the property of the state and its citizens. It's impossible to deny anyone access to the sea. This is highly desirable, as Barbadians love the sea and are strong believers in the healthful benefits of 'de sea baff.' It also ensures that beach cricket, an immensely popular game, can be played, no matter how grand the nearby hotel may be. Some foreign would-be investors have tried to have this restriction waived, hoping to be able to offer their guests a private beach. They have failed.

In the years after the hotel opened in 1961, all the land between the road and the sea that was not required for the hotel and its facilities was made part of the Sandy Lane estate. This was divided into lots for sale, which were snapped up. The buyers were an illustrious lot, Lords Bernstein and Rothschild amongst them. The family Amberikos also invested. Some Americans called Ward built a sort of mini Taj Mahal on one side of the hotel, and a Venezuelan tycoon put up a more modest palace on the other. Julian Byng had a place too. Towards the southern end a beach facility was established for use of property owners, which offered for sale cabanas for storing beach furniture, lilos, towels, snorkelling gear and so on, especially handy for those whose houses were not on the sea. Unfortunately there were not enough cabanas – some owners, in the early days, having wisely bought two or three – for each house to have one. On the rare occasions that they come on the market, the price has gone through the roof and, as roofs go, there are few as high as those on Sandy Lane.

These plots of land, never less than one acre in size, were selling well at around 1US$ per square foot in 1972. Under the covenant, providing the plans were approved, it was permissible to build a house of any dimensions, together with an all-important guest cottage, with a footprint of not more than 1,200 square feet. Winding amongst the houses was the original Sandy Lane golf course, now known as the Bottom Nine. These houses were a good source of customers for my restaurant, only a ten-minute drive away, due to a convention that on the staff's night off house guests would invite their hosts to a restaurant for dinner. They often chose Bagatelle.

This was the miracle Ronnie Tree began in 1961. By the time I discovered it almost ten years later, the hotel, acquired by Trust Houses in 1967, boasted 120 rooms and had become an icon of excellence throughout the world. It was to play a pivotal role in my Caribbean life, socially, recreationally and commercially.

It offered everything I needed: water sports, a place to keep my catamaran, somewhere to moor my water-ski jump, a fine swimming pool with a springboard, tennis courts, a bar, and endless bikini-clad girls. Waiters patrolled the beach, with trays laden with rum punches, rum coolers, Tequila sunrises, Pimm's, Bellinis, and refreshing lime squash in tall frosted glasses. At lunchtime a delectable buffet at US$9 a head – now US$125 – was on offer in the beachside restaurant, with an undemanding dress code. With my current book propped up as ever against an ice bucket invariably containing a bottle of Muscadet, digging into smoked salmon, flying fish, cold roast beef and a vast selection of salads, I was in heaven. After lunch you could pass out on a chaise longue or plunge into the sea. One could visit Dotto's Boutique to catch up on the local gossip and buy the odd Pucci shirt or a pair of Lothar trousers. In the evening, as the land cooled down and the wind died with the sun, one could water-ski in the sheltered bay in front of an admiring audience, thereafter retiring to join friends at the bar for punches and backgammon, keeping a beady eye out for that oft-doubted phenomenon, the green flash.

The world of the tropics is divided into two groups, those who have seen the green flash and those who have not. As the sun sets on a cloudless horizon, just before it disappears, you might see for one or two seconds an apple-green flash slightly above the orb. It does not occur every sunset but it is very real. The best I ever saw was from an elevation of two or three hundred feet, driving down Cave Hill past the University towards the sea. When in 1974 Blake Edwards was making *The Tamarind Seed* on Barbados, his cameraman Freddie Young used to indulge his hobby – every day, no matter where he found himself, he would film the sunset. One evening a hotel guest complained that she had been looking for weeks for this green flash she had heard so much about, in vain. Freddie advised her that if she removed her Polaroid sunglasses she might have more luck.

Commercially, at Sandy Lane, I had landed on my feet. I have moaned and groaned about the iniquitous Modified American Plan (MAP) system which was forced on hotel guests whether they liked it or not, meaning that a restaurant would have been barely viable since the locals rarely dined out. When I arrived in Barbados in 1970, there was no first-class restaurant outside a hotel on the whole West Coast. My only competition, La Bonne Auberge, was in the middle of nowhere and the very devil to find. Now, however, MAP was to prove a valuable benefactor. It was my good fortune that amongst my first customers at Bagatelle was the manager of the Sandy Lane Hotel, Ray Carroll; I doubt if there has ever been a finer hotelier or one more loved by his staff. Ray took a great liking to my restaurant. He knew that many of his guests resented having to dine in his hotel every evening, and that men found the evening dress code on special nights hot and uncomfortable. So Ray instigated a system whereby any of his guests on MAP – which is to say just about all of them – was entitled to dine at Bagatelle once for each week of their stay, an arrangement for which I was most satisfactorily reimbursed by the hotel. Moreover, often these guests enjoyed the informality of their experience at my place so much that they came back, even though they had already paid for dinner at the hotel. I was in clover.

The Irish-owned hotel these days operates under a very different excluding philosophy, which would not, I believe, have found favour with Ronnie Tree. But the Sandy Lane Hotel of those early days holds a place, very dear, in my heart. Now we must return to the building work at Bagatelle. Time and money are running out and Christmas is approaching.

Chapter Twelve

Lined Up And Cleared For Take-Off

A s work progressed I began publicising the imminent opening of my
Bagatelle Great House restaurant – 'the Bagatelle' for short. As far
as official contacts were concerned, thanks entirely to the Leacocks,
I had met the Prime Minister, the British High Commissioner, the American Ambassador, hotel managers, tour operators, suppliers of food and wine,
a friendly bank manager, and journalists. I had met everyone of consequence
I needed to know. My connection with the Diner was helpful; many knew
it as the 'in' place in swinging London, where the food was interesting and
original. The expectation that my Bagatelle menus would be a departure
from the predictable offerings of the local hotel restaurants was a source of
interest and hope. Thus the opening of my place was awaited with lively
anticipation and optimism.

I had returned to Barbados from Jamaica at the end of the high season,
when the snowbirds were going back to the United States and Britain, leaving behind those who lived on Barbados the whole year round. Some, like
Claudette Colbert, had strayed northwards to the less populated parish of
St. Peter, but most lived in St. James, an area of barely ten square miles.
Its smallness facilitated my spreading the word. Many potential customers
were well off, had magnificent houses with swimming pools, maids, cooks,
chauffeurs and gardeners. They were given to entertaining, assisted by a butler – uniquely in Ronnie Tree's case, two. Life without such a man, immaculate in black dress trousers, black bowtie, Persil-white uniform jacket
with gleaming brass buttons – usually wearing shoes but not always – was

unthinkable. There was even a sort of finishing school where butlers could be polished by Ann Amberikos' coveted major domo, Joseph. In many ways the West Coast was a retirement home for those who, having lived and worked in the Old World, were determined to continue to enjoy old-fashioned pleasures in the balmy tropics, where, unlike in left-leaning post-war Britain, they could live in the manner to which they had been accustomed. By choosing to live on Barbados these people had wound back, or rather stopped, the clock.

I was quite a rare bird, a bachelor with no family attachments, an extremely useful beast as far as hostesses were concerned for making up numbers or partnering single female guests. In addition, I had something of a story with which to regale fellow diners. On a tiny island, with its long-standing family feuds, cliques and scandals, fresh – neutral – blood is welcomed, so I received many invitations.

One of these, via Margaret Leacock, was from Sylvia, Lady Brooke. She had been the last Ranee of Sarawak, and everyone called her Ranee. Off I went a few days later to Tuffet Cottage, her home on the Sandy Lane estate, the first of many visits. Ranee was tiny, and wore long floaty chiffon dresses and knitted socks on her feet, the toes of which were, it was said, webbed. She was a charming animated conversationalist with a twinkle in her eye. We often gathered of an evening, sitting around her feet or perching on the arms of her chair, as she talked about life in Sarawak and how the staff would always leave the royal palace before sunset because, when she and her husband the Rajah were dining, they could hear the clatter of knives and forks on plates as invisible long-departed ancestors dined with them.

Only after her death did I learn more. Hers had not been a dull life. She was born in 1885. Her father, Lord Esher, is said to have been insensitive to his children, except his son Maurice, whom he idolised; one of Sylvia's first tasks every day was to tie her brother's bootlaces. So unhappy was she that she attempted suicide twice before her twelfth birthday. On the first occasion she left an opened tin of sardines on top of a wardrobe until they rotted and then ate them, hoping ptomaine poisoning would do away with her. This failed so, ever-inventive, she lay naked for hours in the snow, hoping to catch pneumonia. She didn't, and survived!

In 1911 she married Sir Charles Vyner de Windt Brooke, whose family had ruled Sarawak, in the north-west of Borneo, since 1842, when his fore-bear James Brooke was given the country by the Sultan of Brunei. She was pleased when in 1917 her husband became the third Rajah and she became the Ranee. This meant that they were henceforward His and Her Royal Highness – heady stuff – and answerable to no-one. They occupied them-selves in a casual sort of way in running a country with a population of over two million, a quarter of whom were Dyaks, indigenous natives famous throughout the world for cutting off their enemies' heads, shrinking them and keeping them as trophies – head-hunters, in a phrase.

She also painted, and I offer elsewhere an example of her work[*] – not a masterpiece admittedly – but it is by her hand and may possibly have a sin-ister undercurrent. Unfortunately I never had the chance to ask her about it because it came into my possession twenty years after her death. I say sinis-ter because, during the cruel Japanese wartime occupation, the Dyaks con-fessed that, with malice aforethought, they had sent their prettiest daughters to a pool in the forest to bathe. When the Japanese approached to stare at them, they had crept up and simply lopped off their heads. As card-carry-ing head-hunters, they were naturally good at that sort of thing. During that unwelcome intrusion from 1941 to 1945 the Dyaks did away with over 1,500 Japanese soldiers.

Ranee awarded herself the soubriquet 'Queen of the Head-hunters' and one of her eleven books bore the same title. A fan was George Bernard Shaw, who composed the following verse.

> *Ride a cock horse, To Sarawak Cross,*
> *To see a young Ranee consumed with remorse.*
> *She'll have bells on her fingers, And rings through her nose,*
> *And won't be permitted to wear any clo'es.*

One of the three Brooks daughters married the bandleader Harry Roy. Dur-ing a tour of North American chat shows to promote *Queen of the Head-hunt-ers*, Dick Cavitt asked Ranee why the RADA-educated Elizabeth, grand-

---

[*]   See picture 34.

daughter of a viscount and daughter of a queen, had married a bandleader. With her hands folded demurely and her feet not quite reaching the floor, the septuagenarian answered sweetly, 'I'm told he was very good with his instrument.' She brought the house down.

So I was surprised to learn that, in Sylvia's own words, 'Though I had thawed considerably in the Sarawak sun, I was still, to all intents and purposes, a frigid woman.' Possibly the same could not be said of her daughters who had eight husbands between them.

Ranee was accused of all sorts of things, rarely flattering. Her brother described her as a female Iago. Another man called her the most charming of despots. Someone even accused her of 'raising her daughters like tarts'. The Colonial Office found her to be 'spectacularly vulgar in her behaviour, full of Machiavellian schemes and dangerous'. These last two epithets referred to her tireless efforts to have the law of succession altered so that, since she had borne the Rajah no sons, one of her daughters could rule the country as Ranee.

Ranee died at Tuffet Cottage in 1971 aged eighty-six. There was a well-attended memorial service for her at St. James' church as the sunset; the parish was quite a good place in which to die. All your friends were close at hand to send you on your way with a few kind words. In the church porch there hung a helpful reminder:

> *Every time I pass this place*
> *I pay a little visit*
> *So when at last I'm carried in*
> *God won't say 'Who is it?'*

The West Coast of Barbados was home to the cream of the international gay set, all without exception outrageously talented, witty and waspish, and an infallible source of spicy gossip. Before the Second World War the tone had been set at Glitter Bay House by Sir Edward Cunard, who, you may remember, later persuaded Ronnie Tree to buy land on Barbados in 1945. Oliver Messel and his partner Vagn Riis-Hansen moved there in 1956; Oliver had restored Ronnie's enormous pile, Ditchley, in England, before the war. Two slightly younger Americans, Frank di Buono and Ian MacGregor, were all-year-rounders. Arnold Scaasi – frock designer to Mrs Ronald Reagan – and his companion Parker Ladd – came every winter, as did Elton John, and occasionally London impresario Binkie Beaumont. There were camp followers too numerous to mention.

Then, out of the blue, into this colourful pool of *glitterati* splashed a not-too-ugly man in his early thirties, who had long hair and wore frocks in the evening – *moi*! I was the guest everyone wanted, and I was lionised and spoiled. As it became obvious that I preferred girls to boys the fever died down, but the friendships remained. Perhaps, some hinted, I might one day see the error of my ways? At largely gay dinner parties, while I was being hopefully looked over, we often indulged in party games. 'Let's play charades,' Frank di Buono would pronounce. 'Ian and I are the team captains. Right, let's see who has first choice.' A coin would be tossed. The winner would immediately announce, 'I'll have Nick.' This was followed by a sharp intake of breath from the loser. The men were then chosen, one by one; the women could join any team they liked, since they didn't really matter.

Amongst the home gay team was the wonderfully named George Money, a director of Barclays Bank DCO, and his friend Llewellyn. Anthony Hunte, a horticulturalist, was something of a star. Gregory the hairdresser flounced around outrageously in one of his sister's flimsy shifts, so exciting the late Simon Foster, a loveable dressmaker, that he didn't know whether he was in the West Indies or the West End. However, the undisputed local leader was Victor Marsden, who lived with his boyfriend Mossy, former ADC to the Governor of Barbados, at his gorgeous house at Highclere, the highest point on Barbados. Victor owned the Ocean View Hotel on the South Coast, where every Sunday they offered a terrific buffet called 'Lunch in Xanadu', and where the board truly groaned. The centrepiece was a whole suckling pig, its skin roasted to a deep shining bronze. The chef, in spotless whites and tall hat, would carve thick slices of meat and crackling and smother them with apple sauce, while a large colourfully dressed fishwife fried flying fish over a wood-burning brazier. There were even salads – not a Barbadian speciality – enormous avocados weighing up to a kilo each from the neighbouring island of Dominica, key lime and lemon meringue pies, and piles of mangos, paw-paw and bananas. And, talking of tasty local dishes, lunch was always followed by a cabaret starring the young and luscious Audrey Shepherd, who was inclined to jump up on a table and dance in a deplorably abandoned manner, her skirts flying hither and thither – mostly hither.

My favourite evening restaurant was Greensleeves, owned by Jack and Laura Teller who coined and registered the name 'Apartel' because, rather than conventional hotel rooms, their guest accommodation was in the form of apartments. These were luxurious in the extreme, each boasting a vast sitting room, a romantic bedroom, an extravagantly appointed bathroom, and a shaded balcony overlooking the pool and gardens. They were, it transpired, too good to be viable. The Tellers had invested so much in the lavish accommodation, they needed to charge more than punters were prepared to pay. For a while the restaurant was sufficiently profitable to carry the whole shebang, but eventually even that ran out of steam and the whole thing folded, but not before many of us had enjoyed happy times there. The Greensleeves' only flaw was that, unlike Ronnie Tree, the Tellers had been unable to arrange to move the coast road away from the sea, so to get to the beach and its bar one had to cross a very busy road, which somehow broke the spell. It was a gauntlet worth running, though, for the nearby Gibbs beach, entirely free of reefs, was never crowded. At its southern end the open-sided beach bar sat on a small promontory shaded by swaying coconut palms, just under Jack and Laura's palatial apartment. The bar was ruled – there is no other word for it – by Delsie, an imperious and statuesque black woman, whom we regulars called 'The Duchess'. The kitchen did a line in scrumptious toasted sandwiches; my to-die-for favourite was sausage, bacon and fried egg.

Every day at noon Gran, Laura's ancient but spry mother, sat at the same table reading a detective novel – the sexier the better, she told me. We chatted often, and she showed me photos of her life in China in the late nineteenth century, riding a mule in the hills, wearing a shady hat, and attended by an army of coolies. She sailed merrily past her hundredth birthday.

The bar was conveniently placed so that, when later I acquired my first windsurfer – a novelty in those days – I would sail up from Sandy Lane and skim and tack and gybe over the waves at fantastic speeds. Around one o'clock I would beach the craft in spectacular fashion and saunter into the restaurant, hopefully picking up, as I lunched, a reservation or two for Bag-atelle, and sometimes a profitable game of backgammon.

After a hard day's work at Bagatelle I would sometimes reward myself with the exquisite food and wine and impeccable service at the Greensleeves main restaurant, where Jack and Laura perched elegantly on tall stools, mar-tinis in hand. Where I should sit was smilingly indicated by a wave of a cigarette holder. Laura was a striking slender woman with exquisite facial bones. In the evening she always wore long clinging sheath dresses and very high heels. She had been the Craven 'A' poster girl in the Thirties; in a Peter Cheyney novel she would have been called Zelda. Jack, once a theatrical agent, was invariably immaculate in a white tuxedo. As if going to the thea-tre, you always dressed up for Greensleeves.

In spite of their relaxed appearance, Laura and Jack kept an eagle eye on the operation of the restaurant. Their son Nicolas worked there too, but his par-ents were so much the star attractions that, for all his strenuous efforts, it was difficult for him to make his mark, and I felt rather sorry for him. His current wife Beryl – he had previously been married to the singer Susan Vaughan – was a live wire and adored him. She was later to bear him, at the risk of her life, two fine sons. When all the guests had left or gone to bed, Nicolas, Beryl and I would chuck off our clothes and jump into the pool. Once, as I was ruminat-ing lazily under the stars, my arms draped over the edge, I felt a warm yielding woman's body pressed against my naked back; lips close to my ear whispered throatily, 'Darling, I'm going to pee all down your back.'

'Is that so, Beryl?' I murmured.

There was a strangled cry. 'Oh, no! I thought you were *my* Nick!' Her face glowed faintly pink in the dark as she swam hurriedly away.

Not far north of Greensleeves lived a wealthy American – she owned quite a lot of Sears Roebuck stock – called Verna Hull, who was an artist. She had formed a friendship with Princess Margaret, who dropped in to Barbados from time to time to stay, before flying on to Mustique and her house there, *Les Jolies Eaux*. During one such visit Verna decided to invite the Princess to dinner at Greensleeves.

When she made the reservation she told Nicolas the identity of her illus-trious guest, which was quite enough to set him all a-quiver. He took the waiters and waitresses aside to give them precise instructions – serve from the left, take away from the right, and so on – things they knew perfectly well already. He went on to say that they must not on any account – as they sometimes did – demand, 'Who de fish soup?' or 'Who de flyin' fish?' They must know beforehand which dish was going to which guest, especially the one destined for the royal guest. If they had to speak, they must do so slowly and clearly. Right?

The great evening arrived, the royal party seated, and Nicolas was standing by, hands clasped in a saintly manner, smiling confidently. The first course arrived from the kitchens, and the specially selected waitress approached the table and in a clarion voice demanded, 'Who de Princess?' Poor Nicolas. Collapse of stout party.

Back at the Bagatelle, thanks to Mr Prescott and his elderly team, the building work was ahead of schedule. The furniture had been made. I had my work permit, and believed I had found a chef.

There have always been dogs in my life, so I visited Dr Will Huey, the compassionate Irish vet who also ran the Island's RSPCA, to ask if he had any animals that needed a home. I was in luck; a hotel chef was returning to the United Kingdom and could not afford the expense of English quarantine kennels, about £1,500 a dog in those days, and he had *two*. He felt that, as long-time friends, they ought not to be separated, and so it was that I inherited an Alsatian – 'Allystayshun' in local parlance – and, with some reluctance, a mongrel called Sam. The Alsatian was always escaping and so was named Houdini.

The vet also had a large homeless calico cat that gave me one look and demanded I take her home forthwith. I obeyed. I called her Tara, but when Tara herself eventually arrived it made life complicated, so the cat's name was changed to Mrs T. She lived for another twenty years on a diet mostly of slightly-off shrimps.

Tara's arrival was imminent. The modest bed that had come with the house was, to say the least, monastic, and I didn't think it was suitable for amorous pastimes. Harold Bowen, a brilliant auctioneer with the broadest Bajan accent and a voice like a rook with laryngitis, was to conduct an auction sale at a fine Jacobean house called St. Nicholas Abbey. Harold knew his antiques and was very witty. He stood behind a table and potential purchasers sat on rows of chairs, sofas, anything that could be sat on, in front of him. Elderly ladies occupied the best seats long before the sale began, their bags replete with thermos flasks and sandwiches and sometimes knitting, all ready to enjoy Harold's one-man show. The in-house porter was an enormous lesbian, a sort of human forklift truck, famous for having thrown a man, who had the temerity to make eyes at her girlfriend, through a window – which was closed at the time. In Harold's catalogue I noticed a four-poster bed was for sale. It was more than I could have imagined or desired for my wicked purposes. Off I went to the sale, where my bid secured me the monumental mahogany masterpiece. Mr Prescott erected it. In the event, Tara had to delay her arrival until the New Year, but I was more than happy to be equipped and ready for any opportunity which might arise in the meantime.

I was now at the stage when the menu and recipes had to be drawn up. Almost any ingredient I could wish for was available, either locally produced or imported, at a price. The only limits were my imagination and the culinary abilities of my all-female kitchen staff that came from the next door village, Redmans. Barbados, unlike the French-speaking Caribbean with its spicy Créole cuisine, was not then known for its cuisine. The women were used to cooking little more than chicken necks, rice and fried fish. As for vegetables, with a tradition going back to Africa, they only knew starchy yams and sweet potatoes. Salads were unknown. This unpromising outlook was offset, however, by the gift which Barbadians have in abundance: the ability to copy, be it food, cricket or furniture. They picked up my recipes very quickly. It was nonetheless my hope to find a chef who would lead the team, broaden their culinary scope, and free my hands for front-of-house work.

Dining out in ethnic restaurants in London and enjoying the classic cuisine of France had given me a catholic repertoire. Working in the Diner kitchen had taught me how a professional kitchen works. Any restaurateur who cannot take over in the kitchen is at risk from the demands of his chef, often an egotistical creature, ever ready to exploit his perceived indispensability. At the Bagatelle I was determined to put into practice the Diner philosophy of serving simple, interesting food which could be repeated quickly and consistently. We would have to manage without reductions, ice sculptures and spun sugar.

There was one exotic item which I *had* to include – flying fish. Uniquely in the Caribbean, this was exploited on Barbados, where it is prized as a foodstuff and, as it is exotic and colourful, in advertising for tourism. In culinary terms it is a little like herring, and the very devil to prepare, being full of tiny bones. Fortunately fisherwomen with nimble fingers do this for you. There are even boning competitions! The national dish is flying fish with coo-coo, which is made from corn meal and okra. They are very tasty stuffed with finely chopped garlic, onion, thyme, hot peppers and chives, and fried. Like herring they can also be smoked or soused. And they are cheap.

The Christmas deadline was drawing ever closer. The police, prior to the licensing court hearing, had made a cursory visit. I had received my liquor licence. The very fussy public health people had arrived, with thermometers for testing refrigerated space, and testing standing water for mosquito larvae. They had given me the nod. The kitchen was equipped, the furniture in place, and the storerooms fully stocked. The restaurant inventory – crockery, cutlery, napery and glassware – had been purchased. The car park had been carved out of the jungle, surfaced and lit. The signs were up.

In the midst of all this I was recommended a chef, an Englishman called Nigel Dawson-Hall, who had recently finished his contract at a hotel and was looking for work. He was already on-Island and had his own accommodation. I immediately set about having his work permit validated for a stint at Bagatelle.

But just as I was about to fling wide the gates, two snags occurred. The American former owner of the Bagatelle property demanded to be paid the remainder of the purchase price. I had conveniently forgotten about her – ostriches could learn a lot from me – and the last pennies in the bank account had been spent on the car park. Fortunately the manager of the Royal Bank of Canada, who had attended one of my promotional dinners at the Great Table, believed in what I was doing and immediately came up with the necessary. Saved!

The other problem was much more tiresome. At the last moment Mr Dawson-Hall left me high, dry and seething, with an inexperienced kitchen staff without a leader. I was told he had had a nervous breakdown. Fortunately I had rehearsed the menu so my staff had a good idea of what to do. Importantly, they were unflappable; West Indians don't do panic. Whatever the pressure, I was convinced, they would produce the dishes accurately and on time. But I was going to have to find someone to lead the kitchen and that right speedily.

I found just the man, a Barbadian who had, he informed me, two names: Hamilton Roberts and Shamangoli Forkell; the first, he informed me, represented his material aspirations and the second his spiritual identity. He was very bright and could solve Rubik's Cube in two minutes flat. In the following twenty-eight years, and three chefs later, I never required a single work permit for a foreigner. Barbadians did everything I asked of them and more. In the meantime, however, until Hamilton/Shamangoli was free of his current obligations, I would have to start without a chef, welcoming customers, taking orders, overseeing the cooking and handling the cash. I was going to be quite busy. However, by the time the dust had settled, Christmas and the New Year had passed, and the enormous revenue, the highest of the entire year, with them.

In the second week of January 1971 everything was in place. The planets could not have been more fortuitously aligned. I found myself driven by some force I have never understood to do the right thing in the right place at the right time. I got lucky. Indeed, I found myself surfing on the slope of a powerful breaking wave – the newly independent Barbados, relishing her freedom. Not only was the West Coast ready to go, so was the whole of this reborn country. As a nation it was far more developed than any of its neighbours, with an impressive infrastructure already in place. This was due in large part to one remarkable man, so remarkable in fact, that I am going to devote the whole of my next chapter to him.

CHAPTER THIRTEEN

The Greatest Man I Have Ever Known

On 21st January 1920, in the Barbadian parish of St. John, Errol Walton Barrow was born into a black family of civic and political activists. He was educated at Harrison College, the best school on the Island, to which entry was gained on merit alone. Here he was given the nickname 'Dipper' by which he was always to be known. After leaving in 1938, he worked to earn enough to study privately in the hope of gaining a scholarship to read theology at Codrington College, the oldest such institution in the western hemisphere. He won the scholarship but, just days before he was due to start his religious studies, he told his family that he had joined the Royal Air Force and, with a group of similarly-minded West Indians, departed for England to fight the Nazis.

There is a long tradition, going back to the eighteenth century, of black West Indians serving the Crown in the armed forces. Whilst still slaves, they had been driven to demonstrate that, as soldiers, they were just as worthwhile as their white counterparts. During the war they made a great contribution, working in factories and serving in the Merchant Navy and the armed forces. Seven West Indians have been awarded the Victoria Cross, most recently in 2004 the Grenadian Private Johnson Beharry, who served in Iraq.

Errol Barrow wanted to become a pilot with the RAF but had an eye problem which disqualified him. Instead he trained as an observer/navigator and flew over occupied Europe. Having flown on forty-five bombing missions, he received his commission, becoming Pilot Officer Barrow. His final posting was as personal navigator to Sir Sholto Douglas, who was to become Air Commander in Chief of the British Zone of Germany, and then Air Chief Marshall of the Royal Air Force. (Later, ennobled, he took the title Lord Douglas of Kirtleside, finally becoming the chairman of British Airways.) He recognised Errol Barrow's exceptional abilities and chose him to fill this important role.

At the end of the war Errol Barrow's repatriation to Barbados was delayed to enable him to study at the London School of Economics. Unusually, he was permitted to study degrees in law and economics concurrently, which gives one some idea of his intellectual capacity. He took his Bar finals in 1949, becoming a barrister-at-law, and gained a BSc in Economics in 1950, two qualifications which would stand him and Barbados in good stead.

In 1950 Errol Barrow returned to Barbados, where the political scene was dominated by Grantley Adams, leader of the Barbados Labour Party, who did an enormous amount to advance the rights of black Barbadians. Although a monarchist, Adams wanted a more democratic Barbados, and by 1949 had wrested government control from the planters and secured for women the right to vote. His vision extended beyond his own country. His dream was the uniting of ten Caribbean colonies into a single state, independent of Britain, to be called the West Indies Federation. In 1958 this dream became a reality, with its capital in Trinidad, and Mr Adams – later Sir Grantley – as its first prime minister. But internal political conflicts caused the Federation to collapse in 1962.

It is worth examining, from the racial point of view, the sort of Barbados Flight Officer Barrow returned to. Three main social groups have inhabited Barbados since the seventeenth century. The whites arrived in 1625 and created plantations for the cultivation of tobacco and cotton. Then, thanks to the acquisition of know-how from planters in Dutch Guyana, this was replaced by more profitable sugar cane. Labourers were required to work on the land and as domestic servants, so the planters brought in West Africans who, torn from their families and homes and sold into slavery, that vilest of trades, formed the second group, the blacks. The third group consisted of men and women, many from western England, Scotland and Ireland, who were deported by Oliver Cromwell in the course of the English Civil War of 1642–1651. On Barbados, being landed as slaves or indentured labour, they were known as poor whites or – even more disparagingly – redlegs, due to the effect of the fierce tropical sun on their fair skins.

It is often said with pride that Barbados has enjoyed, after England, the oldest Westminster-model parliament in the world. This is true. In 1639 the Governor of the Island, himself appointed by the Crown, selected sixteen landowners from the so-called plantocracy to serve in the House of Burgesses (later the House of Assembly). As a result, the government of Barbados, its economy and judiciary were in the hands of a small, white and wealthy oligarchy, who were to be notorious – even in the New World – for their racism and cruelty. This unsatisfactory situation remained unchanged for the next three centuries, during which time the planters took full advantage of their autonomy. The slave rebellions of 1645, 1675 and 1692 were mercilessly suppressed. Some alleged participants were beheaded and their bodies dragged through the streets; others were burned alive.

The British government, mindful of the increasing wealth and influence of Barbados, intervened rarely and then only when the wilder excesses of retrogressive policies threatened to disturb the political equilibrium. As a result, the Barbadian government dragged its heels on any kind of reform. The tenets of racial difference continued unchallenged. Even after the abolition of slavery in 1839, nothing changed much; the planters saw to that. They were very conscious of the fact that they were outnumbered twenty to one by African Barbadians, but this did not deter them from encouraging the slaves to breed. On the contrary, after a time, the slave population was self-perpetuating and therefore cost-effective. Importing slaves was expensive. Additionally, the whites pursued a deliberate policy of not allowing the blacks security of any kind, giving them no chance to put down roots or to acquire land. They were not able even to buy sufficient food to do a full day's work. Education, their greatest hope for advancement, was likewise denied them – and I am not writing only about the seventeenth, eighteenth and nineteenth centuries.

The practical effects of emancipation were negligible. More than a hundred years later little, deplorably, had changed for black Barbadians.

And what of the third group, the poor whites? They were unfortunate indeed, for both the planters *and* the blacks had shunned them ever since they first landed in around 1642, and continued to do so long after my arrival in 1970, when most Barbadians would not give them the time of day, let alone have them in their houses. The poor whites found refuge in the Scotland district on the remote East Coast where they clung together, ignored and unloved. The result was a ghetto with high levels of mental retardation, alcoholism and inbreeding. Even so, a few poor white families, by dint of hard work and courageous persistence, have succeeded against all the odds in breaking out of this prison. Some, like the Williams and Goddards, have become so successful that the plantocracy has been forced to acknowledge their existence whether they like it or not. Even today the Scotland district remains a sad place to visit; the blotchy skin and empty hopeless eyes of the feckless inhabitants are haunting and shaming.

As far as colour discrimination was concerned, the Barbados Flying Officer Errol Barrow returned to in 1950 was not very different from the place he had left at the outbreak of war. Some black families, having somehow acquired an education, had made good, the Barrows amongst them. But the racial barriers remained insurmountable. Churches were segregated; the whites sat in front and the blacks at the back or in the gallery. A black person would never dare sit amongst the whites. Areas where well-to-do middle-class whites lived, like Belleville and Strathclyde, were out of bounds to black males after dark. The large hotels, haunts of white society, excluded black people other than as employees. Clubs such as the Royal Barbados Yacht Club, the Aquatic Club, and certain cricket clubs, had an exclusively white membership. Grantley Adams, the First Minister, married a white woman who was a member of the Aquatic Club, but when he drove her there he had to drop her off at the entrance and leave the premises. He, on whose broad shoulders Errol Barrow would one day stand, was not allowed in!

The Royal Barbados Yacht Club was notoriously inaccessible to any black Barbadian no matter of what rank or distinction. In 1957, for the benefit of local non-white sailors, local businessman Ian Gale founded the strictly non-racist Barbados Cruising Club. Errol Barrow, a keen sailor, was a founder member. He, like every black Barbadian, had experienced racism on innumerable occasions. One particularly harrowing experience is recounted in Peter Morgan's excellent book *The Life and Times of Errol Barrow*. In the early 1950s an Englishman, Captain John Hodson, was in the Officers' Mess of the Barbados Regiment on the Savannah in Bridgetown with some fellow officers, when in walked Flying Officer Barrow in RAF uniform. Captain Hodson's widow described what happened:

> *'Due to the unfortunate current ambiance (which Errol was coura-geously breaking through) he was given a very cold reception. John saw him standing alone and quite naturally welcomed him and supported him during the rest of the evening. The next day John got unpleasant phone calls criticising him and threatening resignation. John was even angrier over the fact that most of those officers had never seen active ser-vice whereas Errol had put his life on the line as a navigating officer on bombing raids over Europe.'*

When Captain Hodson died more than twenty years later, Errol Barrow recalled his gratitude for the support he had been given in a letter of condolence to Mrs Hodson.

Many young Barbadians who had joined up and returned home from wartime Britain had witnessed and been inspired by the success of Clement Atlee's Labour Party, and Errol Barrow, having spent five years at the London School of Economics, a veritable hotbed of Leftist thinking, was very much of their view. All these young Turks had initially willingly thrown in their lot with the progressive BLP but became dissatisfied and restless, for Grantley Adams was dictatorial and used to doing things his way. Nor did they agree with his reluctance to borrow money. He was a cautious old-fashioned Barbadian, and they felt he was holding the nation back. Consequently, in 1955 they formed the breakaway Democratic Labour Party (DLP), with Errol Barrow as its leader. In its early days this organisation was viewed as being fundamentally communist and was eyed with mistrust.

In 1961 the DLP, still led by Errol Barrow, won the general election, giving the young bloods the opportunity to realise their vision of a new Barbados. Provided loans could be repaid on time, they were happy to borrow. They had a leader with formal training in economics and, more importantly, a gift for putting it to practical use. Nonetheless, one thought dominated their minds: independence from the Crown. This concept had been included in the DLP election manifesto and became the primary issue the moment the West Indies Federation failed in 1962. The constitutional wheels to effect this seismic change were set in motion, even though the BLP and others disagreed, feeling that Barbados should not go it alone, and that another confederation of the East Caribbean states would be safer. There was the added fear that Errol Barrow would become a dictator. But the young legislators were not deterred. They believed that Barbados had whatever resources were needed.

At midnight on 30th November 1966, the greatest moment in the country's history, Barbados became a self-governing nation, independent of Great Britain yet remaining within the Commonwealth. At last, after more than three hundred years, the vast majority of Barbadians, by whose blood, sweat and tears a vibrant country had been created, would have the opportunity to share in its riches, to educate their children, to build their own homes, and to be free to go anywhere on their Island. Crucially, they now had legal recourse against the racial discrimination that had cursed the island for so long. All Barbadians were truly free and equal under the law.

While it is true that the white plantocracy had taken cruel advantage of its oligarchic rule since 1639, this at least meant that an experienced civil service – often referred to by Errol Barrow as 'the army of occupation' – was already in place. The new administration picked up the reins of power with consummate ease; only the driver had changed. Additionally, black Barbadians had learned – or had had battered into them – an ethic of thrift and hard work, for which they have always been highly regarded all over the world. The national motto is, appropriately, *Pride and Industry*.

Independence meant that Errol Barrow went from being Premier – First Minister – to *de facto* Prime Minister, and for the next ten years he was to fulfil magnificently his destiny as the father of an independent Barbados. In 1969 the Church was disestablished and disendowed by an Act of Parliament. Errol Barrow once told me that, prior to that Act, unless you were well in with the ecclesiastical authorities – a notably racist establishment – and white, you had no chance of obtaining a good job. Regrettably, if the experience of my religious Barbadian friends is anything to go by, it still is, only in the opposite direction – whites need not apply. In spite of this, the Church in Barbados, after a well thought-out transitional period, is successful and self-sustaining.

There was another change. You may remember that, when in 1955 the Sandy Lane sugar estate was sold to Ronnie Tree, the representative of the owning family, Colonel Jack Thorne, scored his first own goal by throwing in the soon-to-become-priceless beach land for nothing. He scored the second when, in his capacity as Secretary to the Royal Yacht Club, he wrote to the Queen asking whether, given the newly independent status of Barbados, the Club would retain its royal warrant. Her Majesty's Chamberlain wrote to the Prime Minister, asking what he wanted to do. Given the Club's past history, you may guess his decision. The lilywhite membership was not pleased. It is now the plain old Barbados Yacht Club.

As a white man I am humbled by the forgiving nature of black Barbadians who have much to forgive. They were torn from their homeland, enslaved, abused, and treated as less than human by the plantocracy. Yet when I arrived on Barbados, only four years after Independence, I met nothing but smiles and politeness; there was no sign of the feelings one might have expected to find simmering not far beneath the surface. And of course many humane white Barbadians behaved as they thought proper and damn the bigots. The Barbados Yacht Club unwisely gave Jack Leacock a place on its membership committee. Shortly afterwards Dr Teddy Cummings, an eminent paediatrician, became the first black member of the Club, and Jack was promptly voted off the committee. For many, such an act would have required considerable social courage. Not so Jack, a great Barbadian admired and loved by his fellow countrymen and women of every creed and colour. He held racists in contempt.

I cannot resist pointing out the irony that the left-wing policies in Britain, which Errol Barrow adopted as his policy for the future of Barbados, were exactly those that had driven Ronnie Tree out of England – to settle in Barbados. By the time I arrived, both men had made enormous contributions to the nation. Errol Barrow, already Prime Minister for six years, had turned Barbados into a country with an infrastructure, social welfare, and educational system far more advanced than those of any other English-speaking nation in the Caribbean. And Ronnie Tree's creation of the Sandy Lane Hotel and Estate and Golf Club had set the benchmark for luxury resorts, both in the Caribbean and throughout the world. However, Ronnie was not only concerned with the future of the Barbadian nation; he was also instrumental in preserving its past by founding the Barbados National Trust in 1960.

That these two remarkable men should have been active in the young independent Barbados at the same time was little short of a divine gift. That they both became my close and supportive friends is a humbling thought.

I met Errol Barrow through Jack and Margaret Leacock early in 1970. I remember a soft-spoken smiling man who seemed genuinely interested in what I had to say. He was one of those rare creatures who listened. He asked many questions. As I was later to discover, he was always inquisitive about the opinions and ideas of those living on Barbados, locals or foreigners. He stored the information away and used it to direct his policies, which for him had but one aim, the betterment of Barbadians and Barbados. In the course of later meetings we discovered two passions in common: cooking and aviation. Inevitably, we quickly got round to one or the other. We never ever discussed politics, although he did from time to time introduce me to West Indian politicians at his home. I remember that he had high hopes for a sparkling young man called P.J. Patterson, who would eventually become Prime Minister of Jamaica.

After three centuries sugar was no longer the source of the immense wealth on which the Barbadian economy had been built. In 1950 the industry employed 30,000 people, who produced in excess of 200,000 tonnes, but by 1999 3,000 cane workers were struggling to cut 50,000 tonnes. It was only the quotas from the European Union-sponsored Lomé convention, with some help from the USA, which made the survival of the industry possible. When these quotas were withdrawn, and Barbados had to compete with other producers – be it derived from cane or beet – the crop was no longer viable.

As Errol Barrow's far-sighted predecessor Grantley Adams had foreseen, the young country needed other sources of revenue. In 1956 the Adams administration passed the Hotels Aid Act, which facilitated the building of hotels by means of tax breaks and importing duty-free materials and equipment. When his turn came, Errol Barrow seized the baton. In 1968 the Barbados Hotel School was opened at the one-time Marine Hotel. It was in 1971, however, that he made a great contribution to Barbados by handing the critically important portfolio of Minister for Tourism to Peter Morgan, a white ex-Gurkha officer who was to be possibly the best Minister for Tourism the Caribbean would ever know. It took a man of Errol Barrow's stature to appoint a white non-Barbadian to such an important and sensitive position. Yet again I marvel – and shall for the rest of my days – at how he, and most Barbadians, did not waste time whinging about past iniquities. They simply got on with building a newly independent Barbados.

The number of tourists – who provided most of my restaurant customers – rose sharply from 17,900 in 1956 to almost 400,000 in 1980. Errol Barrow had put his wartime experience in the RAF to good use, so visitors who flew in now found themselves in a modern airport, with a runway long enough to accept the supersonic Concorde carrying Queen Elizabeth II in 1977. The Sir Grantley Adams airport is now the aviation hub of the southern Caribbean. Those who came by liner landed at the Deep Water Harbour, a scheme initiated by Grantley Adams in 1956 and completed in 1961, which offered sufficient depth for the 70,000-tonne liner *Queen Elizabeth 2* – a frequent visitor – to lie alongside.

On one occasion Errol Barrow fell into conversation with an English tourist called Alex Horsley, and discovered that he was chairman of Northern Dairies, a Yorkshire company (and, incidentally, a neighbour of my family in East Yorkshire; we children used to play together). One thing led to another and, thanks to Mr Barrow, Barbados was soon to have its own dairy business, Pine Hill Dairies, jointly owned by Northern Dairies and the New Zealand Dairy Board. That meant that those of us in the restaurant business had milk, cream, yoghurt and cheese at our disposal, which greatly widened the scope of our menus. Such luxury was unheard of in the southern Caribbean, except on the islands of Martinique and Guadeloupe, which welcomed two cargo flights a week carrying all the foodstuffs a Frenchman or woman expects, wherever they live, from *andouillettes* to frogs' legs and *foie gras*.

I once found myself on the same flight to Toronto as Errol Barrow, who was travelling in a private capacity. Many Barbadians lived in that city and held high positions, most notably in academic circles. We were both going there for a long weekend. On the way back we met in the departure lounge and I asked him how his weekend had been. He gave me the wry smile of a wise, patient man. On arrival at immigration he had produced his driving

1. My mother, wearing the only piece of jewelry she ever cared for, a crown and anchor broach, a gift from my father.

2. My father, scourge of the Hun in both the Irish and North Seas, in mine-sweeping rig.

3. HMS Worcester, *home to 200 cadets. Note on all the masts the maintop platforms, just above the three main yardarms, and the futtock shrouds going outwards around them.*

4. The ears have it! The Hudson boys – left to right – Tony, Richie, me and Peter, all ready for the annual Hull City Hall Fancy Dress Ball.

5. 2nd Lieutenant Nick Hudson, Royal Marines.

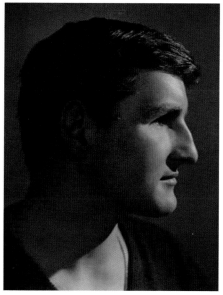

6. The profile Otto Preminger admired (taken by Lotte Meittner-Graff).

Rognons en Pyjamas – £1.20p: Fresh bobby veal kidneys are baked in their own suet with bacon and are served on a bed of well buttered mashed potatoes. This is the only dish we know wherein the innate excellence of calves kidney can be manifest to the wonder of all to behold. Even if this does sound like something from the second chapter of the Acts of the Apostles, it's lovely nosh.

Scallops on a Stick – £1.20p: Succulent Queens Scallops, mushrooms and bits of bacon are skewered on to bamboo sticks, grilled, sprinkled with chives and served with rice and a creamy mustard sauce. It may sound like one of the more hair raising bits out of "The Bridge on the River Kwai", but it really is quite excellent.

La Bourride – £1.00p: A garlic ridden cousin to the Bouillabaise, our Bourride is fast becoming a house speciality. Mixed fish is poached in liquor to which a quantity of aioli is added. It is advisable to share it with your intended other half if one is not to be accused of infidelity with a denizen of the Old Port of Marseilles.

Spatchcock Chicken – £1.20p: a well flattened poussin is flavoured with basil, garlic, pine kernels and Dijon mustard and simply grilled. This is a dish which makes any diet acceptable.

Quail in the Nest – £1.20p: Boned and stuffed quail is served on a bed of Chinese style crispy noodles with a rich brandy and grape ridden sauce of great excellence. Regulars may remember this dish as the one Wine and Food Magazine raved about last year.

Carré d'agneau aux flageolets – £1.30p: Well marinated rack of lamb is roasted with herbs on a bed of those delicious green flageolet beans which have been enlivened with some aromatic tomato and onion concassé. That's the dish: the experience is something else.

Saltinbocca alla Frederico – £1.10p: A "jump in the mouth" of pork fillet, sage leaves, raw ham, butter and marsala: this dish combines lightness with a positive taste, which is so vital in a diet conscious world. The rice we serve it with, after all, can always be ignored.

Osso Bucco – £1.15p: shin of veal is slowly braised with wine and mixed vegetables and becomes a classic, which we powder with a spicy "gremolata" mixture of parsley, garlic and grated lemon peel.

Moussaka Ifield Road – 95p: a savoury mixture of beef and lamb, onions and aubergines, topped with an egg and cheese mixture.

Entrecôtes au Poivre Verte – £1.60p: well hung entrecôte is cooked in butter with

7. The Diner main courses described in my partner Nick's revolutionary resto-speak. Note the recently decimalised prices in 1972.

8. Peter Scott, gentleman thief.

Nick Clarke: "I don't get the same frisson of excitement when royalty book at the Diner."

9. Nick could be pompous but on this occasion he broke all previous records.

10. Heidi my Afghan hound at work, advertising my wine company.

11. Mr Bernard Miles does not look too impressed with my wine.

12. Intrepid aviator, off to Guernsey to give a tasting, clutching an Imperial of fine Burgundy.

13. I swapped my Mercedes Benz 300SL Gull Wing...

14. ...for this treasure, a 1936 Rolls-Royce Sedanca de Ville.

15. *The* Friendship Rose, *the blue-hulled two-master – the schooner – in Port Elizabeth, capital of Bequia.*

16. *Where my adventure began, Friendship Bay, looking towards the south-west.*

17. *Sunfish at play.*

18. *A colourful Barbadian chattel house – the original flat-pack.*

19. *Sold! Bagatelle is mine. Note my Herbert Johnson hat with the snakeskin band.*

20. The new sole prop, with real estate agent extraordinaire Margaret Leacock at his side, surveys his new kingdom.

21. Bagatelle – as I found it in March 1970.

22. Reclaimed by the jungle, a terrace where the Tryhane family's children's tea parties were held as late as the 1950s.

23. The modest cooker on which I created veritable masterpieces — filet de boeuf Richelieu for example.

24. Tara, verily the goddess of peace, in a Berbice chair.

25. The recreational area — with advanced air-conditioning unit and that backgammon board.

26. My bed — the very embodiment of chastity — came with the house. Tara would demand something more romantic.

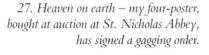

27. Heaven on earth — my four-poster, bought at auction at St. Nicholas Abbey, has signed a gagging order.

28. Holders House with its splendid deep terrace, from which Janet Kidd ruled the world.

29. The west façade of Heron Bay.

30. The fine coralstone Sandy Lane Hotel portico with the glorious blue Caribbean as its backdrop.

31. The green flash. Beware of non-believers, they know not of what they speak.

32. Mrs T – take me home with you, she said, as cats do. I did as I was told.

33. The official logo of Barbados, the flying fish. They can 'fly' for up to 100 metres.

34. A Sarawakan maiden, painted by Ranee of Sarawak and self-appointed Queen of the Headhunters

35. Errol Barrow – RAF navigator and observer – and man of destiny.

36. The Right Excellent Errol Walton Barrow, PC QC, father of the newly independent Barbados.

37. Oliver Messel – a self-portrait, painted when he was aged 19.

38. Oliver's St. James home on Barbados, Maddox, where he lived with Vagn Riis-Hansen, the Great Dane.

39. *The Bagatelle Great House restaurant, a gastronomic oasis in the middle of nowhere.*

BAGATELLE GREAT HOUSE

Barbados
January 13th, 1971
THE SECOND NIGHT
Dear and Most Beautiful Dot, thrilled you could make it.

GARLIC BREAD
Comes by the foot

ESCARGOTS	PIROSHKIs à la UKRAINSKI
à la BOURGUIGNONNE	Little meat-filled pies with
With garlic & parsley butter	Sour cream & a shot of vodka

PÂTE DE CAMPAGNE	AVOCADO à la CRÉOLE
Shamelessly imported from	½ an enormous pear stuffed
France via Martinique	with shrimps in sauce Diable

FRENCH ONION SOUP	CHILLED PERSIAN SOUP
The classical version. Bonkers!	With yogurt, sour cream, fresh
- far too heavy for the Tropics	mint, shrimps, and cucumber

FLYING FISH BAJAN	GRILLED FRESH BARRACUDA
Stuffed with garlic, thyme,	Seasoned & served with Hot Pepper
Basil & marjoram & fried	Sauce & a shot of see-through rum

FILET de BŒUF en CROÛTE	A WHOLE CARRÉ D'AGNEAU
A sort of Beef Wellington	A LA RAVISSANTE DOT
with a cream & mushroom sauce	With Soubise & mint sauces

Our desserts - home-made by our brilliant American neighbours

KEY LIME PIE	LEMON MERINGUE PIE
CRÊME CARAMEL	RUM & RAISIN ICE CREAM

41. *What a way to catch your lunch, a rum bottle's throw away from your chattel house. The fish so netted, jacks, are small like whitebait.*

40. *This is the personalied menu I wrote on the second evening for Dot Morrison; she missed the first. So began a tradition.*

42. *Our musicians Mary and Frank, who impresario Binkie Beaumont tried to lure away – and failed.*

44. *There is nothing you can name…the fabulously raunchy Dana who would do anything for a Bagatelle chocolate mousse.*

43. *The poor woman is doomed, doomed. Surrender now. Nick is playing* Spanish Romance. *Ask Clyde Turney.*

45. *I really took to this birdman lark, which gave Anthony Armstrong-Jones a nasty moment.*

46. *The double-tasking trampoline is just visible.*

47. *My first aeroplane in the Caribbean, the under-powered Sundowner – or was I the under-skilled pilot?*

48. *Ruth at work in America, not long before we met.*

49. *Showing off at a Sandy Lane water gala – compère Jack Leacock. The crowded schooner in the background is the Goddard's Ecstasy.*

50. *Ruth at play with Veronica and Roy Barnes. Ignore the anonymous groper.*

51. *Sweet Melanie, one of kind. She is to be seen on the cover of this book, not wearing much.*

52. *Crossing the pond to Mr Nick's, where a quiet after-dinner smooch made for an agreeable end to an evening.*

53. *Dancing at Mr Nick's. All sort of beasties lived in the coconut-frond roof, sometimes joining in the fun below. Not everyone was amused.*

54. *My modest little road sign. The word 'Smoochery' was fortunately too long to include.*

55. Anna in her favourite woollen dress – no embellishment required.

56. Anna, my friend, my sister, my lover, my everything.

57. Anna at the Bakoua Hotel on Martinique, fully recovered from our near miss.

58. The sapling David Hart and I planted outside the then Troubadour Coffee Shop in 1965 is alive and well and bigger in 2015.

59. David Allison, a great man, a true friend, and a terrific accountant.

61. The cover of Gourmet *magazine, October 1973. As a restaurateur, I have arrived!*

60. Bohemian was belovèd Penelope's favourite style. She adored big Tibetan bangles and baubles.

62. Erin Hall in 1972 when Margaret Leacock showed it to me, before its conversion into Alexandra's Night Club.

licence as proof of identity, but this was not acceptable. Errol had explained that Canadian citizens were permitted to enter Barbados, of which nation he happened to be Prime Minister, using their driving licences. The authorities relented to the extent that he was allowed to enter Canada on condition that he was accompanied everywhere by a police officer. He made no fuss, although he was fully entitled to do so. Like Mahatma Gandhi he changed attitudes solely by pacifist means. He would, however, take a strong line where his fellow citizens were concerned. He was strongly opposed to undue American influence in the Caribbean, and knew just when to engage in some Yank-bashing, especially on the hustings. The Monroe Doctrine cut no ice with him; he believed that the region was perfectly capable of handling its own affairs. He was instrumental in setting up CARICOM, the Caribbean free trade association, which has done so much to unify the participating countries and make them more financially secure.

Errol Barrow was again an initiator when, in the wake of Hurricane Janet in 1955, he and George Money of Barclays Bank revitalised the Barbados Light Aero Club. It was, Mr Money claimed, the only multi-racial club on the Island. They began by having the hangar, blown down by the storm, rebuilt. Thereafter Errol always kept his private pilot's licence current. When I mentioned that I was flying to Mustique to deliver some stock to Basil's Bar, then on to Martinique to lunch and buy a few French delicacies, he asked if he might join me. We took off the next morning and an hour later landed on the tricky narrow little strip on Mustique. Having made the delivery, and with Errol as pilot-in-command in the left-hand seat on this leg, we set off for Martinique, about an hour to the north. We landed, parked the aeroplane, and grabbed a taxi to take us to Fort-de-France and a favourite restaurant of mine, La Grand'Voile. The chef and owner, a native of Lyon, set an excellent table of which we took full advantage. On the way back to the airport we stopped at a supermarket to buy some pâté, cheeses and foodstuffs difficult to find on Barbados. We took off rather later than I had planned and were going to land slightly after sunset – strictly against the rules – but I had done it in the past. The control tower knew me and would make the usual allowances.

About fifteen minutes from our destination we saw a flat brownish dish on the surface of the sea. It was Barbados! Errol remarked with a smile that all proud Barbadians should see this, just to give them an idea of how totally insignificant their home actually was. It was getting dark, and dusk is very brief in the tropics. I was reflecting that, although I had trained to fly at night, only halfwits fly a single-engine aircraft over water in the dark, when the Barbados control tower came on the radio asking for the name of the pilot. I reached for the radio microphone but another hand had got there first.

'Name of pilot, Barrow, E.W.,' Errol answered for me.

'Roger,' said the controller, obviously a member of the Democratic Labour Party of which Errol was boss. My bacon was saved! But I often wonder what would have happened if the controller had been a Barbados Labour Party supporter. He would have been within his rights to turn us back to Martinique.

By now it was dark, so I turned on the instrument panel lights. Or rather, I tried to. Nothing happened. They weren't working. Obviously, when you can't see the physical horizon, an illuminated instrument with an artificial version is essential. Without such information how would I know if the wings were level? And what of the other critical instruments? Were we descending or climbing? What *was* our air speed? This was serious. Then I remembered! When I was training for my night-flying qualification, my instructor Cliff Hammond told me always to carry a torch in my flight bag. I fished around and there it was. So we finished the flight with Errol shining the light over my shoulder, illuminating the instruments for me, and, for the first time, I landed using the instrument landing system which had been installed at the airport on the instructions of a far-sighted prime minister. Praise de Lord!

In the course of that trip he told me something that I never heard him repeat elsewhere. He spoke of his great fear that the military establishment – the Barbados Defence Force – might decide to stage a coup; after all, they had the weapons. He had seen this happen in so many third world countries, not least in nearby Trinidad, where the seemingly unassailable Prime Minister, Dr Eric Williams, had almost been ousted by his military.

Errol's concern was understandable, but in the event he need not have worried. The only real threat came in October 1976, when a Barbadian madman and gun-runner called Sidney Burnett-Alleyne, assisted by 'Mad

Mike' Banks, a known mercenary, planned to invade Barbados and get rid of the current administration. Once installed, he would declare himself Archduke of Barbados. The recently elected Prime Minister, 'Tom' Adams, received word from British security sources, who had learned that special uniforms had been ordered and were ready to be shipped to nearby Dominica, whence the invasion would be launched. Afterwards I heard from a Barbadian military connection that they had been expecting an *airborne* invasion. In view of my national service with 42 Commando of the Royal Marines, I was arbitrarily designated to organise the defence of central Barbados, though with what weapons was never made clear. Burnett-Alleyne was intercepted, on a yacht loaded with arms, off the island of Martinique, where he was sentenced to languish in a French jail for a while.

Errol obtained the Caribbean marketing rights for a small sea-plane. He thought I might be interested in joining him as a partner in the venture, and possibly buy one for our own use. In theory, such an aircraft would make us independent of airfields throughout the islands. We dropped the idea after another pilot, landing a sea-plane in Port Elizabeth at Bequia, struck a floating log which knocked off his floats. The aircraft sank, and he was lucky to survive. So we decided instead that I should sell my Cessna 180 and buy jointly a Shrike Aero Commander, a rather dashing twin-engine job with an alley between the six seats, a very grown-up plaything. Errol's son David was a qualified aero engineer, which skill, we thought, would help reduce the maintenance costs. It was not to be.

In 1986 Errol was again elected Prime Minister, this time by a landslide, winning 24 out of 27 parliamentary seats. The Island had missed his wise guidance sorely. We often found ourselves talking about aviation and instrument landing training, unavailable anywhere in the southern Caribbean, except at the airports on Barbados and Martinique. The latter, being a *département* of metropolitan France and of strategic importance, was well equipped. Pilots from the Venezuelan airline VIASA actually came to Barbados to practise their instrument landings because their system at home didn't work. Errol and I discussed the possibility of establishing a professional aviation school in the sparsely populated north of Barbados, where the topography was ideally suited for a runway, flat with unimpeded approaches and take-offs, and the prevailing trade winds from the east.

Then, unexpectedly, on 1ˢᵗ June 1987, this great man died. He was only sixty-seven years old. When we were last together he had seemed in good fettle, still talking enthusiastically about the proposed school. But his family said later that he had been in poor health for some while.

A lasting memory has to be his 'Mirror Image' speech, delivered two weeks before the recent general election. It is a father chiding his children for their attitude and lack of ambition. The speech ends with his characteristic lack of fuss and fanfare: 'Anyhow, ladies and gentlemen, I done.'*

Here I must add a footnote. Errol and I sometimes prepared Chinese meals for our friends, once producing a mammoth banquet at his beach house, Kampala, in the grounds of the Paradise Beach Hotel. I was especially taken by his version of Sweet and Sour Pork, the real thing, not the Chinese take-away disaster covered in glutinous orange-coloured sauce. Not long after we had buried Errol, the telephone rang, and a deep measured voice said, 'Mr Nick, Nita Barrow here.' Errol's sister, Dame Nita Barrow, was at that time Barbados' Ambassador to the United Nations. She was also appointed to an eight-strong Eminent Persons Group, the only woman in it, which would negotiate the release of Nelson Mandela from his twenty-seven years in a South African prison, which they achieved in January 1990. That same year she would become Governor General of Barbados – the Queen's representative on the Island. For women around the world, Dame Nita represented what an educated community-conscious woman can achieve, and what true service to her country and its people can mean.

Today she had a message for me: 'Errol said he was sorry he forgot to give you his recipe for Sweet and Sour Pork, and asked me to pass it on to you. I shall be sending it shortly.'

I had mentioned to Errol how disappointed I was that he had not included this, of all recipes, in his book *Cooking in the Caribbean,* which he co-authored with Kendall A. Lee. He had not forgotten, nor had Dame Nita. What a lady to remember to call me at such a time!

Errol Walton Barrow was the greatest man I have ever known. He was the pre-eminent national leader in the English-speaking Caribbean, yet,

---

* The full text of this speech can be found in the appendix to this book on page 335. I urge you to look it up.

unlike his colleagues, he never awarded himself a knighthood; he was Dipper to the end. The flourishing, peaceful and self-sustaining nation of Barbados, a proud and independent member of the British Commonwealth, is his legacy.

CHAPTER FOURTEEN

The Blessed Weather Satellite

Every year, mostly between June and October, in this haven of blue skies, white sand and warm sea, some islands find themselves in the path of tropical storms which leave death and destruction in their wake. Some are hit more frequently than others. Over the last three centuries, for example, Martinique has suffered, on average, a direct hit every seven years. Barbados has been more fortunate, with an interval of fifty years between strikes.

You probably feel, as I do, that the vast sums spent on investigating the uninhabitable planets might be better employed for the benefit of a starving uneducated mankind. What *is* beyond question, however, is that the space programme has greatly benefited the tropics and those who live there.

In 1960 – as recently as that! – the first weather satellite was put into orbit so meteorologists could study images of atmospheric systems, particularly anticyclones, with their potential to become hurricanes as they cross the Atlantic from Africa. The information gained, combined with reports from hurricane-hunting propeller-driven aeroplanes that actually fly into the very eye of the storm, allowing precise readings to be taken, enables weather centres to predict the probable development and course of a storm.

One cannot over-emphasise the importance of this graphic, which is an informed attempt to forecast the course of a storm and the degree of danger to be faced by those in its path. The time to prepare is the key when these potentially lethal storms are in the region. Many West Indians live in extremely vulnerable chattel houses. Now, at least, they have time to pull

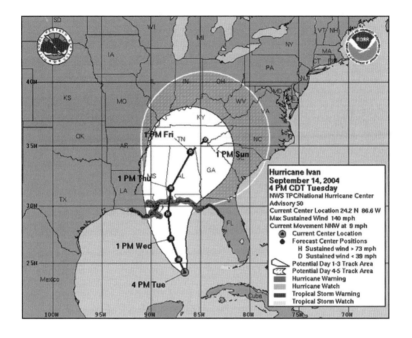

The cone of probability, an indispensable graphic used to alert those in the path of a storm.

their fishing boats high and dry, find shelter for livestock, board up windows, store dried food, fill every possible receptacle – not least the bath – with water. And they must hurry, for shops supplying kerosene, candles and matches soon find their shelves emptied. Electricity is always cut off before a storm, to avert the danger of live cables dangling from downed power poles, so safe refuge must be found in a hurricane shelter – maybe a school or church – before the lights go out. The aftermath of a hurricane is terrible to behold. There are the dead, the injured, the homeless, and a lack of food and safe drinking water. I flew a Salvation Army officer in my light aircraft into St. Lucia in 1979, the day after Hurricane Alan had passed. The inhabitants were as if shell-shocked, wandering lost in a wasteland bereft of once-familiar points of reference.

The great hurricanes of 1779 and 1831 all but destroyed Barbados. The former killed 4,326 people, 5% of the population. Meteorologists estimate its wind speed to have been around 200 mph. The latter caused a storm surge 17 feet above the mean high water mark, which flooded Bridgetown and drowned 1,500 people. The final death toll was 2,500. There was a catastrophic loss of historical documents. If only they had known it was coming, had been allowed a few hours to prepare…

In spite of this dramatic history, I was feeling increasingly at home when I received a timely reminder that there is a price to pay for living in paradise. Late in September 1970 the blessed weather satellite warned Barbadians that a tropical depression was approaching. This category of revolving storm does not reach the speeds in excess of 74 mph that officially define a hurricane, but it does have a very low central atmospheric pressure. This may sometimes be well below 1,000 millibars, which results in torrential rainfall. I was woken up on 2nd October 1970 by a thunderous drumming on the galvanised roof of Bagatelle, unlike anything else I have ever heard. Outside was just sheeting rain; it gave new meaning to the expression 'the heavens opened', for it was if someone up there was emptying a bucket of water, a solid mass with no separate drops. In the next twenty-four hours the forecast depression was to dump 500 millimetres – nearly 20 inches! – of rain on Barbados. Incredibly, not a drop of water entered my seventeenth-century house, but what of my friends in their modern homes?

My friend Dot's house, Toad Hall, had been designed by her husband Ian, not according to tropical tradition, but with open spaces and courtyards, and I doubted if the shingled roof or the drainage system could cope. I raced to my car clad only in my bathing costume – the rain actually hurt! – and set off cautiously down the drive, which was more of a river. I found my dogs Houdini and Sam half-running, half-swimming alongside. I stopped and hauled them aboard. Dot's house might have been worse off; at least the bedroom where I found her and her twin baby daughters, Ashleigh and Sharon, huddled wide-eyed on the bed, was dry. Dot politely rejected my offer of a safe berth at Bagatelle, not wanting to leave the security of her home. All she and the babies could do was wait until the rain stopped. When darkness fell they would have only candlelight. There was no electricity.

Another friend, Veronica Stuart, had a boutique near the sea in Bridge-town. She and her boyfriend Stephen went to try and rescue her precious stock. As they approached the shop, a manhole cover in the road was forced up and the drain suddenly became an enormous plughole. Water swirled into it, dragging Stephen to certain doom. With great presence of mind Veronica grabbed him with one hand and a lamppost with the other, and hung on until the road was drained. Heaven knows where he would have eventually come up, probably in the middle of Carlisle Bay and not in very good shape. Three people died in this storm. Yet without the satellite warn-ing, that figure would have been much higher.

As for direct hurricane strikes, Barbados is living on borrowed time. Fifty years is the average period between strikes. The last was Hurricane Janet in 1955, packing winds of 120 mph. Thirty-five people died. Statistically the Island is in for it. It could prove expensive. Look out Lloyds!

I had never thought of the West Indies as being volcanically active but I have learned from direct experience that they are. Between the islands of Saba in the north and Grenada, four hundred miles to the south, is a line of twenty volcanoes, nine of them on the island of Dominica. Four were active whilst I was living in the West Indies. There were eruptions on the islands of Guadeloupe in 1976/'77, St. Vincent in 1979, St. Lucia in 1980 and – most devastatingly – Montserrat in 1996. I was to be closely involved with three of these.

The most infamous, relatively modern, eruption was that of Mont Pelée on the French island of Martinique in 1902. The capital in those days, Saint-Pierre – 'the Paris of the Caribbean' – was situated in the foothills of the volcano. Governor Mouttet was expecting to win the elections, which were imminent, and did not want his 20,000 constituents to leave. So he asked the owner of the local newspaper *Les Colonies* to broadcast that there was no imminent threat. This he did so convincingly that the smoking volcano became a tourist attraction; the population of Saint-Pierre swelled to 28,000. Troops were stationed on the road to Fort-de-France, the Island's second city, to turn back the less convinced. Then Mont Pelée did erupt and all but three of the 28,000 perished. The best known survivor was Louis-Auguste Cyparis, who was in prison, accused of murder. The prison was the most robust building in the city. The cell in which he survived had no windows, only a narrow grating in the door facing away from the volcano. It may be visited today. Louis-Auguste was pardoned and took himself to the United States to join Barnum and Bailey's circus, where he exhibited the dreadful burns caused by the boiling water and scalding gases that had crept under his cell door.

Another natural disaster threatens Barbados. While the odds on it occurring are long, they are by no means incalculable. In the channel between the islands of Grenada and Carriacou there is an active submerged volcano called Kick'em Jenny. The depth between the surface of the sea and the bottom of the crater is presently 268 meters. From the rim it is 180 metres. If, as has happened in the past, the crater floor rises to within 130 metres of the surface, and if the volcano were to erupt, a 30-foot tsunami would occur. Barbados is only 150 miles away, next door in tsunami terms. Unlike the steep volcanic islands of the East Caribbean, Barbados is a low-lying coral bump, vulnerable to even small increases in the sea level.

The last small eruption of Kick'em Jenny was recorded in 2001. Today there is an exclusion zone 1.5 kilometres in diameter directly over the crater in case of yet another upheaval. On occasion gases are vented from the crater, filling the water with bubbles and lowering its density to the point where even quite large vessels – vindicating Archimedes in spectacular fashion – sometimes sink due to lack of buoyancy. It is a ghastly thought, sinking helplessly into a bubbling, sulphurous void. I have sailed there; the sea is unfriendly, often disturbed and lumpy, the wave patterns quite unlike any others I have experienced. The vibes are bad. I never felt at ease in those waters and was always happy to leave.

Chapter Fifteen

Oliver Messel – Magician

I have already mentioned that Anthony Armstrong-Jones, husband of Princess Margaret, and by this time Lord Snowdon, had been interested in buying Bagatelle. In the event, he did not proceed with the purchase, but when I acquired it, it was arranged that I should meet his uncle Oliver Messel, who had already looked the house over at his nephew's request.

At the time I had no idea of Oliver's stature, his only possible rival being the highly talented Cecil Beaton. They were eternal rivals, but Oliver had pinched Cecil's favourite toy, an artist called Peter Watson, and refused to give him back, and so held – as it were – the whip hand. It further needled Cecil that Oliver's nephew had married the Queen's sister, which gave him easy access to the royal family, whereas Cecil was only allowed in to take his marvellous photos.

Everyone wanted Oliver to work for them. Ronnie Tree relates in his book *When the Moon Was High* how Oliver designed a white muslin tent for the house-warming party he and Nancy threw at Ditchley, their enormous home. The theme was white. Gentlemen, of course, wore white tie. But Oliver, the brightest star in the glittering gay constellation, turned up in a white suit and red bow-tie. A fellow guest was heard to mutter, 'That fellow ought to be thrown in the lake.'

I arrived one morning to meet Oliver at Maddox, his seaside home. As the solid high white-painted gates closed slowly behind me, shutting out the busy West Coast road, I found myself in a magical place.

Oliver had bought Maddox in a very poor state in 1959, and made it a place of pure enchantment. There was nothing grand, nothing big, nothing showy. It was constructed entirely of exquisite pink-tinged coral stone, the woodwork, in the tell-tale Messel pale sage green, predominated. The garden was bordered with dense tropical planting, holding the outside world at arm's length, and there were masses of ornaments – urns, pots, drip-stones and balustrades – all the work of the talented Mr Massiah, the Island's only coral stone sculptor, who had enough orders in his book to take him to the grave and beyond.

One peculiar feature was the lack of an indoor staircase, which, as a set designer, Oliver was not used to including in his designs; its absence was noticed too late. So it was attached – very prettily, it must said – to the exterior.

Maddox was one of the few houses on the Island with an effectively private beach, because rocky headlands to north and south made it inaccessible except by sea. Overlooking the sea was a coral stone terrace shaded by an enormous mango tree.

As I parked my car and approached the house, an enormous man emerged. He turned out to be Oliver's companion of many years, Vagn Riis-Hansen, known as the Great Dane. This latter-day Viking was fiercely protective of his illustrious friend.

Oliver reminded me of an exotic bird. But though delicately boned he was in no way frail. His movements were quick and elegant, and his eyes twinkled mischievously in an elfin face. He was wearing, as was his wont, a blue and white striped top, white ducks and a peaked sailor's cap set at a jaunty angle.

Oliver already had a plan for Bagatelle, which he had devised for his nephew, a deep first-floor balcony extending the length of the west, seaward façade of the house. From each end – he extended both arms wide – a curving balustraded staircase would come rrrrrrrrippling down – he brought his hands down in extravagant, fluttering, descending curves – to a coral stone terrace.

'How much vill all ziss cost?' boomed the Great Dane.

'Oh, about forty thousand pounds,' Oliver answered airily.

'It vill cost tvice as much – ett least.'

In the event, I did not ask him to do the design for me, in retrospect a regrettable decision. Every one of the houses Oliver designed on Barbados and Mustique were highly desirable and hence valuable. Bagatelle had great potential, some of which I was later to realise, and in Oliver's hands, and with an open-ended budget, it would have been a gem. But my funds were limited to £21,000 and whatever I could borrow for doing up the property and opening the restaurant. Had I gone ahead with Oliver I would have been penny-less but asset-rich!

I used to see quite a lot of Oliver and Vagn in the energetic social life of the West Coast. I remember with special fondness taking afternoon tea with them under the enormous mango tree, a popular gathering place for green monkeys that would grab a mango, take a bite, drop it and seize another. Much to the annoyance of their neighbours, these beasts, emboldened by Oliver and Vagn feeding them cake and sandwiches, even pinched jewels off dressing tables.

These monkeys, which have a particularly toxic bite, are destructive to crops, especially bananas. In the nineteenth century there was a bounty on them of half-a-crown a tail. But nobody liked to shoot them because they cried like human babies when wounded. Nowadays they are protected in the wild and others bred in a special unit, eventually to be killed for medical purposes. This practice is widely condemned by animal rights activists, and such an attitude is often commendable; but here's the rub: a substance extracted from their kidneys is an essential ingredient of the Salk polio vaccine, and today polio as a disease has been more or less eradicated.

Next to Maddox was Crystal Springs, a house Oliver had likewise touched with his magic, owned by Arnold Maremont, king of the Maremont Muffler Corporation. His wife Eileen – Gussie to her friends – had previously been married to harmonica virtuoso Larry Adler; she eventually missed her hundredth birthday by just a few days. She and Arnold asked Oliver to design and build a guest cottage, and called it the Tea House. It cost them US$60,000, not bad for a one-bedroom cottage in the early Seventies.

Sometimes the Maremonts invited me to lunch. Once my fellow guests were Maggie Smith and Joan Plowright. I remarked that it must be difficult for their children to be in the same business, having such eminent parents. Not at all, both asserted; to show it had not always been easy for them they had kept the bad reviews. One critic they quoted had advised that Laurence Olivier should abandon the stage and stick to films. I found Maggie, with her fine posture and commanding bosom, incredibly sexy. And that voice!

Further north along the coast was Mango Bay, home of Averill and Pamela Harriman. It was, Oliver told me, his favourite creation. In many cases he adapted older buildings, but this time he had designed and built from scratch. I arrived there one day to deliver some gastronomic goodies – *ris de veau* – which I had flown in from Martinique for Pamela, to find Oliver on his hands and knees, reworking a detailed floor mosaic. It had not been perfectly executed and that simply would not do.

Oliver might have worked on many more houses on Barbados had he not been lured by his friend Colin Tennant to nearby Mustique, where he was involved in at least thirteen of them. For his very first job in 1969 he designed the island's first hotel, the Cotton House, based on the Indonesian 'long house' concept. Most famously he designed *Les Jolies Eaux* for Princess Margaret. One baking hot noon, a story goes, sobbing was heard and traced to the roof of a house which was under construction. There was Oliver, crying his eyes out. Someone had taken away the ladder on their way to lunch.

One day he telephoned me. 'Dear boy,' he said, 'we've decided to sell the Rolls and a man is coming to look at it. Would you please come and explain some of the knobs so we can show him how it works?"

I was surprised they were going to sell the Rolls, which was not required to do many miles a year. Barbados is, after all, only 160 square miles, and Oliver and Vagn rarely strayed from the West Coast. But it did have one important function. The parish in which they lived, St. James, was in the charge of the most practical and effective Christian minister it has been my pleasure to know well, Father Andrew Hatch, who set up an outreach programme called Meals on Wheels to provide food for the poor and lonely. The church supplied the meals and Oliver and Vagn the elegant wheels. The Rolls must have looked extraordinary gliding amongst the wooden chattel houses. Their long-standing contribution, not to mention Oliver's infectious *joie de vivre*, was going to be much missed.

Oliver, dressed as usual *au matelot*, and I sat in the car with me in the driving seat. 'We know how to start it,' Oliver announced, adding proudly, 'and we know how to work the brakes and lights and so on, but all these other knobs – haven't the faintest. Kindly explain them, dear boy.'

'Well,' I began, 'this is the cigar lighter, and this is the interior light, and this is the air-conditioning control, and this lever is for…'

'Stop! Please! That one is for *what*, dear boy?'

'The air-conditioning.'

'You mean to say this motorcar is air-conditioned? Goodness gracious me, we never knew that! You cannot *imagine* how uncomfortable it was, delivering hot meals to those poor people in the heat of the day. And we could have been so cool…'

The Red Cross Society of Barbados had Princess Margaret as its patron. Its annual fundraising ball was held at Holders House, the home of Cappy and Janet Kidd. Although, the royal presence notwithstanding, it was a relatively informal affair, there were certain rules. Indeed, in those days one of the great joys of West Coast life was that *almost* everyone knew the rules. As the Princess circulated amongst the guests, a Canadian man aimed a camera at her. A large Danish paw grasped his collar, lifting the malefactor clean off his feet. He was put down, camera still in position, elsewhere. Not a word was spoken.

Sadly, sometime later this splendid Viking contracted cancer and by the time he died weighed only six stones. I shall remember him for one of his specialities, a decanter of aquavit encased in ice, into which flowers – frangipanis, birds of paradise, bougainvillea and so on – had been frozen. Quite beautiful.

In 1976 Claudette Colbert persuaded Oliver, who was seventy-four at the time and reluctant to leave the Island, to design the sets for a production of *Sleeping Beauty* at the New York Met, something of a re-run of his enduringly famous *Sleeping Beauty*, starring Margot Fonteyn in London in 1946, forever afterwards called the Messel production. Word reached Barbados that, at the time of the dress rehearsal, Oliver had fallen very ill. So I was surprised to meet him a little while later at Jack Leacock's clinic, the very place he had dealt with my burns six years previously. As we embraced, I said, 'I thought you were at death's door.'

The eyes twinkled mischievously. 'I was, dear boy, I was. They even called in someone to say the last rites over me. Well, I opened my eyes and beheld this gorgeous black priest. Love at first sight! I jumped to my feet immediately, cured, and brought him back to Maddox. He's there now.' And there the priest stayed until Oliver died two years later on my birthday, July 13th, 1978. I feel fortunate to have known this remarkable man.

CHAPTER SIXTEEN

The Bagatelle Opens Its Doors

In the last ten months much constructive work had been carried out at Bagatelle. There was to be no formal opening party, no fanfare. I thought it wiser to get the show on the road first, and sort out any problems. People thought I was mad to open a restaurant up in the hills away from the beaches. Indeed, some businesses refused to deliver goods and taxi drivers would think twice before agreeing to bring customers. Yet the punters were straining at their leashes.

What was it that made dining at Bagatelle such a special experience? Why did passengers instruct the QE2's chief purser to make an expensive sea-to-shore call to make a reservation well before they arrived on Barbados, and even to order certain dishes? Why would the Bagatelle within three years grace the front cover of *Gourmet* magazine and the back cover of *Time* magazine? Its success had nothing to do with *haute cuisine*.

Imagine yourself in the softly-lit foyer of the Sandy Lane Hotel. You can hear the surf breaking gently on the powder-sand beach. Under the high *porte cochère,* a commissionaire in a tailored white uniform with gleaming gold buttons is handing guests into one of the large American limousines that serve as taxis. You have a booking at the Bagatelle restaurant. Your dining partner has been told about the dress code – the more beautiful you are, the less you should wear – and looks gorgeous. For the gentlemen, smart and casual is *de rigueur*. You are talking with George Forte, immaculate in his white tuxedo. He has worked at the Hotel since he was fourteen, rising from a lowly kitchen porter to his present executive position. It's difficult to know what George's official job description is. What he actually does is make sure that guests get what they want. He has almost certainly made your restaurant reservation.

Your taxi arrives and you are handed in by the commissionaire and swished in air-conditioned comfort through the manicured gardens and past the imposing gates with their immaculate sentry, also in white and gold. The taxi turns left onto the coast road, then after 300 yards it turns right up a narrow bumpy road leading into the Island's dark interior. Tall sugar cane plants arch overhead, almost touching, to form a tunnel. The cane, ripe and ready to harvest, is dense and impenetrable. The more fearful may wonder: will someone leap out of the dark brandishing a cutlass – a machete? Is the driver to be trusted? The lady pulls her stole more closely about her slender shoulders and moves closer to you. After ten minutes the vehicle turns through a pair of rusting wrought iron gates – I had run out of money by that time – up a driveway overhung with bougainvillea, emerging finally into – lights! At last! The large parking space is dominated by two bearded fig trees, *los barbados*. Their island-wide presence prompted the Portuguese, who landed there briefly in the early seventeenth century, to give the island its name. To your left, in all its Palladian splendour, is the Bagatelle Great House.

You emerge. The driver will not leave the safety of his taxi because he sees, on the steps leading up to my apartment, my Alsatian Houdini, who bares a gleaming fang. It is cooler here in the hills than down on the coast. The ceaseless cacophony of crickets and tree frogs assaults your ears but will soon become an unobtrusive element of the tropical night. When the creatures are not on song, as when a powerful storm is approaching, the night seems empty, and you miss them.

Under the arch you will see a long-haired barefoot figure in a kaftan – me – waiting to greet you. However, before I have that pleasure, imagine for a moment that, instead of making the trip from your hotel in your air-conditioned taxi, you had made the journey in a hired Moke, as many of our brave diners did, through that endless tunnel of clashing sugar cane stalks and rustling leaves, in a tinny open-sided rattle-trap. You would be vulnerable to the ill-intentioned thug hidden in the dark, his razor-sharp machete gleaming in the moonlight. My word, you would feel intrepid! And your hair would be a terrible mess.

I shake your hand and lead you in. You feel you are being welcomed to a private house, an impression which is entirely intentional. The walls are made from the ubiquitous coral stone, far too handsome to be hidden under plaster. Candles in sconces provide soft flattering illumination.

Immediately through the arch, away to the left, a passage leads via a sloping ramp to the main dining terrace. As a would-be architect I am inordinately proud of this feature, which I put in to facilitate wheelchair entry, something which in 1970 was way ahead of its time. We proceed along the corridor. Next to the left you will see the private dining room, with its dodecagonal – twelve-sided – Great Table, cast in stone and finished in polished satin-smooth coral-dust mortar. Blue Delft tiles mark each of the twelve place settings. The massive chairs weigh a ton and are painted black with black cushions. I had noted the success of the private dining room at the Diner, but that one was dark, lockable and good for all sorts of shenanigans; here at the Bagatelle it is open for all to see. I had quickly learned that the famous people who frequently take this room like to be recognised; anything – even having your dinner clumsily interrupted for an autograph – is better than being ignored. The game is that guests pretend not to look, while those at the table pretend not to notice they are being looked at. You might see Ronnie Tree giving a birthday party for Ingrid Bergman, with her children Isabella and Robertino Rossellini, or an outrageously bespectacled Elton John, entertaining Oliver Messel who is telling jokes in camp Cockney and shrieking with laughter. Or it might be a dying Keith Moon on his last legs, his minder hand-feeding him tenderly. In livelier moments you would see Ahmed Ertigan and friends throwing key lime pies at each other – the pie still in the baking tin, by the way – or listen to Tom Jones advising Engelbert Humperdinck what to sing at his next appearance in Las Vegas.

Across the corridor from the private dining room is the bar, domain of Mr Randolph Blackman, a master of his trade. I lead you to one of the banquettes that run around the walls. The barman approaches and asks what you would like, suggesting you might care to try his lethal concoction, Black Power. You sip your drink and look around, wondering whom you might see; at my restaurant, celebrities are happy to be private citizens in a paparazzi-free environment.

Once at your table, you can choose dishes of French, Créole, Russian, Barbadian and other origins – later this will be hailed as fusion cooking, as if it were a new concept! Apart from the wine and food, the service, the atmosphere, and the spotlessness of the loos are clearly of paramount importance, as is the restaurant's underlying feeling of generosity. If you were to complain, your food or bottle of wine would be instantly replaced without fuss and knocked off the bill. Putting something right with good humour and generosity can earn a restaurant far more kudos than serving a perfect meal – and such a gesture is never forgotten.

After your dinner, you might return to the bar for a *digestif*, and then your taxi driver, alerted by Mr Blackman, speeds you back down that long dark tunnel between the cane fields, returning you safely to the welcoming glow of the foyer of the Sandy Lane Hotel. One thing is certain – you have had an evening which you will never forget.

The first night went smoothly. I had spread out the bookings and the customers arrived at their designated times, so the kitchen and bar were able to cope. We were fully booked from that first night until Easter, four months later.

But I had another reason to celebrate. My accountant Paul Harman had had a drink with my father in London, during which Paul brought my father up-to-date with my whereabouts and my plans, something that – shamefully – I had not done myself. Thanks to Paul I recommenced my Saturday morning phone calls to my mother. Like the marvellous parents they were, they forgave me. My mother sent me a congratulatory telegram.

Something happened on the second night which was to prove both my best advertising gimmick and a rod for my back. My bosom pal Dot Morrison, the beautiful sole prop. of the stylish Dotto's Boutique at the Sandy Lane Hotel, missed the first night but made a booking for the second. She was so special to me I welcomed her with a menu I had dedicated to her. In those days, before word processors, all my menus were hand-written. Dot was immensely gratified. The next night another close friend turned up. When I gave her a menu to peruse, she tapped it with an elegant finger. 'Where,' she demanded, 'is *my* menu? Dot showed me the one you did specially for her. I want one too.'

So I rushed upstairs – there are some advantages to living over the shop – and dashed off another menu. Thus began the tradition of personalised menus at the Bagatelle. They became collectors' items and now adorn many loo doors around the world. Hosts who gave parties at the Bagatelle glowed with pride as their guests saw their name elegantly inscribed and a suitably named dish on the menu, just like those handed out to Princess Margaret or Marlon Brando. Once I visited a restaurant customer in New York in his palatial office overlooking Madison Avenue. There, in an enormous gilded frame, was a Bagatelle menu that I had dedicated to him and his wife. On occasion I wrote three or four menus for one evening. One person even sent one back to me, carefully packed in a tube, asking that I refresh the writing which had faded.

I let the restaurant evolve gradually, in its tropical setting, guided by the customers' needs and preferences. In the event, little changed after the first night. The system of taking newly-arrived guests to the bar rather than directly to their table was part of the private-house ambience, as if they were having an aperitif in the drawing room before dinner. There they would peruse the menu and consult the wine list, have their order taken, and await the call to their table. I employed a guitarist, Frank Mossburg, and a lovely singer, Mary Marsden, who would go around the tables, entertaining and smoothing away any delays. On the rare occasions a diner became irate, Mary's sweet voice and gentle smile soon restored the peace, and probably earned her a tip.

I had a clear policy for the wine list. If a customer wanted Cristal Champagne, Château Pétrus, Corton Charlemagne, Brunello di Montalcino, even *Eiswein* from Canada, I made sure they had it. At the other end of the scale, I have always believed in the French tradition, that house wines should represent value for money, so that regulars can dine frequently without being hammered by the cost. I chose good examples of less expensive wines – Côte de Brouilly, Muscadet-sur-lie, Rioja, and wines from Argentina. My mark-up was not excessive – 210%; the extra 10% as to take into account my personal consumption! However, due to its negligible cost, rum-based drinks were the major source of profit.

Every couple of months or so a party of Barclays Bank directors – wearing collars and ties in the tropical heat! – would dine at the Great Table, running up an enormous bill, which would be paid just before they came back for another equally expensive feast. For me the problem was that I never really saw the money because they were forever in my debt; they had effectively awarded themselves a form of revolving credit! Signed bills, before credit cards became the norm, were a real problem. I required around 50,000 Barbados dollars – 25,000 American dollars, quite a lot of money in 1971 – to finance this credit facility, for which I had made no provision in my cash flow projections. To tell the truth, I had not made any such projections anyway. Moneywise I was always running to catch up, since my undoubted ability to make the stuff was only surpassed by my capacity to spend it.

The ideal bachelor – my constant target – should be able to play the guitar I thought. At a party I cornered a Yugoslav called Micky Mikiç, who played the classical guitar at a professional level, and arranged to become his pupil. I bought a guitar and began practising assiduously, starting each day with an hour of scales and exercises. In spite of my lack of musicality – I have to learn every single note as I cannot play by ear – I progressed so rapidly that after a year I was able to give, to the amazement of the local classical guitarists, a tolerable rendition of Villa Lobos' haunting First Prelude. When Frank and Mary were not performing I would sometimes entertain the guests. I had also learned *Spanish Romance*, a popular piece that everyone recognises – the *Für Elise* of the guitar. It soon transpired that it was the only tune many customers ever wanted to hear me play.

A local lawyer, Clyde Turney, surprised me years later when he told me that, if a woman was reluctant to surrender to his amorous overtures, he would bring her to the Bagatelle and ask me to play *Spanish Romance*. Thereafter, he swore, she positively leapt into bed. Sadly Micky, who worked for the United Nations as a town-planning adviser, was posted away from Barbados, a crushing event for me, for no other teacher has been able to discover an iota of musicality – a gift from God – in my make-up.

People sometimes dropped into the bar on the way home from a dinner party. Tony and Joy Bland did so frequently. One evening an American customer had stood on a chair, camera in hand, to get an aerial shot of his fellow diners. The chair tipped over, decanting him and his camera over a wall and into the garden several feet below. With a little help from me he clambered back up, battered and bloody. O Lord! I thought, as I dashed to the bar to telephone for a doctor, Americans are notoriously litigious. This could mean a claim beyond our million-dollar public liability cover. However, in the bar having their habitual Cognac *digestif*, I found the Blands. Tony held the Chair of Law at the University of the West Indies. Could I be sued, I asked? Tony didn't miss a sip. 'Dear boy,' he said. 'No. In a phrase – *volenti non fit injuria*. Long established legal principle. Top us up with more of this nectar, if you would be so kind.' Case closed.

Before Barbados I had never before worked with people of African origin, and, since my entire staff was black, I had to accustom myself to their ways and them to mine. A notable example of different thinking which was forever beyond my grasp – my imagination was plainly not up to it – was when it came to excuses. Africans never approach a contentious matter head on – that is considered to be rude – but obliquely. And if something goes wrong, it is never ever their fault.

At seven o'clock one February evening, at the height of the season, the telephone rang. 'De body is Mr Clarke,' a voice told me. He was one of my waiters.

'Good evening, Mr Clarke.' I invariably addressed all my staff as Mister or Missus.

'Boss, I en't come to work tonight.'

'Really, Mr Clarke, why not?' I asked through gritted teeth, for we needed all hands on deck.

'Boss, de bus missed me.' I reeled slightly before my brain could accommodate the subtle logic. Of course, relatively speaking – ask Albert Einstein – it was true. I missed the bus: the bus missed me. It was one and the same.

'Mr Clarke,' I ground out, 'if you do not come to work immediately, I shall find you, take a blunt knife and…'

'Okay, Boss, I come.'

On another occasion I made a telephone call and asked for the person I wished to speak to. 'Man,' my correspondent said, 'dat body en't live heah. Yo' got de wrong number.'

'I'm sorry to have disturbed you,' I apologised.

'No hassle, man,' he said. 'De phone was ringing anyway.' Spit the pips out of that!

Staff attendance was very good, mostly because the day staff all lived in the next village, Redmans, and I could chase them up if necessary. As for the waiters, I had bought a huge Chrysler station wagon in which, every working day at five o'clock, I sent my reliable driver Carlisle Hicks to their homes to pick them up and bring them to the Bagatelle. At the end of the night's business they were taken home again. This meant that their commuting was simple and cost them nothing, and I suffered minimal absenteeism, so we were all happy. We worked well together and, over the course of nearly thirty years, my staff turnover was negligible. I still miss them, especially my secretary Beverley.

Once in a while, when customers returned to the bar after dinner for a *digestif* or two, and showed no signs of leaving, I would send the waiters home in the Chrysler and take over as barman, a job I loathe – give me the washing up any day. One evening Verna Hull, Claudette Colbert's erstwhile girlfriend – they had fallen out – dropped in with Anthony Armstrong-Jones, who wanted to see what I had made of the place he had once thought of buying. I showed him and Verna around and then we went to the bar. Suddenly a broad form filled the doorway and a slurred voice boomed a thespian, 'Good evening!' It was Oliver Reed, which meant Trouble.

There were two Oliver Reeds. Before ten in the morning he was amusing and interesting. After ten he was invariably drunk, unless his Jacky was on-Island with their daughter, when he remained sober and loveable. Apart from that he was a menace, banned from many West Coast restaurants and bars. Ollie was obsessed with arm-wrestling, and ideally would have beaten every male on the planet. Tonight he was at his curmudgeonly worst. He sat down and eyed Armstrong-Jones belligerently. He once told me he thought his eyes were hypnotic and he had always wanted to play Rasputin. 'What have you ever done except build a bloody great bird cage in Regent's Park?' he barked, referring to the avian extension to the London Zoo that Armstrong-Jones had designed.

'Frankly,' came the quiet reply, 'the remarks of a second-rate actor are of little consequence to me.'

Ollie's eyes almost started out of his head. He was being defied – by this quiet mild man! 'What was that?' he demanded.

In infuriatingly unhurried tones, Armstrong-Jones repeated every word. 'Right!' bellowed Ollie. 'Right! Come outside!'

Armstrong-Jones stood up reluctantly. The poor fellow had only dropped by for a drink and a glance at what I had done to Bagatelle. Now he was being challenged to a fight by a drunk twice his size. And he was not a strong man, having suffered from polio in his youth. But he was unafraid. As Ollie marched towards the door, his face wore a most confused expression. It was dawning on his alcohol-fuddled brain that he, for whom true blue was everything, had just summoned the Queen's brother-in-law outside for a fight. Horrified, Verna looked at me appealingly. But hardly had I got to my feet in the hope of somehow defusing the situation than they came back, Oliver with his arm around Armstrong-Jones' shoulders, his huge round face attempting desperately to obey instructions and smile. 'Ho! Ho!' he carolled like a part-time Father Christmas. 'What a joke! Oh, ha-ha!' He left soon afterwards.

In fact I was soon to be somewhat in Armstrong-Jones' debt. Johnny Kidd and Jack Leacock had purchased a toy, which, they suggested, I might enjoy playing with. I met them on the beach at the Miramar hotel, together with Andre Thomas, who ran the water sports there, admiring an enormous red, white and blue contraption, an aluminium-framed kite. Johnny rattled off the instructions without much conviction. 'You put on this harness, get in the water and put on the skis. Now you hook the harness to the kite, then attach the tow-line from the speed boat to the harness, and take hold of this tow-bar. Finally the boat will start pulling, and at a certain speed you'll take off like a bird. Couldn't be simpler. Absolute child's play!'

My villainous friends strapped me into the harness, and soon I was in the sea, my feet in the skis, clutching the tow-bar. The speed boat crept forward until the line was taut. 'Hit it!' my friends yelled. In a moment I was skimming over the sea, the kite flying above me. The boat's speed increased and suddenly I was airborne, plucked off the water by the kite, a fantastic sensation. I felt comfortable and secure, although the skis dangling beneath me were rather clumsy. The driver went in a big circle with me flying behind. I began making a few tentative airborne cross-cuts above the wake and soon felt quite in control. As we came back to shore I somehow indicated to the driver that I wanted to go round again, but with a difference. On the second circuit, I kicked off one ski and put my free foot in the back binding of the other, a slalom ski. Now I went completely bonkers! I was having the greatest time, swooping from side to side, turning, banking steeply, and sweeping across the wake in the other direction, only touching the sea like a kingfisher in flight. This was the life! As the boat roared along the beach the driver turned a bit too sharply, so that centrifugal force swung me even further out to the side, the kite flapping madly with my greatly increased speed. I looked down and saw startled sunbathers looking up at a huge striped bird with a man hanging beneath it. Then I was over the hotel roof. Fortunately I have an exceptional sense of spatial awareness and hand-eye coordination, and am absolutely at home operating in three dimensions – upside down or right side up, it's all the same. I was disappointed when, after the next circuit, the boat slowed down, put me safely back on the water.

On the beach I was greeted by ashen-faced friends. 'We need a drink,' someone said. Then the story came out. These scallywags had purchased the kite as a syndicate and each of them had tried it out in Carlisle Bay. None of them had managed even to become airborne, and had finished up in the sea in a tangled mess of line, kite and harness, though fortunately not injured. It had been put away in the roof of Jack's garage. One day someone suggested that Nick, newly arrived on-Island and of questionable sanity, might manage to fly the thing. Perhaps it would be better not to mention their own failed attempts. They had been vastly relieved to see me return in one piece, although they had been reassured, they said, by the presence of Jack the Knife, as the surgeon was affectionately known, who would have been able to put me together again in the event of disaster.

I knew this kite lark would end in tears, but my stupid ego would not let me stop just because it was dangerous. Shortly after my first 'flight', my architect friend Ian Morrison asked me to show him the ropes, and in no time at all was taking part in our water shows, drawing 'aahs' and 'oohs' from the spectators, although he did not swoop quite as extravagantly as me. Being the father of beautiful twins, he had responsibilities and more common sense than me. One day he mentioned the kite to Anthony Arm-strong-Jones, who asked to try it out – no milksop he, as we know. I don't know the details, only that he crashed and completely destroyed the con-traption. That solved my problem of how to retire with my reputation for intrepidity intact. Thank you, Tony.

Chapter Seventeen

The Barbadian Banquet

Y ou may remember that early on I had precociously formulated a life plan that involved sailing the high seas and making love to beautiful women. I was denied a life at sea. Making love to beautiful women, on the other hand, has been a different story. It is impossible to imagine anything better than the life of a bachelor on Barbados in the 1970s. The place was awash with girls on holiday, when rules fly out of the window, accompanied by morals, inhibitions and clothing. Once back home girls tended to revert to type. Four thousand miles away from home and anonymous, they were fancy-free; in London or New York they had to watch their step.

I was sitting at the bar at the Sandy Lane Hotel when an extremely pretty girl – nay, a Vision – in a bikini top and a pareo around her slender waist climbed onto the next stool. 'Hi,' she said, 'I'm Cat. And I could use a drink.' Nursing her spritzer, she told me that from the terrace she had spied this hulk sitting at the bar and told her mother she rather fancied him. 'So,' said her mother. 'Go! Fetch!' Cat had wasted no time. Her mother was no slouch either, and I later introduced her to John Bennett, the British High Commissioner to Barbados, who looked just like Pablo Picasso. They had a fling which lasted until the day John died – on the job, the story goes.

Cat was an unfailing source of the best marijuana which she, or rather her young brothers, bought from the Rastas on the beach. Marijuana in those days was mild compared to the dangerous stuff in circulation now. Our trips were giggly affairs, with no after-effects and definitely no addiction. When stoned, Cat was irresistibly drawn to horizontal surfaces and expected action. Not even the Great Table of Bagatelle was safe…

Of special memory was the absolutely gorgeous Dana Gillespie, a one-time water-ski jumping champion, who went on to form her own rock group. She is still performing. Dana would do anything for a Bagatelle chocolate mousse.

Over the years I found that some of my more ardent girlfriends were just as happy to make love to each other as to me. Having exhausted me, the girls would do whatever girls do together and talked about things girls talk about until late in the night. There existed between them that divine continuum between affection and passion, moving effortlessly between one extreme and the other. Being one of a *ménage-à-trois* was quite the most satisfying arrangement imaginable. To be awakened in the cool of a tropical dawn lying on the old four-poster between two lissom female forms, my eyelids caressed by the first tentative rays of sunlight, was sublime. The world of silk and satins, fragrant perfumes, swaying skirts, soft voices, smiles and caresses was heaven.

I know I have banged on about being a bachelor and enjoying the banquet which is Barbados. But it *was* a banquet, and I had positioned my feet well under a board groaning with delectable goodies and countless opportunities which I was in a position to seize. Added to this, my finances were much improved; I had finally paid for Bagatelle and was no longer waking up at four in the morning, totting up what I owed my creditors – fellow self-employed entrepreneurs will know what I mean. In London Paul Harman was slowly sorting out my chaotic financial affairs.

During the high season from Christmas to Easter my social life was constrained by the demands of a busy restaurant. I began work, like most Barbadians, at dawn. One man who helped me in those difficult early days was Bob Wolfe of Atkinson & Wolfe, purveyors of fine foods, and one of the few non-agricultural businesses in the parish of St. Thomas. Sometimes, when there was no money, Bob allowed me time to pay and even continue ordering goods. The other benefactor was my bank manager at Barclays, Tony Thomas. In the darkest days he advised me, when drawing wages on Fridays, to get to the Bank just after noon. He would have left by then for lunch at the Bridgetown Club, and therefore not be available to refuse to cash my cheque. I should go, he told me, to the very pretty cashier, Miss Archer, who would dish out the dosh. These two men made my commercial survival possible.

I once asked a Sandy Lane Hotel guest why he was prepared to pay the very high rates charged over the Christmas season. He replied that the best way to make money was to mix with money; the business contacts he made at the Hotel meant his annual two-week stay was a good investment.

One of the Hotel's most revered guests was the elegant George Stevens, holder of many General Motors concessions throughout the USA, who occupied the best suite at the Hotel for February and March every year. He took a great liking to me and the Bagatelle. He would always ask how the business was doing and, if I said I was not quite full, he would summon the ubiquitous George Forte. The two Georges would sally forth onto the beach and go to work. A guest, relaxing peacefully on his chaise longue, would become aware of a smiling but insistent presence.

The Presence spoke. 'Hello, I am George Stevens. How do you do? Have you been to the Bagatelle?'

'No, I can't say I have. What's a Bagatelle?'

'It's the best restaurant on the Island, bar none. You must go. Your name, sir? Right – got that, George? And your room number, sir?' George wrote everything down. 'Which evening would you like to dine there? It's only ten minutes by taxi.'

In a moment George Forte had all the details he needed to make a reservation.

The newly appointed hotel manager was one Guy MacPherson. He had ambitions for promotion in the Trust Houses Forte group, for he was very able. One day he and I were wallowing in the sea with Peter Moores, of the football pools family, who had a pithy – some would say bitchy – turn of phrase. Hearing of Guy's hopes, he observed dryly, 'You don't have a chance of getting anywhere Trust Houses Forte; your name doesn't end in an *e*, an *i* or an *o*.'

Peter's words were to prove prophetic. Guy's next job in the Group, at some sort of commercial travellers' place, was unworthy of the abilities he had displayed in Barbados. I sincerely hope Guy later moved on – and upwards.

My friends decided that Dot Morrison was just the girl for me. We became very good friends but nothing more. In any case, she was mother to twin daughters, Ashleigh and Sharon, and I was not exactly suitable material for marital stability. However, we were invited to parties together. One of the most generous hosts – he could well afford it, I hear some of you mutter – was Cyril Lord, the 'Carpet You Can Afford' bloke. He was not universally popular in British business circles; it was generally believed that, knowing what was coming – insider trading, as it is now known – he had sold his shares in his company and left the United Kingdom for Bermuda, just before it went bust. My father was of that opinion – perhaps he had been an investor – so I never dared tell him that I had enjoyed the considerable hospitality of Cyril and his wife Shirley at their house on the Sandy Lane estate. He was vertically challenged and inclined to strut, wore Winston Churchill-style boiler suits, and could be irascible. He had an African Grey parrot, a gifted talker that liked to imitate his cough. One of my favourite memories is of Cyril, infuriated by the incessant coughing, shouting up at the bird, 'Shoot oop! Shoot oop!'

The Sandy Lane estate had evolved marvellously well. Many of the plots – never less than one acre in size – had sold at US$1 a square foot. On them had built some superb houses, between which the fairways of the Bottom Nine golf course ran. A covenant regulated the development of the plots, but unfortunately it had been drawn up on the instructions of a gentleman – Ronnie Tree – for gentlemen, and was far from watertight. At first the regulations were adhered to, but three decades later that has all changed, and not for the better. Basically, one was permitted to build on each plot one house of a design and size approved by the Committee, and a guest cottage of not more than 1,200 square feet. Now the covenant is all but meaningless; the days of the gentleman at Sandy Lane are long gone.

In the Season there was a throbbing social life on the estate, with countless cocktail parties and dinners. One could live happily on canapés and Champagne or rum punch. Until I arrived on the scene their choice of restaurants had been limited to those found in hotels, but now they had the Bagatelle. Even better, the hotels often insisted on impracticable dress codes for gentlemen. Not so at Bagatelle, where smart and casual sufficed. Lord Samuel, of H. Samuel Everite Watches, always stayed at the Coral Reef Hotel (forever known as the Coronary Reef after an aged guest drove off from his tee on the Sandy Lane golf course, revolved three times and dropped dead). However, on evenings when Budge O'Hara – late of the Lygon Arms and a pioneer hotelier in Barbados – enforced a rigid dress code, His Lordship dined at the Bagatelle.

I had a recurring problem when it came to presenting restaurant bills. Tycoons do not like somebody else paying their bill, especially another tycoon. I might have to explain to, say, Lord Rothschild that, much as I appreciated the offer of his credit card, Lord Delfont had already proffered his. The old hands would march straight through to the kitchen on arrival and give me their card. Heaven forefend if a lady, even if she was the hostess, attempted to pay. In the case of Pamela Harriman, after the death of her venerable husband Averill, the wrangling became so tiresome that I no longer presented her with the bill; I used to deliver it personally to her at Mango Bay the next day.

After my usual lunchtime feasting from the buffet at the Sandy Lane Hotel, I would repair to the beach and my Hobie Cat. Jack and Margaret Leacock had suggested that I buy this single-sail catamaran and join the non-racist Barbados Cruising Club. I did so, and kept her next to Peter Tomlin's water sports hut at Sandy Lane. This sailing boat, a recent addition to racing fleets in America and Hawaii, was very fast, the longer two-sail versions reaching speeds close to 30 miles an hour. I used to race mine every Saturday at the Cruising Club, and surfed her at the Hilton Hotel beach when the waves were big.

Aboard my Hobie Cat there was room for three – just. My friends Veronica and Stephen and I used to head northwards along the coast to a favourite deserted beach, adjacent to land owned by Ingrid Bergman, who was rarely on-Island, where we would join others for a picnic. The landlubbers would come by car, bringing all that was needed, including a spear gun, hopefully to harpoon a difficult to hit but tasty barracuda for lunch. Whilst one of us was busy hunting, a shallow pit would be dug and filled with coconut husks, always to be found washed up on that beach. They would be set alight. We would cut the fish into thick slices, moisten with a squeeze of lime, and barbecue them over the fire. Served with a lick of hot pepper sauce it was food for the gods. There was no shortage of beer and rum punch.

Our bottle of Muscadet had been hung in a string bag from the forestay and dragged through the cool water. This beach sadly is no longer accessible; the government built an enormous cement plant there, its jetty serving as a conveniently isolated spot well away from police stations, for the landing of contraband at night.

After one such picnic, as we were returning home, the sky darkened ominously and we were treated to one of those intense late-afternoon thunderstorms. The wind was still, the menacing black clouds seeming almost to touch the water, and the flashes of lightning and crashes of thunder were too close for comfort. We sat helpless on the trampoline which was held in a metal frame, which in turn was attached to metal stays, which were attached to the tall metal mast, thus making us integral if unwilling components of an ideal lightning conductor. With an unearthly crash a bolt struck the water very close by, succeeded immediately by a deafening clap of thunder. The air was so charged with static electricity. that I saw Veronica's long thick hair stand straight out from her head, every filament visibly separate. I shouted out a desperate 'Don't touch the frame!' It was some time before any of us dared to do that.

The trampoline had another use, possessing as it did the dimensions of a double bed. Sometimes my girlfriend of the moment and I would sail offshore, well away from prying eyes, drop the sail, cast aside our bathing costumes and have a bit of fun. One day we were so engaged, when we heard a speedboat approaching and a voice yelling, 'Ahoy there!' We ignored it. We had other things on our minds and, anyway, I could hardly have stood up and waved.

'Can I help?' the man bellowed. I suppose he thought we had suffered a rigging failure. The boat came closer, its engine muttering. Then disbelief came into his voice. 'Oh Lord, no! Children, don't look!' And with a mighty roar he was gone.

From time to time the Leacocks organised a water sports show on the Sandy Lane beach. The hotel kitchen created a fabulous buffet, graced with enormous ice and butter sculptures, and everyone was welcome – unlike the exclusion policy of its Irish owners that so jars locals today. Watercraft of all descriptions, packed with spectators, gathered in the bay. We all did our bit on the water, with Jack Leacock giving a witty commentary. Ian Morrison flew the kite, swooping hither and thither. Margaret Leacock, with five girlfriends, skied close to the beach as a human pyramid, with three girls on skis as the base, the next two on their shoulders, and another as the wobbly apex. Cyril from Peter Tomlin's water sports gave a demonstration of slalom skiing. I did a couple of things. First I would demonstrate the use of my shoe skis, which were little over a foot long and made me look as if I was walking on water. Then there was the water-ski jump which we had built, launched and moored offshore. I had jumped on calm inland water at Ruislip under the eagle eye of David Nations and the gravel pits of East Yorkshire, but here I was on the open sea. As I approached the jump at speed, I noticed to my horror that, due to the swell, there was daylight between the leading edge of the jump and the sea. My skis were going to pass under the jump whilst the rest of me continued over it. Not a good idea. I swerved away desperately. The boat towing me made a circuit and approached the jump again. On this occasion the leading edge was beneath the water and over I went, landed and skied on to great applause. What would have happened, had I not noticed the gap, doesn't bear thinking about. I never used the jump again. It was towed northwards to the Miramar Hotel to be used as a sunbathing platform, before eventually sinking in a storm.

Of an evening, after my water sporting activities, I would go to the bar, order a rum punch, and telephone the Bagatelle to enquire who was coming that evening. How many menus did I need to write? With a bit of luck I might join a game of backgammon on the hotel terrace. Then, hopefully slightly richer, I would leap into my beach buggy, drive home, dash off the menus, and prepare to welcome my guests. One evening Alexis Lichine, wine-making husband of the much married film star Arlene Dahl, telephoned. I explained that we would not have a table for him until 9.30 at the earliest. I did none of that first and second sitting nonsense – that was not my way. As a guest in my house you had your table for as long as you liked. There was a pause, then Monsieur Lichine said – people actually do say these things – 'Do you know who I am?'

'I do indeed,' I said. 'I've read your excellent book on the wines of Burgundy. I'm really interested that, although you own Château Prieuré-Lichine (a Grand Cru Classé in Margaux), you seem to have a soft spot for Burgundian wines…'

★

The summer meant that I had time for other pursuits. I had purchased a Yamaha upright piano – I like to have a piano wherever I live. I had arrived in Barbados with a minimum of baggage, but found that I needed a few more bits and pieces. There was only one place to look – Bowen's Auctions.

The sale I attended was packed and Harold was at full speed. Suddenly the voice of one used to being obeyed made itself heard: 'Mr Bowen!' It was no less a personage than Honoria Drummond, who lived alone in the deepest south-east corner of Barbados in a reputedly haunted house. She was quaintly potty. Recently she had arrived at Goddard's supermarket in Fontabelle, wearing a dress but with her corset on the outside. Bruce Goddard, unfailingly urbane and seemingly unaware of the unconventional arrangement of her clothes, accompanied her around the emporium, helping her select various items, then saw her through the check-out and escorted her to her car.

'Mr Bowen,' Honoria boomed, 'where is that silver cow creamer with the scroll feet?'

'It's been knocked down, Mrs Drummond,' a smiling Harold told her.

'But I intended to buy it.'

'Mrs Drummond, I'm afraid you can't. It's been knocked down to someone else. You fell asleep.' Harold did not mince his words.

Mrs Drummond got to her feet. 'You should be in prison, like my son!' she pronounced and marched from the room leaving a shocked audience behind her.

She did have a son, George Albert Harley de Vere Drummond. One day, during a golf match on the Isle of Man, his father, a Drummond of Drummonds Bank, had said to his playing partner words to the effect of, 'I say, sir, would you mind standing as godfather to my sprog?'

'Absolutely!' affirmed his fellow golfer, which is how Honoria's son received the Christian names George Albert, for his godfather, then Duke of York, was soon to be crowned King George VI following the abdication of his brother. When George grew up he was due to inherit a considerable fortune, around nine million pounds. Unfortunately there was a misunderstanding concerning US$100,000 of travellers' cheques, which, unbeknownst to George, had been stolen prior to the final stage of printing. Subsequently George was indeed sent to prison and possibly disinherited.

In the autumn I had to go to London for a couple of days to see my lawyer, Anthony Rubinstein, of Rubinstein & Nash, one of the few in his profession whom I trusted absolutely. I arranged a massage in my hotel and my chatty masseuse told me she was having problems with her parrot that did a life-like – but noisy – imitation of a train hooting in a tunnel. The landlord had said the parrot had to go. By the time the massage was over I had agreed to buy the bird for a bottle of Chivas Regal. I took him to Barbados – no psit-tacosis problems in those days – where he enhanced my life for years. One of his best tricks was to imitate a telephone ringing and his former owner answering it. He would then relate her end of the conversation for minutes at a time. I learned a lot about her unsatisfactory love life and the untrust-worthiness of men.

CHAPTER EIGHTEEN

Return To The Skies

On the Island there was a flying club with a light aeroplane for hire. I had gained my private pilot's licence at Denham in England in 1968, so all I needed to fly the machine was join the Flying Club and have my British licence revalidated by the Barbadian civil aviation authorities. This entailed re-taking exams, written and practical, after which the Caribbean, and its innumerable islands, would be my oyster. Adventure beckoned!

Having a private aeroplane at my disposal meant I wouldn't have to depend on the local airline LIAT, which, despite the beauty of its flight attendants, the charm of its pilots and its excellent safety record, was not, as I have already mentioned, known for its fair allocation of seats. One stood a good chance of being dumped.

Flying out of Barbados was very different from leaving Denham. Once the Island slipped below the horizon there was only water and, obviously, no landmarks. The islands forming the Lesser Antilles, never more than ten miles apart, ran from north to south about a hundred miles west of Barbados. It stood to reason, surely, that if you were heading due west, eventually you had to pass over one of them.

A couple of years hence so thought Jeremy Sisnett, chairman of a large rum distillery and a collector of old maps. He once borrowed a privately owned single-engine Piper Arrow to fly himself and two friends to Palm Island, 120 miles to the south-west. Jeremy chose to fly above the clouds. After a certain time he would descend through the clouds into the clear air beneath, identify his intended destination, and land there.

Down he came, emerging through the cloud base, expecting to see the chain of islands, with Palm Island more or less dead ahead. In fact, what he saw was a great deal of Caribbean Sea in all directions. Had a strong headwind delayed him or a powerful tailwind taken him too far west? He had no way of knowing. If he pressed on, but was mistaken, he was faced with a thousand miles of Caribbean – next stop Central America. If he turned round, equally mistakenly, 4,000 miles of Atlantic Ocean lay ahead. And he had at most 600 miles' worth of fuel. He searched around in desperation, then spotted a tiny blip on the sea at about two o' clock to the right, and altered course towards it. It was his only hope. It turned out to be the island of Tobago, which had an airfield. He and his passengers were safe.

So he had been heading east rather than his intended course of southwest. What had gone wrong? The aeroplane's owner, Art Taylor, a surfing Australian with a death wish and a misguided sense of economy, was to blame. Needing a replacement he discovered that truck alternators were much less expensive than those made specifically for aeroplanes, so he bought the cheaper version. What Art didn't appreciate was that aeroplane alternators are shielded, so the magnetic field generated by the electric current is contained within the unit. The magnetic field generated in a truck alternator is uncontained and had seriously affected the aeroplane's magnetic compass, sending Jeremy dramatically off course. It was fortunate that he spied Tobago; he was in fact on course for Nigeria!

Another consideration is that in tropical latitudes, with such high ambient temperatures, the weather can change quickly and violently. A visit to the meteorologist in the control tower and careful study of the weather radar before take-off are always advisable. The anvil-shaped cumulonimbus clouds towering tens of thousands of feet into the sky might hide vertical winds of 60 miles an hour. It was also unwise to fly between their base and the sea, an area in which powerful lightning strikes were common.

When the engine of a single-engine aircraft fails over land, returning to terra firma *and* walking away in one piece is tricky but often do-able. Over the open sea achieving a satisfactory outcome is more complicated. As any honest pilot will tell you, engine failure is always at the back of one's mind, for neither engines nor engineers are infallible. All you can do is reduce the possibility of failure. This means a meticulous check of all systems. In twenty-five years of flying in the Caribbean every life-endangering problem I have encountered, with one exception, has been because I was in a hurry and skimped on the pre-flight inspection and drills. This says everything about the maintenance carried out by the engineers at Aero Services, Barbados. Thank you, ladies and gentlemen; I owe you my life.

If you do have engine failure over the sea you must have the emergency drill firmly in your head; there is no time to consult the manual. Every thousand feet of altitude gives an unpowered light aeroplane only two miles of glide. I tended to fly at around 6,000 feet, which would give me maybe five minutes before hitting the sea. During that time you have a host of critically important things to do. And, unlike other emergency drills, landing on the sea is not a skill you are able to practice. It was a situation I never had to face, thank heavens.

Now that I was free to fly around the Caribbean, I wanted to revisit Bequia, the tiny island where my West Indian life had begun. Ron and Stan Young of the Friendship Bay Hotel had mentioned that they had a new American residential guest who, they both agreed, was just the girl for me. That was all I needed to know, so I booked the Club aeroplane for a few days.

There was no airport on Bequia, and wouldn't be for another twenty years, so I would have to fly to St. Vincent, and take the schooner *Friendship Rose*. St. Vincent's airfield, Arnos Vale, was not without interest to a pilot who had only landed on conventional runways, which, depending on the wind direction, could be landed on from either end. The approach, over the sea into the prevailing easterly wind, would be simple enough. But there was no possibility, in the case of a missed approach, of going around again; you had to land because dead ahead, at the end of the runway, was a mountain. This meant that take-off had to be downwind, something I had rarely practised. There were other unusual considerations – for example, before an aeroplane could take off or land, the road across the runway – which created a sizeable bump – had to be closed, and cows or small children shooed to safety. I viewed my first take-off there for my return flight a few days later with some trepidation.

My own flight to St. Vincent was uneventful and took just under an hour. I had arrived early in the mistaken belief that the *Friendship Rose* ran several times a day. But the only service was at 12.30 pm. So I took a taxi to the Yacht Club for some breakfast. As I sat munching my toasted ham and cheese sandwich, a man dashed in shouting, 'De cruise ship in!' In a flash the barman rubbed out 'EC$' – Eastern Caribbean dollars – from the price column on the blackboard, replacing it with 'US$', thereby trebling the cost of the food and drink at a stroke. After breakfast I took a taxi to Kingstown, the capital. Already it was its crowded, hot and very smelly self. The *Friendship Rose* was alongside the jetty taking on cargo. I sought refuge in the air-conditioned Hazells Bar where, on my second day in the southern Caribbean a year ago, I had had my first sighting of Colin Tennant. I boarded the *Friendship Rose* just after noon. We cast off and motored out of Kingstown en route for Port Elizabeth on Bequia. Once in the rumbustious channel, the sails were hoisted and the engine silenced, and the cool salt spray blew away the malodorous memories. Bequia, a mere 20 miles from St. Vincent, was another world, free from the brooding presence of the volcano. I was surrounded by the smiling peaceful faces of people whose lives were ruled by the elements. The Island subsisted, apart from killing maybe two whales a year, on boat-building, fishing and, increasingly, tourism. Bequia is a beguiling country. You cannot fail to fall in love with it and its people. But to maintain a tourism industry, and remain unspoiled, is not easy, for tourism is a double-edged industry. The price of the tourist dollar is frequently the dilution of indigenous values. Fortunately the lack of a Jumbo-able airport on Bequia will always protect it from the worst excesses of mass tourism.

Soon I was on my way once more in the island's rickety taxi – its suspension as unforgiving as I remembered – to the Friendship Bay Hotel to find Ron and Stan Young and 'just the girl' for me. We arrived in a cloud of dust and I received a rapturous welcome. This was where my Caribbean odyssey had so painfully begun with nasty sunburn. Nonetheless, it had a special place in my heart, since it was here that the Fates had sent me off in an unexpected direction. We went straight to the bar and armed ourselves with rum punches. Stan disappeared, to return a few minutes later holding the hand of a striking woman in a bikini top, each triangle the size of a postage stamp, and a pareo around her tiny waist. Her face and body were burned the colour of dark mahogany, and her California-perfect teeth gleamed in a welcoming smile. It was the facial bones, though, that took centre stage. They were beautiful, angular and pronounced. Ruth Neumann-Derujinsky, for it was she, had until recently been a top model featured on fashion magazine covers throughout the world. She had fallen ill and was convalescing on Bequia with her little daughter, Andrea. Mother and I hit it off straight away, and I was invited to stay in her chalet.

The morning after my arrival there was consternation at the hotel; no staff had turned up, which was unheard of. Stan drove hurriedly to Port Elizabeth, rounded up the absentees and returned with the car full. The reason for the no-show was, it appeared, my fault. On the way to the hotel the previous day, as the taxi passed over a bridge spanning a deep gully, I had remarked casually, 'I bet there are duppies (ghosts) living down there.' I didn't know that on Bequia duppies are no laughing matter. The driver had put the word around and no-one wanted to cross the bridge. Luckily Stan was able to reassure them that I was an ignorant foreigner making a clumsy joke.

We spent much of the following days on the hotel yacht, a 53-foot Gallant, exploring the Grenadines, dropping in at Mustique and Basil's Bar, the divine Tobago Cays, and Palm Island, where I was introduced to the famous Caldwell family. We were always accompanied by Stan's dog, a Jack Russell. When he went diving for spiny lobsters or sea urchins, the dog would follow him down, as deep as 20 feet, bubbles streaming from his snout.

One evening, as Ruth and I were enjoying a sundowner at the Friendship's bar, Andrea said, 'Mommy, look at my new bracelet,' and held out her arm. Her mother turned pale. We were both struck dumb. The 'bracelet' was a centipede, about six inches long, whose poison, injected by two ugly stingers, can cause severe pain and swelling. For a susceptible adult, if the poison enters the body close to the heart, there may be more serious consequences. For a small child it might prove fatal. Our dilemma was that if we tried to remove the creature, it might well sting Andrea. In the event, our intervention was not required; without a trace of fear she picked up the centipede on her index finger and laid it out carefully on the table. A trembling mother took her daughter, blissfully unaware, in her arms and hurried away.

Although it did not deserve such an end, anything but all things considered, I knocked the insect onto the patio floor and crushed its head with a stone.

The next day, just before the sun rose, Ruth, slender and suntanned, was lying on a snow-white sheet next to me, her eyes closed, hair spread out in a halo. All was peaceful, until a cock crowed. 'Listen to that cockerel,' I said. 'He's far too early.'

Eyes still closed, Ruth enquired sleepily, 'What in God's name is a cockerel?'

I reflected. How should I put it delicately? 'Well,' I explained, 'it's a thing that fucks chickens.'

Ruth's crack of laughter – she had a powerful voice – put an end to any morning calm. Between coughing fits Ruth managed to let me know that in America the bird in question was a 'rooster'.

After several idyllic days it was time to return to Barbados. Stan, who had business on St. Vincent, kindly gave me a lift on his yacht. In the taxi to the airport, I was already rehearsing the downwind take-off. Usually one takes off into the wind so as to reach as soon as possible the speed through the air that allows flight. With a lift-off speed of 70 knots and a headwind of 20 knots, one takes off with a speed over the ground of 50 knots. But with a tail-wind of 20 knots, to get to 70 knots airspeed, 90 knots over the ground are required, quick for a light aeroplane. By the time I had completed the departure formalities, the road across the runway was closed, free of cows and small children. I taxied to the eastern end of the runway and turned round with the mountain behind me. I lined up the aeroplane, the runway stretching far ahead of me downhill to the sea. Spectators sat on the road-crossing gates. I felt sure that they knew this was my first take-off at Arnos Vale, and harboured morbid expectations of an accident. The control tower cleared me for take-off. I opened the throttle to full, waited until the engine had achieved maximum revs, and released the brakes. The machine leapt forward. I had an eye on the airspeed indicator; until that showed 70 knots I could not pull back the control column and take off. Well before I had reached take-off speed the undercarriage wheels hit the raised road where it crossed the runway and tossed the machine into the air, so I had to put it back on the ground. Finally, the airspeed indicator showed 70 knots and I eased back the controls and was airborne – sweating ever so slightly. I made a climb to the east and headed for Barbados.

I was glad to leave St. Vincent behind. Only once, with Alexandra and Noel Charles on board, did I attempt an into the wind take-off; the tail wind was too strong. It nearly ended in tears and we were lucky to escape with our lives.

Over the years I became accustomed to the runway and was never to have a problem there. It was, however, my least favourite destination in the whole Caribbean.

CHAPTER NINETEEN

Invading Hordes

The less hectic summer had given me time to examine at an idea which had been lurking in my mind. Some customers, after dining at Bagatelle, told me they had returned to their hotel feeling that their evening was not quite complete. How might this be put right? The answer seemed obvious – to create an intimate bar with a small dance floor. The ideal spot, in my garden, was a mere step from the tables. Additionally those who had dined elsewhere could also continue their evening at the Bagatelle.

So, before my visit to St. Vincent, I invited back my builder Mr Prescott with his ancient masons and carpenters, and enlisted lads from the village as labourers. The architect was one N. Hudson. Work began without any plans whatsoever – the idea of seeking planning permission never crossed my mind. I decided to name the nightspot Mr Nick's Smoochery. May I be forgiven, but the idea was for people to smooch, and smooch they did. Is there a better way to end an evening?

I had three dozen metal signs made, with black letters on reflective yellow, indicating the way to Bagatelle and Mr Nick's. My irreplaceable Basil travelled with me all over the Island armed with a hammer, a box of nails and a ladder, attaching them to convenient posts. I had a nasty letter from the Barbados Telephone Company threatening awful retribution for misuse of their telegraph poles, but nothing happened. I learned later that the signs were used by tourists to find their way back to the West Coast (signposts were not one of Barbados' strong points).

During my brief absence on Bequia the restaurant had functioned well, with enough customers to cover the overheads. Mr Nick's Smoochery was a building site, swarming with lads shoving wheelbarrows. But it was on track to open before Christmas. I ordered the discotheque equipment – turntables, speakers, lights and so on – and designed and had built a dozen mahogany rocking chairs with especially high backs. The other seating was horseshoe-shaped stone banquettes with my awful black leatherette cushions as found at Bagatelle. I lined the underside of the roof with coconut fronds, which both gave it a tropical atmosphere and hid the ugly – but marvellously cheap and quick to install – galvanised sheets.

With the Smoochery finished, Bagatelle was the complete evening destination. I had an excellent loyal staff and the business was profitable. Not that it ran itself; it did not – successful restaurants require constant attention – so I gave it all the time needed and thoroughly enjoyed doing so. I was also aware that the high season was followed by a long, lazy summer when I would recharge my batteries.

The attractions of Barbados as a winter destination had been known for years to socialites from both sides of the Atlantic. Many had already bought properties on the Sandy Lane estate and along the West Coast where they spent the Season in style. Now the catchment area had increased to include other well-heeled hordes.

The Venezuelans were the first. Their country was a convenient four hours' flight away, southwards down the Caribbean. In the early Seventies its economy was larger than that of West Germany, and the national wealth, as was the way in South America, was shared amongst a small percentage of the population. They were a lively and generous crowd, arriving in twin-engine aeroplanes that they piloted themselves, accompanied by wives, children, nannies, even Mesquite charcoal for their barbecues. Leader of the pack was Erasmo Santiago, who had inherited Yukery Fruits, the biggest orange juice business in the world. He always took the Great Table at my restaurant and entertained lavishly. On one occasion I had a girlfriend, Linda, staying at Bagatelle, who was a jeweller; she had brought with her from New York a collection of exquisite and unique pieces, made of precious and semi-precious stones and silver and gold, to hawk around the boutiques of Barbados. She opened her briefcase on the bar to show me her creations.

At this moment Erasmo came to the bar to pay the bill, noticed the baubles and picked one up. 'How much?' he asked. Linda, well prepared, passed him a price list.

'Spread out these pieces on the bar. And please, don't sell a single thing until I come back.' He returned to his guests. 'Girls,' he announced. 'I want to give each of you a present. Go into the bar and choose a piece of jewellery.'

When, after much squeaking and gasping, the girls had made their choices and returned to their seats, Erasmo asked 'How much do I owe?' I totted up the total on the cash register and it came to a lot of money. He was signing US$100 travellers' cheques for the next few minutes. That was how you often paid in those days.

One of Erasmo's chums was an architect named Johnny Perez-Canto who flew a smart Beechcraft 55 aeroplane. He was married to the volcanic Sylvia Casablancas, sister of the recently deceased John Casablancas who had the famous Elite model agency in New York. When I visited her in that city I noticed a hole in the glazed front door. 'I threw the telephone at my daughter,' she explained. 'But I missed.' She was a gorgeous creature and a dear friend. She had been a member of the international jet set – di Portago, Rubirosa, Schellenberg, Rossi and the rest – and was once engaged to Karim Aga Khan, but refused to become a Muslim so that was that.

They invited me to return with them to Caracas, and Johnny flew us down there. We landed at La Carlotta airport, a joint military and civil field in the middle of the capital. It was at an altitude of 835 metres, which could make taking off in the heat of the day interesting if as pilot you hadn't done your temperature/altitude calculations. Around the Flying Club were marked off parking spaces for members' aeroplanes; the closer to the club-house the more it cost. The most expensive was US$200,000. Having put his aircraft carefully to bed Johnny took me into the club house for a cup of Venezuelan coffee. I took a sip. It was black, thick and very sweet. I might as well have been kicked by a mule, such was the caffeine hit. My heart took several minutes to return to its normal resting rate.

Some years later their marriage ended in tears, and Sylvia expressed her feelings by attacking Johnny's beloved aeroplane with an axe. He would have much preferred castration.

In the halcyon days of the early Seventies the Venezuelans brought much money to Barbados. Then sadly Erasmo, on behalf of his company, borrowed heavily in American dollars, just before the financial crash and consequent devaluation of the Bolivár against the dollar. The rate quickly went from five or six Bolivárs to the dollar to seventy (it is now in the thousands). Since the earnings of Yukery Fruit were in Bolivárs, this created an insurmountable problem and the company failed.

I shall never forget the generosity of my Venezuelan friends. If I had a single complaint it was that they made returning hospitality impossible. On Barbados, if I offered them lunch they would say, 'Nick, we're on holiday. You are our guest.' If I suggested giving them dinner when I was in Venezuela, they would respond by saying, 'Nick, if our friends saw us allowing a guest in our country to entertain *us*, they would be ashamed for us.' I could not win. I wonder what has become of them now, in the socialist state, so completely changed under the late Hugo Chávez.

The charms of wintering in Barbados were also discovered by rock musicians who could comfortably afford the best the Island had to offer. When first I met Elton John and his songwriter Bernie Taupin in 1972, their royalty incomes were of the order of £11 million a year – each. I was introduced to Elton by Bernie, a country lad from Lincolnshire. Each winter season he and his now ex-wife Maxine moved into the Bagatelle Great House. Bernie began to write poems, sometimes inspired by listening in Mr Nick's to recordings of his musical idol Otis Redding. Later Elton arrived on the Island with his entourage and moved into a seaside villa on Sandy Lane. I had my piano sent down and, for the next few nights Elton, with Bernie's poems on the music rest in front of him, composed some of his greatest hits.

And there were parties, fabulous parties. Once I was offered a piece of cardboard covered in what looked like, to an innocent lad from Yorkshire, a miniature ploughed field with white soil. But it was the sort that made you sneeze. There must have been a small fortune on those little trays.

As soon as fans discovered that Elton John was staying at the beach, they crowded the fence, taking away any privacy he might have enjoyed. Having had enough, he and Kiki Dee, a regular house guest, rushed up to the fence on hands and knees, barking like dogs. Their tormentors got the message and retreated.

One day I invited Bernie and Elton to fly to Martinique for lunch. Elton declined. It would, he said, give his insurers a fit if he flew in a machine without at least two professional pilots. But Bernie accepted, as did Dave Nutter, who did the photography for Elton's record sleeves – his brother was the famous Savile Row tailor Tommy Nutter – and Tony King, Elton's very camp fixer-in-chief.

We landed in Martinique and took a taxi to my favourite Grand'Voile restaurant. The meal was as good as ever. The only disappointment was Tony's; he sulked because the serving staff were all waitresses and he had hoped to find, he said, a dark and handsome French waiter to flirt with. At about four o'clock, well fed and too well watered, we took a taxi back to the airport. I completed the departure formalities, and we took off for Barbados. Just as we were about to leave French air space, I radioed the control tower on Barbados. Did I have a night or instrument rating, they asked, because I would be arriving close to sunset? I had done the training, I told them, but not taken the exam. They refused to accept my flight plan, and for the first time I had to turn back to Martinique, landing twenty minutes later, as it was getting dark.

We found a hotel and tried to telephone Elton but could not get through. Surely he would realise that we had decided to overnight in Martinique? So we had another good meal – I don't remember whether we found any waiters for Tony – and took off for Barbados early the next morning.

Once back on Barbados, we belted back to the villa to find a distraught Elton. 'He's been pacing up and down the whole night,' Kiki reported. The previous evening he had called the control tower in Martinique, who told him that, yes, we had left Martinique and had been turned back by the Barbadian controller – and put down the phone. Elton thought that the aeroplane had gone down and that in a single blow he had lost Dave his photographer, Tony his fixer in all things, and worst of all, his irreplaceable genius Bernie. There were hugs, tears and reproaches, Elton calmed down, and soon there was laughter again.

It was the custom for boys in Elton's entourage to be given girls' names. After this little adventure I was forever known as Amanda Hudson-Dare. I was honoured. I was even told that I would get a credit on a record label. Maybe I did. Some years later Tony turned up at my new restaurant, greeting me with 'Hello, Amanda.' I don't suppose its name, La Cage aux Folles, had anything to do with it. Perhaps he thought that I had seen the light.

The last time I was in contact with Elton was when he kindly sent his car to meet me on my arrival in London Heathrow. And what a car! It was a chauffeur-driven drop-head yellow Rolls-Royce with a telephone. Never had I been so warmly greeted by the commissionaire of the Churchill Hotel. I hope I remembered to tip him appropriately.

Barbados held an added attraction for rock musicians. Astutely, Eddie Grant had opened recording studios there so that their holiday could also become a working vacation. Unfortunately, Mick Jagger told me, the facilities were not well maintained, so he and others moved their recording work to Montserrat, 300 miles to the north-west. Eventually this facility, and indeed much of the Island, was destroyed by the erupting Soufrière Hills volcano in 1995.

Alice Cooper came to Bagatelle as Elton's guest. I introduced him to a recent litter of mongrel puppies. He asked if he might take one of them back to America, so I invited him to choose. A few days later, at a party featuring another white ploughed field, I was chatting with Alice. I heard a 'woof', looked up, and saw the puppy on the balcony of Alice's room. The little fellow squeezed himself between the wrought iron bars and confidently launched into space. Without a break in our conversation, Alice caught him.

Many other musicians came to Barbados, and to the Bagatelle and Mr Nick's. Jefferson Airplane, Eric Stuart of 10cc, Nina Simone, Paul McCartney, Ringo Starr – the list goes on – and found the lifestyle to their liking. In return, they, by their glamorous presence, attracted other visitors, and put much money into the country's coffers.

CHAPTER TWENTY

Anna

In 1972 I returned to London to clear up the chaos caused by my unplanned move to the Caribbean. At Nikita's, a Russian restaurant partly owned by Nick Clarke and myself, I dined alone – as I often did. I began with blinis filled with smoked sturgeon and smothered in *sauce Hermitage* – smetana with red caviar – washed down with Zubrówka vodka. This was served in a small carafe wrapped in dry ice. I finished with strawberries Romanoff and another vodka, this time *krupnik* – a Lithuanian honey vodka. Feeling merry and romantic, I felt an urge to visit some old haunts just ten minutes' walk down the road, so I set off. Several years ago, after a jolly weekend, David Hart and I had brought a sapling up from his home in Essex. Late that night, we lifted a paving stone in front of the Troubadour coffee house, planted the tree and went home, taking the stone to use as an unlikely chopping board. Some weeks later, as we sat in the Troubadour, a council lorry arrived and men climbed out armed with tools. Oh no! we thought; they're going to dig up our tree. Not at all – they installed an iron railing around our baby, loaded up their tools and left! Now, in 1972, I wanted to see how it was doing. Soon I was there, and so was the tree (it's still there today).

As I was proudly admiring my sole contribution to urban arboriculture, a soft voice enquired, 'Nicky Hudson?' I turned and beheld a woman of arresting beauty, with hair the colour of pale mink framing her lovely face, whose name...escaped me! To be fair, the vodka can't have helped. The vision smiled and said, 'Anna. Anna Palk. The water-ski club – remember?'

She slipped her arm through mine, said 'Let's have a coffee', and led me, still wordless and in some confusion, into the Troubadour. We sat down, our eyes met. No words were needed. For the next eighteen years we were lovers, confidants, and friends. During those years I lived on Barbados and Anna in London, but this made no difference. Whenever we met, the passion and love were undiminished. We knew neither jealousy nor anger until death savagely did us part.

Anna was married. Her husband Derek Brierley was a stockbroker and they lived in a tall narrow house in Chelsea. Often they had terrible rows, real shouting matches. Anna would shriek like a fishwife from the top floor, Derek would shout back from the kitchen like an angry schoolmaster. Their toy poodle Pompey, in the intervening sitting room, yapped, desperately upset.

Derek quickly accepted my role in Anna's life. His principal concern, he told me, was that she should love him. She did, and respected him too. But her sexual appetite was voracious, and after their son Jonathan was born Derek accepted that he would never be enough for her – nor would any one man. I was by no means her only lover; she had others – we discussed them – but they did not last.

For years Derek had been obsessed with making a film about Wagner, and raising funds for it. He was executive producer of a star-spangled TV series featuring Richard Burton, Vanessa Redgrave and John Gielgud, and an appearance by – curiously – the composer William Walton.

Both Derek and Anna were fond of Edward Heath, whose allure, other than as a courageous yachtsman, eluded me. But Anna liked powerful men and money, and Heath after all had been Prime Minister. So what on earth did she see in N. Hudson, I hear you cry?

We were not horizontal the whole time. We enjoyed antique shops and good restaurants, and we talked endlessly, telling each other everything, like brother and sister. Anna was a busy actress, RADA trained, and worked with Peter Cushing and in some cult movies. In 1971 she was in Michael Winner's *The Nightcomers*, with Marlon Brando and Stephanie Beacham. Her roles were always sexy. When we met in 1972 she was in a series called *The Main Chance* with John Stride, in which she was the first woman to bare her boobs on the BBC.

The house in Cale Street would be my London base for years. After Jonathan's birth there was another occupant – Nanny – who strongly disapproved of me. What made her particularly cross was that, when we needed the house to ourselves, Anna would send her out with Jonathan for marathon walks or on pointless missions. The bedroom by no means sufficed as our playground. We tended to get around the place quite a bit, finding uses for pieces of furniture which might have quite surprised their designer. And we were noisy lovers, especially if the lovely Melanie had dropped by. Then it was bedlam. Melanie and Anna were birds of a feather; I first met Melanie on Barbados when, reluctantly, I made an appointment to meet yet another female selling advertising space in a tourist publication. Into my sitting room came the sexiest prettiest creature imaginable, wearing a miniskirt and a blouse that struggled to conceal fine insolent breasts. She had a mane of black hair, eyes that sparkled and a smile that promised. I definitely wanted to see her again, so I bought some space. I was wearing my tight Lothar jeans and a rather theatrical shirt with leg-of-mutton sleeves, and she thought I was gay, she told me later. That very day we began an enduring, passionate friendship *sine die*. Together we created a sexual perfect storm. When Anna was with us, the windows steamed up. Melanie has gone from commercial success to success, and now owns several tourist-related publications based in Antigua.

But that was still in the future. I left London shortly after our meeting at the Troubadour, but not before it had been for arranged for Anna to visit Barbados as soon as possible. By delicious coincidence Melanie lived on Antigua, not a million miles from Barbados – in fact 300. Next door!

Anna came to stay later that year. One morning I suggested we whizz over to Martinique for a night or two at the Bakoua Hotel. Wanting to reach Martinique in time for lunch, we dashed down to the Flying Club, I checked out the aeroplane, filed my flight plan, and in no time we were lined up and cleared for take-off.

I pushed the throttle to full open. Quickly the airspeed indicator showed that I could rotate and take off. I pulled back on the control column and we rose into the air, climbing left to head north-west for Martinique. Suddenly the indicated airspeed began to fall. I pushed down the nose but it still fell – to zero! This was a most important instrument; if you flew too slowly whilst turning, the aircraft would either spin or stall and dive into the ground. But I was still flying, so my airspeed was not zero. There had to be some malfunction. I radioed a Mayday call to the control tower but got no response – in a panic I had probably dialled in the wrong frequency – and headed back to airfield. I had to guess the airspeed and stayed well on the side of flying too fast. Anna sensed a problem but said nothing. As I prepared to turn on my final approach, I felt the engine lose power, so I opened the throttle. No response. Reduced power, no airspeed information and no radio contact *was* tricky. Still not a word from brave Anna. Fortunately I had enough height to make the runway on, which I landed, and limped back towards the Flying Club parking area. As pilots say, if you walk away from it, you have done good. I got out, handed Anna to the tarmac, and called a mechanic over. I explained my problems. Immediately he clapped his hand to his head, and peeled off a piece of masking tape with which he had covered the airspeed indicator escape hole prior to spraying on paint. He had forgotten to remove it when the job was done. That explained the loss of airspeed indication. He then raised the engine cowling to reveal that the air ducting, which fed air to the engine, had collapsed, imploded. No air. That explained the loss of power. It had been a close call, but at least it had been over land rather than the uninviting ocean. Anna and I hugged for quite a long time.

Rather like falling off a horse, I thought it better to take to the air as soon as possible. Anna agreed, brave girl. The aircraft was repaired and we later took off for Martinique. We were too late to make it for lunch, but would give ourselves a cracking dinner. About halfway across, Anna whispered, 'Darling, how high are we?'

I consulted the altimeter. 'Six thousand five hundred feet,' I informed her.

'How many feet are there in a mile?'

'Five thousand two hundred and eighty.' I knew my weights and measures tables.

'Then we're more than a mile high. Isn't there some sort of club one can join…?' The randy devil! Just when I thought she must still be quaking in her pretty shoes after our nearish miss – I was still not completely myself – she had more important matters in mind! I switched to autopilot…and landed on Martinique with a smile on my face.

After two blissful days we returned to Barbados. Shortly thereafter Anna went on to London.

CHAPTER TWENTY-ONE

Bagatelle Gathers Pace

I was in desperate need of financial guidance. I hardly knew capital from income, and regarded an overdraft limit as a target rather than a barrier. On the other hand I was good at making money, so there was a sort of balance between incomings and outgoings. One day my bank manager pointed out that I was obliged under the law to file annual financial statements – something I had never even considered – and recommended a chartered accountant, one David Allison. He hailed from Canada, which country had, since the seventeenth century, close economic ties with Barbados. David was also a bachelor and we were to share some interesting times. On a practical level, he computerised my accounts, giving me an accurate idea of where I stood every month, something a restaurateur ought to know. He was to become, besides my financial adviser and guiding my business life, a close friend for the next twenty-five years until his tragically early death.

Back in England my father had become chairman of the British Trawler Federation and was conducting the Cod War against Iceland, sometimes from the cocktail bar of the Station Hotel in Hull.

Due to the success of Bagatelle I was invited to take over the Sunset Crest Beach Club in St. James, a large operation. Flattered, I accepted, but it proved an expensive mistake. One of the events was a weekly barbecue. A customer would buy a ticket, be served a steak cooked to their liking, help themselves to salads, grab a bread roll, then exit the barbecue enclosure and choose a table. What could be simpler? But after a few weeks, despite large numbers of people buying barbecue tickets, I was losing money. My bookkeeper, John Payne, identified the problem and suggested I come down to see for myself. One evening, concealing myself in the shadows, I watched a man receive his steak and choose some salad, piling up a substantial pyramid. He stuffed his pockets with rolls and butter portions, and made his way to where three other people were sitting, with plates, knives and forks already on the table. They each took some salad, cut the steak into four, and dug in. Four dinners for the price of one! I eventually extricated myself from this inappropriate commitment, but at some cost. Cash businesses are hands-on affairs and you can't be in two places at the same time, it is as simple as that.

Now my second season had arrived, and with it the snowbirds. Owners returned to their winter nests. Customers from my first season returned. It is *the* greatest pleasure for a restaurateur when people come back. Inevitably friendships result, which is equally rewarding. There were cocktail parties galore, the beach was crowded with beautiful girls, and I heard from Anna in London that she was completing the last series of *The Main Chance* and would be coming to stay again before the end of the year. So, all in all, I was a fulfilled man.

There was not much time to play. Mr Nick's Smoochery was a huge success and, as well as being a bar with dance floor, I began serving food. To simplify the operation I offered only fondues – beef or shrimp – or grilled lobster with garlic butter. The concept went down well. I engaged a Calypsonian, the Mighty Gabby, to entertain the guests. The rock musicians took to him and appreciated his ability to make up rhyming couplets as he went along. The fact that they were often offensive and personal did much to endear him to them. They would slip him 20 dollars, pass on lurid details, and let Gabby loose on some unsuspecting diner. Of course he loved performing to legends of the rock world.

One evening at Bagatelle the art dealer Eric Estorick and his wife Sal ushered in an old lady swathed in chiffon. I greeted her with, 'Good evening, madame'. In the background Eric growled quietly, 'I told you to wear something more masculine.'

The 'lady' was in fact Erté, the Russian-born artist and designer; Eric was his agent. At the time Erté was a young party-going eighty-year-old, eventually dying aged ninety-seven. He used to stay with the Estoricks at their house, Nelson Gay – now owned by the Rausings – in St. Peter further up the west coast. Some time later Eric took me to the guest cottage where Erté stayed, and showed me a fabulous frieze he had painted on the wall – because he was bored, he told his host. Eric was also the agent for the Zulu sculptor of a life-size bronze figure in a hammock which hung between two trees in their garden. I always went to drool over it when I visited the house. I took them a chilled bottle of Champagne which was passed to the butler to open. After quarter of an hour, and no Champagne, I found the butler trying to drive a corkscrew through the metal cap on the cork. I don't think that particular wine was served in that house too often.

My sunset rum punch companion, dear Ronnie Tree, often came to the Bagatelle on a Sunday. Ronnie's guests were a sort of Who's Who of society on both sides of the Atlantic. Sometimes Marietta came too, but as well as being on the board of PanAm and working with the Democratic Party, she was engaged in affairs with John Huston, and later Adlai Stevenson. She was frightfully bossy and bullied everyone at Heron Bay, guests and all, posting lists of do's and don'ts in the rooms as if it were a Brighton boarding house. Like Cappy Kidd with Janet, Ronnie was a different man – a free spirit – outside his wife's powerful gravitational field.

Marietta and Ronnie had a daughter, Penelope, who deeply resented her mother bullying her father, to whom she was closely attached. In 1967, when she was eighteen, Penelope met and fell head over heels in love with the photographer David Bailey. At the time he was married to Catherine Deneuve, whom his hell-raising friends Brian Duffy and Terence Donovan had bet him £50 he wouldn't dare propose to. He did and she accepted! But she had to go when Bailey was captivated by Penelope's unique beauty – no female I have seen before or since has ever looked remotely like her. In a series of brilliant photographs he made her a fashion icon. One Sunday Ronnie brought them both to Bagatelle.

They were an unlikely couple. On her mother's side Penelope was a scion of the Peabody family from the East Coast of the United States, and on her father's side adorned the highest ranks of English society. Bailey, something of an enigma, was an East Ender through and through. He was a huge admirer of the profoundly unlikeable Kray brothers and showed me with pride his pictures of Ronnie Kray's wedding. He also admired David Litvinoff, Rachman's enforcer. He had a strong aversion to inherited wealth and no time for anyone born with a silver spoon in their mouth. He went off me for a while when he found that I was guilty in a modest way of this very crime. But, my word, he could take unforgettable photographs and he was extremely witty and generous.

Around this time Penelope fell victim to a cruel blow, the late onset of acne. As she put it, 'I went from being sought-after to being shunned because nobody could bear to talk about the way I looked.' The damage to her until-then flawless skin did not affect me at all; I was already enraptured. There was a light that burned within her that even the effects of this shattering blow, not to mention anorexia, and later bulimia, could dim. I am not surprised that in latter years she has turned to Buddhism. There was assuredly a spiritual flame waiting to be kindled.

One Sunday Penelope, Bailey, a few friends and I went to lunch at the Kingsley Club at Cattlewash on the East Coast. The menu, which had not changed in thirty years, always ended with key lime pie; the entire wine cellar – three or four half-bottles – could be carried on one tray. This was irrelevant, since the rum punch was so good – and cheaper. After lunch we felt too far gone to drive back to the West Coast, so we repaired to a cottage called Matilda that I had rented in nearby Bathsheba to use as a surfing base; it was just across the road from one of the Island's best – if slightly hairy – surfing spots. My paparazzi-avoiding friends found Matilda ideal as a trysting spot. On this occasion we all collapsed in post-prandial languor. Not for long. A shrill petulant voice instructed, 'Everybody, look at me!' There was one of our number pointing a camera in our direction.

'Oh, for God's sake,' grumbled Bailey. 'Put it away, Dick.' There was a disbelieving silence, followed by a sob. The would-be snapper was Richard Avedon, who was not used to being told what to do with his camera.

Eventually Penelope and Bailey split up; he went on to marry a model, Marie Helvin. I have heard several reasons for the separation, but Penelope once told me that she could tolerate Bailey's beloved parrots being all over their house in Gloucester Avenue but would draw the line if ever there was one in the bathroom. One day there *was* a parrot in the bathroom.

Post-Bailey I took Penelope out to dinner in London. When we returned to her house I suggested that we might take matters further. She declined with such sweetness, leaving my tender ego so unbruised I didn't even feel the bump. We were very close friends. She called me Nickelodeon and I called her Poo. I shall, as I have already said, love her forever.

One customer that year was Marlon Brando, who had just completed the filming of the first *Godfather*. He sat at the bar, his cheeks still puffed out *à la* Don Corleone, although the padding had long been removed. He brooded, rather after the fashion of Oliver Reed, talking to nobody, not even the taciturn blonde who was with him.

I hit it off straight away with a young couple at the Bagatelle, he an extremely handsome and gentle Canadian, she an attractive, exquisitely dressed American. They were Donald and Cherry Marshall, who have played a central role in my life. Donald would shortly become my partner in the Bagatelle.

One evening Lee Radziwill, who arrived in Barbados on board Aristotle Onassis' motor yacht *Christina*, brought to the restaurant her sister Jackie's children, John John and Caroline Kennedy, and their bodyguard (following the death of their father they would be protected by the State until they were twenty-one). I offered the bodyguard something stronger than his soft drink, but he explained that he did not drink on duty. Much later I went to let him know that the party was leaving, and found him slumped over the bar, fast asleep. 'Mr Blackman, what on earth happened?' I asked aghast.

'The gentleman changed his mind,' I was told. He had consumed two of Mr Blackman's lethal Black Power cocktails. One was dangerous enough!

So too were the cocktails at the Hilton Hotel beach bar, where every Saturday I would arrive on my Hobie Cat for lunch before taking part in a races organised by the Cruising Club. They served real American hamburgers with mountains of chips and relishes on the side, and a potent – nay, lethal – cocktail called a Backscratcher; there actually was a wooden backscratcher in the glass to use as a stirrer which you were allowed to take home. I foolishly had three of these one day and fell asleep – actually, passed out – in the middle of the ensuing race.

If I was playing hard, I was working even harder. I began the evening service at the Bagatelle at seven in the evening and often closed Mr Nick's well after midnight. The critics had given me kind reviews and I was starting to appear in syndicated American gossip columns like that of the sharp-tongued Suzy Knickerbocker. My increasingly experienced kitchen staff, under the watchful eye of chef Shamangoli Forkell, meant that I could be more adventurous, and the menu grew more interesting as I became better acquainted with local produce.

Overall, though, a sense of routine was creeping in. I was not good at routine and was inclined to look around for something else to turn my hand to. Importantly, I had yet to learn the importance of paying off business loans at the first opportunity.

CHAPTER TWENTY-TWO

The Most Beautiful Girl I Had Ever Seen

I had to navigate the Christmas and New Year's Eve madness as 1972 gave way to 1973, which involved an invasion of New Yorkers and their uncontrolled children. It was a very profitable two weeks, which is the only thing that stopped me resorting to justifiable infanticide. The parents weren't much better – Mr Blackman was asked for Harvey Wallbangers, Pink Ladies, mint juleps or dry Martinis made with Lithuanian gin, as if we were a downtown Manhattan cocktail bar in the 1930s. Ordering items not on the menu was popular too. Sometimes the nightmare was put off until the bill was delivered to a large table. Actually, they would say, we each want a separate bill. But who had eaten what and who had drunk which wine and how much? It was all very testing.

The biggest cash night of the year was New Year's Eve or, as Bajans say, Old Year's Night. We devised a special menu featuring exotic imported ingredients – oysters, for example, *foie gras* or Maine lobsters. It was the one night in the year that we had two sittings, one at seven thirty and another at ten. Inevitably, some early diners decided to stay on, even though they had been made aware that I had sold their table for the second sitting. It's not easy to persuade someone who has just spent a small fortune for dinner to leave, especially if some celebrities have just come in. I was glad when that night was over. The only good bit was banking the money.

Later in January Barbados switched into grown-up, child-free mode when the snowbirds flew in, and girlfriends dropped by for a night or two, often on the way to Mustique.

One evening two people who had dined together at the Bagatelle introduced themselves to me. He was a photographer called Ronny Jaques, she a travel writer Doone Beal (Lady Marley); they were doing a piece on Barbados for *Gourmet* magazine. They had enjoyed my restaurant and would like to return the next day, interview me, and take some photographs. This they did and I thought no more about it.

One evening I sauntered into the bar, order pad at the ready. Sitting on the banquette seat was a man I knew slightly called Shirley Smith, who had done well for himself with fruit machines, or, more accurately, one-armed bandits. But my eyes settled on his companion, the most beautiful girl I had ever seen. Her features were perfect, her lips generous, and her hair long, blonde and free. She was wearing a simple white blouse loosely tied with a fabric belt, and white trousers. Her radiant smile left me speechless. I was helplessly in love – again.

Within weeks Chérie Hunte had moved into Bagatelle. She was an Island girl, born on Barbados; her father Geoffrey came from a family of Plymouth Brethren, the Barbadian chapter of which was particularly strict. The women wore only brown or grey clothing, their hair scraped back and no make-up. Brethren never dined with non-Brethren, though they would happily do business with them – in fact, they were a commercial force to be reckoned with. However, Geoffrey committed the cardinal sin of marrying an outsider, the lovely Lela, and was forced to leave Barbados with his family and move to St. Vincent. There, Cherie told me, their rented accommodation overlooked the prison yard, and as a young girl she witnessed a hanging, for which that Island was particularly well equipped. Some years previously three men were condemned to death, and it was decided that they should be hanged simultaneously. Accordingly two more gallows were erected and never taken down. Capital punishment is still on the statute books in Barbados, but there have been no executions since 1984, mostly due to the exertions of the human rights lawyer Alair Shepherd.

From St. Vincent the Huntes (it is quite usual in Barbados to add an 'e' to otherwise ordinary English surnames) moved north to St. Lucia, where Chérie was soon much in demand as a model and became the official icon of the Board of Tourism. Hers was a natural beauty, which she had no need to enhance. She never wore make-up or went to a hairdresser. When she entered a room people stopped talking. Having a Barbadian passport, she was able to work in the restaurant as she did not require a work permit, and work she did – if a cook didn't turn up she would take over in the kitchen. In those early days she was as responsible as I was for Bagatelle's success.

An aura of peace surrounded Chérie, warming people in its glow. The customers adored her, as did my African Grey parrot, George. He was very clever and could imitate anything. If he couldn't make a noise with his throat, say car brakes, he would get the effect by rubbing his beak on the bars of his cage. He was free to fly around the garden, but I only had to rattle a teacup on a saucer, and back he came; he knew that meant a sugar lump soaked in tea. His favourite sport was admiring himself, perched upside down, in a car wing mirror. When I was working at my desk he would creep across the floor and bite my toes with his razor-sharp beak. He stalked Mrs T, the cat, too. But when Chérie joined the household he immediately fell in love with her, and would sit on her shoulder, nibbling her ear, crooning and besotted.

I sometimes invited regular customers upstairs to my apartment for an aperitif. When once Harry Secombe and his wife joined me, I put on a recording of *Aïda*, and he joined in, his powerful tenor voice filling the room. ''Arry *bach*, your 'eart,' his wife cautioned him. She was right. Within a year he had a heart attack and had to lose stones in weight.

Brian Forbes and Nanette Newman were especially charming; they and their two children were always a joy. One evening, as the Newmans walked past the Great Table, Brian recognised Cubby Broccoli.

'Cubby!' he yelled, embracing him.

'Brian!' bellowed Cubby.

But as I led the Newmans to their table Brian muttered under his breath, 'That son of a bitch.' Oh, the luvvies!

Brian told me how once, in England, they had been invited to a fancy dress ball at the town hall. Nanette went dressed as Eva Braun and he as Adolf Hitler. To their horror they were seated next to the mayor of Hamburg.

★

One of the characters of the West Coast was Peter Tomlin, a Seychellois, who ran the water sports operation at the Sandy Lane Hotel, where I kept my Hobie Cat. He asked me to fly him and a friend to Mustique, where they planned to dive on the wreck of the SS *Antilles*, which struck a reef in January 1971, caught fire and sank. Much of its rusting superstructure was above the water level and badly disfigured the seascape. When I saw the landing strip, I could not believe my eyes. It was narrow and short, with a hill on the threshold and another at the end of the runway in the take-off path, on the slopes of which was the wreck of a light aeroplane with a French registration. It made Arnos Vale on St. Vincent look like Heathrow. I chickened out, telling Peter I would have to practise landing there alone before taking passengers, and took two disappointed men back to Barbados.

However, pilots who landed frequently on Mustique gave me some useful hints. The most useful was to make a steep approach so that the threshold of the runway, otherwise hidden by the hill, was always in sight. I quickly mastered the technique and thereafter flew in regularly.

Margaret and Jack Leacock were always making my life more interesting, as they had ever since I bought Bagatelle three years earlier. They had just taken up polo. They knew I was a more than competent rider, so why, they now asked, didn't I? So I applied to the Club and promptly forgot all about it.

Then one evening, an Englishman entered into conversation with me at the Bagatelle bar. He said he lived across the road, and seemed surprised that I spoke the Queen's English. He steered the conversation round to what truly interested him – where had one been to school? When I said I had been to Sedbergh, he was overwhelmed with relief. 'Oh, jolly, jolly good!' he said. 'My son was there.' His name was David Mount and he was the secretary to the Barbados Polo Club. The membership committee had decided, he said, before implementing their original decision to blackball the long-haired be-kaftaned applicant – which was to say me – proposed and seconded by the illustrious Leacocks, to find out more. My having been at Sedbergh, like his son, meant apparently that I was a sound chap and fit to be admitted to the Club.

The Leacocks had not finished with me yet. Margaret, wearing her realtor hat, told me there was an interesting property for sale at a 'pretty snippy' price. She drove me to Bishops Court Hill in the centre of Bridgetown, where one found some of the finest mansions in the town. We went up a drive, at the end of which was a large house, locked up, shuttered and obviously unoccupied.

Erin Hall had about an acre of land. In the grounds was a dance school run by a daughter of the Wilkinson family who owned the house and were Plymouth Brethren. The potential of the property was obvious, for everything was right, including the price. It was located nicely between the South and West Coasts, and there was plenty of space for parking, often a problem in urban environments. My only task was to decide what precisely to do with it. My first thought was to convert it into an enormous pub, and I broached the idea with my accountant David Allison. In the meantime, putting my resources to the test, I bought it for BDS$146,000 – a little over £30,000.

At around this time Errol Barrow, the then Prime Minister, found himself at Alexandra's nightclub in Stockholm, home to the international jet set. It was owned by Alexandra Charles, a Swedish woman married to a Trinidadian, Noel Charles, and a quiet American called Tom Macksey. Errol was impressed and thought such a business would enhance Barbados' tourist product, something he always sought to do. Via Errol, I suspect, word of my purchase reached Sweden, where it was agreed that Erin Hall would indeed be the ideal place for a Barbadian version of Alexandra's. It was arranged that Noel would come to Barbados to discuss the matter with me.

Meantime, I had a lovely surprise. The October 1973 edition of *Gourmet* magazine, arguably the most prestigious foodie magazine in the world, came out and there was a dish of mine, Smoked Flying Fish, on the cover! For many Americans, *Gourmet* was the gastronomic bible; they never travelled without consulting it. Doone Marley had done me proud. No amount of money could buy this sort of copy, and for years to come people arrived at the Bagatelle with that very edition under their arms.

As the article said:

'*Quite different in every respect [from Greensleeves] is the BAGA-TELLE GREAT HOUSE, converted from a plantation house, in the hills directly behind St. James. The bar, for example, is in the old cellars, and the whole building has been brilliantly adapted by Nick Hudson, former partner in the London restaurant Nick's Diner. True to Caribbean form, he was one of those who came to Barbados on holiday and simply stayed, absorbing the old-world charm. The restaurant, with stone walls some three feet thick, hurricane lamps on tables, and louvered windows open to the song of the cicadas and to the sky, is enchanting. The food is a tour de force, for Mr Hudson has imported some of the more adventurous ideas from his London establishment and combined them with local fare. One has the feeling of being attended by a host rather than a restaurateur, and Mr Hudson's enthusiasm is infectious. 'Please just try one of these Maine lobsters that were flown in today,' he entreated. But I settled on the beignets de moules, preceded by his version of Callalou Soup, and followed by a superb Rock Cornish game hen stuffed with water chestnuts.'*

Doone's piece confirms to me that I had created the sort of restaurant to which I had aspired, without having to resort to *haute cuisine*.

At about this time – in late 1973 or early 1974 – Blake Edwards and his film crew descended on Barbados to make *The Tamarind Seed*, starring his wife Julie Andrews, Omar Sharif and Anthony Quayle. The cameraman would be, as in virtually all Edwards' film, the brilliant Freddie Young. I never met the Edwardses, but Omar had a generous entertainment allowance and, as he rather took to Bagatelle, I saw quite a lot of him. I thought he should visit an out-of-the-way part of Barbados that he might not otherwise see. So one evening I drove him up into the hills to Mrs Watson's rum shop, the Barbadian version of an English pub. Outside, under the hamlet's one street lamp, was a wooden table on which the locals crashed down their dominos. Inside was Mrs Watson, cosily wrapped in a warm overcoat and her church hat, with floral trimmings, firmly pinned on her head. I told my illustrious companion that he should try a Bajan speciality, a mouthful of ham cutter immediately followed by a swig of Stades' Extra Special see-through rum. A ham cutter is a bread roll basted with margarine and stuffed with a slice of ham liberally plastered with sauce made from Scotch Bonnet peppers, one of the hottest on the planet. See-through rum, as opposed to dark, which has added colouring, is clear and may be very strong.

Mrs Watson put two cutters on the counter, carefully rinsed and polished a glass for each of us, and filled them to the top with firewater – the hooch is so cheap there is no question of measures. I explained the routine to Omar – a bite of cutter followed by a swig of rum. Let's go!

I was the first to take the plunge and, knowing what was coming, enjoyed the powerful assault on my senses. Omar didn't know what to expect. He was zapped first by the fierce pepper sauce and then hit over the head by the see-through rum. I swear his eyes started out of his handsome head. Thereafter, as with an earthquake, everything gradually returns to normal, although there may be aftershocks. But before this could happen, we took another mouthful and another swig, and so on.

Towards the end of filming Omar took the Great Table for a dinner party, to which he kindly invited me. Anthony Quayle told, and dramatically acted out with bulging eyes and savage shrieks, a joke about a Japanese *mohel* – circumciser – who did his work with a Samurai sword, which had us falling off our seats.

As 1973 drew to a close I was able to look back with some satisfaction on my time since arriving in the West Indies. Starting only with £21,000, a backgammon board and a hat with a snakeskin band, I had established a home complete with dogs, cats and parrot, and created an internationally recognised restaurant. Erin Hall was promising. Chérie's beauty and gentleness filled my world with light. I was reconciled with my parents. My way of life was all and more that any young man could hope for. My cup overflowed.

In England my father was still waging the Cod War with Iceland and, so far, not winning. The indefatigable Paul Harman was striving to sell my shares in Nicks' Diner and Nikita's.

It was time for me to talk turkey with Mr Noel Charles.

CHAPTER TWENTY-THREE

Alexandra's

Here a preamble is required, since in July 2013 Noel Charles, who features so largely in this chapter, died. He first met Julian Lennon, Beatle John's son, and then later John's first wife Cynthia, whom he married in 2002. Before he died Noel published his memoirs, *In My House*, which I have read. His version of events differs from mine, but since they occurred almost forty years ago, this may be expected. So I shall be careful to report only from first-hand experience. If I quote from hearsay I shall make it clear. What must be said is that, as the son of a Trinidadian cobbler, Noel had come a very long way.

Following Errol Barrow's initiative we first met in late 1973 to discuss the possibility of establishing an Alexandra's nightclub in Barbados. From the photos he showed me of the operation in Sweden, the Erin Hall property seemed ideal. However, we decided I should visit Stockholm and see for myself. Our planned route was via London, mainly to buy me clothes. Noel was a natty dresser; I was not – my wardrobe consisted almost entirely of kaftans and swimming costumes and no shoes to speak of – so a visit to the King's Road and Carnaby Street was necessary. We departed Barbados with a travelling backgammon set, as he wanted me to teach him the game as we flew. In London we stayed at my usual haunt, the comfortable Churchill Hotel in Portman Square, and hit the shops hard. Noel had excellent taste and I was soon looking very much the part, all unbuttoned tight shirts and flared trousers. I even bought some boots which I still wear occasionally.

In Stockholm I met Noel's attractive wife Alexandra. Also in her flat were her three sisters, Scandinavian beauties who absolutely adored Noel and loved to wrestle with him. I was green with envy as he struggled unconvincingly under a pile of writhing nubile bodies. Girls liked him partly because had two secret weapons. One was the *Eau Sauvage Extrême* with which he perfumed himself liberally before venturing out. The other I am not allowed to mention.

I was taken aback by the sheer theatrical opulence of the club. It was all plush velour, carpeted floors, brass rails, luxurious horseshoe-shaped banquettes and enormous chandeliers, and it was full of beautiful young people. This *was* exactly what Barbados needed and that Erin Hall *was* just the place for it, I was in no doubt. It was run as a membership restaurant-discotheque, which ensured exclusivity. I wasn't sure how that would work in Barbados, with a transient tourist clientele, but a way would be found. The clientele of Alexandra's boasted regulars like ABBA, Björn Borg, as well as the Crown Prince of Sweden. We had a meeting with Alexandra's partner, Tom Macksey, to work out a business arrangement. Briefly, we decided that I would contribute Erin Hall and its land, and Alexandra's would finance its conversion. I would exchange a number of shares in Bagatelle for a number of shares in the Barbadian Alexandra's. The deal also included John Reid, a charming Canadian who already held some shares in Bagatelle. Before leaving Stockholm we were given lunch by the senior executives of SAS, the national airline, which offered special deals for Swedes flying to Barbados. And what a lunch they gave us! I very much enjoyed the herring prepared in many different ways, the *gravad lax* and endless quantities of *akvavit*. My memory of the event is blurred.

Noel and I returned to Barbados, again playing backgammon all the way. I won quite a lot of money. Firstly, I understood the game much better than him. Secondly, Noel was a gambler. He had been a croupier at the Cromwellian Club in the Cromwell Road in West London, and treated backgammon like a gambling game, which it is not; I tried in vain to explain that it is a matter of mathematics. My winnings paid for my whole trip, clothes included. It took Noel a while to pay up but he did in the end.

Our first job was to put together a company, structured as we had agreed in Stockholm. Work on Erin Hall was a massive undertaking; the building would have to be hermetically sealed for reasons of air-conditioning and sound-proofing, since we were in mid-town with neighbours close by. The sound system, of critical importance, was the best money could buy. Alexandra's Stockholm poured in money and know-how until the job was completed.

In mid-construction Noel moved into Bagatelle's guest room, just as the very valuable sound equipment arrived. This would be the last thing to be installed because the gear was so susceptible to construction dust, and far too tempting to thieves. It was delivered to Bagatelle, where we set it up to make sure it was all working. The system was powerful and boasted two amplifiers of 450 watts each. We placed the enormous speakers on the floor about six feet apart, and laid out some cushions between them. Noel produced a mega joint – he always had a good supply of marijuana – and lit up. We lay on the floor, our heads on the cushions, dragging deeply on the joint and passing it on. Noel began to play heavy metal music, winding up the volume until our heads were being pounded by 900 watts of sound. What a trip that was! We did it frequently until the time came to install the system at Alexandra's. How we remained sane – and not deaf – I do not know.

One evening John Reid prepared a *fricassée* of fish for supper. As he set the pot down we recognised the sweet heavy smell of hash. We dug in greedily. After the first few mouthfuls we all felt as if someone had hit us over the head with a sledgehammer. 'I didn't put in *that* much,' protested John, his eyeballs seeming to bounce off the walls.

'You spiked it as well?' said Noel, alarmed. 'So did I!' We were still stoned the next day.

Come the evening of the opening party at Alexandra's, we were running slightly behind, in that the carpet layers were rolling out the last piece of carpet down the entrance hall as the first guests were coming in. But it was a lavish affair which will never be forgotten. It was opened by Errol Barrow, whose initiative had led to its creation in the first place. The Club was a resounding success, full to bursting. The entrance money was pouring in and the restaurant upstairs doing great business, as well as the discothèque. We had a circular table just beyond the bar, only for us owners and our friends, at which places were much sought after. Tom Jones was often there, drinking only Dom Pérignon and tipping the waiters with US$100 bills.

Viv Richards the cricketer, April Ashley – all the usual suspects. And of course the place was awash with leggy blonde Swedes who came over on SAS' special deals. Once, dressed in purest white, a dozen gorgeous young local girls obviously looking for a good time came in and caused a riot. We heard later that they had that evening attended their confirmation service at the cathedral and had escaped via the drainpipe from their boarding school dormitory. These angels were subsequently expelled.

Another girl had joined my household, Gay Beresford from South Africa. She was stylish, a model and looked just like a young Bette Davis. In London she had introduced me to a fellow model, Carina Fitzalan-Howard, daughter of the then Lord Beaumont, who would inherit the dukedom of Norfolk about a year later. I remember being staggered by her diction; it was not at all upper class, much more Essex than Wessex. We weren't snobs, though. Chérie, Gay and I invited her to join us at Bagatelle, where she met Noel Charles.

Shazam boom! They were a number straight away. Carina had a marvellous svelte figure and could wear anything. Since Noel dressed very carefully, they made a pretty picture. They found a house away from Bagatelle and moved in. Carina came to Alexandra's every night, often staying into the small hours, and was terrific company. Some time later I was invited to a chat by her parents Miles and Anne, who asked what I thought would be the outcome of their daughter's liaison with Noel. As a married man he would not be the ideal son-in-law for the holder of the Great Office of Earl Marshall and Hereditary Marshall of England, and the senior Roman Catholic in the Realm. My opinion was that any sort of pressure on their part would be counter-productive and that maybe time would do its job. After this meeting Carina did not speak to me for some time; I suspect that, in her eyes, I stood accused of disloyalty. She did talk to me again when she came back to Barbados with her husband, David Frost, nearly ten years later. This time her chosen mate was the divorced son of a Methodist minister. Poor Miles and Anne just couldn't win.

If the numbers of people passing through its doors, paying handsomely for the privilege, and supporting the bar and restaurant was any indication, Alexandra's was a monumental success – but nonetheless there were problems at the bank. Do I detect echoes of the Diner here? A vibrant operation but no money left over? The Alexandra's overdraft was growing and more working capital was needed. I had no spare cash, and no more was coming from Sweden, maybe because Alexandra had recently parted company with Tom Macksey. Noel canvassed his friends, including a somewhat unsavoury gambling connection he had in New York who wanted a casino in Barbados and was eyeing Alexandra's. Noel gave me to understand that I was in the way, and that if I did not accede to this person's demands – i.e. handing over my shares – my person would be in danger. I had never been threatened in my life, and I have been unable to forgive him until now, for he is gone, poor fellow.

At last one of Noel's friends offered some money. He was an interesting character, one Albert Coxall. Always known as Cox, he was very tough and, I suspect, a left-over from Noel's days in the world of gambling. He was also very likeable and held Noel in high esteem for rising from his humble origins. Cox's involvement in the business meant that I could leave. Noel and I went our own ways. I was glad to be out of it. The finances never did improve and eventually Alexandra's went to the wall.

So, why did what should have been a gold mine fail? One reason I know for certain. Alexandra's in Stockholm was run under the eagle eye of Alexandra herself. She had trained at Cornell University in the USA, knew the business inside-out, and had instigated those tedious but indispensable controls. Noel, like my Diner partner Nick Clarke, had loads of natural ability – creativity, charm, salesmanship, ideas – every quality except an appreciation of the necessity controls which cash businesses have to have in place. Also Noel was working every night until four in the morning and could hardly be expected to run the office in the daytime. I heard from a reliable source that, towards the end, the cost of liquor sales exceeded the actual sales. The back door to the liquor storeroom, forever the Achilles heel in the catering business, must have been unguarded.

A last-ditch attempt was made, I understand, to convert the operation into a casino. Indeed, work started on the project but was not completed. It was only due to the strenuous opposition of the combined churches of Barbados that gambling – synonymous in the Caribbean with organised crime – had never been allowed. Thank heavens – there was quite enough corruption in the Caribbean without that. I went once to Antigua with Noel to a casino run by the Gallos, a New York crime family. The very day we got there the casino had been burned down. When the firemen had tried to rescue the valuable roulette wheels, they were found to be wired to the floor. This, I was told, was part of the braking system which could be used to influence the slot in which the ball came to rest.

When Julian Lennon, who had been marvellously supportive, both morally and financially, during the long illness, announced Noel's death in 2013, he wrote:

> *'It is with the heaviest of hearts that I bring this news to you today, that my mother Cynthia's husband, stepfather to me and friend for over 30 years, Mr Noel Charles, passed away from cancer yesterday on Mother's Day whilst sleeping. He had fought a brave battle for just over two years, but now finds himself at peace, as we are, after a very heartbreaking last couple of months of severe pain and panic.'*

RIP, ex-partner.

Chapter Twenty-Four

Doctor Rat Makes A House Call

The year 1974 was very special for me; in February I was overjoyed when my dear parents came out to Barbados to see what I was up to and had a terrific holiday at the Sandpiper Hotel. My father had been awarded the CBE for his contributions to the fishing industry and the family was very proud. They met Chérie and liked her enormously. They were very happy with what I had achieved at Bagatelle. My selfish transgressions were forgotten.

Early on Easter Tuesday I woke up early and tottered to my study to start the morning's work. Barbados being a God-fearing nation, the banks had closed from Good Friday until after Easter Monday. But restaurants had remained open, for it was still the high season, and it had been a long, hard weekend. Looking forward to banking quite a lot of loot, I cast a loving glance over the filing cabinet in which I had stashed five days' takings. Normally the money would be in the safe in the office downstairs but it was out of action. But wait – wasn't the top drawer distorted around the lock? It had been jemmied open! A desperate search soon revealed that all the money and travellers' cheques had been taken, not far short of 5,000 American dollars for which I had plans. How did the robber get past Rosco, my new Alsatian – Houdini had died – whose very unfriendly nature was widely known?

I made myself a strengthening cup of coffee, turned on the television news, and was informed that the notorious criminal Doctor Rat had escaped a few days ago yet again from Glendairy, Barbados' one and only prison, a vile Victorian institution. He had swum out to a motorboat anchored off the west coast, managed to start its engine, and headed westwards, probably towards St. Vincent a hundred miles away. However, the far-sighted owner had left only sufficient diesel in the tank to get the vessel to the nearby fuelling jetty. Consequently, a mile or two out to sea the engine stopped and the vessel began to drift.

In the meantime the boat's absence had been noted, the police alerted and a launch crewed by armed officers set sail to investigate. When they approached the boat wallowing in the swell, their loud-hailed 'Ahoy there' was answered by a volley of rifle shots from the cornered Doctor Rat. The police retaliation was lethal. They riddled the stolen boat with submachine gun fire until there was no further response. Cautiously, the news report went on, after firing several canisters of teargas into the vessel, the police officers boarded and found a very dead Doctor Rat, and scattered around him a quantity of bank notes and travellers' cheques.

If you don't ask you don't get, I thought. I gathered up the bills and the reservation book relating to the Easter weekend and took myself to the central police station. There I explained to a senior police officer why I thought it was Doctor Rat who had robbed me. Maybe some of the monies found aboard the stolen boat were mine? A constable wearing rubber gloves placed a pile of blood-soaked teargas-stained items on the inspector's desk. And lo! The cash receipts tallied with the monies found, even down to the float, and the signatures on the travellers' cheques matched names in my reservation book. I retrieved every penny I had lost. Overjoyed with the success of my visit, I extracted one of the less stained hundred dollar bills, and handed it to the senior policeman, requesting that it be added to the police fund.

As to how the infamous Doctor Rat had got past my infallible Cerberus, it transpired that he was a friend of my gardener Rupert, who was, of course, known to the dog.

As gardeners go, Rupert went.

In the polo world there are men and women called patrons. They are wealthy – they have to be; it is an extravagant sport – and they finance the polo teams in which they play. One such man was Ronnie Driver, who brought his team San Flamingo to Barbados. He saw me play, was impressed, introduced himself, and invited Chérie and me to England the next year. If I so desired, he would ask his team captain, Julian Hipwood, to coach me for a month at Cowdray Park. I did so desire! Julian and his brother Howard were the two best players in England. That was indeed something to look forward to.

Then the Leacocks struck yet again. 'We have something to show you at Sandy Lane,' they said. We met on the beach, where I saw my first windsurfer, something I had never even heard of. It had only been invented in 1968.

'How does it work?' I enquired. By way of answer Jack launched the contraption into the water, pushed a little way off the beach and clambered aboard. With difficulty he stood up, wobbling violently. Finally he pulled on a rope attached to the masthead, which brought the mast vertical, used the handrail to pull in the sail closer to his long thin body, and caught the wind. Jack fell off into the water. He climbed aboard again, pulled up the sail, went a yard or two, and fell in again. 'Now you have a go,' he said. I did so and fell in. Back on board, and fell in. And again. Each time, though, I went a little further. Whilst I was amusing everyone with my antics, a slender girl came hurtling towards the beach on her windsurfer. At the last moment she gibed about and accelerated away with insolent ease. I gritted my teeth. I'll be doing that in a few days, I told myself. And, by golly, I was!

I bought a second-hand windsurfer from the water sports shop at the Hilton Hotel and, by the time I had sailed it the seven miles back to Sandy Lane, I had mastered the technique. Thereafter I went everywhere on it, wearing around my neck a small watertight container to hold money so I could buy drinks at beach bars. The beautiful hawksbill turtles, undisturbed by my passing, surfaced to watch as I skimmed by. One hazard is that, if you sail, as I did, several hours a day in all weathers, you develop a crushingly powerful grip. Thus, when you shake hands unthinkingly, there is sometimes an agonised yelp. So I had to be careful. No sailing machine of any kind has given me more pleasure than my windsurfer. As a recreation, as a sport, there is nothing to compare for simplicity, low cost and sheer exhilaration. You are directly in touch with natural forces with no intermediary mechanisms. Like playing the classical guitar, when all interaction takes place between your fingertips and the strings – no keys, no levers, no hammers, no pedals. Both activities give me a profoundly satisfying feeling of oneness.

★

As part of our summer holiday Chérie and I were invited by Penelope and Bailey to stay with them in an apartment on the top floor of their Gloucester Avenue house. The household consisted of themselves, Cesar the Brazilian butler, and two enormous black dogs that slept on the black-carpeted stairs and were invisible; one often tripped over them. Models came and went. One was the beautiful Amanda Lear. I was hugely surprised when Bailey – he was always called simply Bailey – told me she had once been a man.

In the basement was a television room with a battery of three televisions permanently on. In another Bailey kept all the expensive equipment he needed for his profession. For insurance purposes security was tight, and one had to be careful to leave the house securely locked. Whilst we were there Bailey locked himself out and had to call the police. A policeman put a ladder up to the first floor window and began to climb. Halfway up he was seized by vertigo and completely froze, and could move neither up nor down. It took his colleagues some time to literally prise his fingers loose and guide him down to safety.

One day I needed a dentist and asked Bailey if he knew of one, explaining that I have always loathed the experience. He said he had just the man, and not to worry. I made an appointment and found myself in the dreaded torture chair. The dentist gave me an injection in my wrist and turned on a sort of electronic kaleidoscope which was hanging from the ceiling, projecting changing brightly-coloured liquid patterns. They became ever more mind-boggling and, by the time the dentist got to work, I wouldn't have minded had he removed my head, I was in such a state of bliss. I believe the shot he gave me was Pethidine – or was it Pentothal? It really doesn't matter. It worked.

Penelope and Bailey were immensely kind to Chérie and me, and we were surprised when, not long after we left, they split up. Did a parrot in the bathroom truly play a part?

Talking of birds, there was a sudden drop in the arrivals of my female birds of passage. The home team, in the form of lovely Chérie, offered somewhat stiff competition. I did not see Anna for a while, as she was occupied with her new baby. But I had found polo and windsurfing, and I was practising the classical guitar assiduously. Every morning began with an hour of comprehensive scales. While playing these I was distracted from time to time by Chérie standing behind me and pressing that divine body against my back, making concentration difficult.

Life, I thought, cannot be better than this.

CHAPTER TWENTY-FIVE

The Magistrate's Court

No piece about Barbados would be complete without a look at the magistrates' court. Here one sees real, unvarnished Barbadian life. One of the benefits of more than 300 years of British rule is Barbados' legal system. It is based on English common law, with a Chief Justice, attorneys-at-law – originally solicitors – and those called to the English Bar, Queen's Counsellors. Each of the Island's thirteen parishes has a magistrate's court which is subservient to the Supreme Court in Bridgetown, where the officers of the court are bewigged and be-robed as if at the Old Bailey. Since gaining Independence in 1966 Barbados has not sacrificed one inch of red tape or carpet.

To understand the court proceedings, a working knowledge of the Barbadian vernacular is essential. Often, well-spoken Barbadians – magistrates, priests in mid-sermon, or politicians – suddenly break into dialect, especially effective for a bit of rabble-rousing. Even Errol Barrow QC, PC, when he felt like doing some America-bashing, would lapse into the thickest accent. Many words are of Elizabethan origin, and when *A Midsummer Night's Dream* was performed at the Holders Festival, the English of that era came quite naturally from the mouths of local members of the cast.

The magistrates' courts issue liquor licences to businesses within their parish boundaries. Every December I applied for this essential document at the St. Thomas magistrate's court. The courthouse, which included the police station, was basic, furnished with the bare essentials – the gated dock, witness stand, benches of an uncompromising hardness, and, on a raised dais, the bench and magisterial armchair. The windows were opened wide since the compound was surrounded by dense tropical vegetation and airless. Everything was whitewashed. The surrounding buildings – stables with a horse-drawn fire engine but no horse, and dormitories – had remained unchanged for centuries. Under the building were the cells into which I peeped one day. Suffice it to say they should be avoided.

The licensing system was simple, with no complicated requirements concerning opening hours or their extension on special occasions. You simply paid a nominal sum which gave you the right to sell alcohol every hour of every day throughout the year.

But though simply given the licence was just as easily taken away, at the whim of the magistrate or the instigation of a vindictive neighbour. The presiding magistrate in St. Thomas, one Theodore Walcott, was in every way a character. Coming from an influential branch of his family, he had enjoyed a privileged education, being taken to school in a chauffeur-driven car in which he sat, until just before the morning assembly when he would join his fellow pupils. At lunchtime the chauffeur would return and little Theodore would eat his lunch in the car. He was then released for the afternoon classes and taken home immediately afterwards. He completed his education with a double First at Cambridge. Not surprisingly, he grew up to be a singular and egregious man. He acted and expressed himself exactly as he pleased, and obviously relished the power his position conferred on him. His word was law but in my experience he administered it fairly, if summarily. Perversely, he heard cases involving family violence, child abuse, attempted murder, arson, torture, bestiality and other forms of mayhem before we innocent applicants for liquor licences were brought before his Worship. We were left standing outside in the shade of a mango tree.

Eventually the massive station sergeant emerged to herd us in to stand in a row before the magistrate, like naughty children before a headmaster. To one side sat a skinny pinched-face couple who had never been known to smile. They were the representatives of the Barbados Temperance League – an unrewarding task if ever there was one – and the very incarnation of Disapproval. They attended every licensing court in every parish every year, opposing the granting of every licence. In a country where the cost of good rum was negligible, they had an uphill battle on their hands.

Mr Walcott would glare at us as if we were murderers who had somehow got away with it. Next he would ask the sergeant if there were any objections to his granting the licences. Bagatelle, incidentally, was the only restaurant in the entire parish; all the other licences were for rum shops. 'None, yo' Worship,' was the unchanging assertion.

'All licences granted,' Mr Walcott would announce. And we would go around the corner to the office of the clerk to the court to pay our annual fee. In return we got a paper to display on the licensed premises. Only once in twenty-eight years do I remember a change in the script. 'Any objections, sergeant?' Mr Walcott enquired.

'Yes, yo' Worship, we have an objection,' came the somewhat embarrassed reply.

'Objection? What objection?'

'Alleyne ent got no roof on he rum shop,' explained the sergeant. Mr Alleyne was assured by his Worship that, once he had a roof on his rum shop, the licence would be granted.

One December day, as I was sitting in the courtroom waiting for Mr Walcott to arrive, I heard the patter of feet on the wooden floor, and there was the man himself in a track suit and trainers. He stopped next to me. 'That was a good dinner at Bagatelle last night, Mr Nick,' he said, then jogged on to the robing room. A while later he emerged and the court, at the sergeant's command, rose. Mr Walcott seated himself in his big mahogany armchair and invited us to sit. 'Right, sergeant, bring de first case!'

'Yo' Worship,' hissed the officer. 'De feet!'

His Worship drew in a sharp breath. He had forgotten to put on his shoes. He retired to rectify the problem, and was soon back in his battered trainers and black magisterial robe, white shorts plainly visible underneath.

Once in a while I found myself before other magistrates' courts, always for traffic offences. On one such occasion I had to answer a charge of improper parking. I approached the station sergeant. 'Name and address?' he barked. I told him and he wrote down carefully in a large ledger: *Nick Hutson, Bagatelle, St. Thomas.* I was always 'Hutson' in Barbados.

'How you plead, man?' he asked.

In Barbados pleading 'not guilty' was seen as a waste of the court's time and was frowned on. By separating those pleading guilty from those not so pleading, the magistrate could rattle through the guilty, dishing out fines as he saw fit. With those out of the way, he could take his time venting his feelings on persons whom he saw as defying the court. The sergeant glanced up at me and resumed his laboured writing. I peered over his shoulder as he wrote in the next column: *White, stout, round-headed*. What? I'm five eleven, dammit, and I can't help the shape of my head. And as for *stout* – the man was a fool. Then I noted the entry before mine – *Eyes too close together* – and felt better.

Ian Morrison, my architect, had bought a Porsche, a vehicle totally unsuited to the Barbadian roads. On the whole Island in those days there was only one straight stretch of road, about a mile long, between Bagatelle and St. Thomas' church, where he could put his foot down for a few exhilarating seconds. This was the occasional site of the Island's only radar trap, so occasional that Ian forgot its existence. Thus he made regular visits to the court to answer speeding charges and would always plead guilty, write out a cheque, and go his merry way. On this occasion Ian pleaded guilty – yet again – and was reaching for his cheque book, when the magistrate stopped him. Mr Walcott had had enough. He had decided, he informed the court, to adjourn sentencing in this matter until the next day. In the meantime Ian was to be remanded in custody in Glendairy Prison! This lawless, convict-run Victorian institution was no place for a pretty rich white boy to be locked up overnight. Ian must have turned ashen. But spend a night in Glendairy he did, and I doubt he ever speeded again. Clever chap, Theodore Walcott.

Again I was before him, this time with two charges to answer – speeding and not stopping at a 'halt' sign. He was in summary justice mode and came straight to the point: 'Did you stop at de halt sign?'

'Er – well – I thought I did, your Worship.' Error! I was wasting the court's time.

'In my court,' he rasped, 'only de ladies can perambulate. Yes or no?'

'No.'

'Guilty as charged! Seventy dollar.' This was around fifteen pounds. The speeding offence was dealt with equally summarily.

After my case I stayed in the courtroom to hear some of the following cases. There was never a dull moment when Mr Walcott was presiding. Station sergeants were terrified of him, of his sharp tongue and considerable powers. How I enjoyed seeing those bullies cringe and stutter. One hard and fast rule for those in his court was to laugh if his Worship made a joke, especially when he made a dig at the policemen, which was often. On this occasion he surprised us all when he looked at his watch, rose to his feet and announced, 'I gone! Clyde Turney foun' me a nice Canadian girl on de *Jolly Roger* an' she sail at ten t'irty.'

Clyde Turney, who asked me to play *Spanish Romance* to his girlfriends at Bagatelle, had shares in the *Jolly Roger*, a fully-rigged motorised island schooner which, dressed up as a pirate ship with skull and crossbones at the masthead, cruised from Bridgetown down the west coast. Tickets were always paid for in cash, making it a floating gold mine. The price included a really worthwhile barbecue and as much rum punch as you could drink. As the consumption of alcohol went up, so inhibitions – if any – fell away. Mr Walcott's carnal expectations were likely to be fully realised.

When he threatened to leave the court the station sergeant was worried. 'What we do 'bout all dese udder people, yo' Worship?'

'Lock dey all up!' instructed his Honour comprehensively. It took some time and a deal of tact to persuade him to complete the court business before taking his pleasure.

One day I found myself in the premier division, the Central Court. Unlike the gloomy Old Bailey, the courtrooms in Bridgetown were open to the trade winds, airy and fresh. Lawyers in billowing black robes, looking like ravens, scurried about trailed by junior clerks with arms full of files. Passers-by would stop at the courtroom windows to listen – the lawyers liked a good audience.

The reason for my presence that day was not in any way criminal. Some time earlier I had agreed to act as trustee of a trust fund. My friend – who was extremely beautiful; I cannot resist a damsel in distress – had given me to understand that it was a simple matter. Her son, a beneficiary, was entitled in her opinion to the lion's share of the assets of the trust. Four other people had suddenly appeared out of the woodwork, thought otherwise and taken the matter to court. With difficulty I dredged up a shirt, tie, jacket and shoes, and called up Egbert, my favourite taxi driver, who duly arrived in his enormous American limousine. 'Where to, Boss?'

'The Central Court, if you please, Egbert,' I told him importantly.

'Boss, you get ketch?' he asked.

'No, no, no, Egbert,' I explained. 'I'm meeting the Chief Justice in his chambers. I am a Trustee,' proudly giving it a capital 'T'. In the event, I was joined by five QCs, one for each beneficiary. Heaven knows if any money was left over to distribute to those for whom the Trust was intended after their fees had been paid.

Every Friday morning at the Central Court was alimony time. The officers who dealt with it were lodged in an office on a sort of bridge spanning the car park. At eight o'clock the window was slid open and the would-be recipients gathered below in hopeful silence. In those days alimony payments were not automatically deducted from the man's pay packet as they are now. The officer would lean out of the window, glance at his list and shout, for example, 'Elfreda Alleyne!'

'Heah!' the chosen one would shout back.

'Nuffink fo' you,' he would tell her, and then maybe, 'Maureen Cumberbatch!'

'Heah!'

'Nuffink fo' you.'

And so it went on. The Barbadian male is notoriously unfaithful, more occupied with creating 'outside children', as those born out of wedlock are called. The women of Barbados, like those of Africa, are the salt of the earth, and I have enormous admiration for them. Nowadays many Barbadian mothers give their child their own name rather than that of the child's father. But this Friday morning all was not lost. 'Beverley Walcott!' shouted the alimony clerk.

'Heah!'

To huge applause from her gathered sisters, Beverley was told, 'Five dollar fo' you!'

Chapter Twenty-Six

Gary Sobers Moves Up, Chérie Moves On

In February 1975 there occurred in Barbados an event of great national importance for which the Queen visited the island. For the first time she would carry out an investiture somewhere other than Buckingham Palace by knighting, on the Garrison Savannah, the toast of the nation, Garfield 'Gary' St. Aubyn Sobers, possibly the greatest of cricket all-rounders. I knew him quite well. There was never a more modest self-effacing man of such prodigious talent. The Queen and the Duke of Edinburgh arrived in Bridgetown aboard the Royal Yacht *Britannia* – surely, together with Concorde, an iconic symbol of British excellence.

The event was covered by the national television service. The commentator was Jeanette Layne-Clarke. As the royal couple descended *Britannia's* gang-plank, she described in some detail what the Queen was wearing. Then she turned her attention to Prince Philip. 'De Dook,' she announced, 'is wearing de uniform o' de Admiral o' de Fleet, an' de pants match de jacket!' I doubt if any event lives on more passionately in the hearts of Barbadians than the sight of Gary Sobers, kneeling to be dubbed knight, in his own country, before his own people, by the Queen.

In those days British West Indians were decidedly pro-monarchy. In later years there was a swing towards republicanism, because they did not view kindly the marital antics of the next generation of royals, Prince Charles and his siblings – three out of four of whom were divorced. This was seen as setting a poor example. But I think it likely that Prince Harry's success in the

West Indies in 2012, especially in Jamaica, and the popularity of the Duke and Duchess of Cambridge and little Prince George, will go a long way to reversing this trend.

I missed a great opportunity that season. The world was beating a path to Bagatelle's door, and one evening Claudette Colbert brought as her guests Binkie Beaumont – who had tried to lure away my guitarist – and Bennett Cerf, big cheese at publishers Random House. I was invited to sit down and tell them something about myself. After I had answered a few questions, Mr Cerf said, 'Nick, I like you. We made Bob (Robert) Carrier. We can make you.' Idiot that I am, I did not follow up this offer.

In May Chérie and I left for England en route for Cowdray Park, where Ronnie Driver rented stables. He had around forty polo ponies looked after by two Argentinean players, twenty girl grooms and a stable manager, Mervyn Barnes. I was introduced to Julian Hipwood who played for England; his brother Howard was captain of the national team. Julian was to instruct me in the basics of the game. He put me on a training device called the wooden horse. Under his critical eye I spent hours on this infernal machine, bashing balls, while Julian chatted with the beauteous Chérie. In fact, I learned a great deal and greatly improved my hitting technique.

One morning Julian brought us breakfast in bed. He leered at Chérie and she smiled at him. After we had finished eating she threw herself upon me with passion. She was not making love to me but to Julian. Tchah!

On match days I was introduced to the rarefied world of polo at sublime Cowdray Park. The top players are often handsome, randy Argentines with enormous egos and extraordinary talents. Their ponies are the best money can buy, and they need to be, as one's ability to play the game depends up to 80% on them. Jet Rangers, the preferred helicopter model, were parked row upon gleaming row. Some players came by road. Michael Butler, who had backed the musical *Hair*, had a stretch limo with smoked-glass windows. As you walked past it, an exotic sweet-smelling smoke would wreath out of a partially-opened window, and giggles could be heard from within. Many marriages did not survive polo, since wives not infrequently went off with rich and dashing Argentine players, famously Ronald Ferguson's wife Susan – and Sarah's mother – who married Hector Barrantes, a big, handsome Argentine high-goal player. Every aspect of the game demanded money, money, and more money.

Putting aside these excesses, polo is the sport of kings and the king of sports. It requires horsemanship, skill, strength, tactical ability, and not a little courage, for it is very physical and injuries are rarely trivial. It began as a war game in 500 BC in Persia with a couple of hundred a side, fighting for possession of a sheep's head. It is now played all over the world, even in China. Its sponsors are apparently immune to, or even benefit from, global financial disasters.

Ronnie Driver introduced me to Viscount Cowdray, who owned an enormous amount of West Sussex – 40,000 acres or so. John Cowdray lost an arm at Dunkirk, but after the war, undaunted, he had an artificial limb made and played on at quite a high level. With his generosity and dedication, he was responsible for the revival of post-war British polo. Playing an evening match on the River ground at Cowdray Park, or watching, pint of Pimm's to hand, with the romantic burnt-out ruins of the original Cowdray House in the background, is an intoxicating experience.

I had made such good progress with Julian that, before I left England, Ronnie invited me to select any one of his ponies, which he would give me and have shipped out to Barbados. I chose a lovely mare, Estrellina. She had played at international level. She arrived in a large wooden crate on the deck of an Elder & Fyffe banana boat at the Deep Water Harbour in Bridgetown. I went with a borrowed horse box to collect her and take her to her stable at Holders plantation. She was led on deck, a sling was passed under her belly, then she was hoisted into the air and swung out over the harbour wall. At that moment the hooter sounded, announcing the noon lunch break. The winchman downed tools immediately and there poor Estrellina hung, swinging in the tropical midday sun, until the one o'clock hooter sounded. When at last her hooves touched the quayside, her legs all but buckled, and she was shaking with terror. The dock workers were unmoved.

Chérie did not pass unnoticed at the Club. She couldn't pass unnoticed anywhere. One day she was coming to watch me play but could not find a top she liked, so, in desperation, grabbed a loose-weave dishcloth, wrapping it around her and tying it in a knot behind.

After the game David Mount, the Club secretary, came up and fumed, 'It's disgraceful – have you *seen* what Chérie is wearing?'

'Yes, I know,' I said cheerfully. 'It's a dishcloth. She was a in a hurry.'

'I suggest you look more carefully!' I did and saw the problem, if problem it was – her nipples were peeping sexily through the holes in the loose weave.

On August 29th Ronnie Tree took the Great Table for a party to celebrate Ingrid Bergman's sixtieth birthday. Noel Charles offered to make the cake. I didn't even know he could bake – other than hash brownies – but I left him to it. Although there were twelve guests, the only ones I remember, apart from Ronnie and Marietta, were the actress and her pretty fifteen-year-old twins Isabella and Isotta. They seemed to exist as a family, quite apart from the other guests, as if they carried their own world around. I have never forgotten the feeling of being so completely excluded.

Chérie and I spent a lot of time with her family in St. Lucia, where her brother Christopher worked with father Geoff in their wrought iron business. We were all very close. Chérie was a very sensuous girl; having her as a lover was like having a Picasso or a Rembrandt – everybody wanted it, males and females alike. Women were important in her life, possibly more so than men. One girl, Dany, was very influential, and came between us from time to time. But Chérie did what came naturally to her. As a child of nature she was without malice and devoid of greed. Her material needs were minimal. Her paintings were intensely feminine and ethereal, often depicting pale green hills and valleys shrouded in mist, sinuous purple rivers and brightly coloured birds. This was her secret world which satisfied her undemanding needs. An aura of calm protected her from a materialistic world.

But our time together was not to last. Chérie decided to move on and live with some handsome but lazy trainee legal beagle. I really cannot blame her. When we discussed her leaving, she said that she had been hoping I would ask her to marry me, something I had not done; I knew myself too well. I knew she wanted to have a child and I cannot imagine a better mother. But my own dear mother and father had demonstrated what it takes to be good parents, and I did not believe I had that in me. I was far too selfish and self-indulgent. There was, I suppose, always the chance that, were I to become a father, I might change. But I was not prepared to risk a broken family and the attendant misery.

Cherie leaving Bagatelle was a terrible wrench. She had added so much to my life, my family adored her, and she was instrumental in Bagatelle's success. To this day I do not know if our marriage would have worked. Without the light of her presence, her peace and transforming beauty, my home was terribly empty and I was miserable for quite a long time. She finally married Renato Venturi, by whom she had a daughter, Lianna.

A few years after Chérie left I received a letter. Her handwriting on the envelope, which I had been hoping to see since the day she left, set my heart pounding. The letter contained devastating news. Her brother Christopher had been installing security bars in a bank in Castries, the capital of St. Lucia. Unfortunately he had drilled into a live power cable, received a heavy electric shock and collapsed. Nobody knew the appropriate first aid so he never recovered consciousness. Chérie worshipped her brother, an especially beautiful, kind man. It was an unimaginable loss and my heart went out to her.

Chérie still lives in St. Lucia, with Lianna close by, painting ethereal scenes giving glimpses into her secret world. And she lives in my heart and will do forever.

Chapter Twenty-Seven

Perfect Shipmates

In 1976 Barbados celebrated 350 years of unbroken British rule. The horrors of a particularly cruel slavery notwithstanding, this was a defining factor in the conservative character of black Barbadians. No other Caribbean country can claim this continuity and it is what sets Barbados apart from other island states. The transition from colony to independent nation was, as a consequence, commendably uneventful and smooth. It was business as usual.

For me, this was going to be another busy year, but I was not prepared for the first event. Tired of Chase Manhattan Bank, I had negotiated a fresh mortgage with Barclays Bank DCO. It was a good deal, and I went to New York for a few days at the Plaza Hotel by way of celebration. It was January and bitterly cold. There were excellent restaurants in the hotel. Trader Vic's served extravagantly garnished Polynesian cocktails, though not of the same potency as the lethal Black Power at the Bagatelle; at the Oyster Bar I could enjoy Oysters Rockefeller followed by Lobster Thermidor; in the Oak Room the black and blue *Tournedos Rossini* was succulent and memorable. I one evening braved the extreme cold to dine at the *sans pareil* Sichuan Pavilion, which uniquely boasted two Chinese chefs who, before the revolution, had been classed as of Superior Rank. It was here that I tasted Bang Bang Rabbit and Whole Deep Fried Sweet and Sour Bass for the first time – and not the last.

I returned to Barbados a couple of days later, refreshed and ready for the Season. Arriving at Bagatelle, I climbed the steps to my apartment, but the door was padlocked, with a chain through the louvres. I looked around and noticed a scruffy fellow sitting under one of the bearded fig trees, with a heavy stick resting across his bony knees. I went down the steps and approached him. He was there, he told me, on the instructions of the receiver and was to admit no-one. The receiver? What about my brilliantly negotiated new mortgage with which I had secured fresh financing?

I was very cross and informed the man that this was my home, and, unless he opened it to me immediately, I might have to break his scrawny neck. He must have believed me because he let me in without arguing and ambled off down the drive.

I found out what had happened quickly enough. Having been informed that Barclays had agreed to my mortgage, Chase Manhattan demanded the funds to pay off their outstanding loan to me. Sorry, said Barclays, we haven't yet cleared the title so you will have to wait. No, said Chase Manhattan, you have already had the deeds for six months; pay up or we will foreclose immediately. Barclays refused, and foreclose they did. It was soon sorted out, but not before the official receiver, a notoriously grasping chartered accountant, had charged me the earth.

Not long afterwards I told Donald and Cherry Marshall, who had by now become intimate friends, what had happened. In no time at all Donald had agreed to buy shares in Bagatelle. It was a vast relief to have the business properly capitalised, but that was only the start.

We had always got on well ever since they came to the Bagatelle on their honeymoon. Cherry was beautiful, and her laughter filled the room. As a pianist she could have reached concert standard had she not met and married Donald. His business, based in the World Trade Center, involved moving huge sums of money around the globe and taking a tiny percentage on each transaction. He was enormously successful. His manners were impeccable, his charm huge, his generosity limitless, his compassion boundless. Soon two boys were born, first Scott and then Mark, and it was my joy to watch them grow up. Donald was the perfect partner but, in truth, Cherry was part of it too.

On July 14th the country lost a great friend and benefactor when Ronnie Tree died. I have already written of his immeasurable contribution to Barbados during the thirty years he had lived there. At the same time I, too, had lost a man whom I loved, admired and respected. Towards the end of his life Ronnie suffered a stroke which deprived him of the power of speech. A speech was engaged, a compassionate man named Ben who, incidentally, was a talented wawa guitarist. His treatment was effective and Ronnie made good progress. I quite frequently went down to Heron Bay at sunset to be with him, and we talked as best we could. The fact that he was precious Penelope's father made this even more rewarding, for their spirits were entwined, and I felt even closer to her. I have not seen Penelope for years, during which time we have spoken only once, but that makes no difference.

One evening at the Bagatelle I found myself in conversation with a feisty woman with wild red hair and a Texan accent, and an archetypal Englishman, slim and moustached, probably with a military background. They introduced themselves as Billy Mitchell and John Wainwright. They were on their way back to Mustique where they both lived and worked. The conversation turned to an event being much discussed in social circles, Colin Tennant's fiftieth birthday party due to take place at the end of November. Guests were coming from all over the world, and anyone who was anybody wanted to be invited, but numbers were strictly limited. For the fortunate English contingent, air fares and accommodation were included in the invitation. The party theme was The Field of the Cloth of Gold, and Princess Margaret was to be guest of honour. Perhaps I would like to be invited, they enquired? And how! They would arrange for me to receive an invitation. I would stay with Billy at her house, Firefly. The party was scheduled to last almost a week. A few weeks later my 'gold'-encrusted invitation arrived.

But that was still several months in the future. One day in August there was a rattling of my front door, which I opened to reveal my old muckers Johnny Perez Canto and the ever-volatile Sylvia. They were in a party of Venezuelans who had flown themselves up from Caracas to give their children a holiday. But the Perez Cantos had no children and were bored. Could they stay with me for a while? Of course! On television that evening we saw images of volcanic activity from La Grande Soufrière on the French island of Guadeloupe, some 250 miles north-north-west of Barbados. The western part of the island was being forcibly evacuated by troops, as an eruption was possible. Johnny and I looked at each other. We did not even have to speak. We had to go and investigate. We were both familiar with those extraordinary images in *Life* magazine and *Paris Match* of eruptions with vast amount of flaming material being flung as high as 10,000 feet. If, we mused, we were to circle Soufrière above 10,000 feet, and the volcano did erupt, imagine the pictures we would have to sell to the international press. Johnny had his Beech Baron 55 parked at the airport. Starting with full tanks, we would have over an hour over the island before having to head back for home.

We actually managed to convince ourselves of the feasibility of this idiotic plan. The next morning we set off, and in under two hours were over Basse-Terre, the western part of Guadeloupe. Military vehicles were moving about, clearly visible. There was not a civilian to be seen; sixty thousand of them, much against their will, had been evacuated to Grande-Terre in the east. We climbed to 11,000 feet, levelled off and began to circle, looking down into the very innards of the grumbling, smoking volcano. There was a stench of sulphur. We readied our cameras and waited for the eruption. It did not come. If it had I would not, of course, be writing this. Aeroplanes flying above erupting volcanoes are unlikely to survive. After an hour, it was time to head back to Barbados. *Life* magazine, *Paris Match* and their readers would have to manage without our priceless photos.

I had seen the famously eccentric Colin Tennant in Hazell's bar in St. Vincent six years earlier, but had never met him. Mustique, which he bought in 1958, was a small island – just over two square miles – mosquito-infested and arid; its only inhabitants were fishermen, and its heyday, farmers when sugar was valuable long gone. I knew something about Colin from Oliver Messel, who worked with him on the Island.

Colin's inspired wedding present to Princess Margaret and Tony Armstrong-Jones, a plot of land on Mustique, attracted international attention. *Paris Match* had adored Princess Margaret ever since her doomed romance with Peter Townsend, and chronicled her every move. As I have learned from Nicholas Courtney's excellent biography of Colin, *Lord of the Isle*, she could be astute. When told of his gift, rather than expressing overwhelming gratitude, she enquired whether or not a house came with the land. What could he say, poor fellow, but yes?

I flew in on the eve of Colin's birthday party, to find the small parking apron crowded with light aeroplanes, most of them with Venezuelan registration marks. Billy Mitchell met me in her jeep and drove me to her home well above the coast.

Some years ago Mitch Mitchell, whose family owned much of the Mitchell and Butler Brewery, was a well-off young man-about-town who liked to drive racing cars. At the outbreak of war he joined the Royal Air Force and was sent to train as a fighter pilot in Texas, where the weather was always good. There he met Billy, a girl who claimed one-eighth Cherokee blood. He took her back to Cheltenham as his wife. With her flaming red hair, hourglass figure and Texan drawl – not to mention her tender age – the new Mrs Mitchell scandalised the sleepy country town. In time, Billy and Mitch were divorced, and she used a part of her settlement to have built in Hong Kong a yacht, inexplicably named *Nosegay*. Accompanied by her Swedish seafaring boyfriend Bo, her daughter Suzie and baby granddaughter Luna, she sailed across the Indian and Atlantic Oceans to the West Indies, finally dropping anchor off Mustique.

Billy fell in love with the Island and bought a plot of land which overlooked Britannia Bay and the lurking Montezuma reef. She designed and built there Firefly, a lovely airy house ideally suited to tropical living. It was to this house that we were now on the way.

She took over the running of the Cotton House and employed Basil Charles, a young Vincentian, whose life had been saved by Hugo Money-Coutts in the aftermath of a bad motorcycle accident, as barman. Mustique was taking shape and Basil was to be one of its principle shapers. Sanity was not the long suit amongst the denizens of Mustique; Basil Charles, however, was impressively sane. Having started at the Cotton House, he has gone from success to success. His is a blend of ability, hard work, charm, imagination, business sense, and financial honesty. He is sincerely devoid of racism, a rare quality. Yet when I think of him what stands out is his unfailing generosity. Nobody else has benefited more from the success of Mustique than Basil, but then nobody, Colin excepted, has contributed more to that success than he has.

★

Colin's birthday party was a rave. Those whom he had invited considered themselves fortunate. It was a very hot ticket. There were lunch parties, dinner parties, and boating excursions every day and every night. The ravishing Dana Gillespie, who would do anything for a chocolate mousse, sang at the Cotton House.

In the dying embers of one soirée I spotted a most exotic Chinese creature, with hair down to her shapely bum, dancing with a man – an artist, she told me later. But I wanted her, so I rather elbowed him aside and took her in my arms where she simply melted. She was called Val Lau.

The next morning I woke up *chez* Billy with this gorgeous girl next to me. Over breakfast of papaya and lime juice we decided that we needed some time alone, away from the crowded parties, so I flew us up to Martinique, where we stayed at the Bakoua Hotel, only venturing out of our beachfront room for the occasional swim and the delectable Créole cuisine. Our bed was covered in golden glitter, since, as Colin's party had gold as its theme, gold was sprayed everywhere. Wherever we had been – cars, beds, beaches, aeroplanes – sparkled.

We returned, refreshed and in love – again, I know – to rejoin the revellers on Mustique, looking forward to The Big One, the Caribbean Spectacular at Macaroni Beach. Gold gleamed everywhere in the light of innumerable *flambeaux*. Guests entered, one after the other, under a golden triumphal arch to the applause of fellow guests. Everyone – we thought! – had made their entrance, except the star turns, Princess Margaret, to be followed by Colin, our host. We waited, but there was an unaccountably long delay and we were getting restless. Then all was explained. Through the triumphal arch there emerged into the light of the *flambeaux* – guess who? – Bianca Jagger. I'm sure she looked a million dollars but I don't remember because (a) we were all hopping mad that she, a commoner to boot, had made us wait, and (b) she was immediately totally eclipsed by Princess Margaret in a shimmering gold kaftan and turban. What took my breath away was the enormous flawless diamond which burned fiercely over her left breast. Macaroni rocked to enthusiastic affectionate applause.

Then our eyes turned back to the golden arch, anticipating the entry of a man whose dream we were all living, a seemingly impossible vision – to create out of a waterless mosquito-infested island a place like no other. Now a palanquin was carried into the torch-lit arena, supported at each corner by tall handsome black men in gold cloaks and codpieces – coconut shells sprayed gold – their splendid muscular bodies oiled and shining. Sitting atop, cross-legged and dressed as the finest nabob under the sun, wearing a fabulous bejewelled turban, a smiling Colin waved regally to the manner born. He was indeed King of Mustique, as Princess Margaret dubbed him, surrounded by admiring and adoring subjects. This climax to an unforget-table birthday party represented the realisation of Colin's most extravagant dreams and exotic imaginings. From what I have read since, I suspect it was the climax of his entire life. Maybe it was this very realisation that sent him slightly off the rails, searching in vain for another unique triumph. He was to go on and create another resort on nearby St. Lucia. But that night on his beloved Mustique was his finest hour. If only he had stopped there.

It was with sadness that I left the next day, but I was determined to return as soon as possible. Before taking off for Barbados I invited Val, who lived in Trinidad, to join me at the Bagatelle. She said she would be with me early in the New Year.

CHAPTER TWENTY-EIGHT

Val Comes Alongside

Val timed her arrival perfectly a few weeks later in mid-January, in the lull between Christmas and the really high season. She did not come empty-handed; she brought a complete edition of the *Encyclopædia Britannica*!

Billy Mitchell, my hostess at Colin's birthday party, owned the Mustique village store which sold a bit of everything. She asked if, for a price, I could fly to her goodies from Martinique. This fitted well with my own plans for my new venture, the Gourmet Shop, which I was to stock with French goodies unavailable in Barbados – pâtés, terrines, Normandy butter, mussels, Perrier-Jouët Champagne (especially for Robert Sangster), French cheeses (Reblochon for Robert as well) – even bread and croissants – which I would fly in. Returning to Barbados via Mustique would be no problem. I always enjoyed visiting the Island. As for Billy, she had a wealthy, discerning, but captive clientele; the cost was irrelevant.

This meant fairly frequent visits to Mustique, and I came to know its inhabitants rather better. Colin was usually there. Probably I knew him at his finest, basking in the success of his birthday party. I always found him amusing, charming and waspish. Apart from the odd manifestation, his eccentricity stayed on the right side of sanity.

On one occasion, as I was enjoying the renowned lobster with garlic butter at Basil's Bar, Colin joined me. As I ate he kept pinching bits of lobster to pop in his mouth. Charlie, his son – sad, sad Charlie – also sat down, his eyes wild and restless. He produced a packet of cigarettes and tipped them out, inspecting each minutely until one made him smile. He lit it, and chucked the rest on the floor. Then he headed to the entrance, but stopped apprehensively at the threshold. He put a foot across it, then pulled it back. He tried again and retreated. He must have tried ten times to cross that spot which he viewed with such fear. All of a sudden he threw himself beyond the entrance and departed. This behaviour, I am told, was a symptom of his cocaine addiction.

As we finished lunch Colin told me that a Mrs Bosenkamp had invited him to look around her new house. Would I care to join him? This lady had been an au pair *chez* Mr Bosenkamp in the States, but before long had deposed the incumbent, becoming herself Mrs Bosenkamp the Second. Nice work! It was evident that Colin was not mad about the current Mrs B., and the way-over-the-top home was not to his impeccable taste at all, but he was his usual charming self. We found ourselves in the gold-tapped bathroom where our guide, a far cry from the slender au pair of yesteryear, went all coy and said in a little-girl voice, 'Von day I am going to bathe myself in meelk.'

For Colin this opportunity was irresistible. 'Asses' milk?' he enquired archly.

At the centre of the web of intrigue which was the social life of the Island was Cassandra, who manned the telephone switchboard. She had a soft, inviting voice which made one want to meet her. She knew everyone's movements. If I rang for Billy from Barbados, Cassandra was quite likely to say, 'She's having tea with Princess Margaret. She ought to be home by six. I'll tell her you called.'

For a long time, Cassandra only was a voice. Then one day, I was playing backgammon at Basil's Bar with Mario Spinella, an Italian architect. He was designing a Japanese-style house with paper walls and blocks of wood for a pillow for Mick Jagger. Kibitzing our game was a very pretty girl who only had eyes for Mario. He was apparently immune to her charms; I was hers for the asking. I asked Mario to introduce me. 'Mr Nick, this is Cassandra,' he said. 'You've probably spoken to her. She handles the island telephone exchange.' So this was the divine body which went with the voice.

As we played, Mario indicated with a jerk of his thumb that I should look over the side of the bar, which extended on wooden legs over the beach and the limpid Caribbean. There on the sand, quite alone, was Princess Margaret, wearing a black one-piece bathing costume, lying on her right side. As she turned to her left, the structured peaks moved first upright then over to the left, to be followed by a veritable avalanche of splendid Hanoverian bosom. It was a remarkable sight. I waited for a while in case she turned the other way. No such luck.

Another resident of Mustique was Dr Charlie Manning, a Barbadian. It was he who in the early days had organised draining the swamp where mosquitoes bred, thereby rendering the island habitable. Dr Manning was the only source of on-Island of medical advice and treatment, since the closest hospital was on St. Vincent, which meant a bumpy boat trip or an expensive aeroplane ride to get there. For more serious emergencies the patient would have to be taken to Barbados. His was an important role.

One evening, just after dusk, I was talking to Marilyn, who managed Billy's village shop across the road from Basil's Bar, when we heard a motorcycle approaching, then an urgent honking followed by a crash, as of metal on tarmac. I dashed down to find a man lying beside the machine he had evidently been riding. Blood was spurting in an arc from his wrist. Obviously he had severed an artery, possibly on the shattered red rear light. I ripped off my T-shirt – a treasured present from Penelope Tree – found a stick, and created a tourniquet around his upper arm, turning it until the bleeding stopped. A bystander offered to drive us both to the doctor's surgery, where Charlie, forewarned by Marilyn – via Cassandra of course! – was waiting. We laid the injured man on the examination couch, and Charlie discovered that the broken glass had also severed a tendon. He administered a local anaesthetic and set about fishing out the upper end of the tendon, which had retreated into the man's forearm. Eventually, with a little assistance from me – second MB failed – he managed to reattach it to its distal end, which had retreated into his hand.

Some time after returning to Barbados I called Charlie for an update and was told that the patient had recovered and regained the full use of his hand. Well done, Charlie! I had harboured faint hopes that there might be some words of thanks – after all, we had saved the man's hand and probably his life. But my hopes were soon dashed. The prevailing sentiment amongst the locals was that, if he had been a white man, he would have been flown immediately to Barbados. The fact that Mustique's runway was unlit, therefore unusable after dark, counted for nothing. Ah, well.

In 1977 the Queen carried out the Caribbean leg of her international Silver Jubilee Tour on board the Royal Yacht *Britannia*, accompanied by Prince Philip. As her last official port of call was Barbados, it seemed reasonable for her, in a private capacity, to visit her sister Princess Margaret on nearby Mustique. Accordingly, on 30th October the royal yacht dropped anchor in Britannia Bay off Basil's Bar. The visit was a major event and Colin and Anne Tennant, and the inhabitants, made them feel very welcome indeed.

Later that night *Britannia* set sail for Barbados, where Concorde was waiting to take the royal couple back to the United Kingdom. This would be the Queen's first supersonic flight. I was on the Sandy Lane beach that morning when this graceful bird, her nose dipped, coming to pick up her royal passengers, idled down the West Coast, her Rolls-Royce engines growling powerfully. British breasts swelled with pride and we all cheered wildly. In December 1989, when scheduled flights began, the supersonic aeroplane left London Heathrow at 9.30 am and arrived in Barbados three hours and fifty minutes later. How proud Errol Barrow would have been! The cost of a ticket was £10,000 each way, but that proved no deterrent. It was important that people knew you had arrived in this unique flying machine, but it would be vulgar to mention it, so a code was established; you simply said, 'We flew in on Saturday morning.' No other international flights arrived at that time of the day. Being one of only a handful of scheduled Concorde destinations was a fine feather in the cap for Barbados, a third world country with a population of a meagre 250,000 souls.

The following year, 1980, I had a girlfriend called Jan, a flight attendant on Concorde. When she learned that I was to fly on Concorde from London to New York, unbeknownst to me, she arranged that I was on a flight on which her friend, Captain David Brister, was pilot-in-command. Just before take-off, a flight attendant asked me, without any explanation, to follow her. She led me forward down the narrow aisle, opened the door onto the flight deck, and invited me to enter. Me! In the holy of aviation holies, the flight deck of Concorde, just before take-off. There I found the engineer, the co-pilot and David, who introduced himself and shook my hand briefly; at this time the flight deck crew had an immensely heavy workload of routine checks. He indicated the trainee pilot's seat behind his, and I strapped myself in. We were cleared for take-off, and David shoved forward a fistful of throttles, unleashing 152,200 pounds of thrust. The acceleration pressed me back into my seat. We seemed to be going extremely fast over the ground before he raised the nose and we were airborne. 'Christ!' said David. 'Another bollocking for noise.' He explained that the Noise Abatement Society monitored every Concorde take-off on behalf of those living close to Heathrow. Today, he said, the air was still, so he had to use full power, a noisy affair. As Concorde had no wing flaps this meant that we had been going over the ground at 250 mph to attain the necessary airspeed. For a Jumbo it would have been 140 mph.

I was still in that seat when, 4° west of Greenwich and clear of the west coast of Ireland, we went supersonic – Mach 1.0 – while still in the climb! I could hear applause from the passenger cabin where there was a speed read-out. Finally, at a little under 60,000 feet, we levelled out, at which height seeing the marked curvature of the earth made one feel like an astronaut. Before returning to my seat, I tried to thank David for an experience beyond price. If you read this, David, thank you again for giving me one of the great experiences of my life. I would thank Jan differently.

Val and I were bracing ourselves for the usual New Year's Eve madness when there was a knock on the door, and there were Johnny and Sylvia, grinning sheepishly. It was always a pleasure to see them and the guest room was at their disposal. Val and I had been invited to Basil's New Year's Day party at Macaroni Beach, so I telephoned and asked if I might bring my friends. Unfailingly he said yes, he looked forward to meeting them. Never was there a more generous host.

The flight plan was for me to take off first, and then Johnny would catch up in his much faster aeroplane. His Baron landed at quite a high speed so I warned him he would have to be careful landing on Mustique's short and tricky airfield. No problem, he assured me, he knew it well. At about noon I arrived over Mustique. No sign of the Baron. Then Johnny's plaintive voice came over the radio. 'Where's the runway? I can't find it.' I searched around, and finally spotted Johnny circling an island some six miles away. 'Johnny,' I told him over the radio, 'you are over Bequia. We're over Mustique, six miles to the south-east.'

'Oh yes, of course, I see you. Be with you in a moment.'

'I'll go in first and show you the way,' I radioed. 'Remember, it's a short field for a Baron. I recommend a steep approach.'

'Roger. See you on the ground.' This could be amusing.

I landed and parked, then Johnny banged his aeroplane down hard on the threshold and braked heavily in clouds of dust, before taxiing to the apron. Sylvia did not enjoy flying over the sea in a light aeroplane – she was by no means alone in this – even though it did have two engines and Johnny was an experienced pilot. She preferred Jumbos. This had been a hairy landing. As her feet touched the asphalt, her knees buckled and she clutched the wing. Johnny passed her a hip flask, from which she took a couple of healthy swigs, and slowly her legs straightened. The intrepid pilot descended nervously. 'Oh yes,' Sylvia mimicked Johnny. 'I know Mustique *so* well. *Cojones!*' she spat. 'You didn't even know where it *was!*' They barely spoke to each other before leaving for Caracas later that afternoon.

Val and I had a marvellous time, for Basil's parties on Macaroni Beach were always lively affairs. Colin introduced us to many people, some of whom had been Diner customers. I met a lady with my favourite surname in the world, Lady Jane Vane-Tempest-Stuart. Colin also introduced me to someone I had admired for years, the concert pianist Moura Lympany. 'It's because of you,' I told her, 'that I play the piano. We had a record at home of you playing Chopin's *Fantaisie-Impromptu*. It so haunted me that I took up the piano, and have never stopped playing since. Thank you.'

She was obviously touched by this, and we chatted for a while. The next morning I went alone to Basil's Bar for breakfast. Miss Lympany was sitting with some friends, her back to me. A little while later she stood up, and sat down at a nearby piano. The instrument was a wreck, corroded by the salt air, and I doubt if it boasted one complete octave. In tune it surely was not. Nevertheless, this world-renowned pianist played the *Fantaisie-Impromptu*, not the simplest piece, on it. When she finished I applauded, and she turned and recognised me. Her eyes widened, for she was genuinely astonished. I *know* she was not aware of my being there, listening to her playing. To this day, recalling that strange event gives me goose-flesh.

Basil was held in awe by the locals, for his was a particularly charismatic personality. Some believed him to be an Obeah man – the southern Caribbean equivalent of voodoo – who, possessed of magic powers, flew up and down the Caribbean in the form of a goat.

I have often wondered if Basil might go into politics, since he has much to offer the nation of St. Vincent and the Grenadines, especially in the field of tourism. He enjoys the vibrant life on Mustique in the winter season, and in the summer the hospitality of friends and admirers all over the world. He is a very popular and knowledgeable guest, and a great ambassador for his country.

CHAPTER ONE

An Eventful Year

Early in 1978 Peter and Debbie Barbor, long-time friends from Yorkshire, visited Barbados. They were keen windsurfers, so we decided to spend a couple of days in Martinique at the Hôtel Bakoua. Since the winds blew out of the east across the island and over the bay, the waves had no fetch and so could not build up. The result was strong winds and relatively calm water – ideal conditions for windsurfing at speed. On my last visit to Martinique I had noticed lying on the beach at the hotel water sports something I had never seen before, a three-masted windsurfer. Such a vessel promised exciting sailing. All one needed were three experienced windsurfers.

We arrived at the hotel, and were soon galloping down to the beach. Yes, the craft which I had been raving on about to my friends, was still there. Launching it, and getting us all on board without capsizing, was not easy, but we made it, and set sail. After half an hour of trial and error and numerous duckings, we got the hang of it and were soon slapping across the bay, at speeds pushing 30 knots.

The rest of that year saw tremendous comings and goings on-Island. The Monty Python team had rented Heron Bay. They were working on *The Life of Brian* and hoping that the impresario Bernard Delfont would help finance it. Unfortunately, Mr Delfont had his eye on a peerage and declined, thinking the controversial subject matter might damage his chances. Penelope was staying in the Pink Cottage with her husband-to-be, Ricky Fataar, a musician with the Beach Boys, who was to be the father of their daughter, Paloma.

Verna Hull called one day to say that her house guest, Princess Margaret, would like to dine with a friend at the Bagatelle, but would rather I did not broadcast the fact. Assured of my discretion, she made a reservation for guest and Roddy Llewellyn. The Princess arrived first and Mr Blackman made her favourite cocktail, which involved a yellow liquor called Galliano; we always kept (an impossibly tall) bottle of it just in case. It languished; nobody else drank it. While she awaited her unpunctual dining partner, I gave her the menu, personalised of course. She glanced at it and said, 'Mr Hudson, Roddy is a *proper* singer, not a *pop* singer.' Roddy had recently sung with Petula Clark, and I had written that he was 'the world's newest pop star'. Eventually Roddy arrived, having kept his royal paramour waiting for at least quarter of an hour. There were no reprimands, just a radiant, loving smile. This was not surprising since, although she could on occasion be quite a stickler, she was so mad about the man but he could do no wrong. Her personal detective may have been hiding in the bushes but I never saw him.

Gay Beresford invited me to join her and her new boyfriend, Ivor Boofty, for a day or two at La Semana Hotel on the island of St. Martin. It was a three-and-a-half hour flight, during which I would fly just to the east of the Lesser Antilles chain, keeping the islands in sight.

As I approached Montserrat I experienced, for the first time in my life, symptoms of vertigo, which was unexpected as I have always loved heights, showing off up trees or high in the rigging of the *Worcester*. I descended to 2,000 feet so that, if I found myself unable to continue, I could make straight for the nearest island. In the event, the symptoms went away, I arrived safely on St. Martin, and a good time was had by all.

On the return journey I decided to drop in to St. Lucia and see Chérie, who still put my heart rate up. She had a boutique in a hotel managed by my friend Alex Oostenbrink. That evening we dined with him and his brother, a doctor who specialised in aviation medicine. I told him of my experience.

'What was your altitude?'

'Ten thousand feet,' I told him.

'For how long?'

'Three hours.'

Unhesitatingly he said 'vertigo', brought on by acute anoxic anaemia – too little oxygen in my blood – as a result of flying for too long in that rarefied atmosphere. I would bear this in mind in future.

Mick Jagger was on-Island and came, as usual, to Bagatelle. He is cricket-mad, with a considerable knowledge of the game and its history. Even in the Seventies, years ahead of his time, he was looking into the possibility of putting on limited-over matches in covered arenas in the USA. The Australians were about to play the West Indies in Barbados. He wondered if I might be able to get tickets for us. These were the days of Richards, Greenidge, Haynes, Lloyd, Kallicharan, Roberts, Croft and Garner, so tickets for Test matches were rare as hens' teeth. But thanks to Margaret and Jack Leacock, members at the Kensington Oval ground, I was able to buy two.

The match was notable for two events. First one of the umpires made a decision that infuriated the crowd, who threw beer bottles onto the field; an old man, ashamed of such behaviour, courageously went out under a hail of bottles to gather up the missiles. The miscreants were shamed into inactivity. Then the very fast Australian bowler Jeff Thompson became incensed – I know not why – when bowling at the legendary batsman Viv Richards. Tommo's fury was such that he achieved what no other bowler had ever done – he had Richards ducking for cover and soon had him caught for twenty-three. But it was to no avail, for the West Indies won by nine wickets. The local newspaper the next day carried on its front page a big photo of my face and the back of Mick's head. It was captioned: '*Rock star Mick Jagger at the Kensington Oval*'.

One day the telephone rang. It was J.M.G. 'Tom' Adams, the Prime Minister, who asked in his polished BBC-trained voice to make a reservation. I seized my chance. 'While you're on the line, sir,' I said, 'I have applied for citizenship of Barbados and heard nothing back.'

'How long ago?'

'About three months, I would guess.'

'I'll look into it, Mr Nick.'

A few days later the Prime Minister arrived with his dining partner. I greeted them under the arch at the restaurant entrance. The Prime Minister, smiling, offered me his hand. 'Good evening, Citizen Hudson,' he said. Shortly after this I received my Barbadian passport, of which I am so proud. I do feel I had earned it.

One of my fellow amateur pilots was Art Taylor, whose misguided use of a truck alternator in his light aeroplane was so nearly to do for Jeremy Sisnett. Art had arrived in Barbados from Australia by way of South Africa, crewing on a yacht to cross the Atlantic. Somehow he obtained a work permit to teach surfing and build surfboards. When he launched his first board at Accra Beach, it sank! Undaunted, he started a business making beachwear. His Beach Baggies shorts were such a success that he widened his product and customer range, eventually selling to other islands. At first he used the Flying Club Cessna 180 as his delivery vehicle, and then decided he needed his own aircraft. He arranged to buy a second-hand Piper Arrow in Tamiami, Florida, and asked me help him fly it the 1,600 miles back to Barbados, which would take about three days. Art hired a professional pilot to get us through the heavily-trafficked Miami airspace as far as Puerto Rico. After leaving Nassau in the Bahamas, we headed for the Turks and Caicos Islands. We took, like Jeremy was to do, the 'VFR over the top' route, and, using our ADF (automatic direction finder), headed south. Beneath us was a sea of white cumulus cloud, but above was clear blue sky. The ADF works on the simple principle that you dial in the radio frequency of a transmitter located on the target destination – in our case the Turks and Caicos Islands. The needle always points to that transmitter and therefore your destination. You simply follow the needle. After a calculated period of time you reduce power, descend through the cloud base, and there is your destination – in theory. We descended at the planned time, emerged from the clouds, expecting to see the Turks and Caicos directly ahead. But like Jeremy, all we saw was blue Caribbean in all directions, a singularly nasty feeling. Our professional pilot became quite excited and, in his anger, bashed the ADF instrument on the control panel. The dial needle immediately moved to point ten degrees off to the left of dead ahead. The explanation was simple. Due to engine vibration, the ADF had backed out of its power socket, turning off the device and rendering the reading meaningless. Fortunately, we had not gone far off course and soon were landing on the island of Caicos. Two days later, via Puerto Rico and Martinique, we made it safely to Barbados.

Ray Carroll, before leaving to take charge of the Grosvenor House Hotel in London, threw a party at the Bagatelle and Mr Nick's for the entire staff of the Sandy Lane Hotel and its numerous associated enterprises – all of them! We agreed that a price per head – something in the order of BDS$34 – would be fair. Ray would greet everyone personally at the entrance to the Bagatelle – that is the sort of manager he was – and I would note the numbers. The first guests arrived at seven o'clock and kept coming and coming. I was desperately multiplying the numbers by $34, trying to calculate how much I was going to make. Everyone came – waiters, chambermaids, caddies, beach staff, kitchen staff – and their mothers and fathers as well. They were not going to miss what was, for most of them, the chance of a lifetime – a do at the world-famous Bagatelle Great House. In the end there were more than six hundred guests. It was an enormous success, and it gave Ray the chance to thank his loyal staff and for them to show their appreciation to their capable and considerate boss.

Tony O'Reilly, the very young CEO of Heinz, invited me to stay with him and his family at their lovely house in Pittsburg. Heinz's commercial HQ had the address P.O. Box 57, of course. Tony and his wife Susan – yet another Australian blonde! – had six children. They had only planned for four, but on the last confinement Susan produced triplets, which must be one of the few times Tony's plans did not work out. I was marvellously spoiled and taken to a fundraising ball for the Pittsburgh Steelers, the Irish Fund Ball at the Waldorf Astoria, and all sorts of other events. Under Tony's youthful direction, Heinz was flying.

He took me to dine with some business contacts in New Jersey. We were whizzed in the Heinz corporate jet from Pittsburgh to La Guardia, and thence in a limousine to a house in deepest New Jersey. We were greeted by an elderly man, Albert Lippert, and his wife Felice. We had cocktails, then, repairing to the dining room, we ate a substantial dinner. No business was discussed at the table. Afterwards we thanked our hosts, climbed back into the limousine, and departed for La Guardia. Once back in the air Tony demanded offhandedly 'What did you think of that dinner?'

'I enjoyed it. There were a lot of courses and they were very tasty, but I don't feel as if I've eaten much.'

Tony smiled, well pleased. In 1963 Albert and Felice had gone into business with Jean Nidetch, founder of a company called Weight Watchers, and Heinz were thinking of making an offer for it. Our meal there was by way of fact-finding. Heinz subsequently paid almost 72 million dollars. Since then Weight Watchers has become a household name. A few years later Tony told me that the deal had turned out even better than he had expected – leaving franchisees were obliged to offer their premises to Heinz first, who then enjoyed real estate appreciation as well. H.J. Heinz & Co. flourished under the youthful leadership of Tony O'Reilly.

Following the death of Ronnie Tree, Marietta had decided to sell Heron Bay with its unique 22 acres of West Coast land. An American, a certain Mr Fischer, put down a deposit of a quarter of a million dollars whilst he sorted out some personal matters. The time expired and he deposited another quarter of a million. In the event, he could not complete that transaction either and forfeited his deposits, but blessedly for Barbados, Sir Anthony Bamford, of JCB fame, and his wife Carole bought the property for a comparative snip of US$1.7 million. And Marietta had pocketed the extra half-million as well. However, Ronnie had not done much to the house since it was built in 1947, and there was a great deal of maintenance to be carried out, not least replacing the roof. The Bamfords were the perfect buyers for this iconic residence. They had the money, taste, desire and vision to restore fully Ronnie's masterpiece. He must be smiling in his grave.

On my birthday, 13th July, the West Coast lost another of its founding fathers when Oliver Messel died aged only seventy-four. We shall not see his like again. His exquisite contributions to Barbados and Mustique are fortunately cast in stone. The world of fine arts will forever be the beneficiary of his genius.

Later that month I hopped across to Mustique to see Mick Jagger, who had recently returned from the Rolling Stones' tour of the USA. He was exhausted and, to keep out the sunlight from his house, had lined the windows on the inside with silver foil. I took naughty Mary O'Brien with me; she was thrilled to meet the legend. Mick told me they made more money on the tour from selling T-shirts and other merchandise – in excess of 40 million dollars – than from tickets.

In the autumn Johnny Perez Canto turned up, alone on this occasion, and by arrangement. He had bought in Barbados a wooden motor sailer of about

35 feet, called *Anola*. He wanted me to help him sail her to Los Roques, an archipelago of 350 islands, cays and islets 80 miles north of Venezuela, and now a national park. However, there was only one island boasting a landing strip on which wealthy Venezuelans could land their aircraft. This was Grande Roque, and permission to build there was no longer granted. Homes rarely came on the market, and so were exclusive. I understood that it was Johnny's intention to anchor his newly-bought boat there, affording him a place to stay close to his very rich friends on the otherwise inaccessible island – a nifty wheeze.

I agreed readily – too readily – to skipper *Anola*. I had not examined the charts for the waters we would navigate, nor had I cast my eye over the boat, nor had I swung the compass. But it was only 600 miles, and after the first hundred miles to St. Vincent we would always be in sight of land, and the trade winds would be almost dead astern as we headed westwards along the north coast of South America. Six days, sailing only in daylight, should suffice. My planned course took us due west to St. Vincent, then south, keeping the Grenadines to starboard. After passing Grenada we would alter course hard a'starboard to due west again, passing through Los Testigos – the Disciples – leaving the resort Isla Margarita to port. Los Roques lay ahead. The trickiest navigation was going to be in the region of Los Testigos, where the currents between islands, influenced by the outflow of the nearby mighty Orinoco River, are powerful, sometimes reaching seven knots. Another consideration was the real risk of piracy. Since we would not be carrying firearms, we would have to hope for the best.

We met on board *Anola* in Bridgetown at the careenage, myself, Johnny, Val, and a likeable Venezuelan friend of Johnny's. Cucurulu – his stage name – was the top honcho among *copleros*, Johnny explained. In Venezuela, two *copleros*, each accompanied by a guitarist, alternately make up and sing offensive rhyming couplets – hence *coplero* – each responding immediately with his own offensive couplet. These popular events could go on for hours, with the supporters of one *coplero* mocking the efforts of the other. When one was lost for words, and could not immediately come up with a responding couplet, he was the loser.

We cast off and Johnny, no sailor, insisted on taking *Anola*'s wheel. We narrowly escaped two serious collisions before we had even left the careenage. At sea I took command and we hoisted the sails, cut the engine, and headed due west for St. Vincent. The wind was dead astern, the most uncomfortable point of sailing, as the ever-present danger of an unintentional gybe – the boom swinging from one side across to the other – requires the constant vigilance of the helmsman, if that spar is not to earn its sailor's nickname, the 'widow-maker.' The following swell gave the vessel a nasty corkscrewing motion, not good for already queasy stomachs. Since we were well clear of land, we sailed through the night, keeping a bright look-out for other shipping. At dawn the mountainous island of St. Vincent was where it should be, 30 miles dead ahead.

As the sun came up so did the wind, but from another direction, causing the mainsail to jibe with a crash; the main sheet block fixing was pulled clean out of the gunwale. Examination showed the wood to be rotten, not only there but in other places as well. The very safety of the vessel was in question, and I didn't in the least fancy taking on Los Testigos' tide races without reassurance as to *Anola*'s seaworthiness. I recommended we put into St. George's, Grenada, and get a professional assessment from the Grenada Yacht Services. A few hours later we entered the fine harbour, which looks much like a West Indian Naples, with houses crammed onto the hills surrounding a basin filled with yachts. The harbour master found us a cosy berth. We would consult a shipwright the next day.

The atmosphere on board was tense. Johnny thought he might have been sold a pup and I was inclined to agree. There's no-one a shipyard owner would rather meet than a person who has bought a wooden boat that 'might need a little work'. That often translates into expensive repairs. He also thought that I, as the designated experienced sailor, was at fault. He was correct. Before setting sail I should have swung the compass. I should have made a general assessment of the boat's condition. I should have checked the life-saving equipment. I should have done so many things. As it was, the comparatively short voyage had begun with an engine which started instantly – which is by no means always the case – seducing me into complacency.

Val and I went for a walk to give Johnny time to simmer down. Looking around the harbour I saw a tall varnished wooden mast and wanted to know to what yacht it belonged. We found her lying alongside, and attached to her counter was a sign – *For Sale* – and a contact address – Grenada Yacht Services – GYS. Oh dear, oh dear! I was smitten again.

I spent a sleepless night. First thing in the morning I was on the doorstep of GYS to arrange, besides a shipwright to check out *Anola*, an immediate viewing of my new love. She was, I learned, called *Kentra*, and her owner was Joanne Leary, wife of Dr Timothy Leary, the famed guru of psychedelic drugs.

Briefly, *Kentra* was 84 feet long, had a beam of 11 feet and drew 11 feet of water. She was a yawl, designed by my favourite designer and boat builder, William Fife of Fairlie in Scotland. She had been used by Yves Saint Laurent, whose silver tea service would be included in the yacht's inventory.

I made an offer – subject to survey – of US$89,000, which Mrs Leary accepted. I arranged to have *Kentra* hauled out on the rare screw lift in the harbour and surveyed. The results would be forwarded to me in Barbados. Johnny was his good-natured self again, admitting that I could not be blamed for *Anola*'s condition. He decided to leave her in Grenada for repair, and send a yachtsman from Venezuela to complete the trip to Los Roques. He left for Caracas with Cucurulu, and I returned with Val to Barbados to await surveyor's report. Rectifying any major problems in such a massive yacht would have made restoration, even with my unbridled optimism, unacceptably expensive. No such problems were found. I could proceed with my purchase.

As 1979 began, my head was buzzing with plans for a life aboard *Kentra*. In early February I signed and posted the contract to buy her, and arranged for the deposit of US$20,000 to be transferred to GYS. The balance of $69,000 was standing by.

I intended to charter her at the very top end of the market, based in Grenada or Antigua. In addition to a general refit – she was a tired old lady – I would install a desalination plant, and lots of refrigerated space to stow all the gastronomic goodies bought in Martinique. Finding a crew would be no problem, except for a cook. This was the highest paid and toughest position on a charter vessel, and they earned every penny – working in a ship's galley in a seaway below deck in the tropics is no fun, and charterers demand a 24-hour service. Helpfully GYS had a job vacancy notice board, locally known as the 'Crew and Screw'. I would give that a try. I was impatient to take possession of the potentially magnificent *Kentra*.

63. *The incomparable Chérie, who played a crucial role in the success of Bagatelle.*

64. *Chérie, the official face of St. Lucian tourism, dressed in the national costume.*

65. *Gay (left) and Chérie, two thirds of my Bagatelle ménage.*

67. *Thanks to Ronnie Driver, I am aboard Estrellina, my string of one polo pony. She knew more about the game than I did.*

66. *Rosco – make my day.*

68. *Val smouldering gently – I pinched her from an artist on Mustique at Colin Tennant's fiftieth birthday party.*

69. *Sunset in Martinique, land of the delectable p'tit ponch and les crabes farçis. Old Nick is a well-known rum…*

70. *My windsurfing friends form Yorkshire, Peter and dishy Debbie Barbor, at Cockroach Palace.*

71. *Alexander and Clair Hesketh at my Tarts and Pimps party at Bagatelle. So who has the best legs then?*

72. *Basil of the bar. He was the crown prince of Mustique – now he is the king.*

73. *The imperial parrot of Dominica – the sisserou.*

74. Kentra, *built in Scotland in 1929.*

76. Kentra, *a grande dame of the high seas. She might have been mine – but at what cost?*

75. *Hobie Cats, apart from offering other useful opportunities,* can fly.

77. Serendipity *(ex Ultima II) – just about right for seven guests, with in-house adagio dancer.*

78. The usual suspects taking a liquid lunch chez Dot. Val (left), Dot (centre) and Carina.

80. Hurricane Allen in the Gulf of Mexico, with wind speeds of 190 mph, and an atmospheric pressure of 899 Mb.

79. The very generous and somewhat baffled Sammy is not happy. The morose bird on his left is the non-smoker.

81. Donald and I at Cockroach Palace with Anna, unaware of the sword of Damocles hanging over her head.

82. The sitting room in the much improved El Slummo.

83. Relaxing by my plunge pool at El Slummo; the design I borrowed, via Ian Morrison, from the Costa Smeralda.

84. With Donald and Cherry, over whose head also hung that twice-damned sword of Damocles.

85. Suzie and I hamming it up at the first La Cage aux Folles.

86. Lovely Luna, a selfie.

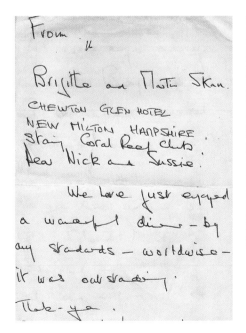

88. With Donald Pleasance, a far cry from Adolph Eichmann.

87. A treasured note from Martin and Brigitte Skan – who knew their onions from their shallots.

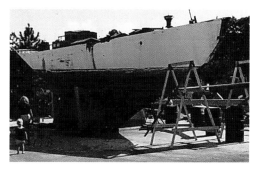

90. Spirit *hauled out. Let the restoration begin.*

89. *How I found* Spirit *in 1984 in a backwater, a once elegant Edwardian lady who had fallen on hard times.*

92. *The saloon, before John Valentine had worked his magic…*

91. *The owner done to a crisp, working on* Spirit *unprotected – no mast, no awnings – in the scorching Floridian sun.*

93. *…and after: the Edwardian splendour of* Spirit's *saloon, a John Valentine masterpiece.*

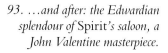

94. *A labour of love. Suzie sanded all 80 feet of* Spirit's *main mast, and then gave it at least four coats of varnish.*

95. *I name this yacht 'Spirit of Carib'.*

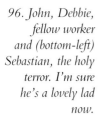

96. *John, Debbie, fellow worker and (bottom-left) Sebastian, the holy terror. I'm sure he's a lovely lad now.*

97. In an unusually benign Mona Passage where I am alone with my mistress, the sea, at last.

98. Michael Deeley, movie producer extraordinaire and husband of the inspiring and lovely Ruth, pottering around the waters of Cape Cod.

99. Spirit stretching her legs on a lazy broad reach.

100. *Veronica, in her London mode.*

101 *Veronica with her new friends and guardians, Zen (left) and Lulu; Little Lil is on her lap.*

102. *Feeling rather better, Veronica lunching under the mizzen awning with John.*

103. *A mermaid emerges from the surf at the Crane beach.*

104. *The unique great table at La Cage aux Folles II. Oggie the budgerigar is on my shoulder.*

106. *At our wedding reception there were three generations of Mitchells – Luna, Suzie and Billy.*

105. *May 8th, 1992 Veronica and I are married – all my worldly goods included. My friends told Veronica she was mad to marry me.*

107. The
de luxe version,
reclining at Casa
di Pablo after
tea and before
several Black
Russians.

108. My 60th birthday party at the great table at Bagatelle
with Cherry, Veronica and Patricia – all nicely bronzed –
in attendance.

109. La Rouquette,
our first home in
south-west France.

110. Limeuil, 'L'un des Plus Beaux Villages de France'. We were captivated at once.

111. Canoeing on the Vézère river with gentle Lucy and fiercely competitive Natasha.

113. Ready to go, to entertain, and to inform spectators at the Holders polo field, Barbados.

112. A crayon drawing of Anna made by a man whilst serving his time in prison.

114. Blossom, a Hudson Bay terrier and veritable treasure.

115. Spaggers – our best friend who could all but talk. We still miss him dreadfully.

116. Archie (left) and Lola, the darlings with which we now share our home.

117. With the love of my life, precious Veronica, anything is possible.

I heard nothing for a few weeks, then GYS called – Mrs Leary had changed her mind! She had fallen in love with her Finnish skipper, who said that, if *Kentra* went, so did he. So *Kentra* stayed. I was heartbroken. I found a photo of her recently,* fully restored to her original design as a gaff-rigged yawl, and on the market for US$3,239,880.

One outcome of this disappointment was the realisation that I needed a change from my life as a restaurateur. After nine years, I was taking more and more time off from the Bagatelle; this indicated that I was finding the demands of running the restaurant tiresome, which would not do. I had seen too many restaurateurs fall into the same trap.

So I began to scheme. I was reluctant to sell the Bagatelle because, apart from the two profitable restaurants, there were also five acres of land, and the value of land on the West Coast of Barbados was on the up. I conceived the idea of renting out the businesses and began to cast around for suitable restaurateurs. Mrs Shirley Browne, a Shetlander given to wearing fishnet stockings with seams, took over Mr Nick's, renamed it The Hideaway, and made a huge but noisy success of it. I was now left with finding someone to take on the Bagatelle restaurant.

In the meantime the Sandy Lane Hotel had a new manager, the likeable and witty German, Norbert Petersen. Fortunately, like his predecessors, he also took to the Bagatelle. When eventually Trust Houses Forte moved him from Barbados back to England, knowing of the success of his predecessor Ray Carroll's mega binge, he threw one of his own at the Bagatelle, again for the entire hotel staff.

On Good Friday, April 9th, the air was thick with reddish-brown dust, so dense you had to use windscreen-wipers in your car. St. Vincent's volcano, La Soufrière, the television news told us, had erupted. The lake in the crater had been rising for some months, as observed by a party led by Richard Goddard that included Margaret Leacock – my word, how that girl got around – who climbed up through dense forest to the crater to have a look. At that point the water level was almost up to the rim. The volcano was to erupt a few weeks later. Although the trade winds blew easterly, and St. Vincent was downwind of Barbados, the volcanic ash had

* See picture 75.

risen 11 miles into the troposphere, where the winds blew in the opposite direction.

A few weeks later I flew Billy Mitchell's daughter Gala from Mustique to Martinique on a shopping expedition. Over St. Vincent we had a good view of the still-smoking volcano. The slopes, before the eruption, had been densely forested. Now there was only grey ash, not a sign of a single tree. The lake in the crater had evaporated, and the boiler house smell of sulphur dioxide was very strong. Gala wanted to take a closer look, so I flew in low over the crater. Peering into the very bowels of the earth, I felt like an intruder in a place where I ought not to be, and tried to fly away from this awful chasm. Nothing happened! It felt as if gravity had somehow become stronger, that we would be dragged down into some hellish Oblivion. I pulled back on the control column further and opened the throttle to full. Fighting for every foot of altitude, we skimmed the crater rim too closely for comfort and fled, relieved to escape that malodorous Hades.

What had happened? Possibly the mixture of gases above the volcano was less dense than normal air. That would give the aeroplane less lift and hence the impression of a greater gravitational force. There is a parallel here with Kick'em Jenny, the underwater volcano, where vessels can sink through lack of buoyancy. I mentioned my experience some time later to Hugo Money-Coutts, a fellow pilot and Colin Tennant's business partner. Curious, he too had ventured in and, only escaping with difficulty, had been badly frightened.

In April 1979 the Central Bank of Barbados played host to the Central Banks of the Caribbean at a regional conference. The final event was to be a dinner at the Bagatelle. The Governor of the Bank, the urbane Dr Courtney Blackman, booked the Great Table for his distinguished guests, for 9 pm. Some of the party did not arrive until 11 pm. In a charming letter Dr Blackman explained that they had had:

> '…a drunken and completely disoriented driver', and thanked us for 'the very professional manner in which your staff coped with an unexpected and extremely upsetting situation'. He went on, 'While we waited, your staff showed their appreciation of our predicament and allayed our anxi-

eties concerning the lateness of the meal. Your receptionist was especially sympathetic and accommodating. When we finally sat at 11.00 pm, we were served graciously and promptly, as if coping with emergencies of this nature was an everyday occurrence for your staff. Needless to say, our guests took with them an opinion of Bagatelle as a "first rate" restaurant.'

I was the receptionist.

That summer Anna and Derek were invited to join their friends Micheline and her partner, Sammy Johaninoff, on his motor yacht *Serendipity* for two weeks cruising in the Greek Islands. Derek was preoccupied gratifying large Thespian egos and raising money for his *Wagner* epic. Anna asked me to go in his place. At the last moment she rang to say that Jonathan had contracted chickenpox and she could not leave him. But all was not lost, she said. Her girlfriend Angie Grant, whom I already knew, would join us in Piraeus.

Angie, an actress who was in several 'Carry On' films, possessed a knock-out body, but I gave her mixed reviews. Whilst being a marvel between the sheets she could be infernally unpredictable. I did not fancy being confined with her on a motor yacht for a week or two. I resolved to jump ship in Piraeus.

I joined *Serendipity* in Monte Carlo. I could hardly believe her size – 258 feet long with a deck crew of seventeen and a vast vase of gladioli on the afterdeck! There were eight suites with accommodation for sixteen guests, so it was unlikely that our party of seven would unduly strain the cabin crew of fifteen.

We were an interesting lot. Sammy Johaninoff, an oil man, was involved in a legal battle with his brother, and was rarely off the satellite telephone – £7 per minute. I never saw him smile. Micheline was his loyal and loveable companion. Then there were two girls, who were very friendly and a source of comfort to either sex, whose names escape me. Sammy bought presents for them both. To one he gave a Cartier gold watch. She thanked him with a kiss. To the other he gave a lighter, not any old Dunhill lighter, but a model called the Gold Nugget, plated in 14-carat gold. Disappointed, she said plaintively, 'But I don't smoke.'

Another guest, John, told me he was 'an adagio dancer' – whatever that is. Every evening he played loud orchestral music in the saloon, conducting with a baton he happened to have brought with him for the purpose. The last guest was an Israeli doctor, there in his professional capacity, who was charming but whom we rarely saw.

The food was superb, immeasurably better than the fatty lamb dishes found on shore (and the less said about Greek wines the better). *Serendipity*'s wine list was modelled on that of the Mirabelle restaurant in London. But Sammy's perpetual gloom meant that conversation at the table was minimal. I took a picture of the moment when, infected by Sammy's gloom, we hit an all time low.** In spite of the fraught atmosphere we were about to enjoy a delicious saffron-infused bouillabaisse on toasts thick with spicy Rouille.

By the time we were approaching Piraeus I was ready to leave. In any case, the Caribbean hurricane season was approaching and I wanted to be at home. The last such storm to hit the Island was Janet in 1955. Statistically Barbados was due for a bloody nose. And Angie, another really dangerous if beautiful storm, was coming aboard. It was time to scarper.

Two months later, thanks to the blessed geo-stationary weather satellite, we were warned of the advent of a beast of a storm named David. On 27th August it was officially classified as a hurricane and was likely to hit, or pass close to, Barbados. Predictions of storm tracks, most of which tend to swing towards the north-west, can only be approximations. Rarely do they turn south towards South America.

I was not too concerned about David. Bagatelle had survived such storms for centuries. I stored lots of fresh water, checked stocks of candles, matches, torches and tinned goods, and made sure no branches overhung the roof. I invited friends who lived on the vulnerable low-lying West Coast to take shelter with me. Only one family came; Sally Fischer and her three children camped in the library. Her husband Karl was in Venezuela on business. Just before the expected strike I shuttered and barred all windows. The electricity had already been turned off by the local power company as a precautionary measure.

***

** See picture 79.

Mercifully, David passed 75 miles to the north of the island. Poor Dominica took the 150-mph category 4 storm head-on; the most severe category – 5 – comes in at 156 mph. This island was relatively undeveloped and many of its buildings frail and vulnerable. Homes and commercial properties were literally flattened. The country was levelled. To rub salt into the wound, the Dutch company that carried much of the insurance did a runner. The national bird, of which Dominicans are so proud, is the imperial parrot, the sisserou. A spectacular bird, 18 to 20 inches long, it is much sought after by parrot fanciers. The trees having been defoliated, the parrots had nowhere to hide, and were hunted, captured and sold on for as much as US$20,000. A few pairs remain and every effort is made to protect them and increase their numbers. Smuggling them is dealt with severely. Fortunately, the birds may live for up to seventy years.

Further north Hurricane David, with sustained wind speeds of an unimaginable 175 mph, and well into category 5, killed more than 2,000 people in the Dominican Republic. David was removed from the list of hurricane names.

After the storm had passed, I went to check on my Hobie, which I had moored to a manchineel tree well above the beach at the Sandy Lane Hotel. As I drove down I could hear, a mile or more away, the thunderous sea pounding the bejesus out of the Island. When I got there I could hardly believe my eyes. The waves battering the beach were enormous, the biggest by far I had ever seen there, with a heavy spume hanging above them, boiling like a giant cauldron. I felt very small.

The breaking point of a wave depends on the height of the wave and the depth of water beneath it. With a long even-shelving seabed, a wave builds up gradually and breaks well off shore. The seabed off the beach at Sandy Lane was almost flat, only in the last 20 yards angling up steeply. Suddenly, therefore, in the final seconds, the waves would rear up 20 feet and more, and crash down vertically, sending leg-breaking boulders of abrasive coral hurling all over the place.

There were a few relative breaks in the surf, mainly at the north end of the beach. The prevailing trade winds blow from the east but, due to the influence of the hurricane, they had been sucked round, coming from the south. Huge swells were running northwards in the open sea, their crests breaking spectacularly in the howling wind, their fronts steepish but not too steep for my devious purposes. My word, Nicholas, the Sirens whispered, imagine surfing on *those*! A seductive picture was taking shape in my thrill-seeking mind. Occasional lulls in a boisterous sea, a beam wind from the south, huge ideally-shaped running swells offshore, and a sailing boat specially designed for surf…this rare combination of circumstances was irresistible. Would it ever occur again? Attaboy!

The feeling of catching a wave is like no other. You give yourself up willingly to the forces of the sea, and become at one with nature, hurtling wildly, barely in control. The possibility of revelling in that experience overruled all rational considerations. I summoned up the blood, dragged the Hobie Cat on to the beach to just above where the waves were reaching out greedily, and checked the rigging, rudders and tiller with care. This was no time for a failure. I hoisted the sail and sat on the forward transom, waiting for a lull in the pounding surf. The sail slatted noisily in the strong wind, ready to be sheeted in and to drive me through the angry sea. Adrenalin poured into my blood. I had the beach all to myself. Fools rush in…

There was a lull, and no time to waste. I jumped onto the sand, seized the forward transom, and pulled for all I was worth down into the sea until the boat was afloat. I scrambled onto the trampoline, locked down the rudders and close-hauled the sail. As the catamaran accelerated into the surf I threw myself flat, head foremost, steering with the long tiller extension with one hand, grasping the forward transom with the other. Just in time! The first wave broke on my back, as if trying to wash me overboard. But there was enough sail above the foam to keep driving the boat forward. All of a sudden I found myself beyond the breaking waves.

I had the time of my life, surfing on the steep north-facing slopes of the spectacular swells for quite a while. Then I went about, crashing southwards through breaking crests, shrieking hymns at the top of my voice. I was acutely aware that Nature, with a snap of her all-powerful fingers, could snuff out me and my puny boat in a moment. Yet she chose not to, instead granting me a brief sojourn amongst the gods. I was untouchable, at one with the elements, careering over the tempestuous sea. I saw Heaven that day. However, if I did not take care of earthly matters immediately, I was likely to arrive there earlier than I had intended. It was time to go home.

I looked shoreward, and my heart stopped. Along the coast, as far as I could see in the weakening light, was an unbroken line of massive breaking waves with that unholy cauldron boiling above them. Through the spume I identified the Sandy Lane Hotel, and with difficulty picked out Peter Tomlin's water sports hut, my only possible point of re-entry. If I came in just a few yards too far north I would be shredded on the reef's razor-sharp coral fangs. Thirty yards to the south and the towering waves would do for me. Little daylight remained and time was running out. I took up station pointing towards the hardly visible hut, my sail flapping wildly.

I called upon every iota of my knowledge of the sea. I let wave after wave go by, until one seemed just right. I had a quick word with God, hauled in the sheets and felt that immense power lift the stern and urge me forward. There was no going back. I had to strike a critical balance between staying ahead of the menacing mountain of water astern and not allowing the vulnerable lee bow to be forced underwater or driven into the back of the wave ahead. That would have caused me to pitchpole, which is to say go base over apex. With a mighty roar, my wave broke just behind me and I was hurled forward. I was actually airborne for a moment – Hobie Cats *can* fly – then I felt the hulls grinding on the fine coral sand. I leapt over between the hulls, grabbed the transom and, like a madman, dragged the boat up the steep beach as the tentacles of the receding wave reached out to drag me back into the surf. All of a sudden both I and the boat were high and dry up the beach. Behind me the surf,, deprived of its prey, retreated, sulking. With my remaining strength I hauled the catamaran beyond that dear, dear hut, dropped the sail and hugged the mast. As the last shreds of daylight were swallowed by the boisterous night, the surf roared a mocking farewell. And my knees began to shake.

One day I answered the door and recognised immediately the smiling face of Les Williams. It was with him and Robin Knox-Johnston that I had agreed ten years earlier to be a partner in a yachting venture. I had let them down badly, disappearing without a word. Here, now, was my Nemesis. Les came in and sat down. I gave him a drink and launched into apologies, expecting a severe well-deserved dressing down. There was no need. All was forgiven, Les said. He and Robin had replaced me with Clement Freud and the money had been no problem. *Ocean Spirit*, as the yacht was named, had taken line honours in the inaugural Cape Town to Rio de Janeiro race. I was vastly relieved. Then I remarked that he looked tired. 'Well, I only got here today,' he said. Then he smiled sheepishly. 'My yacht's crewed by five women!' Les is the strong quiet type that ladies seem to like.

Now I found someone willing to rent the Bagatelle restaurant – Nick Ashworth, who had had a restaurant on St. Lucia. We met and I gave him all the financial details in one of the computer print-outs that David Allison put together every month. We agreed a rent. Nick wanted to move in straight away with his wife Sharon, and took over my apartment completely furnished. He bought my beloved four-poster on the understanding that, when I repossessed the business at the expiry of his licence, I would buy it back at the same price.

I felt very happy because now I was going to receive two good rents from my restaurants whilst keeping their freeholds, which were every day increasing in capital value. With no need to work I could do as I pleased.

Yet again I reflected how well the life of a bachelor suited me. I was free to change direction at a whim without having to consult a wife or take into account the needs of our children. I was free to go wherever the winds of chance might blow me.

CHAPTER THIRTY

Cockroach Palace-On-Sea

With the Ashworths now occupying Bagatelle, my next home was a wooden shack on the beach a few yards north of the Greensleeves beach bar. It earned the name Cockroach Palace when, during my first night in residence, I turned on the lights at three in the morning and there was a clattering stampede, as hundreds of the revolting beasts dashed for their nooks and crannies. The next day I bought half a dozen canisters of Baygon's finest insect spray and spent three days squirting, almost gassing myself – I got an awful headache – and sweeping up carcasses. That was only a temporary reprieve. The moment I stopped my daily offensive they were back in strength.

In fact, I tried without success to buy Cockroach Palace. The landlord, Mr Soodeen, was keeping it for his daughter, the lovely Neysha. Later, when she had taken possession of the property, she told me she intended to sell it for a few hundred thousand dollars. I advised her to wait. When I last saw her she thanked me profusely. It is now worth in excess of seven million dollars, and she has such illustrious neighbours as the tycoon Sir Martyn Arbib.

The first thing to do was to sail my windsurfer down from the Sandy Lane beach and prop it up against Cockroach Palace. To be able to get up in the morning, launch my board, and sail for hours was exhilarating. When I returned at lunchtime, next door was the Greensleeves Beach Bar and Restaurant, where Delsie the Duchess ruled supreme. It was also a good hunting ground for games of backgammon, which I tended to win, my opponents having frequently had too much of Delsie's rum punch and not being at their sharpest.

Val went to London to continue her studies in accountancy. She had been a marvellous companion, wise and beautiful. Unfortunately, once in England, she fell very ill with a severe chest infection and required major surgery. But Ronnie Driver was enormously helpful and generous, arranging for her to have the best possible treatment at the Royal Marsden Hospital at his expense.

Val left me with many happy memories and the *Encyclopædia Britannica* – all thirty-two volumes, an indispensable resource before the arrival of Google. She also discovered in me a knack for preparing Chinese dishes. We went to Trinidad, which has a large Chinese population, and bought all the necessary paraphernalia – a wok, steamers, chopsticks and so on, and the special ingredients unavailable in Barbados. The first dish Val taught me was a simple stir-fry, chicken with hoisin sauce and cashew nuts. And I was off! I bought the *Time-Life Chinese Cook Book* and within the year, to the great joy of my friends, was producing authentic Peking Duck, pancakes and all. Since then my restaurants have all benefited from this new dimension to my repertoire. Val's introduction to this art was a gift beyond price, both professionally and personally, for which I shall ever be grateful.[*]

And, as I did not have a live-in girlfriend, there was, you might say, a job vacancy.

For the first week or two I revelled in my freedom from the demanding business of running the Bagatelle. I loved belting out onto the beach my favourite music at a huge volume. Top of the list was Sviatoslav Richter playing Rachmaninov's Second Piano Concerto and Yehudi Menuhin's exquisite rendition of Beethoven's Violin Concerto conducted by Fürtwängler. Not far behind came Bob Marley and *No Woman No Cry* and Carlos Montoya playing his flamenco guitar. In no time, windsurfing every day, I

---

[*] It was only in June 2007 that the wok we bought together in 1975 gave up the ghost, when, worn thin, a pinhole appeared in its shapely curved bottom.

was as brown as a berry and fit as a fiddle. Socially, there were endless parties both at lunch and dinner.

Soon, though I had a problem. I am a doer and I quickly become bored. I was renting VHS videotapes – all the rage then – from an attractive and somewhat pneumatic Belgian friend who rejoiced in the name of Jeannine Cipolata. She spoke an amusing Franglais – when I asked her if she had been water-skiing, she replied, 'No. I went down to the beach, but il faisait trop de choppy.' Her business was in a wooden chattel house opposite the Treasure Beach Hotel on the West Coast road, a perfect spot for passing trade. She complained to me of the unfair – not to mention illegal – competition from similar shops which peddled pirated versions of the most recent films. Jeannine always stuck to the rules.

I was looking for something to do other than playing. My subconscious went to work. I had an aeroplane at my disposal. Houses on and around Sandy Lane had owners with sophisticated tastes which the local supermarket did not satisfy, while Martinique was bulging with gastronomic goodies. Billy Mitchell, who had the only food shop on Mustique, had already expressed an interest in my supplying her with certain items. So why didn't I fly to Martinique, bring back lots of foodstuffs that were needed on-Island, and sell them at a profit? And what better retail outlet could there be than Jeannine's shop, so perfectly located? Thus I took over Jeannine's lease and the Gourmet Shop came into being. To make sure the enterprise did not completely tie me down, bringing me effectively back to square one, I employed Ken, who had been my butler at the Bagatelle, to mind the shop. I purchased a large freezer and a chilled display unit, had a sign made, flew off to Martinique and came back loaded with whatever had taken my fancy.

When I returned to Grantley Adams Airport I would park the aeroplane well away from the terminal building, clear immigration, health and customs, return to my machine and taxi across the runway to the Flying Club. There I would transfer the goodies to my car, and drive back to the Gourmet Shop.

None of the airport officials could be bothered to walk across the windy tarmac to see what I was carrying. If they had I would have explained that the goods were for my personal consumption. This might have worked the first two or three times, but then questions would be asked. Only many years later did it occur to me that I had been running a fairly large smuggling operation! Even so my swanning airily through customs had not gone unnoticed. One day a man approached me and said, were I to carry a tightly wrapped package weighing exactly one kilo and deliver it to a person beyond the airport perimeter, I would earn myself thousands of dollars. I could do this as often as I liked. I declined. Barbados is on the drug highway from South America to the USA, and many officials at airports, unable to resist the chance of easy money, have been corrupted. The daughter of the manager of the Barbados Hilton told me that there were pushers at the very gates of her school, Queen's College, the most prestigious in Barbados. None of the girls dared say anything for fear of having their faces carved up – or worse.

On one buying trip, at about five in the afternoon, I was heading back to Barbados where I expected to arrive yet again just before sunset. However, my departure from Martinique had been delayed by incoming flights. My machine was crammed full, laden with goodies for my Gourmet Shop, and the tiny cabin was filled with the lovely aroma of still warm baguettes; there was hardly room on the seat next to me for the obligatory life raft.

As I flew, I could see the island of St. Lucia a few miles to my right. The weather ahead had deteriorated unexpectedly. This had not been forecast by the French Met officer at Lamentin, the Martinique airport. I was going to have to decide – did I bash on to Barbados in the hope of finding clearer weather and arriving just before sunset? If I had to fly round storm cells, making my journey longer, I risked arriving late and being turned back, having to fly to mountainous Martinique in failing light. The decision was not difficult. I would divert immediately to the Vigie airfield on St. Lucia, only ten minutes away. I informed the Lamentin control tower of my change of flight plan and headed towards my new destination, where I landed a few minutes later.

Fortunately, my old friend Alex Oostenbrink, manager of the La Toc Hotel, was on- Island. (It was his brother who explained to me the effects of anoxic anaemia.) Alex would always find a room for me, and he had fridges and freezers in which I could store my perishable purchases overnight. I would leave, refreshed, for Barbados at first light.

Within an hour I was installed in a room at the hotel, my cargo safely stored in the kitchens below. Having an urge to spoil myself, I consulted the Champagne section of the room service wine list. They had Taittinger Comtes de Champagne Blanc de Blancs, my absolute favourite. I couldn't believe it! I ordered a bottle. In a few minutes I opened the door to admit a waiter with an ice-bucket, bottle and a glass – no bill. He showed me the bottle. Mumm Cordon Rouge. 'But I ordered Taittinger,' I said.

'Us 'en got dat one.'

'Which one have you got?'

'Dis one heah.' He pointed to the bottle on the tray.

My restaurateur's nose smelled a rat. There was a whiff to this transaction. I have always made a point of telling professional colleagues if I think I have spotted a racket in their operation. Of course, I needed evidence – without it the waiter could deny my accusation. I made a silly offer and got the bottle of Champagne for almost nothing. He could hardly argue or report me to the management. I tried unsuccessfully to make contact with Alex.

Having downed most of the bottle, I went downstairs for dinner. I was tired and wanted to avoid the floor show, the usual tourist fodder – limbo dancing and fire-eating –featuring the exotic Madame Volcano. As I was returning to my room after dining, coming along the corridor was a vision, a barefooted female in a long skirt of garishly coloured feathers, and a white scoop-necked blouse. Around her neck was a splendid Mayan necklace with semi-precious stones. Her fingers were much be-ringed and her arms jingled with bangles. On her head there was an intricately tied headscarf. By local Créole tradition the number of knots in the scarf indicates the marital status or aspirations of the wearer. White teeth flashed in a glowing black face. A pair of challenging eyes looked at me boldly. She wasted no time, asking in a husky voice, 'Man, you stayin' heah?' I had met Madame Volcano.

She was the hotel's resident cabaret artiste and limbo dancer, who could insinuate her lissom body effortlessly under a bar placed across two Coca-Cola bottles. 'You wan' some fun?' she demanded. 'Only twenny dollar – American dollar, o' course.'

By way of defence I came over all British and proper. 'Most kind of you I'm sure, but I'm afraid I'm terribly tired. I'm going to my room to sleep.'

'Man, I wake you up,' she promised. I eased past the dusky temptress with an outside break and accelerated towards my virgin bed.

When I got back to Barbados the next day, I telephoned Alex and told him about the suspicious room service of the previous evening. A few weeks later he called to tell me he had set a trap, which proved that the waiter and the barman were pocketing much of the room service sales. I had saved his hotel quite a bit of cash. I also mentioned Madame Volcano's offer of hospitality. He laughed and said that she did pull a few tricks in the short interval between her first and second performances. No wonder she had been in a hurry!

My next visit to St. Lucia later that year was to be under very different circumstances. On 30th July a tropical depression approached Barbados and the islands of the Lesser Antilles. By 2nd August it had become Hurricane Allen, with sustained wind speeds of 127 mph. Thanks to the weather satellites – yet again – those in its path were given two invaluable days' warning.

Allen was to become the second most powerful storm since records began. It passed a mere 38 miles north-west of Barbados, grazed the south point of St. Lucia six hours later, then continued into the Caribbean, eventually reaching sustained wind speeds of 190 mph. At one point its barometric pressure was down to 899 millibars. It killed 269 people.

St. Lucia, although not suffering a direct hit, was badly damaged. There was no power or clean water, roads were blocked with fallen trees, and villages were cut off by landslides. One particular threat were diabolical phenomena called spinners, which the hurricane threw out as it advanced. These were extremely tight whirlwinds – tornados – with internal speeds of close to 300 mph. When Hurricane David had passed just north of Barbados, one rocketed through Janet Morrison's garden on Barbados, neatly defoliating half of a tree – it was as tight as that – and carving out a piece of hillside like a giant knife. To survive such conditions requires luck, no matter what your preparations.

After Allen had moved on, the Flying Club called me. A man from the Salvation Army was anxious to get to St. Lucia, but the local airlines had suspended all flights. Could I help? I dashed down to the Club, met the man, and off we flew. It was a bumpy ride. The residual atmospheric conditions could best be described as disturbed. Strangely, though, the visibility was good, which permitted me to fly within the rules. In under an hour, we landed at Vigie airfield. My passenger had been met by a Red Cross representative and whisked away to do his humanitarian work.

I climbed the stairs to the control tower and entered. This space was designed to give all-round visibility, enabling controllers to monitor traffic movements in the air and on the ground. The large windows on all sides, however, turned it into a greenhouse. With the local power turned off or disabled, the control tower was functioning on its emergency generator, which could supply the radios, but lacked capacity to run the air-conditioning system as well. I asked them how I might help. The response was unanimous – I could bring them ice! None was available because of the power outage. So I took off for Barbados to beg my hotelier friends for help. They raided their ice machines and gave me as much as they could spare, and I returned to St. Lucia with as many insulated boxes packed with ice cubes as would fit in my aeroplane. The controllers were very grateful indeed.

Quite by chance I began an unlikely and unanticipated career. One day the commentator failed to turn up at a polo match. So I found myself, microphone in hand, describing the match. I could never have imagined myself as a commentator, having suffered from a severe stutter in my teens – I still do today to a lesser extent if I am very tired – so I had never considered speaking publicly about anything. What is odd is that when I spoke into that microphone, there was no trace of a stutter, and now I am relatively famous in the job. I have commentated for thirty years, in Barbados, Florida, and in England at the Cowdray Park and Cheshire Polo Clubs.

In November the Jaggers' divorce went through in London; I should imagine Mick was vastly relieved because another lady had entered his life, Jerry Hall. Mick was one of my first guests at Cockroach Palace on his way to Mustique. He made quite a few telephone calls, dutifully recording each one. When the time came for him to leave we went through the calls and estimated their cost. He paid me with a cheque. When I next saw him he said he'd noticed that I had banked his cheque. I told him, of course, Yorkshiremen always bank cheques. 'Possibly so,' he rejoined. 'But some keep them for my signature.' Which is true, and they are worth more, much more, than the cost of those telephone calls.

★

I hopped across to England, first to visit my parents in Yorkshire, then to spend some time in London with Anna. She and I had the house at Cale Street to ourselves. One summer afternoon we were on her bed in the sun-filled room, the crisp white sheets in glorious disarray. She was lying on her back, hands behind her head, breasts lifted high, eyes closed. I was resting on my elbows, muttering sweet nothings, whilst exploring the hills and valleys of her gorgeous body. On the perfect undercurve of her right breast I encountered a small bump. I mentioned it. Yes, she whispered, she had felt some time ago but had put off going to the doctor. Maybe she should make an appointment, I suggested…

She went to the doctor.

Tests were carried out.

I was back in Barbados by the time Anna called to say the lump was malignant. I was numbed. But all was not lost. Women may survive cancer of the breast if it is detected in time, and the lump which I had encountered had been tiny. Anna underwent surgery, which did not involve a mastectomy, although her lymphatic system was found to be infected. But the surgeon was hopeful that he had excised all the cancerous tissue.

Once home from hospital my beloved Anna, defiant and courageous, went straight to war, fighting the vile disease tooth and claw. Apart from surgical procedures and unpleasant conventional therapies, she was tireless in her search for a cure. She consulted mystics in Machu Picchu and witch doctors in Brazil; she lived and prayed in nunneries, made large financial contributions to dubious churches and, *in extremis*, even went on a grape diet. Throughout she remained undaunted, her libido undiminished. No matter the weird paths along which my rackety life led me, Anna – witty, beautiful, passionate and loving – was unfailingly there. I prayed that she would win the battle.

CHAPTER THIRTY-ONE

From Cockroach Palace
To El Slummo

Y ou would be hard-pressed to think of a better life than the one I was enjoying at Cockroach Palace. My ever-ready windsurfer was propped up outside against the wall, the Caribbean was my garden, and Greensleeves was a bottle's throw away. I had my books, my guitar, and flocks of the most delightful girlfriends flew in and out. My most special guests were Donald and Cherry. One of their fringe benefits for holding shares in the Bagatelle was the use of a villa on the Sandy Lane estate whenever they felt like it, so they came down from New York quite often.

Fifty yards or so behind the Gourmet Shop, there was an ugly bungalow with rubble for a garden and enclosed by a rusty chain-link fence. I put in a very small offer – US$10,000 cash – which was accepted. I named it 'El Slummo', and began to have it made habitable. It did not take long. El Slummo was an apt name, but I made it comfortable for very little money. Since the house was not on the sea, I required some sort of outside bathing facility. There was no room for a swimming pool so I unleashed Nicholas the Architect on the problem, and he came up with the idea of a plunge pool with curved stone edge. I moved in. It was with some sadness that I moved out of Cockroach Palace, but I was not going to suffer. Across the road from El Slummo was the new Treasure Beach Hotel, which had an excellent kitchen, and my Hobie Cat and windsurfer were back at the Sandy Lane Hotel five minutes away. I had moved from one paradise to another.

My new freedom meant that I had time to read. I struck gold twice. First I found myself reading a book by an American author I had never heard of called Rex Stout, creator of the private detective Nero Wolfe and his side-kick Archie Goodwin. Stout's books are endlessly re-readable. He is the most published American author, living or dead; when he died in 1975 aged eighty-eight, he had over 200 million books in print. Here are three of his titles as starters – *Some Buried Caesar*, *The Doorbell Rang* and *Too Many Cooks*. You will thank me for this introduction. A lifetime of reading pleasure lies ahead for you, female and male alike.

I was able to increase my collection by a great stroke of luck. I had met Eric Idle in 1978 when the Monty Python team, while working on *The Life of Brian*, had rented Heron Bay. When I met him again, he had a problem. He had to attend a critical meeting in New York at short notice and all flights out of Barbados were full. I offered to fly him, for a nominal fee, up to St. Maarten, so he could catch a flight from there. He accepted, and, with his girlfriend Tania, we flew up to that half-Dutch, half-French island, eating Smarties all the way. They flew on to New York, and I went to grab a lobster lunch.

Afterwards I wandered into a shop that sold all sorts of things. The owner had recently done a house clearance and had found there about forty Nero Wolfe novels, both hardbacks and paperbacks. She had priced them all at one dollar each. I snapped them up. My collection of the Wolfe novels was all but complete.

Second I found another book in Bridgetown's only bookshop worthy of the name, a popular science volume called *Einstein's Universe,* by Nigel Calder. Since leaving medical school I had been intellectually lazy. My sort of restaurant did not require much in the way of mental effort, only hard work, good humour and long hours. I practised the piano and classical guitar fairly assiduously. I had kept my Russian language alive, listening to tapes in my car. Apart from bridge, there you have the extent of my intellectual endeavours. Delving into Nigel Calder's book had a powerful effect on me. The floodgates opened, and I was all but washed off my feet. It was as if my intellect, starved of nourishment, had suddenly found a source of the very sustenance it craved. I could not get enough of Albert Einstein, the man, the humanist, the philosopher, the thinker, and the theoretical physicist. For years now I have grappled joyously with his two theories of relativity, and have read Abraham Pais' definitive biography of him, *Subtle is the Lord*, three times. I have wondered where this passion for theoretical physics came from. I remember my mother being so proud of her father who, although a builder by trade, studied Euclid and got as far as understanding his Third Book. Maybe I inherited it from my Welsh grandfather.

I was really enjoying doing the polo commentaries, and making a name for myself. I met the daughter of the patron of a visiting polo team called San Flamingo, a girl with a huge belly laugh, the voice of a foghorn and the vocabulary of a stevedore. She was ten years old at the time and I was forty-four. We got engaged. She was called Minnie Driver. I bet she has forgotten.

More and more of the horsey crowd were coming to Barbados. The advance guard was led by the Australian jockey Scobie Breasley, who in the Sixties bought a house on Gibbs Beach not far from Cockroach Palace. He trained race horses in Barbados with great success, particularly those of local tycoon David Seale. Lord Porchester, the Queen's racing manager appeared, as did Jeremy Hindley and many others in the trade. Indeed, Barbados was soon known as Newmarket-on-Sea. Robert Sangster, top breeder and the then owner of Moores' Football Pools, bought an enormous house, Jane's Harbour, next to the Sandy Lane Hotel. His friend and partner, John Magnier, built a house on the other side of the hotel. It was separated from the sea by a single house owned by Lord (Sidney) Bernstein. To the frustration of Mr Magnier, who was desperate to have direct access to the beach, Lord Bernstein – and subsequently his son – refused to sell to him at any price. A possible alternative, the house next door to Lord Bernstein, did not offer much hope either, being owned by Lord Rothschild, who could well, one might assume, afford to say no.

Messrs Magnier and Sangster initiated a pro-am golf tournament and were founder members of a group known as Sangster's Gangsters. Their names read like the cast of a Damon Runyon play: Mike 'Lunchtime' O'Sullivan, the Widow Grey, Sam 'The Slammer' Torrance, J.P. McManus, and the charming stockbroker and banned part-time racehorse trainer Tony Collins. Tony had been part of a Runyonesque plot that involved swapping a horse called Gay Future in a race for a lesser nag, the idea being to make a bob or two. Tony and his fellow conspirator's daring exploit so excited the admiration of the judge, they almost got away with it.

The Gangsters were all golf-mad and rampant gamblers. In the tournament's first year and before the last round, they lunched at tables outside the Gourmet Shop. This was to become a tradition for several years. Nice Peter Allis lurked, Stevie Cauthen loved the game, as did Willie Shoemaker. Charles Benson, alias racing correspondent The Scout, was a key, if frequently impecunious, figure. Not very nice Tony Jacklin was never far away; I say not very nice because, at his request, I went to some lengths to prepare for him a Chinese feast – for which he never thanked me. That, in my book, is not very nice. Over the years the tournament has grown. The Gangsters have been immensely generous in supporting the Island's charities, as well as local restaurants. Robert Sangster was a kind and generous man; when he died in 2004, at the young age of sixty-seven, the Gangsters, Barbados – and I – lost a true friend.

Chapter Thirty-Two

A Dream Comes True

I was flying so much now it seemed best to buy my own aeroplane. I learned through Aero Services, who owned and serviced private aircraft, that their single-engine Cessna 182 and a twin-engine Beech Baron were both for sale. I went to discuss financing a purchase with Lloyd Roberts, a director of Barclays Bank. My casual approach to banking was not exemplary, so I did not rate my chances of success very highly.

So I was surprised when he positively beamed at me. Would the Cessna be big enough, he enquired? Surely the Beech, with its six seats in a cosy club configuration, would be preferable? And weren't two engines safer than one? The Bank would be more than happy to lend me the funds, whichever I chose. Slightly bemused, I settled for the Cessna and the loan was arranged. On 22nd July I and Nick Ashworth – my licensee at the Bagatelle who became my partner in this venture – had our own aeroplane. We even obtained a nifty registration – 8P NIX, the 8P denoting Barbados. Only later was all explained. Barclays had purchased Aero Services Limited and were anxious to sell off any aircraft that did not suit their masterplan. They were more than happy to offload the Cessna and the Beech, financing the buyers if necessary – whatever the likelihood of their repaying the loan.

Also working at the Bank was Richard Barclay, of the Barclay family, who lived in Barbados with his wife Alison. They had sold a Great Dane to La Toc Hotel – wherein lurked Madame Volcano – in St. Lucia, where it would do the rounds with the security personnel. He asked if, for a fee, I would fly the dog out to its new owners. I would be accompanied by a professional dog handler. I agreed. Before putting the beast in the aeroplane, the handler injected him with a tranquilliser. This was very necessary; the prospect of a dog weighing 160 pounds becoming excited in the confines of the tiny cockpit did not bear thinking about. I asked the handler how you could stop dogs accepting food from strangers. Chucking poisoned meat to a 'bad' dog – i.e. a dog that attacks robbers – was a nasty West Indian habit. 'Simple,' he said. 'Put a car battery somewhere on your property, attach to it two leads and insert their terminals into a lump of meat. The dog finds the meat, bites it, and gets a shock. Once is usually enough. Twice certainly is. After that he will only take food from you'

In April 1982 President Reagan decided to spend Easter in Barbados, taking the opportunity to visit his fellow thespian Claudette Colbert at her house in St. Peter. Just to be sure their President would be safe, the US security services had flown in, in the belly of an enormous military cargo aeroplane, three armoured limousines and a brace of helicopters. As an additional precaution, a US Navy gunboat was anchored offshore with a complement of secret service agents, who, laughably disguised as tourists, buzzed around in inflatable dinghies.

Mr Reagan was staying in a house on the Sandy Lane estate. Each morning he was whisked off by helicopter to be with Mademoiselle Colbert, a five-minute flight. Both choppers were always in the air at the same time to confuse those who might want to shoot down the President, halving the odds as it were. When he returned home after dark, the pilots used as a landing guide the floodlights on Ronnie Driver's tennis court, on which we frequently played after dusk. We noticed what the Americans were up to, so, as the choppers approached, we switched off the lights for a short while, then on again, and then off. A man standing in the chopper door shook his fist at us. It was childish behaviour on our part and could have ended in tears.

The President and Claudette spent much of their time picnicking on the beach, a large stretch of which had been closed off to the public, to the annoyance of her neighbours. Under the law beaches belonged to the Nation and were sacrosanct – Barbadians celebrated public holidays on them, playing cricket, splashing around in the surf and swigging Banks Beer. The Island's beaches played an important role in the everyday recreational life of Bajans. One day, on a whim, the President suddenly leapt – well, clambered – to his feet and tottered into the sea. His bodyguard, legally obliged to stay within a certain distance of his charge, had to plunge after him into the briny, suit and all.

Since this was a private visit, the President had no official engagements. The sole exception was when he attended church on Easter Sunday in one of the three limos at his disposal. The locals were very amused, watching the police dogs sniffing behind the gravestones. Later, questions were raised on Capitol Hill when it transpired that this jaunt had cost the American tax-payer 3.5 million dollars.

Before the visit the American authorities made it known that, not trusting Barbados' third world ability to provide an adequately secure telephone system, they had installed their own. After the President's return home, an authoritative letter in *Time* magazine announced that the Barbadians had monitored all the presidential calls! We believed that the CIA had been carrying out background checks on persons they thought might pose a threat. To test this conclusion some American acquaintances of mine, who were staying at the Miramar Hotel, telephoned some compatriots holidaying on another island and mentioned a 'plot' to kidnap the President. Within the hour they were visited by unsmiling men with jutting jaws, steely eyes and bulges at the shoulders of their well-cut suits.

On 15th August 1982 my dear father died. I had spent the last precious weeks of his life with him. As he lay in bed in the Hull Royal Infirmary, I was closer to him than at any time in my life. Whatever may be the advantages of a public school education, getting to know one's parents is not one of them. He gradually lost the power of speech but I generally managed to interpret his signals. Not long before the end he became extremely agitated, but I could not make out what he wanted. In desperation I wrote out the alphabet on a piece of paper. He stabbed at this with his index finger three times. G–I–N! I spoke to his nurse, who spoke to the ward sister, who in turn spoke to Matron, who gave her immediate assent. I went to the off licence and bought a bottle of Gordon's Gin and one of Angostura Bitters. Until the day he died my father had his favourite pink gin on demand, often served by his beautiful nurse, something he greatly appreciated. He was not sad to die, he told me, having achieved all the targets he had set himself by the time he was seventy, and seen his beloved wife well provided for. My father was the finest of men, a Christian, compassionate, and of unimpeachable integrity. He left his estate in perfect order. My brother Richard discharged his duties as executor so admirably that, when probate was granted, the Revenue wrote to congratulate him on the excellence of his work.

In the late autumn of 1982 Suzie Blandford, Billy Mitchell's younger daughter, entered my life. She was a feisty redhead with a terrific body and our life in bed was passionate and adventurous. Not long after she moved in, I began to detect the familiar symptoms of an affliction to which I thought I had become immune. However, after waiting patiently for two years, my Heart detected that the conditions were favourable for another successful incubation of that affliction. Already in place were a successful track record, an international reputation and a loyal following, but an indispensable ingredient had been missing. No longer. Between the Gourmet Shop and El Slummo, on the West Coast road and close to the Island's best hotels, was a parcel of unused land. Location! Location! Location! screamed my Heart. I was defenceless against the bug. Doctor! Help! I feel a restaurant coming on.

Quickly Suzie and I erected a simple building using the cheapest materials – block work walls, a concrete floor, post supports of wallaba – a dense tropical hardwood – and a galvanised iron roof, camouflaged underneath by coconut fronds. The builder called it 'the shed'. The modest kitchen cost less than US$2,000. Originally we were going to call it La Gare du Nord, since it was so close to the noisy West Coast road, but the film *La Cage aux Folles* so stole our hearts that we gave it that name instead, which led to a few misunderstandings in the gay community. In the corner of the unpaved ill-lit car park, between the dining room and the kitchen, there would be a man cooking on a barbecue – me. There I would prepare the best *filet de bœuf à la Béarnaise* anywhere.

This restaurant would repay my capital investment in a single month's trading. You don't have to spend a fortune to create a successful restaurant.

Given, above all, a good location, an unfailingly high standard of welcome, service, staff, food and wine suffice. For some obscure reason, seediness actually sells, as was the case twenty years earlier with the Diner, which was *really* seedy. First-time customers at La Cage aux Folles thought they were slumming it, yet once inside they might rub shoulders with any number of well-known people more used to frequenting the upmarket restaurants of London or Manhattan. The whole world beat a path to our modest door.

Before Ronnie Tree blazed the trail in the 1960s, much of the West Coast land, as I have written, was considered to be uninhabitable and worthless. There was even a small swamp next to La Cage. Sometimes crabs – swamp-ies, as they were called – would sidle into the restaurant, menacing fighting claws the size of my fist held high. I literally had to boot them out. On one occasion, in the middle of the service, I swung my foot at such an unwel-come invader. The crustacean flew through the air and landed in the middle of a table full of *Daily Telegraph* Travel Section writers, my shoe in its claw.

In October Nick Ashworth and I sold our aeroplane, and I truly can't remember why. Possibly it was because I now had at my disposal both Art Taylor's less-than-reliable Piper, and Bernie Weatherhead's immaculate Cessna, with its grown-up retractable undercarriage.

At the Bagatelle everything was apparently going swimmingly. Nick Ashworth was paying the rent on time, as was the Hideaway. La Cage aux Folles was flourishing and Suzie and I were having a great life together, trav-elling to France and Thailand. I was giving polo commentaries locally and internationally, and playing as well. My windsurfer kept me bronzed and fit and I continued to do masses of flying to stock up the Gourmet Shop, which was filling a real need. It was a good life.

In early 1983 our household at El Slummo increased by one in the form of Suzie's ten-year old daughter Luna, who had been living with her granny Billy in Mustique. Luna was a striking child, and took to collecting mirrors in which to look at herself. At the last count there were thirteen of them, scattered around her bedroom and bathroom. Her favourite pastime was to roar along with me in my beach buggy, her long blond hair streaming behind. This caused heads to turn which was, of course, the idea. In all the thirty years I knew her, not once did Luna allow seawater to touch her crowning glory.

In England, following the death of my father, my eldest brother Peter bought the family home, Equerry, named after the minesweeper our father commanded in the war. My mother moved to a delightful mews house in the centre of Beverley, and I went to help her settle in. But there was a fly in the ointment, a seventeen-stone fly.

Early one morning the telephone rang at my mother's house. On the line was my charming neighbour Jim Lambie. The time in Barbados was 3 am. Was I aware, he asked, that there was to be an auction sale at the Bagatelle that very morning, at which, according to an advertisement in the local newspaper, *The Advocate*, the entire contents of my upstairs apartment were up for grabs? I was not.

I got through to my lawyer Barry Gale the moment he entered his chambers. I explained that I had rented out my apartment fully furnished, the only exception being my treasured four-poster which was the subject of a separate gentleman's agreement. I asked Barry Gale to stop the auction. He said he couldn't – why, I have no idea. Ashworth was effectively selling my personal possessions and trousering the proceeds. Gale did have some items removed from the sale but not my irreplaceable bed.

As soon as I could I hurried back to Barbados to Bagatelle, and dashed upstairs to the apartment, only to be attacked by thousands of fleas. When Ashworth left he had taken his dog with him, so I was adopted as a satisfactory substitute host by the pests. I beat a hasty retreat, slapping and squashing, hastened to the nearby rum shop – where they sell everything, as well as rum – bought several cans of flea spray, and thoroughly sprayed the apartment.

Later that day the telephone rang. The caller was a man called Richard Richings. He was staying with his brother Michael, a restaurateur on St. Lucia, whom I knew slightly. He had heard through the grapevine that the Bagatelle restaurant might be available for rent. Could he come to Barbados and look it over? A day or two later I met him at the airport and drove to the Bagatelle. Apart from my foray into the flea-infested apartment, it was the first time since Ashworth did his runner that I had looked around the restaurant area. Having shown Richard the bar and dining rooms, we went into the kitchens. I opened a fridge door and speedily slammed it shut. It was crawling with maggots and the stench was awful. Cautious investigation revealed that all the refrigerators and freezers were equally putrid. The unspeakable Ashworth had turned off the electricity without bothering to remove the perishable foodstuffs.

I would not have been surprised if Richard had hopped on the next aeroplane back to St. Lucia. But he did not. On the contrary, he rolled up his sleeves and helped me clean out the fridges and freezers before even discussing a possible business arrangement. He truly wanted to take over the restaurant. Profoundly upset by the foul condition of the kitchens, I had forgotten for a moment the high esteem in which my restaurant was held.

Richard and his brother Michael hailed from Shrewsbury, where, since leaving school, they had worked in the family hotel business. They had decided it was time to show their father they could run their own shows. Michael, the first to fly the coop, had taken over a waterside restaurant on St. Lucia called Doolittle's, on the water's edge at historic Marigot Bay. I had dined there and remember his delectable *steak au poivre flambé* – fillet steak, double cream, fresh ground black pepper and Cognac, which he prepared with panache over a burner at your table.

Richard was hoping to emulate his brother, with whom he had been staying when Ashworth returned to St. Lucia, his wallet bulging with the proceeds of the sale of *my* goods. In spite of the deplorable condition in which Ashworth had left it, his mind was made up – the Bagatelle was exactly what he was looking for. Soon after, his father and mother came from England to cast their experienced eyes over the business, and both liked what they saw.

We struck a deal, a renewable licence. Richard and his wife Val – a talented artist – two sons and two daughters joined him from England, and they moved into the now flea-free apartment. What of the unspeakable Ashworth? He had never complained about the rent nor hinted at any problems, and ran the Bagatelle satisfactorily. I can only guess that when an opportunity in the form of The Charthouse, his new business, presented itself in St. Lucia, he grabbed it. I finally got through to him. 'These things happen,' was all he managed by way of explanation, before putting the phone down.

I started legal proceedings to recover the moneys he owed me.

★

Towards the end of 1983 Billy became bored in Mustique and felt the urge to return to the sea. Living on an island of just over two square miles, where fresh water is scarce and expensive, and with maybe 500 fellow human beings with nothing to do but gossip, the need for change of air and company is never far away. She had happy memories of the freedom she had enjoyed sailing *Nosegay* on the high seas and chartering her in the Caribbean. She wanted to return to that life.

Her plan was to buy a suitable yacht, have it restored to her specifications and offer it for charter with herself again as hostess. I strongly suspect that she had Bo, her Swedish lover, inked in as skipper. It so happened that Suzie's last boyfriend, a Yorkshireman called John Valentine, specialised in the restoration of vintage yachts. Indeed, he had bought and painstakingly re-built an 1893 gaff pilot cutter, which he had sailed from England to the United States. He was now living with his American wife Debbie and her son Sebastian in Florida. Billy asked him to scout around for a suitable vessel, which she would buy and he restore. She would then sail the boat to the Grenadines and put her out to charter. John began his search among the boatyards found in the innumerable inlets and rivers of the Floridian coastline. In the meantime Billy would put her property, Firefly – now one of only two hotels on Mustique – on the market.

In February 1984 John found a possible candidate anchored in Tarpon Springs, a small town known for its sponge diving industry and Greek immigrants. It was on the Anclote River a few miles upstream from the Gulf of Mexico. She was a Camper and Nicholsons yawl launched in 1912, 69 feet on deck, with a mainmast 80 feet high. She needed work. Her name was *Cariba* and the asking price was US$18,000. This included two lock-ups full of machinery, rigging, winches, vintage fittings and a full set of usable sails.

It's hardly surprising that this news fanned the embers of my yacht-owning ambitions to a healthy red glow. Camper and Nicholsons – *tick!* 1912 – *tick!* Yawl – *tick!* 69 feet on deck – *tick!* $18,000 – *tick! tick! tick!* Once again battle was joined between Heart and Head, and poor Head didn't stand a chance. Your businesses are going well, there's money in the bank, cooed Heart; think how proud your grandfather would be. And Suzie would be the perfect first mate. She is an experienced ocean sailor. This is your dream.

You only live once… A wooden boat is a hole in the water into which you pour money, intoned Head, but no-one was listening.

Billy was still vacillating. She was aware of the open-ended financial commitment restoring large wooden boats entailed, never mind one seventy years old. She suggested I go to Florida to meet John and inspect the yacht. If I fell in love with her, she was mine. But before I took the plunge, she advised, I should have the vessel professionally surveyed and obtain from John a detailed estimate of the cost of restoration. Leaving La Cage aux Folles in Suzie's capable hands, I flew to Tampa – the best-designed airport I know – and drove to Tarpon Springs, where I met John, a spare and somewhat dour Yorkshireman, and Debbie. They took me to the quay where the yacht was moored. *Cariba* was not much to look at but I was immediately struck by her classic lines. This old lady was built for powering her sleek teak hull to windward; she could ride out any storm. Her mahogany deck housing, in spite of its peeling varnish, still echoed her lost Edwardian elegance. I imagined her at anchor after an exciting day's sailing in the boisterous trade winds, and myself sitting on the long overhanging counter, the star-filled tropical sky overhead.

Those yachtie embers burst into flame, and restraint and common sense were reduced to ashes. Heart *would* have its way. I arranged for a survey, although my mid was already made up.

As I was to learn over the next several years, surveys of very old sailing vessels were practically meaningless, no matter what the aim of the survey, whether it was to assess the vessel's value as an asset, or to estimate how much she would cost to restore, or to calculate her resale value once restored. The first task in *Cariba*'s case was to assess the true state of the vessel, a complex integrated structure comprising several different woods nearly one hundred years old, with several tons of lead in the keel. To uncover the deepest secrets of her hull, one would have to dismantle her, which was hardly practical. Thus much of a surveyor's report must consist of guesswork, guided by experience. The state of engines, winches, generators, sails and rigging, being accessible, can be more accurately assessed.

The surveyor found *Cariba* to be generally sound and noted that, notwithstanding the fact that the seller had recently put US$50,000 into essential work, he valued her at US$60,000. The selling prices of vintage yachts, even in mint condition are, as I would discover, in cloud-cuckoo-land. If they sell at all, the price depends on finding a buyer as obsessed as me, or one for whom cost is irrelevant – and even they might change their minds after a few years of meeting a yacht's running costs. For example, a couple of years later, John called to say that he had found a mainsail winch 'going cheap'. Might he buy it? I agreed, because we had to have it. The old one was shot. Only later did it occur to me that, for what I paid for that winch, I could have bought an almost new Mini Cooper.

But even had I known all this in April 1984, it would have made not a jot of difference. I would have bought *Cariba* anyway.

John's 27-page survey was thorough. His estimate for the restoration, of $84,053.25, which included $10,000 contingencies, was:

> '...*an estimate only, and until work progresses, cannot be relied upon as an accurate costing, and the final costs could exceed these figures by a wide margin. However, we will do our utmost to keep within 25%...*'

As is my wont, if I want something, I look at estimates and projections in the most optimistic light. A beautifully restored Edwardian yacht would earn money chartering – wouldn't she? Should the need arise, she had to be worth more than my investment in her. The surveyor had given a replacement figure of US$710,000 and I was going to restore her regardless of cost. Even with a bad sale, my money was safe – surely? Attaboy! urged Heart.

Cariba was hauled out for inspection on 7th April 1984. On 11th April, for $18,000 (the surveyor's previous valuation of $60,000 was ignored); I became the proud owner of a yacht begun by Fays and completed by Camper and Nicholsons, two of the finest builders in the realm. I headed home, delighted with my negotiating skills, in blissful ignorance of what was to come. The purchase price was the smallest bill I was to pay in the whole restoration.

Cariba sailed currently under the American flag, and I wanted her plying the high seas under the British red ensign. But the name *Cariba* on that registry was already taken; I would have to find another. Eventually I settled on *Spirit of Carib*, which expressed the essence of what I was trying to achieve, and on 28th February 1986 succeeded in registering her in Jersey in the Channel Islands.

★

Back in Barbados I bumped into my friend Mike Conlon. He had been in St. Lucia with Albert Coxall – Cox – who, you may remember, was once a close friend of Noel Charles at Alexandra's nightclub; indeed he had come to Noel's financial rescue. His day job was collecting debts, a milieu in which welshing was viewed in a stern and unforgiving manner. Mike and Cox had gone to The Charthouse, Ashworth's new business after Bagatelle, for a drink. Ashworth saw them and, Mike told me, the blood drained from his face. He knew what Cox did for a living, and something of his collection methods, and surmised that Cox was there on my behalf. He feared the worst.

On this occasion my lawyer, Barry Gale, got it right. Some months later I was invited to meet Ashworth's solicitor in the robing room of St. Lucia's Central Criminal Court. His client was not present. From his brief case the solicitor produced bundles of used – non-sequential as they say – American dollar notes and invited me to count them. They totalled something in excess of US$22,000. I signed a receipt and a release and departed. I did not drop by at The Charthouse.

Later that year Richard and Val Richings began to run the Bagatelle with considerable success. The outdoor Barbadian life suited their children and they had the added advantage of the excellent local school system. To this day many Barbadians living in the United Kingdom send their children to school in their country of origin. Places in the best institutions are gained solely on merit. All pupils proudly wear the school uniform and truancy is not tolerated. There is a long queue of eager children waiting to take up the places of those who fall by the wayside. In an independent Barbados nothing is more highly valued than a good education, something so long denied to the majority of the population.

In 1984 Sangster's Gangsters again took over La Cage aux Folles for the lunch before the final round of their pro-am golf tournament. Suzie and I did them proud with a veritable feast. The tournament had begun with the traditional dinner on the eve of the first round. Each year, when the meal was over and everyone thoroughly oiled, Charles Benson would stand up. Having been unbelievably rude about his host and benefactor Robert Sangster – who had on at least three occasions paid off his gambling debts – he would turn auctioneer and sell the players. As the tournament progressed, shares in the players, still in the knock-out tournament and valued on their current performance, were traded for considerable sums. By the time of the La Cage aux Folles lunch, this had reached fever pitch. One man who seemed impervious to the tension was Sam 'The Slammer' Torrance, so called because of his favourite tipple which involved pouring liqueur into a glass, topping it up with Champagne, slamming his hand over it, causing the concoction to fizz violently, and drinking it in one. He got through several of them at the lunch.

Mike 'Lunchtime' O'Sullivan held the book, and fixed the odds on the players' chance of winning the tournament. From time to time he miscalculated, and, like Charles Benson, was rescued by the unfailingly generous Robert Sangster.

After the final round, the winner was declared. At the prize-giving, while talking to Susan Sangster, I had a nasty feeling; I was being drilled by a laser beam emanating from the eyes of a woman not far away. I mentioned this to Susan.

She was vastly amused. 'That's Mrs Brian Barnes, Max Faulkner's daughter. She had a gorilla (£1,000) on her husband to win. Brian went into the last round comfortably in the lead, but she blames you for getting him so drunk at the lunch he could hardly hit the ball and so slipped down the field. She thinks you owe her a gorilla.'

When the Gangsters were in town life was never dull, and they were inclined to let their hair down in the unstuffy atmosphere at La Cage aux Folles. On one occasion Robert and Susan Sangster hosted a dinner there for twenty guests. The dinner began peaceably enough, when suddenly voices were raised. Well before the soup, never mind the loyal toast, Robert's bloodstock agent Billy MacDonald had lit an enormous cigar, enveloping the table in a cloud of smoke. A Mexican woman sitting next to him had asked him to put it out. He may have been good at choosing bloodstock but Billy was an aggressive little man. He refused, telling the lady in precise anatomical terms what he would do with his cigar if she didn't shut up. Billy was sent from the table and was later reported as having a punch-up with a hotel doorman just down the road. He ended up in a cell at the best-avoided Holetown nick – again.

Every restaurant needs a show table. At La Cage aux Folles it was in the centre of the restaurant, surrounded by a small moat and visible from all sides. It had its own little roof and seated four people. Celebrities, we know, like being seen but not hassled. Once it was taken by Oliver Reed and Donald Pleasence. Oliver's wife Josephine and Donald's wife Meira, an Israeli folksinger, were both far younger than their husbands. They were no shrinking violets. A fellow diner, an American, recognised Oliver, and asked me to offer him and his party after-dinner drinks. Not a good idea – Oliver was the last person in the world who should be having after-dinner drinks.

However, the offer was accepted, and Colin Babb the barman delivered the order to their table. When their American benefactor saw the drinks had been safely received, he stood up, raised his glass and shouted, 'Okay, Oliver, let's go lay the women of the town!'

'Don't waste your time,' announced Josephine in a carrying voice. 'He's the worst fuck in the world.'

This unkind observation elicited from Donald, in reality the kindest of men, a crack of laughter so sinister it chilled me to my bones.

La Cage aux Folles continued to receive plaudits. Barry Took wrote in British Airways' *High Life* magazine:

> *'The island hotels are excellent and restaurants abound. If I had to pick only one it would undoubtedly be La Cage aux Folles, which is near the Sandy Lane Golf Club. Here the menu is international and of a standard to be found only in the best restaurants in the world.'*

Such success did not come easily. Constant attention to the smallest detail is the name of the restaurant game, and maintaining that for five years is enough for many proprietors. Living next door made this task much easier for Suzie and me. We were always immediately available and could keep a beady eye on things.

Chapter Thirty-Three

Spirit of Carib Is Restored

I have frequently taken on a project without considering what is involved – cost, time, feasibility – or even visualising the outcome. But often the results have wildly exceeded my expectations. This restoration was no exception. But, as with my purchase and development of Bagatelle, Heart carried the day. I *had* to do it.

The work to be carried out in Tarpon Springs involved the entire vessel – hull, deck, spars, anchor capstan, rigging and sails, electrical systems, and the engine. The interior would be made habitable and the galley workable. This done, *Spirit* would make the sea passage to the Caribbean, where the interior would be completed on which island exactly had not yet been decided, although probably St. Lucia.

We were starting from scratch, the $50,000 invested by the previous owner to rescue the ageing hull having been swallowed up with little to show for it. So it is with old wooden boats. John Valentine, with Debbie's indispensable input, was to lead a team of men and women, and to inspire them by his example, to meet his demanding standards – in short, perfection. John's attitude to the humble screw gives an idea of the standard of workmanship he expected. In the boat-building tradition of Camper and Nicholsons, all screws – of which there were tens of thousands – were counter-sunk, the grooves in the heads aligned fore and aft, and masked by a wooden teak cap. If the head was scratched, the screw was rejected. John was to demand, and be given, such minute attention to detail until the last coat of varnish was applied to the last mahogany panel in the saloon three years hence.

The two lock-ups included in the purchase price were stuffed with all sorts of bits and pieces which had earlier been stripped from the yacht. They were from the Edwardian era and essential if the restoration was to be authentic. Some items were in need of refurbishment or repair, but at least I had them.

Two matters were quickly dealt with. John received his work permit and so could work in the USA legally. And he had unearthed a company in England, C&N Supplies, which held the original documents relating to Camper and Nicholsons hull drawings, sail plans and rigging details, essential to the restoration.

I left my yacht in the skilled and caring hands of the Valentines and their team for her to be made seaworthy to sail the 1,200 miles to the Caribbean. In the meantime I made innumerable decisions concerning the project, with Suzie and I going up to Florida whenever possible to take stock of progress and assist in the demanding physical labour. Finally, I had to make available on demand the necessary funds, a job made so much easier by Debbie's meticulous accounting and John's planning. She and John had taken on a daunting task, but they were committed to seeing it through.

Towards the end of 1984 I began to suffer a nasty pain in my lower back. This surprised me because I had not suffered any injury I was aware of. I went to Dr John Gibling in St. James, who quickly diagnosed kidney stones. He warned me of the pain to come, even recommending with black humour that I bite on a piece of wood when it got really bad. More helpfully he prescribed a cocktail of painkiller, anti-spasmodic and diuretic medication. He was right about the pain; when the stones moved in my urinary system it was excruciating. On a flight home from London Heathrow, just after take-off, I felt the dreaded symptoms, and within a few minutes I was in agony. I could hardly writhe in my seat with fellow-passengers on either side; and when the pain starts it's impossible to sit still. I went to the loo – fortunately for the other passengers there were several – and stayed there all the way to Barbados, emerging from time to time so the flight attendants would know I was not dead.

Never was so much pain caused by something so small. My method was to drink enormous quantities of coconut water, which I bought from the local Rasta at one Barbados dollar a gallon. Unlike tap water you can drink literally gallons of it, and it did actually blast out the horrid pebbles, but at a painful price. I spoke to my friend Ian Wilson, who was a surgeon. He referred me to an urologist, Mr P.R. Riddle at the Royal Masonic Hospital in London, whom I consulted in February 1985. Working every night, he surmised, in a hot tropical kitchen, with my only fluid intake being Muscadet, meant constant dehydration leading to the production of kidney stones. He carried out a small ureterotomy, as it is called, and told me to drink four to five litres of water a day. I have not quite achieved that target but there has been no recurrence of the problem, thank heavens.

The season came to an end. Suzie's mother Billy moved into El Slummo. The hospitality industry was second nature to her and, importantly, she understood West Indians, and they liked her enormously. She confidently took over the running of the restaurant, which enabled Suzie and me to get away more often to Florida to join in the work on my yacht.

It was tough work, for without a mast there was no way of rigging an awning, and laying the teak deck in the roasting Floridian sun was punishing. Suzie had taken on a monumental job, volunteering to restore the colossal main mast, all 80 feet of it. First she sanded off endless layers of old varnish down to the bare wood. She then applied a layer of fresh varnish and sanded that, then applied another and sanded that... She did this seven times, a labour of love if ever there was one. The end result was a glorious spar which in any marina stood out magnificently amid a forest of characterless synthetic poles.

I was luckier in that I was mostly working below deck, removing and replacing the obstinate hull fastenings installed in Edwardian times.

We found some respite at the weekends when we took ourselves to the nearby city of Tampa, where the Hyatt hotel boasted fantastic room service and very good restaurants, the perfect antidote to a gruelling week of work.

★

Towards the end of July I found a beautiful feline creature lying on a banquette in the bar at La Cage aux Folles, long blond hair falling over her face, and a man sitting next to her grinning broadly. Mr and Mrs Jagger – who had wrecked my unwreckable bed in Matilda cottage in Bathsheba a couple of years ago – were in town. Jerry raised a languid hand to be kissed and drawled a Texan welcome. They were overnighting in Barbados on their way to their house on Mustique.

A few days earlier I had watched on television the Live Aid concert in Philadelphia. Mick was performing. Suddenly he appeared to spot Tina Turner in the audience and beckoned her to join him on stage, where they gave a blisteringly raunchy performance to thunderous applause. I expressed my admiration for them, putting on such a show without any rehearsal. He gave me a pitying look. 'Without any rehearsal?' he snorted. 'We rehearsed that gig for three weeks!'

Preparations for making *Spirit of Carib* seaworthy for the journey southwards had been coming on apace. Launching her would require a transporter lift to pick her up from where she had stood for two years, move her about 200 feet, and lower her into the water. This could only be done at a spring tide, which would provide sufficient depth for her 9'6" draft. The operation was by no means straightforward. The lift, dwarfed by the yacht, would be carrying its maximum authorised weight – rather more, in fact.

On 22nd April 1986, *Spirit of Carib* was at her finest, dressed overall, her splendid hull and varnished spars gleaming in the sun, a far cry from the sorry spectacle she had presented two years earlier. The mobile crane picked her up in its slings and, watched by the entire workforce of the boatyard – which looked empty when she had gone – positively tottered over to the dock, its tyres almost flat under their burden. Suzie could not be present but Billy had asked that we observe a Chinese custom, as she had done in Hong Kong with the launch of *Nosegay*, so joss sticks were burned close to the dock. It fell to me to name her *Spirit of Carib* and break a bottle of Champagne on her stem, soaking myself in the process.

Finally she was lowered slowly into the water, and the fine old Edwardian lady was once again back in the element for which she was created.

The next stage was to tow her to a marina where she would be made ready for the passage to Barbados. By this time Bo, who had been languishing in Darwin, Australia, had joined us, and was setting up the rigging, a complicated task. We lost one or two hours of his working time since he suffered from what I have come to call the Scandinavian disease – alcohol. Virtually every Swede and Finn I met in the Caribbean drank like fishes. It must be the long dark days. However, he did find time to make me a beautiful piece of scrimshaw, depicting *Spirit of Carib* in minute detail.

In addition to the comprehensive structural restoration from truck to keel, the yacht was now fully up-to-date in terms of equipment. Besides the conventional machinery found in an ocean-going yacht, I had installed a sat-nav. This inexpensive device is invaluable, no matter how good one's navigating skills, when sailing in coastal waters abounding with unmarked coral reefs and wrecks and few navigational aids.

Also I had installed a water-maker. This device, by means of a process called reverse osmosis – consult your 'A' level physics notebooks! – converted seawater into fresh water at the rate of 15 gallons an hour. It is difficult to convey, to a person used to all the fresh water they want, the luxury and freedom a constant supply of it confers on a sailor. It is nothing short of a miracle. Clothing soaked in salt water never truly dries out unless washed with fresh water. Being awakened at four in the morning to go on watch, and having to pull on damp sticky foul weather gear, would become a misery confined to the past. To compound this blessing, John had created a wooden hip bath in a space next to my cabin, in which Suzie and I intended to luxuriate.

One evening John called on our new-fangled mobile device the size of a young suitcase. A hurricane in the Gulf of Mexico, which I had been tracking, was moving towards the Florida panhandle, and the rising water in the Gulf would send a tidal surge up the coastal rivers. An increase of 15 feet at Tarpon Springs of the Anclote River was predicted. John warned that since my yacht was moored to a pontoon which rose and fell with the tide, even 12 feet would put the vessel higher than the supporting poles. She might then come down on top of them, be holed and sink. He had already sent Debbie and Sebastian ashore. Did the insurance cover such an eventuality? Would it be considered an act of God? What should he do?

I told him that if the pontoon rose even close to the tops of the poles he must go ashore and rejoin his family. He could do no more. Problem analysed. Logic applied. Executive order given. Problem solved. Well done, Mr Hudson. Officer material, obviously.

At around four in the morning the telephone rang again. John's voice was tight. He had kept an eye on the pontoon being raised inexorably by the tidal surge. It was now close to the top and the poles threatened the hull. It was time to abandon ship. But there was an unforeseen snag. As the water reached the level of the walkway, the wooden slats – on which one walked – had floated off and been washed away by the tide. Unable to walk on water, John could not get off the boat. He couldn't possibly plunge into the swollen waters of the Anclote River and try to swim ashore. I had no answer. I ought to be reduced to the ranks.

In the event, the tidal surge had reached its zenith, the water receded, and all was well.

Several weeks later Suzie and I arrived to sail *Spirit of Carib* to Barbados. We assembled a crew of six. John stowed in the forecastle all the tools he would later need to complete the restoration in the Caribbean, cramming the space up to the fore hatch. Suzie brought on board sufficient ship's stores to feed the crew for a month. We were ready to set sail.

CHAPTER THIRTY-FOUR

To The Spanish Main And Beyond

Our course from Tarpon Springs to Barbados was over 1,200 land – not nautical – miles in a south-easterly direction. It would take us into the prevailing north-westerly current that sweeps up from the equator. We would also have the trade winds on our nose for the first thousand miles, which meant we would have to tack – zigzag into the wind – for most of this leg. By the time we reached our destination we would probably have logged close to 3,000 miles.

We set sail in November 1986, emerged from the Anclote River into the Gulf of Mexico, and headed south. Ten miles offshore we touched bottom, a very nasty feeling indeed, and my heart stopped. But it must only have been a sand bar for we were soon moving on. We resumed our course towards Cuba, keeping a bright look-out. Fishing boats in these waters trail astern baited lines as much as 45 miles – yes, 45 miles – long. They catch fish indiscriminately, inedible and endangered species included, and their use is the height of environmental irresponsibility. It is quite possible to foul such gear and never see the vessel towing it.

Aboard *Spirit* – as we came to call her – we were a crew of six: Suzie and me, Bo and three Americans. I regret that I remember them only as the woman, the student and the sailor; their names are in the ship's log but, years afterwards, when the yacht had been sold, in a fit of pique John refused to send it to me. Whatever the rights and wrongs of our contretemps, the log is the property of the owner for the period it covers. If John happens to read this, I hope he will see fit to restore it to me at Journiac in France.

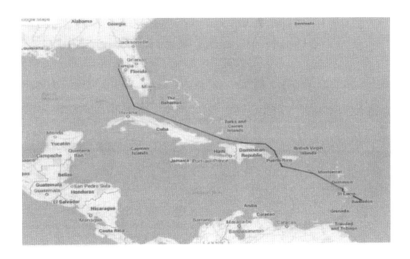

The passage of Spirit of Carib *from Tarpon Springs, Florida to Bridgetown, Barbados – about 1200 miles.*

I divided the crew into three two-man watches, to be on watch for four hours and off for eight. Claiming *droit de seigneur*, I awarded to Suzie and me those covering 0800–1200 and 2000–2400 – the forenoon and first watches, in old money. The others paired off and divided the rest between them. It was a comfortable arrangement.

John, Debbie and Sebastian would follow later in their gaff cutter, *Luke's Minnie*, to Rodney Bay in St. Lucia, where they would complete the restoration of the interior. Their boat was smaller, therefore slower, than *Spirit*, so it would be a demanding trip, months rather than weeks, and they would need to make quite a few stops on the way. They made it, but I never enquired how they managed the watch-keeping. Since there were only two adults on board, they would only have a four-hour rest period.

We skirted the western limits of the Florida Keys, crossed the Straits of Florida, approached as close to Cuba as we dared and turned eastwards. The idea was to sail close to Cuba's north coast to avoid the worst of the current sweeping up into the Gulf of Mexico. I had not appreciated that Cuba is nearly 800 miles from east to west – a hundred miles more than the combined length of England and Scotland – of which we had to traverse 700 miles. Every port tack took us close in shore, putting us well within Cuban territorial waters. Our American student became quite agitated, imagining himself on the cover of *Time* magazine, languishing in a gaol in downtown Havana, or becoming an item on CNN news.

After several days we left Cuban waters unchallenged, and began to cross the northern entrance to the Windward Passage. Guantánamo, the US naval base, was just around the corner. Suddenly a United States military helicopter appeared and hovered overhead, the downdraught playing havoc with our sails. A man at the door of the aircraft signed that we should make radio contact. I did so, as usual on channel 16, before switching to another frequency. He was abrupt and bossy as American officials so often are in the Caribbean. They think they own the place, that it is their 'back yard', and that the hated Monroe Doctrine gives them the right to behave as they please. The nearby Turks and Caicos Islands had been granted certain privileges if they permitted the American military, for reasons of immigration control and illegal drug interdiction, to overfly their territorial waters, and generally throw their weight about. We were well south of that area and in international waters, so I got shirty too, pointing out that we were sailing under the red ensign – kindly note flag flying proudly on stern – and said, somewhat facetiously, that if they did not improve their behaviour, I would set Mrs Thatcher on them. In those days she was everywhere perceived as being akin to Boadicea. They went away! Rule Britannia!

The sailing on the reliable trade winds was very agreeable. There was not much steering to do except when tacking, as the autopilot was slaved to the sat-nav and kept the vessel on course. This combination of systems was marvellous when it worked, but no electrical system on board an ocean-going yacht ever works all the time. Of all difficult marriages few can compare with that between electricity and seawater; it is as bad as they come, but they have to stay together for the sake of the child – the yacht.

After crossing the Windward Passage, we saw to starboard the island of Hispaniola, the western part of which is Haiti, the poorest nation in the western hemisphere. This poverty is not of its own making. The country gained independence from France in 1804, thanks to an ex-slave, Toussaint L'Ouverture. It has been burdened by debt since 1825, first to its colonial master France, and later the rapacious international financial community, only paying off its crippling indemnity in the late 1947. Never was a country worse treated. It is yet to recover.

In another 150 miles the Dominican Republic, the eastern part of Hispaniola, was off our starboard beam. One hundred miles further still, we arrived at the town of Puerto Plata, where we planned to stay for a day or two and take on fresh water. We moored stern on to the marina and I trotted down the gangplank and onto the pontoon to find that, after a week of sailing, my legs were unused to land. Terra was not firma at all. I was rolling around like a drunken Jack Tar and it took me half an hour to return to my normal gait.

Puerto Plata had been part of the Spanish Main. Once-opulent buildings with long colonnaded façades bore witness to the good old days of gold and silver seizure, piracy and slave-trading. Now they were shuttered, sadly dilapidated. As far as one could deduce two industries flourished in Puerto Plata, prostitution and amber. The girls on the street gave the impression of being happy in their work. Indeed it had become an export. As far south as the Dutch Antilles, it was the ladies of the Dominican Republic who staffed the strictly regulated brothels sanctioned by the government and the Catholic Church. I knew the Dutch were worldly, but had no idea the leaders of the Church of Rome were such realists. The girls went there on a limited-stay work visa, and in three months earned far more than they could in a lifetime at home – and in Yankee dollars to boot! Campo Alegre on Curaçao was the biggest house of ill repute in the Caribbean. The one on Aruba was set up in one of the wartime US Air Force bases that were built in the Caribbean, so that submarine hunters could attack the U-boats that sank so much allied shipping. Hewanorra airport on St. Lucia was another such base. The centre of Nazi Caribbean operations was Martinique, then part of Vichy France, and U-boat pens were built there. The submarine hunters required very long runways, which have since proved very useful for handling tourist-laden Jumbo jets.

That evening, on the Puerto Plata marina, I was enjoying a sundowner on the counter of *Spirit* when a swarthy man, with a cap covered in enough scrambled egg for an Admiral of the Fleet, came up the gangplank. He was, he announced, the harbour master, though his authority was somewhat diminished by his string vest, dirty white shorts and bare feet. I gave him a Scotch and paid him for the water we had taken on board that afternoon. He admired my shoes, a rather smart pair of deckies, and said he would like to 'buy' them. I tried to convey that as they were the only pair of shoes I possessed – which was true – I was unable to do without them. He finally took no for an answer and slunk away.

The next morning, taking advantage of a hosepipe on the pontoon, I took a good long fresh water shower, probably the last before Barbados. My word, it felt good! I soaped myself luxuriously and reached for the hose to rinse off the gleaming torso – and the water stopped. I stood on the deck like a model for pink Camay. Next to the standpipe, hand on tap, stood the harbour master, grinning fiendishly. I had no intention of using any of our valuable fresh water to finish the job and only a fool dives into that foul harbour, which is little more than an open sewer. So I waited until we were well clear of Puerto Plata, and plunged over the side.

Within half an hour we were becalmed. As there was no sign of the wind getting up, my only option was to resort to the engine which, for a change, fired up immediately. I engaged the gear, we moved ahead briefly, and then the engine cut. Ever since leaving the Anclote River we had towed a Walker log, a device that trails astern, spinning, and records via a cord to a counter on the stern rail the distance traversed. I had unthinkingly set the yacht's propeller turning, forgetting that since the vessel was stationary the line was hanging straight down, and it had become entwined around the shaft. An enormous swell was running, a condition I particularly dislike, and the sloppy disordered sea was causing the yacht to pitch violently, the counter rearing up, then slamming against the water with a crash. We were drifting towards the rocky shore and needed to free the propeller. I was gathering up courage to take the plunge – which I did not fancy in the least – when Bo dashed below, came up with a mask, flippers and knife, and dived down to the propeller, almost ten feet under water. Hanging on grimly to the rudder post he sawed away at the entangled line, all the time being raised up and dashed down, the sea foaming around him, snatching a breath of air when he could. It was an act of great courage, for he could have been badly hurt, even drowned. At last he was on the surface, breathless, but able to give a thumbs-up. We hauled him aboard, restarted the engine, and moved smartly away from the menacing rocks.

The breeze picked up, I cut the engine, and we resumed our easterly course. Our next change of course would be almost due south into the Mona Passage, which separates the Dominican Republic from Puerto Rico. What a stretch of water it is! Part of the important shipping route between the Panama Canal and the Atlantic Ocean, it is the principal connection between the Caribbean and the Atlantic. It has a terrible reputation in yachting circles and is reckoned by some to be one of the most difficult and dangerous passages in the world. Merchantmen barrel through on autopilot without a look-out on the bridge. Humpback whales use it on their way to and from their breeding grounds. The North Atlantic current pours into the southern end causing strong tidal currents to flow in unpredictable directions. Sandbanks reach far out into the main channel. The mountains on either side mean that the winds are fluky, the weather unstable and powerful electric storms frequent. It is no surprise that the advice to sailors is not to take the Mona Passage lightly.

I had been there before in 1976, when Art Taylor and I flew his single-engine Piper Arrow from Tamiami, Florida to Barbados. One of our refuelling points was San Juan in Puerto Rico, so our flight path took us over the Mona Passage. The meteorological conditions had forced us higher and higher as there was no way round the cloud mass. Eventually, at 14,000 feet, we had clear air ahead. The service ceiling of the aircraft was 16,200 feet, so it was gasping for oxygen. I noticed that when we spoke of our voices sounded much higher than usual, whether for physiological reasons or because of dreadful apprehension I do not know. I *do* know we were glad to land at San Juan International Airport.

Many yachtsmen wait at Samaná on the north Dominican coast for a favourable weather window, then make a dash for it. I went for it anyway. The weather was kind, the wind helpfully backing easterly, so that we did not have to tack.

Once clear of the Mona Passage, *Spirit* powered her way out into the Caribbean Sea, where we headed eastwards to Charlotte Amalie, capital of the US Virgin Islands, where the American woman and the student would catch a flight back to the States.

Just after leaving Puerto Rico, south of the small island of Vieques we observed columns of water erupting to the north, as though we were being bombarded. I dashed down to examine the chart. We were indeed being bombarded, for we had strayed into a firing range. We did not hang around. Sat-navs can make one complacent and lazy about referring to the charts as frequently as one should. Once anchored at Charlotte Amalie, we conveyed our shipmates ashore in the inflatable dinghy and wished them farewell. They had been good companions, and never complained about the Spartan conditions below deck.

Charlotte Amalie apparently served only one purpose – as a vast shopping centre. Every couple of hours an enormous cruise liner, perfectly disguised as a floating block of flats, would spew out into waiting taxis torrents of garishly dressed persons carrying large shopping bags. They went directly to huge warehouses full of duty-free shops, where they shopped till they dropped. All food and drink was included in the cost of the cruise and they dined on board, so any other attractions the Island might have offered, not least the restaurants, went unremarked. As each departed another moved in, and another three or four would be waiting just outside the harbour. Thus it is that the Caribbean has 80% of the world's cruise ship business. We watched aghast from *Spirit*, knowing that the only beneficiaries of this trade were the taxi drivers, duty-free shops and harbour authorities, and the senior pursers aboard who took enormous amounts of commission. Meanwhile the island's infrastructure took a terrible drubbing.

We set sail two days later with just me, Suzie, Bo and the American sailor on board. We continued with the same watches; Suzie and I kept 0800–1200 and 2000–2400, and Bo and the sailor each stood the other two alone but with help always at hand. Our penultimate port of call was Martinique. The course was a comfortable south-south-east, which meant, although we were hard on the wind, we could make good our heading without tacking. And ever since we had left Florida, in the heavens dead ahead were Orion, his Belt and Betelgeuse. Stars, unchanging and infallible, beyond the reach of worldly influences, are a great comfort to a navigator.

★

This leg of 350 miles was uneventful except for the early evening line squalls, which could be quite lively. The brief downfalls, which gave us the chance to wash salt off our bodies and brine-soaked clothing, thoughtfully, announced themselves well in advance as a long line of fierce low black clouds. Occasionally lightning, in the form of thick braided golden cords, lit up the boiling undersides of the clouds. Strangely, there was no thunder. These disturbances sometimes packed very strong winds, but we always had time to shorten sail until they had passed. They were part of our daily routine.

Two days later we approached Martinique from the north-west. The peak of Mont Pelée, the dormant volcano, dominates the northern end of the island. We kept a wary outlook, as the mountains can impart to the trade winds from the east a considerable vertical factor – williwaws as they are known – in the lee. These may cause knock-downs when yachts' sails are forced down flat on the sea. We headed southwards along the west coast, passing Saint-Pierre, and soon saw on our port beam the town of Fort-de-France, which replaced Saint-Pierre as the capital after the eruption of Mont Pelée. It is protected by the massive ramparts of Fort Saint-Louis, where France's national gold reserve was stored in the early 1940s when the Island formed part of Vichy France. I knew the town well and its restaurants even better. We would overnight here before tackling the last leg to Barbados. Conveniently, on the water's edge, was a dive run by an ex-jailbird called Henri. It was dusty, dark and probably dirty, illuminated by strip lights inside pieces of bamboo drilled with holes and candles on the tables. The food was so good that there being no menu, no choice, and no change ever whilst I frequented the place, did not matter. Henri charged whatever he felt like but he was never greedy. The first course was a mousse of squid dotted with tiny pieces of hot Scotch Bonnet pepper, the main course rabbit in mustard sauce, and the pud was *crêpes Suzette*, which Henri flamed with his own version of Grand Marnier, with strong rum as the active ingredient. We returned to *Spirit* in a happy frame of mind.

We set sail at noon the next day, leaving Martinique to port and St. Lucia to starboard, and, once in the Atlantic, headed directly for Barbados. Again the wind was hard on the nose but we were able to make good our course of south-south-east without having to tack. The North Atlantic current was also heading us, but my old lady bashed into it with glee. Since the forecastle was full of equipment, we were heavy in the bow, so rather than go over the waves she was more inclined to go through them. We would emerge with water pouring along the deck and out of the scuppers, but not a drop went below, a tribute to the work of John Valentine and his team. Apparently, after Suzie and I turned in at midnight, the weather turned very rough indeed, so Bo and the American sailor had to hand (take down) the mainsail and sail 'jib and jigger' with the staysail and mizzen, a configuration unique to yawls and ketches, and ideal for such conditions. I didn't wake up once.

Early the next afternoon, our Barbados courtesy flag with its broken trident flying on the starboard shroud, we tied up at the Deep Water Harbour in Barbados. We were home!

CHAPTER THIRTY-FIVE

Uncharted Waters

Having cleared my yacht with the port authorities, we sailed up the West Coast, anchored off the Treasure Beach Hotel and went ashore to El Slummo to be reunited with Billy and Luna. Bo was left on board in charge of *Spirit*. He was a victim of the Scandinavian disease but had sworn not to touch a drop of the stuff during the trip, and had kept his word. But now he returned to his old ways. His efforts to navigate the inflatable dinghy through the surf and clamber aboard *Spirit* after a night's carousing were mostly unsuccessful. Often he would knock on the door at El Slummo in the small hours, sending the dogs wild. For all that, he was a fine and courageous man.

It was very jolly having *Spirit* so close – literally across the road – allowing me to take my friends cruising along the coast. Amongst my guests were two of my dearest friends, Michael Deeley and his terrific wife Ruth. Michael was, to say the least, a successful film producer, with *The Italian Job*, *The Deer Hunter* and *Bladerunner* to his credit.

For insurance reasons I had to have *Spirit* professionally valued locally. Admittedly the marine surveyor had no similar vessels with which to compare her, but his figure of US$60,000 seemed hardly less than derisory. I was starting to mistrust marine surveyors as valuers.

We were now into the 1987 Season. Out of the blue I had a telephone call from Mick Jagger. He and Jerry had taken a house in the parish of St. Peter, and had with them their two young children, Elizabeth and James. Would I care to drop round and admire the little nippers? And how! I hopped round and gave them a prod. Ronnie and Misty Driver also had a youngster called Charlie, so I thought of arranging for the children to get together. Misty suggested a children's tea party at about four o'clock the next day at San Flamingo, their home next to the polo field. Mick, Jerry and their children would come past El Slummo and I would escort them there.

The next afternoon I waited…and waited…and waited. This was surprising, for Mick is meticulously punctual. It was not until the next morning that I heard from a very distressed Mick that Jerry was in prison. Apparently she had asked her butler on Mustique to send her in Barbados, via Mustique Airways, some things that she needed in Paris where she was going to do some modelling work. The Grantley Adams Airport Customs had rung, saying they had a package addressed to her. She went to pick it up but the package looked nothing like the one she was expecting, and she declined to open it. The Customs officer insisted. Under protest she obliged. It contained 20 pounds of marijuana! Jerry reiterated that it had nothing to do with her. Even her name was misspelled, she pointed out.

They did not believe her and she was locked up in the Oistins police station, charged with possession of an illegal drug. Still protesting her innocence, she was arraigned before the Oistins magistrate and spent the night in a wretched cell. Most Barbadian police stations were built in the seventeenth century and the wind of change has not blown through them. By the time she was released on BDS$5,000 bail, threatened with a $50,000 fine and two years in prison, had surrendered her passport, been instructed to report to the Holetown police station twice a day, and had the charges dismissed, Jerry had lost fourteen pounds in weight. In the event, she was found not guilty and set free. Not surprisingly, en route to Mustique in future years, the Jaggers did not stay in Barbados a moment longer than necessary.

Whilst Suzie and I were sailing *Spirit* down from Florida, Billy had really enjoyed running La Cage aux Folles and creating a garden around El Slummo. She had even managed to get a jade vine to grow. Her granddaughter Luna shared the house and they got on well together. I was in love with my yacht and Suzie maybe was in love with me. We decided to try to arrange matters so everyone got what they wanted. Billy would buy La Cage aux Folles for US$93,000, which I would invest in finishing off *Spirit*. Suzie and I would live aboard her, chartering in the winter months and cruising the Caribbean and beyond in the summer. Billy handed over the money and took over the running of the restaurant.

Then she decided she didn't want to buy it after all; *la donna è mobile*. Well, Billy was anyway. She wanted to go back to Mustique and make more of Firefly instead. But by then the money was either committed or spent. So I agreed to pay Billy interest of 8% per annum until I could repay the principal sum. The way the dollars were pouring in, I could easily amass $93,000 in a couple of years, I told myself. In the event, I paid it off eleven years later.

In St. Lucia John and Debbie had nearly finished the interior of *Spirit*. When finally she was ready, I offered John a job as skipper and Debbie as cook. At first he declined, saying that he had no experience of such a large sailing vessel, and pointing out that having a permanent crew of only two, increasing to three when chartering, meant that she would frequently be short-handed (in John's original 1984 survey he wrote that *Spirit* needed a crew of six, even for day sailing). I persuaded him that, given the modern equipment we had installed, he and Debbie would be able to manage well. He relented, we agreed a salary, and they set sail. They inevitably encountered severe weather but they came through unscathed. John was a cautious sailor, as one would expect of a man skippering someone else's yacht. For example, he usually sailed with a single reef permanently in the enormous mainsail. When I was on board, we immediately shook out!

On 18th December John's elder brother, a doctor, became the first to charter *Spirit*. John and Debbie, assisted by their Canadian first mate Scott McDougal, proved natural hosts. The remarks in the visitors' book all glowed with praise for the yacht herself, the crew, and Debbie's scrumptious cooking – whatever the weather.

Then, in January 1988, a honeymooning couple sunbathing on a beach in southern St. Lucia saw a fine yacht anchored offshore, and – on the husband's suggestion – swam out for a closer look. They hailed, 'Ahoy there, *Spirit of Carib*.' No reply. 'Let's take a peep anyway,' the man said.

He climbed up a ladder, then helped his apprehensive wife on board. They surveyed the spotless teak deck, polished brass fittings, giant winches, and the table and chairs on the counter, shaded by the mizzen awning. As they stood there, awestruck, an inflatable dingy came alongside and its three occupants climbed aboard. The wife was mortified and began to explain. One of the new arrivals raised a horny hand. He said it was flattering that they found *Spirit* so irresistible – perhaps they'd care to come for a short sail? The anchor was weighed, the sails set, and off they went, soon to be overhauled by the hotel water-ski boat with their luggage. Of course it was a put-up job, arranged between John and the husband, and the newly-weds sailed into the sunset to spend a blissful honeymoon in the Grenadines aboard *Spirit*.

Suzie and I had been together for five years, and had many interests in common, but our bed life was running out of steam. We both had a bit on the side now and again, but sleeping in the same bed had lost its point. Following the death of my father Suzie had drawn very close to my mother, and was extremely supportive of her in her early widowhood, but I had always known that I would never marry Suzie.

I decided to move back to the apartment at Bagatelle. Richard and Val Richings had made such a success of the Bagatelle that they had been able to buy from the Kidds a plot of land overlooking the Holders polo field, where they had built an attractive house into which they now moved. Suzie seemed happy to stay on at El Slummo with Luna. What a clever fellow I was, I thought, to extract myself in such a way that a woman, who not always easy to please, accepted my new arrangements without protest. Over the years in Barbados I had joined a sort of club. It had no rules, no membership list, and no subscription fee. Its existence was never mentioned. It just *was*. Being part of it meant that anywhere in the world – Barbados, Mustique, New York, Paris, London, Antigua, even Yorkshire – where a fellow 'member' resided, provided they were expecting you, you were made welcome. And you invariably woke up with an attractive bed companion. I have always thought of it, but never said in so many words before writing this book, as the YNSA – You Never Sleep Alone. Thus travelling single once again was the greatest fun, and cost half as much.

I decided to give myself a moving-in present, and bought an 1889 Bechstein concert grand piano, which I had completely restored by the talented Michael Gibbons, a member of the hyper-conservative Barbadian Plymouth Brethren. Even before the restoration, the piano's rich dark-chocolate bass register set my heart beating. Never mind how poor a pianist you may be, there is nothing quite like playing on a concert grand – lid up, of course. It was an inspiring addition to my 60-foot drawing room and proved irresistible to musically inclined guests.

My fiftieth birthday was approaching and I decided to spend it aboard *Spirit* – where better? I borrowed Bernie Weatherhead's aeroplane – the sexy one with the retractable undercarriage – and flew to St. Lucia, where I boarded the yacht in Rodney Bay. The next day we set a southerly course towards the Grenadines 70 miles away. Our first stop was in the lee of the Pitons, the iconic twin mountains of St. Lucia, where I went ashore to do a little exploring. Not for long. Along the beach came an elephant, flapping its ears in an undeniably threatening manner. I beat a hasty retreat. Apparently Colin Tennant had imported it to Mustique. But elephants eat about 300 pounds of vegetation a day so, to preserve what remained of the Island's scant vegetation, he had been deported to this land under the Pitons, which Colin owned with the intention of developing it. Two young West Indian mahouts were rumoured to have taught the beast to dislike white people, and he had learned well.

We sailed on the next morning and anchored in the Tobago Cays, a divine spot surrounded by reefs. The entrance is quite tricky and eyeball navigation the only safe way to enter; a crew member wearing Polaroid sunglasses is hauled up to the lower spreader, from which the reefs are clearly visible, to shout and hand-signal steering instructions to the helmsman. Tragically, nowadays it is an overcrowded anchorage, the seabed covered in Coca-Cola cans.

That evening we rigged the barbecue and cooked a barracuda we had caught on a line trailed astern. One of the more gruesome sights aboard charter boats is an attempt to kill a recently caught fish. A winch handle is often used to bludgeon the animal to death, and gore splatters everywhere. The simple, humane and mess-free method is to pour rum into its gills; that does the trick in a moment.

The next day we continued southwards to the island resort of Petit St. Vincent, where accommodation is in comfortable wooden bungalows, each with a veranda and a plunge pool. Each unit has a flagpole. If you need something, you hoist a flag and a waiter is dispatched on a Mini-Moke, otherwise you are left undisturbed. This was where I had intended to have my birthday dinner, but a very strong current was running through the anchorage and we decided it would be foolhardy to leave *Spirit* unattended. We dined on board instead and Debbie worked wonders in the tiny galley.

Over the next few days we meandered northwards, anchoring here and there. Once the routine of putting *Spirit* to bed was completed, I would cruise amongst the yachts on my windsurfer looking for boats I knew, and enjoy a sundowner with their crews. One of my favourite ports of call was the tiny island of Mayreau, west of the Tobago Cays. A short walk up from the beach was Denis' Bar, where the conch mousse was to die for, and best washed down with a shot or two of Jack Iron rum. The acid test for this bootlegged firewater was simple – if an ice cube didn't sink, as through a vapour, you sent it back for being below strength. Denis had a very pretty English girlfriend. A year or so previously a yacht had anchored at Mayreau and the two couples aboard had repaired to Denis's Bar. When they left they were only three; one of the wives had decided she preferred a life with Denis on Mayreau to one with her husband in Birmingham.

I arrived back in St. Lucia relaxed and refreshed. I had greatly enjoyed my yacht. All the equipment was working perfectly, a rare state of affairs on a sophisticated yacht. Debbie had been in top form in the galley. John, a Yorkshireman through and through, insisted on meat, spuds and two vegetables every evening, whatever the weather. He was a man with all the flexibility of a crystal walking stick, yet totally dependable, loyal, and fearless. He and Debbie were good shipmates.

In a year's time the lease at La Cage aux Folles would be due for renewal. My landlord Norman Green lived in Harlem in New York. Conveniently we shared a lawyer, Sir Henry Forde, whom I asked to arrange for a ten-year extension. I heard nothing. Eventually Sir Henry told me that Mr Green was not going to extend the lease, which was surprising. I had, at my own cost, built a restaurant – primitive, but world-famous – on his land, with his permission. I had paid the rent on time. When last he dropped by for a drink, he appeared perfectly amiable. His refusal was something of a mystery, and highly inconvenient. This was our milch cow, the golden-egg-laying goose that allowed me to run my yacht (the nett income from chartering her nowhere near covered the overheads). I persisted, for I had built up much good will. But Mr Green would only communicate through Sir Henry and refused to budge.

Disturbingly, John, just returned from another successful charter, reported two savage attacks on yachts in the Grenadines. In one, the father of the family was now in the intensive care unit on Martinique with a broken jaw and fractured skull. In another, in the Tobago Cays, two yachts had been boarded, everyone robbed at gunpoint and a young girl raped. Closer to home, John and Debbie woke one morning to find *Spirit*'s inflatable dinghy, which had been tied up alongside, gone. Robbers had swum out and cut it adrift, then, well away from *Spirit*, in another boat, they had taken the outboard engine and slashed the inflatable, at a cost to me of more than US$2,500. John went on:

> *'You can imagine our feelings during our nights at anchor in the Grenadines; without firearms we are defenceless, so perhaps the time has come to consider carrying weapons… As you can imagine we are extremely depressed and are beginning to wonder what is happening down here, the lawlessness is out of control; every day we hear of some other incident of theft or assault.'*

It looked as if my dream of a life of cruising and chartering was turning into a nightmare. John was not given to exaggeration or scaremongering, but he had a wife and stepson. The immaculate *Spirit* reeked of money and was a likely target, and her charterers would be at risk too. I could not envisage the necessity for bearing firearms as being part of an idyllic holiday afloat.

One solution as a defence against being boarded was provided by the legendary yachtsman Joshua Slocum. Whilst he was making the first single-handed circumnavigation, the bare-footed savages of Tierra del Fuego were inclined to creep on board his yacht *Spray* at night to steal things. So before turning in he would scatter tintacks on the deck. But that was hardly a long-term solution.

The next event on my yacht calendar, the Antigua Charter Yacht Show, would be the equivalent of *Spirit*'s Queen Charlotte's Ball. There she would meet her peers, all dressed in spotless white and ravishing, ready to be introduced to suitable charter booking agents. At the last moment Debbie had to be in the USA. I was not best pleased, as I liked to entertain agents with lunches and dinners on board. Further, I spent comparatively little time aboard my yacht, and fully expected that when I did so the full crew, whose wages I paid whether I was on board or not, would be there for me. In the event, John and I did a good job. New York journalist Erla Swingle later wrote to me:

> '*The Antigua Charter Yacht Show will always make a good story, but my day with you on* Spirit of Carib *is the stuff of great memories. My friends are already thoroughly sick of hearing me talking about it.*'

That was the magic of the yacht I rescued from the backwaters of Florida and brought back to life.

At the Show Alexander Laird, who worked at Sotheby's, told me that the auction house was for the first time thinking of holding an auction sale of classic yachts the following summer. *Spirit* would make an attractive lot in the sale, he suggested. The violence in the Grenadines, reinforced by Debbie's absence, compounded by Mr Green's refusal to extend my lease, all led me to promise to think about it. In the meantime, as a result of contacts we had made at the Show, we picked up several charters at nearly $4,000 per week, which was handy.

I decided to put *Spirit* into Sotheby's sale, which was scheduled for 31st May 1989. In March I had her professionally valued, and the figure was US$400,000, which sounded about right. I paid £800 to appear in the catalogue, and went to London to attend the sale, sitting in the front row reserved for sellers. *Spirit* had an estimate of £230,000–280,000, and the saleroom was full. But, in the words of *The Times*' art market correspondent, Sarah Jane Checkland, '*Sotheby's suffered a fiasco at its first sale of full-scale yachts last night when only eight of 28 on offer sold.*' And a spokesman for Sotheby's said,

'Clearly the yachting world isn't ready for us yet.'

I was no longer bothering to add up how much I had spent on *Spirit*; it would have been pointless and distressing and, as it transpired, irrelevant. After the sale I put her on the open market, advertising in several yachting publications. No-one expressed interest.

That June Barbados celebrated 350 years of unbroken parliamentary rule, a statistic which, combined with the national motto *Pride and Industry*, went a long way to explaining the great success of this tiny nation. I felt prouder than ever of my Barbadian nationality.

In October I went across to England, first to Beverley to see my mother in her new mews house. She was well looked after by Mrs Grey, who had been with the family for decades – indeed, she *was* one of the family. My brothers and their wives were also very attentive and caring, something for which I, living so far away, was extremely grateful.

Whilst there I bumped into my childhood friend Jill Chatterton, and asked – as I always did – for news of our mutual friend Veronica Nicholson. She was married for the second time, Jill told me, to a successful business-man called Ron Howard, and they lived in Bedfordshire. And yes, Jill did happen to have her telephone number.

I went to London to stay with Anna and Derek at Chelsea Green. At the first opportunity I called Veronica. Her husband answered. His wife was out, he said, but he would pass on my number. Later the phone rang. There was no mistaking Veronica's voice, although we had not spoken since I had dined with her and a friend twenty years before. I had wanted to see her again, but her then fiancé, an actor called Bill Ellis, would not allow it.

Way back in 1958 I saw her once, or thought I did; I was on the up esca-lator at Piccadilly underground station. Going down, I swear, was Veron-ica, dark hair falling over her left eye as usual, a secret smile on her lips. I waved frantically but she looked fixedly ahead. I galloped up the escalator and down the other side, but she had vanished. Thirty years later Veronica confessed – it had indeed been her. She was wearing her favourite citrus yellow coat. That day had been very hot, so, such was the naïveté of this leggy young thing from Yorkshire, rather than abandon her favourite garment, she had sashayed around the West End wearing nothing under it but bra and panties.

Now we were speaking again. I asked if we might meet for dinner. As it happened, Ron was out that evening, so we arranged to meet at the cocktail bar at the Sheraton Park Tower Hotel. I was sipping a drink, remembering the dark-haired beauty of my childhood, when I heard an enquiring low-pitched voice – 'Nicky Hudson?'

And there she was, elegant in a perfectly cut burgundy and black check suit, and even more beautiful than I remembered. The intervening years melted away. Nobody and nothing else existed for us at that moment.

We had dinner at my favourite restaurant, La Poissonerie in Sloane Avenue. I was all too aware that Veronica was a married woman, but managed to keep my feelings under control. As I put her into a taxi after dinner I asked if I might write to her. She said I could. We both knew in our hearts that this was meant to be, that we had to be together for the rest of our lives.

I was in uncharted waters.

CHAPTER THIRTY-SIX

Changing Of The Watch

I was elated. Veronica had decided to leave Ron and join me as soon as possible. We would spit out the legal pips later. But my telephone bill, thanks to gouging Cable & Wireless, took a terrible hit in the meantime.

I also had another matter on my mind. Richard Richings had made an offer to buy all the shares in the Bagatelle business. This suited me, as I needed some cash to create La Cage aux Folles II, negotiations to extend my lease having proved fruitless. Donald Marshall decided not to sell his shares. He shared with his wife Cherry a passion for golf, and the on-Island golf scene was improving year by year, so the fringe benefits he enjoyed, thanks to his shareholding in Bagatelle, fitted in very well. Richard and I agreed a price for my shares. The deal also allowed me to continue living in the apartment at the Bagatelle.

Planning permission to change Summerland House – a property I had purchased on which to create a new La Cage aux Folles – into a restaurant finally came through. I put together a team of builders and work began. The job was to take almost a year.

Meanwhile, in England Veronica was having a torrid time, having told her husband she was leaving him. Belatedly, he had realised how much he needed her to help him ascend the social ladder, something for which he was ill-equipped. For Ron life was all about money. Veronica's desires and aspirations were of secondary importance, and her exceptional talents in the performing arts, antiques, horticulture and writing were never allowed to flourish – that would have meant she had less time for him. She had longed to have children but failed to do so. Finally she had gone through the exhaustive adoption process. When at last a suitable baby was found, Ron refused to let her adopt it. He could not have dealt her a more shattering blow. He did admit many years later, when they were somewhat reconciled, that he had got his priorities wrong.

Veronica went to live with a girlfriend until it was time to leave for Barbados. I sent her the money for an airline ticket, and on 13th February 1990 I drove to the airport to meet her. Walking from the aeroplane, although painfully thin, she somehow managed to look radiant. With a quick wave she disappeared into Immigration and Customs and emerged, with the single suitcase she had brought with her, some time later. There had been a problem at Immigration. Never doubting that she would not be returning, she had bought a one-way ticket, not knowing that non-Barbadians must have a valid return ticket before being admitted to the country. Then she remembered – Ron had given her a return ticket in case she changed her mind! The immigration officials accepted this and all was well. What a cruel irony it was for Ron that the ticket he had given his wife, to enable her to return to him, allowed her to remain with me.

When we arrived at Bagatelle Veronica was overwhelmed by the classic Palladian façade of the Great House. I introduced her to my two Dobermans, Zen and Lulu. The poor girl was terrified. She had never lived with dogs and this breed had an unjustifiably bad reputation. But they all quickly became bosom pals. I had prepared my darling for the minimal nature of the furnishings of my home by sending photos. Very much the bachelor, I had only bought pieces I really needed. She was amused to see birds nesting in the Georgian chandeliers in the drawing room. We stopped only to grab a bottle of Champagne from the fridge before flinging ourselves on the new four-poster. The angels sang divinely.

I felt I ought to introduce Veronica to Suzie. After all, she was my business partner, and until recently had been rather more than that. So we invited her to lunch. It didn't go well – surprise, surprise! I see you shaking your heads in disbelief – how could I be so naïve? But Suzie and I had parted amicably, I thought; we had continued as friends and business partners, and she had a new lover – why wouldn't she and Veronica get on? Why indeed? As a lifelong bachelor, of course, I knew all about women. I used to tell anyone who would listen that a man who thinks that, because a woman no longer wants him, any other woman can have him is an idiot. But I had somehow forgotten that.

Towards the end of lunch Suzie left the table. I found her in the east gallery crying her eyes out. I should have understood that she hadn't realised my fling with Veronica was serious.

Veronica later complained that I had not told her about Suzie's role in my life. There were two reasons for this. First, Suzie and I were no longer a number so it did not seem relevant. Second, bachelors' lives tend to be compartmentalised, unlike the sharing transparent family life of a married couple. Since I am an intensely private person, I instinctively played my cards close to my chest. I had found that living on a need-to-know basis avoided misunderstandings.

In England Anna was fighting for her life but still making plans for the future. She and Derek were moving to a spacious apartment at Ranelagh Gardens next to the Hurlingham Club, close to the Thames. Her letters were always upbeat and witty. Since the cancer had invaded so much of her body, sleep was difficult. The most painful position for her was on her back which amused her, since, as she wrote with wry humour, that had always been her favourite.

In late March she arrived for a visit. She wore a wig, which made her weary face seem even smaller, but the desire to survive burned fiercely in her. She and Veronica got on well. Both had been born in North Ferriby in East Yorkshire, and both had attended RADA before going on to become actresses. Anna achieved great success, but it did not work out for Veronica as a career. They were both my ideal woman – intelligent, sensuous, beautiful and witty, and I loved them both. There was never a hint of jealousy or possessiveness. Indeed Anna was happy that Veronica and I were together, every day and every night, something her familial circumstances had never permitted. We three spent many happy hours at the Royal Pavilion Hotel swimming pool, where Veronica and I embarrassed Anna dreadfully by shouting at her from the pool in broad Yorkshire accents.

This visit was the last time I would see my precious friend alive. It was the end. Derek rang a few weeks later to say that Anna had died. Would I come to London to be there with him and Jonathan? I was on the next aeroplane, leaving Veronica, Zen and Lulu to hold the fort. The funeral service was to be at Holy Trinity Brompton in Knightsbridge. Derek asked if I would read the lesson, a glorious passage from Revelations chapter 21. Of course I agreed, and marvelled that the husband of my mistress should entrust me with such a task. The next day Derek, Jonathan and I were led by an usher to the front pew to join the family mourners. When the time came I walked to the lectern, a monumental gilded eagle, its spread wings supporting the Bible, and adjusted the microphone. Ever since entering the church I had been thinking about Anna, her widowed husband, and her son who no longer had the mother he adored. Now the sea of faces before me brought me smartly to my senses. Every pew was filled, all eyes turned towards me. But I had rehearsed the lesson until I knew it by heart, and read well; kind comments were made later. Derek, Jonathan and I walked behind the flower-covered coffin to the great west door, passing pew upon pew of Anna's friends and fans. They all knew of her ten-year battle with cancer and were filled with admiration and love and a sense of great loss.

On my return to Barbados I occupied myself in creating La Cage aux Folles II. The property – Summerland House – needed a lot of work, but thanks to my recently sold interest in the Bagatelle, I was flush with cash, and inevitably financially irresponsible – a bank account in the black always had that effect on me. The flat within the building became Suzie's apartment; stables were to be built close by. Her new passion, in which she intended to invest her savings, were Haflinger horses. Haflingers are used as working animals by the Amish community in the United States; they are chestnut with white manes – in a word, palomino – and have exceptionally sweet dispositions. Suzie hot-footed it to America to buy a stallion, a mare-in-foal and a foal, and arrangements were made to transport the animals to Barbados. At the same time she bought a cart, a sort of surrey with a fringe on top, and harness, brushes – everything. A few months later the horses were safely landed on Barbados. She was in business.

The old La Cage aux Folles restaurant had already been bulldozed. However, we managed to rescue the Gourmet Shop. It had once been a chattel house, so we dismantled and re-erected it in the Summerland grounds, where it doubled up as Suzie's tack room.

From time to time female members of the YNSA turned up at Bagatelle, but Veronica, sniffing the wind, always got to the front door first and sent the poor women packing – charmingly, of course! This marked, for me, the demise of YNSA but the memories – and, I have heard, the YNSA itself – lived on for a while.

I was keen that Veronica should sail aboard *Spirit*. The yacht was on the market and I would be sad if she were never to enjoy something that meant so much to me. We flew to St. Lucia and joined John and Debbie at Rodney Bay. The next morning the trade winds were lively. We weighed anchor and set course for Martinique 30 miles to the north-north-west. The moment we were out of the lee of Pigeon Island we felt the full force of the strong easterly wind on our starboard beam. *Spirit* dug in her lee rail and tore along, rejoicing in her natural element. I was at the helm, happy as could be. I turned to make sure Veronica was equally elated – oh dear! There was a distinctly greenish tinge to her complexion and, in spite of a gallant attempt at a smile, no sign of elation. She tottered to the lee rail – good girl! – and was sick. Out of kindness she had not told me that this happened sometimes. However, she recovered quickly and was soon able to enjoy the sail and the delightful Créole cuisine of Martinique. On future sailing expeditions, our discovery of Stugeron pills meant that seasickness was no longer a problem.

Our friends Nick and Ollie Horsley invited us to spend the Christmas of 1990 with them at their house, Broadreach, on the Sandy Lane estate. This was the first time in twenty years that I did not work through the Christmas holidays, and it was a welcome change – once we opened La Cage aux Folles II it would be business as usual. While *chez* Horsley I had a call from John Valentine. Some Germans had made an offer of £80,000 for *Spirit* – was that acceptable? My decision was not difficult but it was painful. I needed the money. By the time I had paid John the 10% I had promised were he to find a seller, I would be left with £72,000, say US$107,000. As a financial venture the restoration had been a disaster. As for its nett cost, after deducting charter revenue, I doubt I would have much change out of $250,000. The fact is the price achieved for the sale of a vintage yacht can only be what a person, equally obsessed as me, is prepared to pay – and they are few and far between. The following figures, professional valuations for *Spirit,* speak for themselves.

In February 1983, in the USA, she was valued at US$65,000. After fourteen months, her value had dropped to US$60,000. It was still US$60,000 three years later in Barbados, by which time I had already invested $250,000 in her.

Then, encouragingly, in July 1989 a British marine surveyor gave a value US$375,000, or £280,000. The harsh reality was, when she was sold, she fetched a mere US$119,000, or £80,000.

Would I do it again? Absolutely not, even were I to live aboard – the only good reason, in my opinion, to own such a sailing boat as *Spirit.* Unless you become self-sufficient in the maintenance of the engine, electronics, navigation instruments, water-maker and the rest, you have to rely on shore-based expertise. And pay for it! Another reason is that there is no privacy on a yacht. I came across a man in Antigua who owned a fine 92-foot Fife-designed yacht. When his girlfriend came down from New York he chartered another boat for his crew so that he and she could be as noisy as they liked.

Having said that, was *Spirit* worth it? Yes, she was. Resoundingly. The memories of sailing through the Mona Passage, cruising in the Grenadines, riding out powerful storms in comfort and safety, giving pleasure to yachtsmen whenever they set eyes on her, entertaining my friends on board – these I treasure. Best of all are memories of coming into a safe anchorage having completed a difficult passage, putting the old girl to bed, retiring thereafter to my hip bath, rum punch in one hand, Nero Wolfe novel in the other, and a pretty girl in my cabin. The wind sighs in the rigging, and waves slap gently against her side, as *Spirit* moves restlessly around her anchor. For me this is heaven on earth.

To restore her to her original glory, something I *had* to do for irrational yet passionate reasons, was vastly rewarding. The yacht I had found rotting in the backwaters of Florida is again sailing the high seas, restored to her rightful place in the great British maritime heritage, a monument to

Edwardian splendour and craftsmanship. In 1992 I found an advertisement placed by yacht broker Jolyon Byerley, possibly the best boat handler in the entire Caribbean. A testament to the skills and dedication of John and Debbie Valentine, it reads in part:

> *'Perhaps the prettiest and most perfect mid-sized classic available anywhere…kept like a new pin by her perfectionist owner…utterly delightful interior…if you could bear to let anyone else go aboard her…she could be yours for £125,000 [US$185,000].'*

The last sighting of *Spirit* was in 2002, when my friend Chris Hale saw her in a harbour in Minorca, with an armed guard protecting her. He found out that the new owner had the engine moved from under the saloon sole (floor) forward to the forecastle. The power was transmitted thence to the propeller via an hydraulic link. He sent me a photo in which, I am so happy to see, *Spirit* remains her immaculate self.

I dedicate the memory of *Spirit of Carib* to the grandfather I never met, Colonel Charles Hudson, Royal Engineers – extra master mariner, adventurer, and gentleman – whose life the sea took in the Fastnet race of 1931. I dedicate it likewise to his son, my father, who instilled in me a love and respect for the sea, and to my mother, my never-failing champion. I like to think they would be pleased with what I achieved.

CHAPTER THIRTY-SEVEN

Time To Set Sail?

With *Spirit* off my hands I could turn my attention to other matters. Throughout the alterations at Summerland House, there was time to skim along the coast on my windsurfer and drop in on friends. There were lunch and dinner parties every day. One could quite easily have lived on cocktail canapés alone and become the size of a house. To escape the crowded West Coast Veronica and I would take ourselves to the Crane beach on the wild south-east coast. This never-crowded windswept stretch of sand is partly protected by a reef from the brunt of the Atlantic rollers, and the residual surf provided superb bodysurfing.

Formerly, the Crane Beach Hotel on the cliff was owned by Julian Masters, a gentleman of great ability and charm. Daily in the high season he offered a Lucullan luncheon buffet, best accompanied by one of his banana daiquiris, immediately followed by another. Since Julian is no longer with us, I feel I can pass on his secret: add a shot of Cointreau to any recipe for a banana daiquiri – there are many – and raise it from the memorable to the sublime.

A few years ago we returned to Crane Beach intending to catch a few waves and a banana daiquiri or two. We couldn't even find the sea, let alone the beach, the whole area having been built up in less than five years. Those who have invested in property there will face a real problem – the air is laden with salt spray against which only glass and wood are proof. Even aluminium survives but a while before rotting; cars disintegrate before your eyes. Unless those properties are continuously maintained, it will soon be a question of ashes to ashes and rust to rust.

★

The news from England concerning my mother was not good. Making sure she had 24-hour nursing kept my marvellous sisters-in-law, Judy, Carol and Jo, fully occupied. Many of the nurses were compassionate and competent, for which I am eternally grateful. Others, if they turned up at all, were ill-suited for the profession, and some were downright cruel and dishonest. Towards the end of January I heard that Mother was very ill, and flew to be with her. She was in an airy rural hospital, surrounded by trees and flowerbeds and birds singing, and the staff looked after her well. We, her four sons, were with her at every possible moment. Just before the end I was alone with her, and she looked at me with a love which seared me. All signs of her illness had fallen away, and she was young again, her soul already at rest. On 9th February 1991 she slipped away peacefully to be with her Lord. Such was her Christian faith that this was an outcome she never doubted. She had been the best imaginable mother, always ready to intercede on my behalf when I disappointed my father, to whom she was a devoted wife. The epitaph which would have pleased her most was that she left four sons who got on famously well.

I stayed on in East Yorkshire to deal with the formalities that follow a death, and returned to Barbados towards the end of the month. Suzie and Veronica had been working well together on the now well-advanced restaurant. Suzie was preparing for the birth of her foal and had a television camera relaying pictures from the mare's stable to her bedroom.

Veronica and I decided to move out of Bagatelle and to rent 'Poachers', the grown-up tree-house on the Sandy Lane estate that had been Ian Morrison's – my Bagatelle architect's – first commission. Then we began our house search. It needed to be on the West Coast and close to La Cage aux Folles II, for a restaurateur's hours are long and late. The Sandy Lane estate was the preferred choice.

One evening Johnny and Wendy Kidd came to Poachers. Just before dinner we noticed a strange sac under the tail of Daisy the dog. After dinner we discovered that the sac had contained a puppy. All mess had been cleaned up by the proud mother – not a spot anywhere. We hadn't even known she was pregnant. So Blossom came into the world, with feathered ears and the prettiest stern in Christendom.

On 15ᵗʰ August 1991 the new restaurant was ready to open. I had poured a lot of money into this building and the surrounding acres, now enclosed by a handsome coral-stone wall with a fine gated entrance.

The restaurant began well, but did nothing like the numbers I was used to. The usual complaint was that it was far too posh, not nearly seedy enough, as the first La Cage aux Folles had been. When I had opened the Bagatelle Great House twelve years ago there had been no competition. Now there were several good dining establishments, and in better locations than La Cage aux Folles II. That extra mile from the hotels, requiring a taxi, made all the difference. Location! Location!

John Cleese dined with us one evening with his fiancée, Alyce Faye Eichelberger, and her two children. The other guest was Michael Winner, who, maybe to the surprise of some, would join them on their honeymoon the next day in St. Lucia. They were to stay at Colin Tennant's new palace near the Pitons.

Our first guests at Poachers were my eldest brother Peter and his wife Jo. She told us that her husband had been diagnosed with pancreatic cancer. The prognosis was not good. Peter was not yet aware of the seriousness of his condition and Jo's awful dilemma was when to tell him. Their marriage had been a stormy one but she was determined that they should be reconciled. Every two days we made up for them half a gallon of rum punch. Usually you fill a glass with crushed ice, top it up with punch, add a few drops of Angostura bitters, grate some nutmeg, embellish with a Maraschino cherry and stick in a straw. Peter and Jo drank the punch straight and undiluted. We told them how it was usually done and they compromised – reluctantly – by dropping a nominal ice cube into the glass and filling it to the brim with neat punch. The nutmeg, bitters and cherry didn't get a look-in. The half-gallon still only lasted two days, but they were happy days. Peter and Jo had a marvellous holiday and left us, at peace with each other, fully reconciled.

Lying in bed on the morning of 14ᵗʰ February, I passed Veronica an envelope. This time she opened it, and found a Valentine card with a message of love and, at the bottom, PTO. She turned it over and found another message – '*Will you marry me?*' It was a good thing she was lying down. When she recovered the power of speech she said, 'Yes.'

Father Andrew Hatch, the incumbent at St. James church where we wanted to be married, told us that, since Veronica was twice divorced, we had to obtain special dispensation from the bishop. This was granted and we fixed the wedding day for 8th May 1992.

Meanwhile Peter's condition had deteriorated, so we went to England for a blessing on our forthcoming union in All Saints' Church in Hessle, only a few minutes away from his house, where the Hudson family had worshipped for four generations. Indeed, there is a plaque there dedicated to my yachts-man grandfather who had been a church warden there, and a handsome baptistery donated by my parents.

The big day came and all went extremely well. Suzie drove a ravishing Veronica to the church in her buggy bedecked with flowers and drawn by her Haflinger stallion, Marco Polo. Sharon Morrison, Dot's daughter, was the lovely best girl. When I met Veronica on the chancel steps I all but fainted for love of her. We sang *Cwm Rhondda* with my Welsh mother in mind, and Donald Marshall gave the bride away. When, prompted by Andrew Hatch, I had to promise to endow Veronica with all my worldly goods, there was a palpable pause before I could get the words out; it did not go unnoticed by my wife-to-be. The organist belted out Widor's stirring *Toccata in F* as the recessional music.

Our friends were waiting to welcome us at Poachers. Marvellously, my brother Richie and his wife Carol had come all the way from England to be with us. The tone was raised by the presence of His Excellency Mr Emrys Davies, the British High Commissioner to Barbados, and Julian Sacher's generous gift of three cases of vintage Bollinger rosé, which made sure we were off to a flying start. Donald in his speech asked how he could possibly give Veronica away, since he hadn't had her yet!

For our honeymoon we chartered a bareboat yacht and sailed down the Grenadines with a boxed set of *Round the Horne* and a game of Scrabble for company. On the return journey to Bequia, just north of Canouan, we were struck by hurricane-force winds. I had to secure something in the dinghy which we were towing, leaving Veronica at the helm with specific yet absolutely undoable instructions as to how to pick me up if I fell into the boiling sea. She was more than glad to see me safely back on board.

Peter was now very ill. In the earlier stages of his illness he had worked at the Dove Hospice in Hull, helping those who were too sick to help themselves. Now he found himself in the same position. Finally he was sent home to spend his last days surrounded by his loving family. I was there too. As the end drew near Peter suffered the most dreadful agony, in spite of being able to give himself morphine whenever he needed it. His death was a merciful relief, and Jo's grief was terrible to behold. Their stay at Poachers had truly reignited their love for each other. The hospice had provided a male nurse, a man of great understanding and compassion, and did everything possible to minimise my brother's suffering and to comfort his stricken family. When I die, the Hospice will be a beneficiary in my will.

Jo and her son Phillip died well before their allotted three score years and ten, and only two siblings – Sarah and Adam – of Peter's family of five would survive to the end of the millennium.

Early in 1993 estate agent Pixie Mahon showed us a property on the Sandy Lane estate which we both liked and could afford. Our offer was accepted. Situated next to the pond on the ninth fairway of the Bottom Nine golf course, it had been built by Jim and Ann Swanton. Jim was the doyen of cricket writers and a survivor – in spite of contracting polio during his imprisonment – of the infamous Burma Railway. Like all Sandy Lane houses ours comprised a main house, built of rose-tinted coral stone, and the all-important guest cottage. There was a pool with a witty notice which read, ''OOL – *there is no p in our pool. We would like to keep it that way*.' With the assistance of Dave Hindley, we modified the property to our liking and moved in.

Sometime later Suzie asked if I thought Father Hatch might be prepared to exorcise the La Cage aux Folles property, having lost two dogs there to unexplained causes and concluded that evil forces were at work. A few days later Andrew arrived with no less a personage than the diocesan Bishop of Barbados, Rufus Brome, in purple cassock and crucifix – Suzie was wearing only a colourful bathing costume and green wellies. She expressed her fears to His Grace, who listened attentively and produced a small bottle containing water he had already blessed. We proceeded around the whole property with Suzie pointing out places where she believed evil spirits lurked. The Bishop sprinkled holy water as directed, saying a prayer as he did so. I don't think she lost any more dogs in suspicious circumstances. But she took to haunting La Cage aux Folles II, creating a baleful atmosphere, which customers sensed, and the business suffered accordingly.

La Cage aux Folles enjoyed some good times, and old friends like James and Patricia Campbell and Robin and Trisha Bradford were very supportive. One evening I found the Bradfords dining there, grinning like Cheshire cats, and asked what was so amusing. Glancing surreptitiously at the broad back of a nearby diner, they whispered that it was Michael Winner; I had visited *their* table first. I never had any problems with Michael. An influential critic, he was the scourge of restaurateurs and a bully, given the chance. I never gave him either a reason or the chance. Having seen his tenderness towards his then girlfriend, Jenny Seagrove, when she was sick, I also knew that there was a kind man behind the bluster. Michael told Veronica and me that Brillo Pad – Andrew Neill – had offered him a column as restaurant critic in the *Sunday Times* for, as he put it, peanuts – £150 a week. It meant he could bully restaurateurs and chefs to his heart's content, and he made the most of it. Cleverly, and gleefully, Michael published the letters of his critics, who easily outnumbered his admirers and provided him with useful copy. Many readers bought the *Sunday Times* for his column alone. At any rate, he wrote some kind things about me. Since his demise, in my opinion, amongst food critics only A.A. Gill has approached his readability and waspish appeal.

Long-standing Sangster's Gangsters, Billy 'The Beast' MacDonald and Tony 'Colonel' Collins, came for dinner to La Cage. With them was a lady whom Billy introduced, prophetically as it transpired, as 'the future ex-Mrs Tony Collins'. Once a very good-looking lady left a table of Gangsters, requested a pen and paper, and asked me to deliver a note to a gentleman dining alone. I obliged. He read the note, and demanded to know who had sent it. I nodded towards the woman by the bar. He glanced at her briefly – she was easy on the eye – and said, 'Tell her, yes.'

I asked him, 'Forgive me for asking, but what does the note say?'

'*Bored to tears*,' he replied, ' *Conversation all about golf. May I join you?*' And she did. I have often wondered how it ended.

As my reputation as a polo commentator grew, I was invited to do other jobs. I covered a garden party at Government House, a Janet Bradshaw-inspired fundraiser for Codrington College at Holder's House, and a charity auction – I really enjoyed auctioneering – among others. An upmarket tour company organised a private luncheon for some of their high-flying clients at the Sandy Lane Hotel. Would I, they asked, for a free lunch introduce the guest speaker, the cricketer Geoffrey Boycott? I agreed and did my homework. Geoff had scored 151 first-class centuries, so there was no doubt the lad could bat. At the lunch I was sitting next to him at one of three round tables with a dozen guests at each. When the coffee had been served I was invited to say a few introductory words. As I sat down again, the dour basher of cricket balls whispered nervously, ''Ell's bells, my speech isn't for lasses, y'know.' He was right. It was a self-aggrandising rant, as vulgar as may be, more suitable for a working men's club in downtown Bradford late on a Saturday night after the staff had left. He didn't change one word. I was surprised none of the beautifully dressed ladies of Sandy Lane walked out.

One day a couple of Gangsters were on the ninth and final green. One of them was trying without success to play out of a bunker. As he tried yet again he heard a voice exclaim in a broad Yorkshire accent, 'Ee lad, you've got that all wrong. Oh dear, oh dear.' It was the great cricketer himself, who, despite having only recently taken up the game, proceeded to lecture the fuming golfer on how to play the shot.

The level of business at the restaurant, where the atmosphere was increasingly downbeat, was barely profitable and no fun for us. Veronica was bending over backwards to maintain friendship with Suzie, but Luna was naturally on her mother's side, and Billy had quite obviously also taken us into dislike. Something had to change.

Meanwhile, on 26th February 1993 a powerful bomb exploded in the car park under the North Tower of the World Trade Center in Manhattan. The idea was to cause the North Tower to fall against the South Tower, bringing them both down. It failed, but six people died and more than a thousand were injured, one of whom was my partner, Donald Marshall. The blast travelled up the lift shafts to where Euro Brokers, the company that Donald founded in 1974, had its offices at the very top of the building. Unable to go higher, the blast emerged from the shafts and gave all the occupants a severe shaking. Donald was ill for quite some time.

There was more bad news in 1994. Derek Brierley called me, in tears. His son Jonathan had won an art scholarship to Oxford, but had begun to suffer from depression, so he had been rusticated for a year to recover. Father and son had been chatting in the sitting room, but when Derek went to the kitchen to make coffee Jonathan jumped out of the window and fell four floors to his death. I was unable to attend the funeral service, which, Derek told me, would be exactly the same as that for Anna four years previously, also at Holy Trinity Brompton. Poor Derek never recovered from losing them both, his sole reason for being alive. The flat became something of a mausoleum, with photographs of Anna and Jonathan in every room. On occasion he played recordings of her voice – very spooky.

Billy finally sold her house on Mustique, Firefly. She had designed and built it in 1970 when she and the wildly talented dream team – Hugo Money-Coutts, Oliver Messel, a Swedish electrical engineer known as Junior, Charlie Manning and Arnie Hasselquist – were helping Colin Tennant to realise his dream. On Barbados Billy found a lovely small plantation house, Little Buckden, previously owned by the colourful Honoria Drummond, mother of the even more colourful George. It comprised a main house and several outbuildings. Living on Barbados meant that Billy could be close to Suzie and Luna, who was herself about to have her first child.

The situation at La Cage aux Folles II had become unbearable, so Veronica and I decided to buy Suzie out. I made her an absurdly generous offer, wanting her to leave our relationship of ten years with her finances in a sound state. Amongst other assets, and with no legal obligation to do so, I offered her El Slummo. Additionally I offered her an income for the next few years whilst she was making her horse and dog businesses profitable. But I was yet to realise that I could never give her enough; she wanted my head, preferably on a platter. So we were reduced to the unpalatable extreme of leaving it to the lawyers to make arrangements.

Eventually an agreement was thrashed out. Suzie would be paid for her shares in La Cage aux Folles, sign the appropriate release and leave, giving us vacant possession. One day, just before she left, she met Veronica in the restaurant car park. Our small black mutt, Lilly, had died that morning. Suzie gave Veronica a hug and said, 'I suppose this is the last time we shall ever hug.' And so it was to be. Thereafter her behaviour was inexplicable, and profoundly saddening, for we had achieved much together.

Suzie departed, taking her horses, dogs, furniture and stables, and a good deal more which we believed belonged to the business. We presented a list of those items to the police station at Holetown and to the two lawyers, on the understanding that the funds to purchase Suzie's shares would be held in escrow by Barry Gale until the company property had been restored. To our astonishment, without Suzie returning anything, Gale paid her the money! When Veronica asked why, he replied that perhaps we should not pursue the matter. This was *our* lawyer, acting for *us*!

I had always wondered why Mr Green, my landlord at the first La Cage aux Folles, had refused to extend my lease which was so profitable for both parties. At last the mystery was solved. He told my neighbour Jacky, who had an antique shop near the original La Cage aux Folles restaurant, that in the restaurant bar he had heard Suzie make what he took to be a racist remark. That sufficed, true or false. Race is the most sensitive subject. If it was true – and I have no idea – Suzie had shot herself in the foot, for that business was a goldmine. That did not concern me too much. The problem was that my foot had been next to hers, an expensive and unfortunate juxtaposition.

With Suzie out of the picture, Veronica and I decided that La Cage aux Folles II needed to be closed down and completely revamped. We re-opened it as Hudsons. The setting was less formal than La Cage aux Folles II, but comfortable in a clubby sort of way. It was to be, from the gastronomic point of view, my best restaurant yet. I was greatly assisted by Veronica and her considerable culinary experience. The waiting staff was my old team, with Colin Babb as barman, and the experienced cooks were overseen by

Veronica. The menu was broad in its appeal and the wine list comprehensive and reasonably priced. The opening night was intended to be low-key to give us chance to iron out any glitches. Our friends, however, aware that we had been through a torrid time, and wanting to give us a flying start, arrived *en masse* on the dot of seven – Campbells and Kidds, Monkhouses and Rothschilds, Bernsteins and Byngs – with their friends, all dressed to the nines. It was the worst night of my professional life! Apart from everyone arriving at the same time, the head chef-elect failed to turn up. Veronica, in all her finery, had to cope in the kitchen and had an evening of hell. Our hostess, whose job was to see to the smooth running of the restaurant, ran out in tears. The diners and drinkers were hopelessly mixed up and no-one was served properly. Johnny Kidd unhelpfully ordered items not on the menu. It was hell. At front of house I was fielding justified complaints from unhappy punters. This nightmare, born of our friends' best intentions and compounded by our chef's treachery, would never be forgotten. My greatest sadness was for my darling Veronica who bore the brunt in the kitchen. The resulting trauma took her a long time to overcome.

A few days later our housekeeper Doris arrived with a cardboard box with a puppy in it. Dorkie would remain with us for nearly eighteen years, the first of which was spent mostly in the dressing-gown pocket of either dear Trish or Robin Bradford.

It soon became all too apparent that Hudsons restaurant was not a success. Failing restaurants – my first ever, by the way, in a career of thirty years – are very expensive; overheads are high and require a concomitant turnover to sustain the operation. So we decided to close and to sell the building and land separately. The restaurant became a private bank and the surrounding land sold some six years later for a healthy sum. To help make ends meet we rented out our home, Coralita, and the guest cottage, and moved to a house next to the Bradfords, the best friends anybody ever had. Veronica and I will never forget their love and loyalty at a time when, in the restaurant at least, such things were in short supply.

We opened a tiny lunch restaurant at St. Nicholas Abbey, but that too was doomed. It was not as if I was a tyro in the restaurant business – I knew what I was doing – I just seemed to have entered one of those phases when, whatever you do, the spiral is downward.

This was not the case with our social life, which was active and entertaining. We oscillated mostly between the residences of James and Patricia Campbell and (Countess) Carla Cavalli and (Count) Theo Rossi (di Montelera). Both homes, Canebrake and Casa di Pablo (where Ronald and Nancy Reagan had stayed), were havens of luxury, laughter, and milk and honey.

Carla, in particular, loathed repetition; there had always to be something new happening. There was one exception, her afternoon tea parties. At four in the afternoon this *grande dame* of a certain age would swan, immaculate, onto the terrace and hold court, having only risen at noon after going to bed at two or three in the morning. After a traditional English tea, as the sun set, the peerless butler Emerson would be dispatched to organise the lighting of hundreds of candles around the garden, creating an instant fairyland. Carla was greatly diverted by learning English idioms and, with a heavy Italian accent, bouncing them off her English guests. She liked to refer to bores as 'pins in de harse' – *they* never came back – or she would say, 'I seenk I will 'ave zee ozzer 'alf', and shriek with laughter. Her gatherings were a veritable tower of Babel with a gabble of Italian, English, French, German and Spanish. As an amateur linguist it was heaven for me.

With the candles lit, the Earl Grey would be replaced with Black Russian cocktails, two parts vodka and one part Kahlua poured over ice, to which I had introduced Carla. Cocktails would morph seamlessly into dinner. Rarely did fewer than two dozen guests sit down. Everyone was welcome, provided they were amusing, stylish and bearers of gossip. One *had* to contribute something humorous or diverting – spicy gossip was well received. It was not enough to sit there looking beautiful. Best of all was to come up with a theme for a party. Veronica and I put on a Russian party for her, which was a wild success. Apart from many exquisite zakuskis and Russian and Georgian dishes (Veronica's crystal-clear gold-flecked chicken consommé was unforgettable) we made several vodkas – pepper, honey, saffron, bisongrass and others – and served them ice-cold. Guests dashed their glasses to the floor in traditional style and we danced on broken glass and felt no pain. The vision of Jack the Knife dancing with Simon, our gay frock designer, was particularly memorable.

Dear Theo Rossi had been Carla's boyfriend for many years. Italians in their circle did not divorce. He had been a playboy of the old type, a contemporary of Juan di Portago, Porfirio Rubirosa, Johnny Kimberley, Keith Schellenberg, Karim Aga Khan *et al* – all handsome, attractive, daring, charming, adventurous, and necessarily very rich. The explosive Sylvia Casablanca was of their number too. When Theo began to show signs of mental impairment, Carla became somewhat impatient, remembering the man she had fallen in love with, who had captained the Italian bobsled team and raced powerboats, besides running the mega-conglomerate Martini and Rossi. Occasionally we would invite Theo to our house to taste a few wines. Away from Carla he became animated and talkative. One evening we were introduced to his niece who was – one should have guessed – Signorina Cinzano! That family surely had cornered the vermouth market.

These were the last days of Ronnie Tree's Sandy Lane, where gentlefolk lived by the spirit of the law without complicated covenants to govern their behaviour. How fortunate we were to have lived that life. The only remaining flag-bearers now, although not quite on Sandy Lane, are Anthony and Carol Bamford and a handful of others, including, of course, dear Margaret (now Lady) Leacock up at Sharon Hill, who gets younger every day.

The definitive changing of the Sandy Lane guard was signaled by the arrival of the new owners of the Sandy Lane Hotel, Dermot Desmond, a wealthy Irishman, and his co-investors John Magnier and J.P. McManus, Irish super-heavyweights from equine circles. We were given a taste of what was to come when Mr Desmond threw a party at the hotel to introduce himself to the estate property owners. He began his speech with the words, 'I am Dermot Desmond. You may have heard the expression $E = mc^2$. Well, in my case, the E stands for ego.' He was not joking. In the process of levelling the Sandy Lane Hotel to the ground, before rebuilding, he and his co-investors enraged locals by chopping down the lovely old mahogany trees which graced the gardens. These majestic hardwoods had taken hundreds of years to grow and were protected under town-planning legislation. However, the fine for destroying them, a few hundred dollars per tree, was peanuts to the Irish – so down they came.

On 19th April 1997 I had a telephone call from our lawyer Barry Gale. David Allison was dead. I was devastated. He was indestructible. David had been driving with a friend to the airport earlier that morning. Coming the other way was a large agricultural vehicle, with a steel basket attached in front, from which spikes projected. The vehicle suddenly swerved across the road and the spikes impaled David through his chest, killing him instantly. His passenger was unscathed. As was explained at the inquest, water had been put into the vehicle's enormous tyres to improve traction. The driver had applied his brakes unevenly, causing the water to swill forward on one side, dragging the vehicle into the path of David's car. He left behind a wife, a son and a daughter. David's widow, Lynn, asked if I would deliver the eulogy at his memorial service. Naturally I agreed, but I only just made it to the end before the tears came. I had lost the finest friend, accountant, adviser and guide anyone could ever have.

Veronica and I were now in limbo, except for managing Donald and Cherry's recently acquired house, Windrush, slap in the middle of the Sandy Lane golf course – their idea of heaven. We decided that after we sold Coralita we would move to England or France. Barbados had given me a terrific innings and rewarded me with my treasured citizenship, but Veronica had never felt entirely settled there; she was always 'Nick Hudson's wife', not Veronica Hudson. It was time for us to start a new life together, for her to flourish on her own merits. We thought we might give England a go and put in a half-hearted offer for a small house next to my brother Richie's Georgian pile in Beverley. Thankfully it was not accepted. Somehow, going from Barbados sun, rum and bare feet to Yorkshire didn't feel quite right. We thought France might be a more promising choice.

We gave our last Christmas party at Coralita. Among the guests were the Leacocks and the Monkhouses. During dinner Jack asked Bob what he did for a living. The response from the great wordsmith was prompt and witty – 'I comede.' He also treated us to an extraordinary performance, demonstrating what he had seen in his shaving mirror one morning having suffered a mini-stroke during the night. He somehow contorted his face into gruesome asymmetry whilst at the same time making us laugh. Unlike so many comedians there was nothing tragic about Bob. He faced problems, including death, head-on.

Early in 1998 Pixie Mahon found a buyer for Coralita. A price was agreed and the transfer of ownership set in motion. We would look at France, since we both liked the country and spoke French reasonably well. On 13th July 1998, my sixtieth birthday, Donald and Cherry Marshall gave me a dinner party at the Bagatelle at the Great Table, where my Barbadian odyssey had begun twenty-eight years earlier. It had been an adventurous journey, vastly enhanced and at times enabled by having Donald as my supportive and generous partner. Only dear David Allison was missing.

I won't bore you with the details but will only say that the sale of Coralita was highly unsatisfactory and that Veronica and I disagreed violently with the handling of it by – guess who? – Barry Gale.

In August we left for France – Coralita as yet unpaid for – with Dorkie and Blossom and eleven pieces of baggage. We travelled via Martinique, thus avoiding England and the expensive and unnecessary quarantine hoo-ha. When we arrived in Paris we proffered documents painstakingly assembled by the Barbados government vet; the French authorities didn't even give them a glance. On the grass outside the terminal building, after seventeen hours of abstinence, the dogs peed and peed for France.

CHAPTER THIRTY-EIGHT

French Leave

Eventually we found ourselves in south-west France. In the bank were, at last, the nett proceeds from the sale of Coralita, rather less than we had anticipated; our worldly goods were in a container in Bordeaux, attracting all sort of unforeseen charges, and we were looking for a new home.

We had a contact in the *département* of Corrèze through friend and hotelier Tim Kemp, and decided to start our search there. There were a few near misses – we were very seriously tempted by a lovely fourteenth-century house with monumental fireplaces and a broad stone staircase – but we but did not conclude any deals. Then, after a timely nudge from an old friend, Richard Hanlon, we found ourselves in the Dordogne, looking at properties between the villages of Lalinde and Limeuil. In an estate agent's window we saw details of a place we both liked in the village of Limeuil. We met the agent at the house, looked at it from the outside, liked what we saw, and said *we'll have it* without going in, it felt so right. Thus we purchased La Rouquette, situated on the edge of a beautiful village where the Vézère and Dordogne rivers meet. Limeuil has *appellation* – official recognition – as One of the Most Beautiful Villages in France.

In early January 1999 the house was ours, and by Easter, three months later, after some alterations and redecorating, we moved in. We were greeted by a magnificent bouquet of white flowers from Carol and Anthony Bamford, who had bought Ronnie Tree's Heron Bay, with an affectionate note telling us how much we were missed in Barbados. We were very touched.

We loved our new home, which came with an unexpected bonus. One minute down the road, towards the village – we were just outside the walls – was the church of Sainte Catherine, where Anglican services in English were held every Sunday and many other days besides, thanks to the Roman Catholic cleric in nearby Le Bugue, who gave the Chaplaincy of Aquitaine the necessary permission. The French only used it once a month for Mass and a few major festivals. Gatherings commemorating the two World Wars and heroes of the *Résistance* also took place in front of the nearby war memorial. Memories of the German occupation in World War II remain vivid. In a nearby village there is a monument to the 'victims of Nazi barbarism'. Accusations of collaborating with the Germans seventy years ago still linger in the minds of some of the older villagers.

Veronica and I are both practising Christians and this church community plays an important role in our lives. The early years of 1998–2000 were stormy, since the congregation comprised many religious persuasions – Lutherans, Methodists, Quakers, Welsh Chapel, Church of England, American Episcopalian, and others. Christian tolerance and forgiveness were not much in evidence; arguments over which litany should be used, and how frequently, tore at the fabric of the Church. One Chaplaincy AGM ended with the chaplain being escorted out in tears. But nowadays compromises have been made and the Church offers spiritual comfort, support and guidance, as well as a place in which to meet fellow expatriates. The Anglican church in Aquitaine is a blessing.

One question which exercised my mind was what to do with my time. I was only sixty, and unused to doing nothing – the word 'retirement' is, and always will be, anathema to me. I decided to try and sell some of the local wines – those of Bergerac, Pécharmant, Saussignac and Monbazillac – in England. Thanks to Nick Ryman of the office supplies chain, and those who have followed in his footsteps, the wines of the region are often good, some excellent, and the perfect accompaniment to local delicacies such as *magret de canard, foie gras* and *cèpes*. Patricia Atkinson's honeyed 2003 Clos d'Yvigne Saussignac, obtainable at the time of writing from Justerini & Brooks, is a marvel of wine-making. Initially Patricia was guided by Nick Ryman, but being a very beautiful workaholic with a quite exceptional palate, she quickly enjoyed great personal success, as she has with her writing. I had sold wines with considerable success in my Diner days. In my new venture my family and former clients in Lincolnshire and Yorkshire were extremely supportive. On this occasion, it transpired, although I thoroughly enjoyed the work, it was not worth my while financially. Bizarrely, customers could not believe the prices compared with our fashionable neighbours in Bordeaux. I really ought to have organised, *à la* Stephen Spurrier, a blind tasting, the *only* way to assess a wine's true worth.

1999 went out with a bang. On New Year's Eve France was hit by a hurricane and many areas were devastated. Close to Limeuil, at Audrix, the anemometer went off the scale and self-destructed at 200 kph (125 mph). The country lost over 350 million trees. Though our house actually shook, and dust flew out of the old walls, we only lost three tiles off the barn roof. Fortunately, lovely irascible Beverley of *La Maison de la Presse* in Le Bugue had warned me about the imminent storm, so I had time to close and bar the shutters. Veronica and I woke up on New Year's Day with no electricity, the bedroom at 10°C, me at 102°C, and both with the 'flu. The fever was not too great a problem since our GP, the irreplaceable Dr Jacques Candau, made a house call that very morning and charged us the princely sum of 30 francs (£3) – house calls are still a fact of life in our part of France. The power was out until 7th January, so we had no lighting, no central heating and no running water. The roads were blocked by fallen trees, so there was no escape. Our lives were saved by recycling hot water bottles – a gift from our friend Marlène – filled from the nearby spring, and heated on our gas hob.

In September 2001 we took a holiday in the Algarve, my first venture into Portugal. I was watching the television news in Portuguese as I dressed for dinner. I saw an aeroplane flying at, and hitting, one of the towers of the World Trade Center. Surely it must be a feature film? This could not be happening. I was unable to take in the far-reaching implications at the time, except that it was where Donald, my partner and dear friend, had his offices, somewhere between the 93rd and 100th floors. He had proudly showed me his own office with its breath-catchingly spectacular view. We had popped up to the 106th floor to the Windows on the World restaurant for lunch, taking advantage of its famously extensive wine list. The date in Portugal was

11th September – 'nine eleven'. My fears were unfounded, as I discovered when at last I got through to him, recuperating at his home in New Jersey. A few years previously he had left Euro Brokers, the company he founded, and joined another company who moved him down to the 22nd floor. Everyone in the higher offices, now belonging to Marsh & McLennan Companies – 295 employees and 63 contractors – had died. One of his lasting memories, he told me, was of firemen dashing fearlessly up the stairs, never to return. When eventually the survivors were given permission to flee for their lives, he dashed down the stairs – the lifts, of course, were out of action – to the South Exit, and ran until he could run no further. He stopped, out of breath, and looked back. People were standing just outside the exit, looking up at the building. It was the last thing they were to see as the tower collapsed on them.

On Barbados the rebuilt Sandy Lane Hotel had opened at an astronomical cost. I obtained one figure for the cost of the rebuild and tried to calculate how much that worked out at for each of the 113 rooms, but it gave my hand-held calculator indigestion – too many digits. I should love to have sight of the balance sheet. I doubt if the profit and loss figures are rosy but that would not be of much concern to the extremely wealthy investors.

The days when the Hotel, under the management of Ray Carroll and his successors, as well as being the iconic hotel in the West Indies, was a club for the locals – offering superb food and drink, water sports facilities, a place to meet friends and to play backgammon – they were gone. That was the Sandy Lane of Ronnie Tree, when an atmosphere of exclusivity was achieved not by gates, guards and gargantuan prices, but by the clientele. Mr Desmond and his colleagues see it differently. Of course, with the money they have shelled out, they have every right to do so. He who pays the piper…

CHAPTER THIRTY-NINE

An Answer To Our Prayers

In 2000 Veronica and I were looking for ways to use our skills and abilities, praying for an opportunity to help others. Two new members of the congregation at Sainte Catherine, Graham and Carol Froome, had belonged to a charitable association in the island of Guernsey that organised holidays for Belarusian children, their immune systems weakened by exposure to radiation, following the catastrophic events at Chernobyl in neighbouring Ukraine in 1986. They wanted to start a similar organisation in France and needed volunteers. Bells rang!

I had continued my Russian studies, unable to bear the thought of letting the language slip into disuse. I had my Michel Thomas CDs in the car and had made the BBC Russian Service my homepage on my computer, so that I was reading the language whenever I went online. I put a free-download translating site on my toolbar in case, as happened frequently, I could not understand a word. This had enlarged my vocabulary and improved my fluency quite dramatically.

Russian was spoken in Belarus. Maybe I could help by interpreting or translating. Also, ever since my fruitless attempts to work for UNICEF all those years ago, I had always wanted to work with children – as opposed to fathering them. In no time Veronica and I were fully involved.

The Association had clearly defined criteria. The children must come from poor backgrounds. If sick, they must be well enough to travel. They must never have left Belarus before. They must be pre-pubertal. They should bring with them their medical histories and family details.

They could each only come once so as many children as possible could benefit.

June of the following year, 2001, saw the arrival of Lucy, aged eight, and Natasha, aged nine. They had travelled in a coach, in which they ate and slept, 2,000 kilometres from Minsk. Their luggage was a small bag containing a pair of knickers and a present for us, something their families could ill afford. When they arrived they were timid and unsure of themselves. Not for long! Within a day or two they had the bath – the first they had ever seen, never mind bathed in – overflowing, and the hair-driers, which they had never used before, howling. Their hair was the only luxury these girls possessed and they spent hours washing and brushing until it shone. We gave them each a disposable camera, and towards the end of the holiday had the film developed. They set to work putting the snaps, together with captions and drawings, into an album to take home – it was to be their most treasured possession.

Veronica and I busied ourselves with fundraising, administration, finding host families, transportation and so on. The most time-consuming task was obtaining permission for the children to leave Belarus, which was sometimes delayed until the very day of departure; once the accompanying teacher/translator was turned back at the airport. Every June we welcomed two more girls (after a couple of difficult experiences we had decided to take only girls), and they had a great time. Swimming was their favourite activity, for there were no public pools at home. Meeting other Belarusian children and sleepovers were popular. We gave them each a small shopping allowance, which they invariably spent on buying presents for their families. When it came to food, they would happily have lived on ice cream. They were wary of vegetables because of the radiation they contained at home, although wolfed down cherries by the kilo. They were unused to choice; at home the same things were put on the table, only sometimes including protein, three times a day. Any mention of vodka shocked the children, for, with no work, the fathers drank to excess and families broke up. It was the mothers who ran the families, together with *babushka* – granny.

To inform ourselves better about the children's families and how they lived, in 2003 Veronica and I went to Belarus, so that, with firsthand knowledge, we could make it clear to possible donors that we knew what we were talking about. Consequently we were never short of funds. We experienced with the families, however briefly, their extreme poverty. The water supply was a tap in the wall. There was no bathroom; the toilet in a shed at the bottom of the garden. As I sat on a plank with a hole in it, amid swarms of flies, a pile of torn newspapers at my side, I reminded myself that winter temperatures of -30°C and lower were usual. You quickly learned to take advantage of a WC in, say, a school. In their homes there was no such thing as a bedroom; everyone slept in the living room where sofas became beds. Yet the welcome was warm and the hospitality generous in the extreme. They gave so much of the little they had; the parable of the widow's mite became reality. At the modest table I was able to propose toasts in Russian; seeing the pleasure it gave my hosts made my studies worthwhile. Before knocking back a shot of vodka it was traditional to propose a toast followed by the words *chut' chut'* – 'very little'. We began with toasts to our hosts, parents, children and Belarus. By the end of the meal anything – the ceiling, a door – would do. The children looked on disapprovingly.

We made sure the families were better off for our visit. Hard currency – American dollars or euros – was put carefully aside, immune to the ever-devaluing Belarusian rouble, to buy medicines, and we always carried vitamin supplements and cod liver oil capsules with us. In the countryside employment was scarce and the pay negligible. One of our interpreters, a multilingual teacher and interpreter, needed to hold down three jobs in order to raise her two children. The mother of one of the girls laboured in a potato field for a month to earn the equivalent of twelve dollars. I am never far from tears when I think of the poor of Belarus.

In 2006 two more little girls came from Belarus, but these ones had quite a few clothes, rather nice spectacles and cameras. These were town girls as opposed to our usual country lasses, and had already holidayed in Europe and North Africa. For Veronica and me, the original criteria – they must be poor, possibly sick, never have left Belarus before, and must bring a medical history with them – were sacrosanct. We were quietly upset. However, we were aware of the difficulty of arranging matters to getting one's way in a dictatorship like Belarus. You *have* to toe the party line and some official always expected to be paid off – or you get nowhere.

By 2007 our Association had joined forces with another based in Limoges, a little more than a hundred miles away. There was one major difference between the two – they brought the same children back year after year, ours only came once. Transport costs had now reached 1,000 euros per child, and we decided to send a coach, from Limoges to Gomel in Belarus, and on to Novozybkov in south-west Russia, on three consecutive journeys. Each journey would be around 6,000 kilometres and would transport fifty or so children. Veronica went on two of the trips and I went on three. Each leg involved two nights sleeping on the coach and a night in a hostel. Although I am not designed to sleep on narrow charabanc seats, I managed. We carried our own provisions which we ate by the roadside. In Belarus, a country devoid of usable public lavatories – except McDonald's loos in Minsk, where the queue of desperate women stretched into the street – toilet stops were made in the forest. The children would be given the order 'Girls left! Boys right!' and they would melt into the forest.

On one trip we were held up at the Poland/Belarus border by stony-faced authorities wearing high-peaked caps which Rommel would have envied. The children were confined to the non-air-conditioned coach in the summer sun from four in the morning until three in the afternoon, for who knows what reason, with only one loo visit allowed. Attempting to bribe an official could have landed one in a Communist jail, though on occasion an officer hinted at what he or she wanted, and we would cough up. Wine, which we always carried, was popular.

The trips also gave us the chance to see for ourselves the forgotten town of Novozybkov, heavily irradiated by the fallout from Chernobyl. There was no work for the men, who, like their Belarusian neighbours, turned to vodka to escape their wretched existence. President Putin, in his wisdom, had announced that there was no longer a Chernobyl-related problem in the region, and cut off the extra aid and removed special concessions. The pollution was so bad that more than 40% of babies born there had some sort of associated defect. If you held a Geiger-counter close to a rainwater butt, it chattered like a tribe of monkeys. And this was twenty years after Chernobyl had gone up.

In 2008 I resigned as president of the Chernobyl association. Veronica and I had given our all for seven years. Helping, and growing to love, the children and their families had been hugely fulfilling, and in some cases their health had greatly improved. The Association took all our time and energy and there other things we wanted to do. Throughout those seven years the children – all fourteen of them – were our life, and our families and friends were marvellously supportive and generous. We are still in touch with Lucy and Natasha and some others. These children stole our hearts and we counted ourselves blessed. Our prayers had been answered.

Those years also saw great changes among our families and friends. In April 2002 my brother Tony called from England with dreadful news – my godson Adam, brother Peter's surviving son, had taken his own life. He had been gravely depressed, I learned, by his inability to find a job. Before Peter's death in 1992 theirs had been a lusty family of five. Now, with Adam gone, only Sarah, the sweetest girl in the world, remained. I have never forgiven myself for failing as a godfather, a role I had accepted without giving it much thought. Apart from losing both parents, Adam had also lost two siblings. If ever there were a need for a godfather *in loco parentis*, this surely was it. My only, albeit feeble, excuse is that most of the time I had lived 4,000 miles away.

In that same year we had great news – Jack Leacock had been knighted for services to Barbados. Never was an honour more deserved; never was a nation better served by one of its sons. Everyone, black and white alike, knew Jack, and many had reason to be grateful to him.

Jack died the following year, on 24th August 2003. He had rejected high academic and professional honours to devote his life to his mother country. Jack had been a founding figure in the then-innovative family-planning unit, which reduced the national birth rate to an acceptable level. He amused the nation with his outrageous column in the local newspaper, *The Advocate*. When finally he decided he had had enough, he drank only water until he passed away. He died, as he had lived, a confirmed atheist. He left this heartrending poem, which his daughter Mandy read at the wake following his cremation.

PRESCRIPT, POSTSCRIPT

So here it comes at last, so long delayed,
That turbulence in the chest, and then the silence.
One time a cough would clear it, not today.
Not long to go now. Memory seems to crawl,
To lose its treasures. That grey tunnel beckons,
With dimming, deceptive brightness at its end,
Its end the end of me, my end of time.

I wish I'd got each single thing cleared up.
At least there are no debts to cramp your style.
But I have debts in plenty. To my wife
For much love and adventure, and for joy,
For cherishing a body in its ills,
For struggling in computer wilderness
With ready help, most often with success.
Farewell, dear love, enjoy each flying year.

And proudly to my daughters, who have shone
In fields far distant and far different
With boldness, enterprise and nesting skills,
And given their father a well-mixed blend
Of bullying and charm and cheerfulness,
Stirred in a golden pot of filial love.

And now, before I shut up, to my friends
I send my thanks for many happy meals
And far more happy drinks; even for their
Affection, gladly and so generously given.
Lastly, to my colleagues and to readers all,
Whose eyes, I hope, have never quite been ruined
By reckless, rotten verbiage in print;

317

To all, from me, goodbye, good luck, good life:
I wish I could be there.
Earth to earth, ashes to ashes, dust to dust.

However, also in 2003, more great news came from Barbados – the land surrounding La Cage aux Folles II had sold for BDS\$1 million (US\$500,000). I had replaced Barry Gale with another Barbadian lawyer, Mark Greenidge, who handled the matter. By the time everyone had taken their cut, and anti-money-laundering regulations been complied with, a goodish sum was remitted to France. It would have been even more goodish, had the euro not slipped from 80 cents to the dollar in 1998 to 1.35 euros in 2004. When the money arrived I immediately bought a second-hand BMW station wagon with heated seats. It was a mistake; it was too big, too shiny and totally unsuited to south-west France. I was soon cruising around in an ancient Peugeot, feeling much less conspicuous, and not giving a damn if it was bashed, as occurred frequently in supermarket car parks.

In June of that year Blossom, who arrived unexpectedly that evening when Wendy and Johnny Kidd came to dinner at Poachers, was very ill. Her lungs were incurably infected and she was in danger of suffocating to death, so we had no choice. The little darling died in my arms and I felt her divine soul fly free. I have never been closer to a dog. To those who think dogs don't have souls, think again.

In July 2005 Derek Brierley called from London to tell me that he had inoperable cancer. He had no intention of being treated, having witnessed Anna's suffering, and anyway he had no-one left to live for. Would I come and say goodbye? I caught the first available aeroplane, only to learn from his sister when I arrived that the dear fellow had died whilst I was in transit. His funeral service at Holy Trinity Brompton was exactly the same as for his wife Anna and his son Jonathan. We emerged from the church into a London under siege. It was 7th July and the terrorist bombings had just taken place. At the wake Derek's sister Susan asked if there was anything I would like to have to remind me of the Brierley family. Indeed there was. An inmate in Hull prison had seen Anna in *The Main Chance* television series and had fallen in love with her. Whilst still locked up, he had drawn her portrait and arranged for it to be given to her. I asked if I might have it.

While Veronica was away in India with Richard Hanlon & Co, I saw on the vet's bulletin board a card with *Home sought for Westie-type dog* and a phone number. We wanted another dog as a companion for Dorkie. This one was irresistible – such a hound! Thus Spaggers the wonder dog, a West Highland terrier/Bichon Bolognese cross, joined us at La Rouquette.

In March 2007 we heard from Donald Marshall that a large malignant growth had been detected in Cherry's lung. So began a four-year battle, with Cherry undergoing hellish treatments and Donald always at her bedside. Theirs was a marriage made in heaven and he did not want it to end.

13th July 2008 was my seventieth birthday, and Veronica arranged a terrific party at La Rouquette. My dear brothers Tony and Richie and their wives, Judy and Carol, came from England. Abol Zahir – my friend from Earls Court and London Hospital Medical School days – and his ravishing wife Keyvan drove up from Provence. We made it known at the party that we planned to sell La Rouquette, buy a barge and cruise the canals of France in the summer. In the winter we would hibernate in a *pied-à-terre* in the immediate region to be close to our friends. We put our house on the market

In 2009 we heard that Jackie Monkhouse had died. We were surprised, because when we saw her in 2008 she was fit and well, at least physically. But she was unhappy. Since Bob's death, she said, she had been ignored socially and had to invite herself to events – not the first time one has heard of widows suffering this heartless isolation. Jackie was a good friend to us and instrumental in Bob's success, and Veronica and I regretted not having been more supportive of her after his passing.

The major event for us in 2009 was giving our financial advisers, Siddalls, the order of the boot. We had many complaints about their Mérignac office, which I set out in a detailed letter to the compliance officer. We received a reply denying that Siddalls were at fault. And who do you think the so-called compliance officer was? The CEO of Siddalls' parent company in the United Kingdom! Is this usual practice? If it is, it could be improved on.

We wanted to proceed legally against Siddalls, but such had been the nervous strain that I found myself grinding my teeth whilst I slept, to the extent that I loosened a wisdom tooth which my dentist, Dr Guignard, extracted easily without anaesthetic. The stress of litigation would have been appalling, for who knows what it would have cost, and there could be no guarantee of our winning. So we dropped the matter, instructed Siddalls to sell the investments they had made on our behalf, and started again.

I do not think myself particularly stupid, but being overly trusting is certainly one of my many shortcomings. From the very beginning, from the eye specialist when I was on HMS *Worcester* onwards, I have been given much rotten professional advice. They seem to confuse your best interests with theirs. The highly capable professionals I have come across – my first lawyer Anthony Rubinstein, my accountant David Allison and our latter-day financial adviser Stéphane Quintana – have been rare creatures.

After many years of annually appreciating local house prices, the market had gone flat, even fallen. The euro did not inspire confidence. But at last, we found buyers for La Rouquette. Our good friends from Barbados, Michael and Judith Adda, came to stay while they looked for a home to buy, and decided La Rouquette was exactly what they were looking for. Why look any further? The sale, in its straightforwardness, honesty and speed, restored our faith in human nature. They are still living there now. However, due to one thing and another, we found ourselves prematurely committed to buying a townhouse in the hill village of Belvès. Further, having incurred losses in liquidating our investments combined with a weak stock market, we could no longer buy the handsome Dutch barge of our choice. Nevertheless, with the help and advice of another friend, David Snitch, we did up the town house beautifully and, after a sojourn *chez* Richard Hanlon in Limeuil, moved in with Spaggers and Dorkie.

Although closely resembling a Chelsea mews house, the interior was very small. But it was a good place, free of distractions, for us both to write in. Veronica made great progress with her poems, her boundless imagination free to explore fantastical realms inhabited by endearing creatures. I scribbled away in my attic study with a glorious view over the Périgourdine countryside. But from the outset we were never really happy there. The garden was across the road, so we had to walk the dogs down the street, clutching awful black plastic poo bags. Come the summer we were miserable and longed to move, but the local property market was in even more dire straits and few houses were finding buyers. We listed our property with many estate agents, telling ourselves we would have to be patient. There was someone out there, our friends reassured us, whom it would suit perfectly.

In 2011, I'm not sure why, I decided to study Mandarin Chinese by means of a course of CDs in my car. I purchased the Michel Thomas Mandarin Foundation Course, the system which had proved so helpful with my Russian. This course proved equally rewarding, including notes on the Chinese way of life, their unique perception of time, and social mores – all sorts of interesting things. Not long ago, at a Chinese restaurant near Portsmouth, I took the plunge, speaking for the first time in Mandarin to a Chinaman (before this I had only spoken to the dogs in the car). When the waiter brought the bill I said I thought the food had been very good. The poor fellow positively reeled – the last thing he expected to hear was a Barbarian speaking his language. He recovered his poise and complimented me. Fortunately I was ready for that; I knew that the Chinese think it boorish to accept compliments. So I played down my very limited skills, and he was even more impressed. Enormously encouraged by my negligible triumph, I immediately bought the Advanced Course. Studying the more difficult material was a real thrill. I am on the Vocabulary Course – the final – course now.

On 14th September 2011 we heard from Donald that his beloved Cherry had finally succumbed to the cancer. Throughout her illness he was forever at her bedside, doing everything in his power to help her. Our hearts went out to this gentlest and kindest of men. Cherry had been his life.

The year 2012 began with a novel experience. Ever since we left Barbados my good friend Eddie Nimmo-Smith had looked for polo commentating work for me. He had heard me working in Barbados and had liked what I did. He worked for some Russian bankers who every year sponsored a team at the Kitzbühl International Snow Polo tournament – yes, polo is played on snow as well as on grass and indoor arenas, too. He arranged for me to join the party of bank customers who had been invited to the event. This went on for four days, all expenses paid, with invitations to matches, parties and peripheral events thrown in. I would be asked to explain (in Russian) to these customers the game of polo, its history, rules and so on, and would also be able to investigate the chances of doing some commentating there myself. The tournament was a very glamorous affair. There was an enormous tent with boutiques, bars and buffets, and an army of waiters in attendance. The delectable buffet – lobster, fillet beef, scallops, salads and pastries – was topped up all day. Vodka and Champagne flowed endlessly. Outside was the snow-covered polo field, a third the size of a standard grass field, the Austrian Alps providing a majestic background. The standard of play was high, the players skilled and vain, and the specially schooled ponies agile and brave. My generous hosts, Russians and Georgians, were welcoming, warm and amusing, and the hotel was first class. I sang for my supper in an additional role, as a sort of in-house Englishman. The guests – mostly Russians – seemed to like the way I spoke and took the opportunity to practice their English on me.

In August 2012, at a fortieth wedding anniversary party given by Michael and Judith Adda (who had bought La Rouquette) I found myself in conversation with a gentleman called Derek Russell-Stoneham. We had much in common, not least revelling in the Swinging Sixties – fast cars and fast women – in London. The difference was that Derek, better known as Puz, tended to marry his girls, whereas I did not. He is still at it today, doing the school run forty years later with another ten years – not children – to go, and loves it. He was very involved at the Cowdray Park Polo Club, the home of British polo and the Mecca of the sport for a commentator. He hoped he might be able arrange for me to cover some matches there. If he succeeded, it would mean I had reached the top of my career in the Great Game. He also thought that I had a story to tell and would like to be involved in its telling.

In September Veronica heard from the trustee of the estate of her recently deceased second husband, Ron. He had bequeathed her a considerable sum of money, far beyond her expectations. It did not make us rich but it changed our lives.

I was invited back to the snow polo at Kitzbühl by my Russian banker friends. The event this year was even better because there was plenty of snow (in 2012 they had had to resort to a snow-making machine). The hotel, the food and the wine were as extravagant as ever, and the women were lush and beautiful. The polo was again of a very high standard. Whilst we were watching, a lady floated past us, aloof and unattainable, in a full-length fur coat. Close by was a man with a Jack Russell on a lead. Some wit amongst us pointed at the coat and whispered to the dog: 'Cat!' The terrier flung itself at the fur, growling, biting and shaking its enemy to death. We had some trouble prising it loose. The lady was not amused.

Puz Russell-Stoneham, as he had promised, arranged for me to give some commentaries at Cowdray Park. I covered a couple of matches, although the weather was abominable, very cold with driving rain, and there were few spectators. I could hardly see the ponies or recognise the players. It was – as polo patron David Jamison, Paddy Bingham (who manages the Cowdray Park Polo Club) and others very kindly put it – a test by fire.

By now Veronica had compiled a volume of poems, *The Family Cat and Other Verses*, which was published under her full name, Ann Veronica Hudson, and I had embarked on writing this book.

In August our darling Dorkie died aged almost eighteen. She was our last connection with Barbados. We buried her in the garden and planted a tree next to her grave. Spaggers was now an only dog.

In September I was again at Cowdray, commentating on the last match of the season. This went down quite well. I am still not convinced that I can do a job entirely to my satisfaction until I have immersed myself in the polo world there. Knowing the riders, recognising their styles, being up-to-date with the local scandal – this depth of knowledge is essential to my style of commentating, which, I like to think, is slightly akin to that of the late John Arlott, doyen of cricket commentators. That would mean living at Cowdray for two or three months during the polo season, being part of the local scenery and becoming a recognised figure. If I can so arrange my life, I *shall* do a good job. This final match was followed by my commentating on the annual Dog Show, an hilarious event when everyone lets their hair down after months of seriously competitive polo.

Veronica and I were less and less happy at Belvès, sick and tired of passing traffic bashing our wing mirrors at £100 a time. The fact that most of our friends lived 20 kilometres to the north did not help. We advertised with many estate agents, but they were already overloaded with properties and were not inclined to over-exert themselves. French estate agents tend to sit on their bottoms waiting for their 7% commission to fall into their laps. We lowered the asking price by 25%, on the assumption that, when at last we were in a position to purchase another home, the sellers would also have had to lower their price.

Enter stage-left a knight in shining armour and estate agent, one Harris Raphael, with clients – a charming couple from New Jersey – in tow. They came, they saw, and they bought! Mr and Mrs Tator were the perfect buyers. The combination of their integrity and the professionalism of Harris, who had perfectly matched clients to property, meant that, in no time at all, they had contracted to buy the house. We would soon be on the move again.

CHAPTER FORTY

Escape To The Country

Immediately the contracts had been signed, we enquired after the lovely fourteenth-century house we had so wanted to buy a year ago, and much to our surprise – for it was most attractive, with a fully furnished *gîte* included in the deal – it was still on the market. Admittedly it was tired and needed work, but we saw well beyond that. Gratifyingly, the asking price was lower than previously; there had not been a single offer all year. Ours was accepted, and we went through the legal procedures quickly, for the seller, whose husband had recently died, was as anxious as us to complete the deal. We really wanted that property. The legal formalities of selling our house and buying the new one would take place on the same day, 23rd February 2014. The property, in the village of Journiac (pop. 414), we knew was going to be ours. Thanks to the legal system, gazumping does not happen in France.

Early 2014 saw us packing up the Belvès house. Initially we were given safe haven by our good friends, David and Victoria Relf. We camped luxuriously in one of their cottages for four weeks, then moved into our own *gîte*, from where we oversaw the renovation of our new home. Since it had been a school in one of its incarnations, as well as the Mairie and Presbytery, we called our house 'La Vieille Ecole'.

Towards the end of March, Spaggers suddenly fell seriously ill. The vet removed a malignant tumour the size of an orange, and we bought him home to recuperate. Within a week there was another, equally aggressive growth. As we carried him into the clinic, Spaggers communicated to us – as if he had spoken the very words – that he had had enough. And so, on the last day of March, he fell asleep under our loving hands, at peace and out of pain. Those who have had to make that decision, which one may be duty-bound to do, will know what we went through. Spaggers was a remarkable being – loving, giving, forgiving, sharing – the complete companion.

The very next day, 1st April – a date they had chosen as a date easy to remember – Donald Marshall married his friend Tina. Fate has dealt Donald some shattering blows, but he has always recovered and never complained. It is good that he is married again. Tina is a treasure. Cherry would be pleased, that I know.

In early June 2014, thanks to our master of works, the indispensable David Snitch, La Vieille Ecole was ready. The removers came and went, and we moved in.

Our new home is everything we could have asked for. It is at the very centre of a peaceful village and shares the *place* with the church, the school and the war memorial. Just across the road are the Mairie and the Salle des Fêtes (village hall). We are blessed with charming neighbours. The days are punctuated by the angelus ringing out at 7 am, noon and 7 pm. The main house is perfect for us – three up and three down, and one room wide, so the rooms are flooded with light. The ceilings are high. We have enough cellar space to start a storage business. Our two-bedroom *gîte* is a nice little earner, but we are selling it and will use the money raised for travel. The garden is a comfortable 800 square metres (8,611 square feet) and there is a functioning well, so we water our plants for nothing. Twenty minutes to the north is the A69 motorway, placing the glorious city of Bordeaux a mere two hours away. Eight minutes to the south is Le Bugue, with its Tuesday market and brilliant fish stall with everything from rascasse to sole to salt cod to salmon.

But there was a serpent lurking in this Garden of Eden. Growing up, I instinctively avoided anything addictive – tea, cigarettes and alcohol – but I remember the moment when the last-named slipped under my guard. Aged twenty-one, I was in the Royal Marine officers' mess at Hamworthy. A fellow officer asked me to help him choose the wines for a mess party that evening. Down in the cellar he drew the cork from a German wine, Rüdesheimer Rosengarten, poured some into a glass, and invited me to taste. I took a sip. My body reacted instantly. It was as if it had rediscovered a dear and long-lost friend. Although I didn't realise it at the time, this was the awakening of the latent alcoholism from which my instincts had tried to protect me. From that moment on my metabolism demanded a permanent, minimum level of this substance in my blood.

While I was active in sports and restaurants I was not aware of this need. Later, with more time on my hands, my sickness – for that is what it is – became more apparent, especially in the misnamed Happy Hour. This was when, telling myself that I deserved a glass or two after a testing day, I would hit the rosé, a disastrously swiggable wine for me. The result was I often fell asleep immediately after, if not during, dinner. When I woke up I was grumpy and argumentative and had to be persuaded to go to bed. It was all very disagreeable for Veronica.

I made repeated attempts to stop drinking, believing I would reduce the chances of suffering a stroke and even lose some weight as well. I wanted, above all, to be able to care for my wife in later years. I would remain abstemious for a few weeks – 'Look, I can stop drinking whenever I want' – but inevitably I would give way to the insidious craving and finish up by drinking more than ever. Then one day, in my doctor's waiting room, I saw a poster.

ALCOHOL
TALK ABOUT IT
IN ORDER TO FREE YOURSELF FROM IT

Bingo! This struck a resonant chord and I took the first step towards the solution I had been seeking. I began to talk about my problem, not only with my wife but with others. There is no doubt that bringing the issue out into the open, rather than pushing it out of sight, was helpful. My second step, born possibly of instinct, was to replace wine with something non-alcoholic. I sat down one evening with, instead of a goblet of rosé in my hand, a glass of Veronica's homemade elderflower cordial diluted with chilled San Pellegrino water. I drank it – aided and abetted by a copious bowl of dried fruits – and felt no desire for wine. There was not a squeak of protest from my body. It was, I swear, as simple as that. Maybe other people's bodies will react in the same way as mine. I hope so.

It is critically important that an unfailing supply of a cordial, chilled fizzy water (in my case) and nibbles are always available. Never run out. That is the keystone. Forget the habit of a lifetime, reaching for the corkscrew. Of course elderflower cordial is all sugar, and I have now replaced that with zero-sugar lemon squash, and the fruit, also full of sugar, with roasted pistachios, which nutritionally are very good news.

I fall off the wagon from time to time. However, if the next day I see a half-empty bottle of rosé winking seductively at me in the fridge door, I pour it down the sink. It took a month or two for any benefits to manifest themselves, during which time, I suppose, my body was eliminating the accumulated toxins. After that, the difference between a body intoxicated for over fifty years to one more or less free of alcohol, has been vivid indeed. My blood pressure is 120/80. I sleep through the night, do not snore (I am told), and wake refreshed. Nowadays I can write in any of the twenty-four hours of the day and enjoy an increased clarity of thought which frankly amazes me. I no longer suffer from indigestion or that vile phenomenon, gastro-oesophageal reflux. I am told I look ten years younger. And I have saved possibly the greatest benefit for the last.

Before adopting my new regime I suffered from that most embarrassing and inconvenient condition, incontinence. I now state unequivocally, after conclusive tests (details available on request), that very little alcohol in my blood means no incontinence, at least for a male of the species; I suspect female plumbing ages better. I had assumed this embarrassing condition was an inevitable consequence of growing older. I have found this is not so. It has been, one might say, a profound relief.

If my resolution suffers from more serious wobbles – on holiday, for example, or when we have guests – I only have to think of the many benefits of my regime and I am back on course. If I ignore these, I tell myself, I am betraying a body which, in spite of being continuously intoxicated, has worked faultlessly throughout my adult life, the odd sports injury notwithstanding. Added to this, were I to lapse, I would reduce the chances of outliving my wife, or – far worse – I would become an invalid, dependent on her. My *amour propre* will not allow that.

I am slowly but steadily losing weight. I had not realised (a) how much sugar a body deprived of alcohol demands, and (b) how wily it is in getting its own way. I am not the thin type – my love of smoked salmon, creamy sauces and mayonnaise means I shall always be a bit rounded at the corners. But these are only skirmishes. In my seventy-seventh year I am relishing victory over my lifelong enemy. I have my foot on his neck, and, if he stirs, I shall do whatever is necessary to silence him.

I include these thoughts in case what I have discovered helps even just one reader who is facing a similar struggle. I appreciate that many people have no trouble handling their alcoholic intake; they can stop and start as they please. However, if you have been hounded all your life by this addiction, you might try my regime. You may be surprised just how easy it is to win the battle. I repeat that it is vital that *you never run out of your preferred non-alcoholic drink and nibbles*. I would like to add that I regret writing, somewhat mockingly earlier in this book, of the two dedicated members of the Barbados Temperance Society who attended the liquor-licensing courts. I apologise to them and their colleagues. They have a point.

The prime beneficiary of my new regime is my understanding and tolerant wife who told me I had become a different man. That will do for me.

There was only one thing missing at La Vieille Ecole, someone with whom to share our good fortune. Memories of Spaggers' last days were less distressing now, so we decided to find a puppy, hopefully a West Highland terrier. We discovered one at nearby breeding kennels, called him Archie, and took him home, a ball of white fluff. We also rescued at the same time a six-year-old breeding bitch that had done her stint, and called her Lola. Now our household was complete.

Now that this book is finished I have other things I want to do. I have set my sights on improving my Mandarin and tackling Chinese calligraphy. I find the concept of creating Chinese characters with brush strokes has a strongly sensuous appeal. Calligraphy is a deeply satisfying art form. My Russian is alive and well and the BBC Russian Service remains my homepage. Both languages are on cassette courses in the cars. As I sit here in my study I am looking at my dusty and under-used piano. That will not do. I shall never forget Moura Lympany's rendition of Chopin's *Fantaisie-Impromptu* on the honky-tonk piano in Basil's Bar in Mustique many years ago.

It is a piece I would like to play one day, however badly, although I rather doubt if I will get beyond the haunting *largo.* I have much reading planned. I am awaiting the delivery any day now of the first of three volumes of the Collected Papers of Albert Einstein. I shall wallow in those. Our collection of Nero Wolfe novels is literally falling apart; both Veronica and I re-read them endlessly. I have to replace almost all of them. I have just reread Joshua Slocum's inspiring book – I'm a great re-reader – about sailing his sloop Spray around the world single-handed. That certainly had the Sirens singing at the top of their voices. My guitar languishes out of tune, so there is work to be done there.

There is much to do outside my study. I help a little in the garden, turning the odd sod and cutting grass mostly – and NOT on a sit-on mower. Our garden is Veronica's ultimate source of joy and fulfilment. She is a gifted gardener and has a way with roses. She writes poetry most days, and her first volume, *The Family Cat and Other Verses*, has been well received – and deservedly so. Her verses are both witty and touching, and enjoyed by children and adults alike. One of her poems, *The Ox's Story*, specially commissioned for the event, reduced the Carol Service congregation to tears. There are two more volumes yet to come – *Joan the Intelligent Camel and More Verses*, and another, as yet untitled.

Entertaining our friends is a perpetual joy. Veronica is a Cordon Bleu cook, and I do a spot of Chinese and have a nifty way with *magret de canard*. A quarter of an hour away is blessed Sainte Catherine's church, wherein dwells our lighthouse, Gill Strachan, and the inspiring Charlotte Sullivan. They look after my spiritual wellbeing. Thank you God for women priests. I am equally blessed physically thanks to the Magali Institute, a perfumed paradise in the nearby town of Le Bugue. It is here that I receive regular massages. I am mad about massage. Absolutely love it. Given that the skin is the body's biggest organ, surely one ought to take great care of it. Added to that, when one is getting on a bit, it is good – without being vain, perish the thought! – to be aware of how one's body looks. Walking Archie, something I am sternly encouraged to do, helps. Lola is our *poule de luxe* and sees no point in taking exercise.

Once, on Barbados, Veronica and I met in a restaurant a retired undertaker with whom we shared a pew on the transept of St. James parish church every Sunday. He was standing alone, as if waiting for someone, smiling gently. We asked him what the source of his serenity was. 'I speak to God every day,' he said. I liked that. I do the same thing now and it truly is a source of peace.

The insistent Sirens notwithstanding, Veronica and I do not see ourselves ever leaving this house. I have already chosen a spot for a lift or, failing that, have noted in the *Oldie* magazine advertisements for second-hand chair-lifts! We feel that coming to live in La Vieille Ecole is rather like, having climbed through a forest, with adventures good and bad on the way, we have happened on a sunlit clearing with a view below of the terrain which we have traversed. In the peace which surrounds us, we have the opportunity to reflect on the richness of our lives in the Périgord.

CHAPTER FORTY-ONE

Lying At Anchor – But Not Laid Up

An important time in my day has always been about four in the morning. Just having woken, lying in bed, my brain immediately whirring, I am somehow able to examine levels of consciousness inaccessible to me when I am fully awake. My life is laid bare, stripped of camouflage, and undistorted by false optimism. I am faced with the truth – which is not always unpalatable! I allow my mind to freewheel, go where it listeth, and sometimes I hear the patient Sirens – singing, singing…

Recently Veronica and I explored one of the many tidal inlets that pierce the north-east coastline of the tempestuous Gironde estuary. Across one such inlet a lock-gate had been constructed. This was opened to admit the rising waters of the flood tide, and then, when the ebb began, closed to retain them in the basin. Vessels were able to enter and leave at close to high water. In this region of France all activities pay tribute to the remorseless tides; here the sea is the sole provider of mankind's every need.

As we were walking around the yacht basin I spied two varnished wooden masts. The Sirens' voices rose like a swell on the ocean and filled my head. I had to know in what vessel these spars were stepped. I hied – nay, galloped – thither to investigate. A few minutes later I was gazing at an exquisite wooden-hulled schooner – hence the two masts – around 50 feet in length, and built, I guessed, in the early part of the twentieth century. She was immaculate and well-equipped with all modern devices. Her sweet lines, the rake of her masts and proud stem let you know that she could take you anywhere on the high seas. Look! I could hardly believe my eyes; attached to the shrouds was a notice – *A Vendre* (for sale) – and a telephone number.

I called the owner, seeking vicarious pleasure rather than intending to buy. The price asked was extremely reasonable, but, as I knew from experience, it is the ongoing running costs of vintage yachts that must be the prime consideration. In addition we had just moved house, upsizing in the process, and were still settling in. More to the point, there was nothing left in the coffers. It was with some sadness I had to accept that the idea of buying her was dead in the water.

But I also know full well that the Sirens do not give up. Once They have chosen you, you are Theirs forever. So I still dream in the small hours of sailing with Veronica to the balmy Caribbean, to white sands, blue waters, and pareos for clothing. And I look back on the voyage of my life and see a strange paradox: that it was never supposed to be like this. Nor am I done yet. By no means. For I really was always meant to go to sea.

Errol Barrow
And The Mirror Image Speech

13th May 1986

'What I wish to speak to you about very briefly here this evening is about you. About yourself.

I want to know what kind of mirror image do you have of yourself? Do you really like yourselves? There are too many people in Barbados who despise themselves and their dislike of themselves reflects itself in their dislike of other people.

Now what has bothered me in this society is that every time after elections, people expect certain things to take place. And although the law says that he that giveth is as much guilty of bribery and corruption under the Corrupt Practices Act as he that receiveth, we know that even on polling day, people were given envelopes with $100 bills in them.

So what kind of mirror image would you have of yourself? If there are corrupt ministers in Barbados tonight, you have made them corrupt.

I am not trying to make any excuses for you, but I realise what has happened in this society. I look around and see people who have not done an honest day's work in their whole lives driving around in MP cars, having an ostentatious standard of living, unlike my poor families in St. John, who the Welfare Officer gives $50 to feed a family of ten for a whole week.

What kind of mirror image can you have of yourself?

You so much despair of this society that your greatest ambition is to try to prove to the people of the United States Consulate that you are only going up to visit your family… And you are surprised when the people at the United States Embassy tell you that you do not have a strong reason to return to Barbados. And you are the only person dishonest enough with yourself to realise that you do not have a strong reason to return to Barbados, because Barbados has nothing to offer you. You are not being honest with yourself, but you tell the man down there, 'Oh yes, I'm returning.'

When I went to Mexico, I had to make a decision, and I returned. I had a strong reason. My reason is that I did not want to see my country go down the drain but you who are not in politics don't have a strong reason.

Your ambition in life is to try and get away from this country. And we call ourselves an independent nation? When all we want to do is go and scrub somebody's floors and run somebody's elevator or work in somebody's store or drive somebody's taxi in a country where you catching your royal when the winter sets in?

What kind of mirror image do you have of yourself? Let me tell you what kind of mirror image I have of you. The Democratic Labour Party has an image that the people of Barbados would be able to run their own affairs, to pay for the cost of running their own country, to have an education system which is as good as what can be attained in any industrialised country, anywhere in the world.

In the state of Texas, the government of that state has asked to make the teachers pass an examination. To see if they can read and write! The gentleman of the Texas teachers' union came on the news and he said that he was proud of the result because only eight per cent of the teachers couldn't read and write!

If Reagan had to take the test, I wonder if he would pass. But this is the man that you all say how great he is for bombing the people in Libya and killing little children… This is the man that you all go up at the airport and put down a red carpet for, and he is the President of a country in which in one of the more advanced and biggest states eight per cent of the teachers cannot read and write, and he feels that they are better than we. And you feel that we should run up there and bow.

What kind of mirror image do you have of yourself? When a government steals from people in the way of consumption taxes and takes that money and spends it on their own high lifestyles, and unnecessary buildings, then that government not only has contempt for you, but what is most unfortunate, you have contempt for yourself, because you allow them to do it.

What kind of mirror image do you have of yourself when you allow the mothers of this nation to be beasts of burden in the sugarcane fields? In Mexico where people suffer under a lower standard of living than in Barbados, they use donkeys to freight canes out of the fields; in Antigua, they use a small railway; but here the mothers of the nation are used as beasts of burden. What kind of image do you have of yourself?

I was inspired by the work done by the late Mr Ernest Bevin, who went to work at eight – I don't mean 8 o'clock in the mornin, I mean eight years of age – and those dock workers in London used to turn up during the winter and summer from 5 o'clock in the morning waiting for a ship, and if a ship didn't come in for three weeks or three months, they wouldn't get any pay. And Ernest Bevin introduced the guaranteed week for dock workers. I set up a commission of enquiry into the sugar industry and made the examination of the guaranteed week for agricultural workers one of the terms of reference, and the commission reported that nobody gave any evidence before them in support of this recommendation.

What kind of mirror image do the people of the Workers' Union have, either of you or themselves? I had to wait until there was a dispute in the sugar industry and say, well these will be the wages from next week and…I went into the House and introduced the guaranteed wages for agricultural workers. Why should only one man have a mirror image of you that you do not want to have of yourself? What kind of society are we striving for? There is no point in striving for Utopia, but you do not realise your potential.

I lived in a little country when I was young, the Virgin Islands. That is a small country. But there is another small country. That country has 210 square miles; it is 40 square miles bigger than Barbados. If you took the Parish of St. Philip and put it right in the little curve by Bathsheba that would be the size of the country of Singapore.

But you know the difference between Barbados and that country? First, Barbados has 250,000 people. You know how many people Singapore has on 40 more square miles? Over two-and-a-half-milion, on an island just a little larger than Barbados.

They don't have sugar plantations; they don't have enough land to plant more than a few orchids. They don't have enough land to plant a breadfruit tree in the backyard and nearly every Barbadian have some kind of fruit tree in the backyard.

They have developed an education system but they are teaching people things that are relevant to the 21ˢᵗ century. They are not teaching people how to weed by the road. They are in the advance of the information age.

But you know the difference between you and them? They have got a mirror image of themselves. They are not looking to get on any plane to go to San Francisco. Too far away. The government does not encourage them to emigrate unless they are going to develop business for Singapore.

They have a mirror image of themselves. They have self-respect. They have a desire to move their country forward by their own devices. They are not waiting for anybody to come and give them handouts. And there is no unemployment.

Is that the mirror image that you have of yourselves?

Anyhow, ladies and gentlemen, I done.'

Index

References to images and maps in the text are given in italics.
References to images in the picture sections are given in bold and prefaced by **Pl**.

More quality biographies from
Bene Factum Publishing

www.bene-factum.co.uk

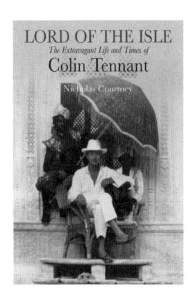

LORD OF THE ISLE

Nicholas Courtney

Bene Factum 2012
ISBN: 978-1-903071-64-9
£20.00

The Extravagant Life and Times of Colin Tennant

"It is so typical of Colin Tennant, the 3rd Baron Glenconner, that a biography of him does not end with his dramatic death outside the hospital in Souffrière in St Lucia for, as in his eventful life, his story twists and turns in many diverse and unexpected directions…"

Lord of the Isle is the much anticipated biography of the late Lord Glenconner, who was often unconventional and always newsworthy, even after his death.

Nicolas Courtney honestly and affectionately tells the story of his close friend Colin Tennant who lived a life of indulgence and eccentricity. This is the untold and fascinating tale of how Colin bought the island of Mustique in the West Indies and turned it into one of the world's most exclusive holiday destinations, frequented by rock stars and royalty alike.

From first-hand accounts of amusing anecdotes, remarkable escapades and legendary parties, to previously unseen family papers and photographs, this book reveals the truth about a life that was sometimes tragic, frequently entertaining and always exceptional.

IT'S ALL GOING TERRIBLY WRONG

Michael Parker

Bene Factum 2012
ISBN: 978-1-903071-65-6
£20.00

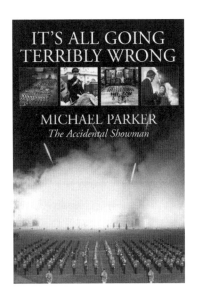

The Accidental Showman

Foreword by Sir Cameron Mackintosh

Forty-six highly entertaining years of organising royal celebrations, military tattoos and charity events.

Who would have guessed in the 1960s that Michael Parker, a typical young Army officer, would turn into one of the most remarkable showmen of his generation? It's All Going Terribly Wrong is a wonderfully funny account of the many different events he has staged around the world. Michael Parker's creativity and originality – all too often achieved in the face of stifling bureaucracy – along with an ability to organise down to the last detail meant he was in continuous demand for Royal jubilees and weddings, G7 conferences, victory commemorations, ship launches, charity events and the world's largest military tattoos.

It's All Going Terribly Wrong captures the author's successes and mishaps in a thoroughly amusing series of anecdotes that cover his remarkable life.